PETER THE GREAT

VOL. I.

PETER THE GREAT.

PETER THE GREAT

EMPEROR OF RUSSIA

A STUDY OF HISTORICAL BIOGRAPHY

BY

EUGENE SCHUYLER, Ph.D., LL.D.

AUTHOR OF "TURKISTAN"

IN TWO VOLUMES

VOL. I.

NEW YORK / RUSSELL & RUSSELL

FIRST PUBLISHED IN 1884
REISSUED, 1967, BY RUSSELL & RUSSELL
A DIVISION OF ATHENEUM HOUSE, INC.
L. C. CATALOG CARD NO: 66−24757

PRINTED IN THE UNITED STATES OF AMERICA

PREFACE.

WHAT is said in the following volumes is founded on the diligent—and I hope the impartial—study of original documents in the archives of various countries, of the Russian collections of laws and state papers, of the memoirs and accounts of Peter's contemporaries, of the works of Russian historians, and of most of the important books written on the subject by foreigners.

My views of portions of the history of the times under consideration differ in some respects from those generally entertained. I have not thought it necessary to emphasize them by attempting to refute the views of others, or by disproving anecdotes and stories in such common circulation as to have become almost legendary. I have told the story of Peter's life and reign as I understand it, and I hope that my readers will believe that there is good evidence for every statement that I make.

The books consulted are very many, and it has been impossible to cite them all. As continual references to authorities which are chiefly Russian would appeal to very few of my readers, I have thought it best to avoid them, and have mentioned only my chief authorities at the end of the chapters. Historical students and those conversant with the literature of the period will in this way readily find whence I have taken my facts.

For the convenience of the reader, I have avoided as far as possible the use of purely Russian words and titles, and where the English forms of proper names are not used, an accentual mark has been placed to facilitate pronunciation.

As circumstances have compelled me to live in five different countries since I began this work, often away from public libraries, and with only my own books and my notes to rely upon, I must ask pardon for many deficiencies and slips.

I owe especial thanks for their kind criticism and assistance to Professor Bestúzhef-Riumin of the University of St. Petersburg, and Professor Brückner of the University of Dorpat, whose works I have had frequent occasion to cite, and which often put me on the track of authorities that I might otherwise have overlooked; and more particularly to Professor Claes Annerstedt of the University of Upsala, who has been of great aid in procuring rare Swedish books for me.

The portrait of Peter the Great is engraved after that by Carl de Moor, painted at the Hague in 1717, which was the picture most liked by Peter himself, and preferred for engravings. It was for many years supposed to be lost, but I discovered it at Amsterdam in the possession of a private family, where it had come by inheritance from the painter Liotard, to whom it had been sent by the artist himself.

EUGENE SCHUYLER.

LEGATION OF THE UNITED STATES, ATHENS:
Thanksgiving Day, November 29, 1883.

ERRATA.

Page 1, line 23, *for* Pskov, *read* Pskof.
" 11, " (*twice*) " Sóltykofs, *read* Saltykófs.
" 45, " 10, " Tcherkássky, *read* Tcherkásky.
" 53, " (*twice*) " Sóltykof, " Saltykóf.
" 59, " 4, " had given, " sent.
" 105, " 37, " Praskóvia Sóltykof, *read* Prascovia Saltykóf.
" 124, " 20, " Oriékhovo, *read* Orékhovo.
" 138, " 23, " Lutzk, *read* Lutsk.
" 210, " 3, " Lubomirsky, *read* Lubomirski.
" 215, " 29, " Theodore, " Yury.
" 216, " 26, " Sóltykofs, " Saltykófs.
" 221, " *last*, " Captain, " Colonel.
" 279, " 2, 14, " Pskov, *read* Pskof.
" 296, " 14, " Thessing, *read* Thesingh.
" 298, " *add* 'Despatches' of Polish Agent Bose in Dresden Archives. 'Coll. of Russ. Imp. Hist. Soc.,' xx.
" 311, " 14, *for* von, *read* zu.
" 323, " 27, " Massálsky, *read* Masálsky.
" 334, " 25, ⎫
" 335, " 2, 10, 13, 15, 18, 20, 24, 27, 33, ⎬ *for* Kayserling, *read* Kaiser-
" 336, " 3, 7, 8, ⎭ lingk.
" 371, " 5, 23, *for* Cardis, *read* Kardis.
" 385, " 17, " III., " IV.
" 396, " 27, " Karlskrona, *read* Carlscrona.
" 409, " 3, " Sóltykof, " Saltykóf.
" 434, " 27, " Kopórié, " Koporié.
" 443, " 20, " Lagau, " Lage.
" " " " " Dec. 2, " Dec. 13.

CONTENTS.

LIST OF ILLUSTRATIONS.

FULL-PAGE ILLUSTRATIONS.

ILLUSTRATIONS IN THE TEXT.

At the end of Volume.

Russian Flag of Peter's Time.

THE INTRODUCTION OF CHRISTIANITY INTO RUSSIA.

PETER THE GREAT.

INTRODUCTORY.

A BROAD, open plain, with scarcely a hill, but everywhere
intersected by navigable rivers, with its three zones of arid,
saline steppe, of rich and fertile arable land, of forest and
frozen moor, fitted in every respect to be the home of a united
and homogeneous people, we find Russia a thousand years ago
sparsely inhabited by disunited Slavonic tribes, frequently at
war with each other, and unable to cope with their neighbours
of Finnish and Turkish race. Scandinavian heroes, as the
legend runs, are called in; civilisation and strong government go rapidly hand in hand; and a distinctively Russian
nation is born from the two centres of Nóvgorod and Kíef.
Christianity is introduced from Constantinople, and with it
Byzantine ideas of law and polity, which have never disappeared, and of which the influence is still felt. Then comes
the appanage period, when the whole of Russia is divided into
independent yet related states, each governed by its Prince of
the House of Rurik under the general headship of the oldest
member of the family, the power passing, not from father to
son, but, as now in Turkey and the East, to the oldest male
member of the family.

The absolute power of the princes was, in some measure,
controlled by the popular assemblies which existed in most of
the larger towns. Pskov and Nóvgorod had already been
greatly developed, and Russia seemed to have entered early

862.

that path of progress which would in time have rendered her a free and constitutional country. Trade, especially with the west of Europe, through Nóvgorod and the Hanse towns, had received a great impetus, and the court of Kíef displayed a high civilisation, when the whole country, overrun by the Mongols and the Tartars, was obliged to submit to their yoke. The effect of the Mongol supremacy was not felt in mixture of race and very little in corruption of language, but chiefly in the arrest of all political and commercial development, and in the introduction among the Grand Dukes of new maxims and methods of government. The Russian states were not ruled directly by the Mongols: they were merely vassal. The Grand Dukes received their confirmation from Tartary, but the only Tartar officials in Russia were those who resided in the larger towns for the collection of tribute. The greatest positive effects produced by the Tartar supremacy were the separation of Russia from Europe and its withdrawal from Western influences, the gradual union of the whole country under the Grand Dukes of Moscow and the establishment of autocracy, which was indeed necessary to this union and to the expulsion of the Tartars. One state after another was swallowed up by the Grand Duchy of Moscow, and even the free cities of Nóvgorod and Pskof were mulcted of their privileges and received the tyrant. After the autocracy had justified its existence by unifying the country and freeing it from the Mongol yoke, it reached its highest development under Iván the Terrible, who succeeded for a time in entirely breaking up the power of the aristocracy of boyárs and in realising what has so often seemed the ideal of the Russian state—an equal people under an absolute monarch. The Russian people had suffered so much from their lords, the landed proprietors, the officials, and almost the whole of the noble classes, that they had become convinced—as ignorant persons are apt to be—that it was only the nobility and the boyárs who 'darkened the counsels of the Tsar' and prevented their happiness. For this reason Iván the Terrible, in spite of his cruelties, was very popular among the masses of the Russian people, and even now his name is mentioned rather with affection than hatred. The death of Iván, who left only feeble

1237-40.

1533-84.

RUSSIAN HOSPITALITY IN THE TIME OF IVAN THE TERRIBLE.

and minor children, gave a blow to autocracy and brought back
the nobility into power.

The firm hand of Borís Godunóf, the usurper, for a time
kept order, and accomplished what the nobility then thought
absolutely necessary to their existence as a powerful class—*i.e.*, reduced nearly the whole of the 1598–1605.
Russian people to serfdom, an institution then first legally established. Then came the Troublous Time—that period of
commotion, distress, and invasion, when pretender
vied with pretender, and the son of the King of Po- 1605–13.
land was crowned Tsar of Moscow. The strength of each of
these pretenders was the measure of the hatred which the common people bore to the nobility. That mysterious prince who
bears in history the name of ' the false Dimitri,' in spite of his
foreign ways, was popular among the people, although the old
nobility stood aloof from him. He was overthrown, not by the
force of popular commotion, but by the plotting of the nobles.
Basil Shúisky, who was placed on the throne by the voice of
the nobles, was unable to maintain himself there, because the
general sentiment of the country, which had not been consulted
in the matter, was against him. Finally the Poles were turned
out, and at the Diet, or general assembly, in which all classes
and all districts in the country were pretty fairly represented,
the young Michael Románof was elected Tsar.

The whole reign of Michael was a struggle to rid the country of the Poles and the Swedes, who were attacking it from
without, and to put down the bands of robbers and
marauders who were making disturbance within; for 1612–45.
the Troublous Time had left a great legacy of difficulty to the
new ruler. The country was poor; every one needed money,
and no one more than the Tsar himself; for officials and soldiers were loudly clamouring for arrears of pay, and for indemnity for the losses they had sustained during the wars. In
order to raise money, and in order more firmly to establish the
power of the Tsar, it was found necessary to have frequent recourse to the States-General, especially during the early part
of the reign. Legislation was directed in part to providing for
the administration of the government, but chiefly to settling
the difficulties caused by peasants running away from the estates

of their lords during the Troublous Time. As years went on and Michael became more firmly seated on his throne, recourse was less often had to the States-General, and the aristocracy to some extent regained its power. In the latter years of Michael's reign the government was practically carried on by a single noble, the Prime Minister, or Favourite, or, as the Russians of that time expressively styled him, 'the man of the hour.'

In the reign of Alexis the States-General were seldom convoked, and only for the settlement of the most important questions, such as war with Poland and the protectorate over the Cossacks of the Ukraine. At one of these sessions the Tsar procured the ratification of his well-known code, which went further than anything had ever done to establish autocracy on a regular basis, and to legalise arbitrary government. Even then no discussion was allowed. The 315 deputies present were permitted merely to listen and to sign, and the majority of 160 that protested were exiled to the Solovétsky Monastery. Henceforward the Tsar managed all matters, both great and small, according to his own will and pleasure.

1645–76.

1648.

The Tsar Alexis was a man of good impulses, and of such gentle and amiable character that he was called by his subjects 'The Most Debonair.' But his very good qualities rendered him one of the worst sovereigns of Russia. The power was exercised by his favourites—Morózof, Ordín-Nastchókin, and Matvéief, and under the rule of the boyárs everything seemed to go from bad to worse. The country was impoverished and in places almost depopulated ; the administration was defective and disorganised, and the officials were corrupt. Taxes were high and exactions frequent. A sedition broke out among the distressed people at Moscow ; the Judge Plestchéief and the Okólnitchy Trakhaniótof had to be given up by the Tsar to the furious populace, and were judged and executed by the mob. Morózof, the Prime Minister and brother-in-law of the Tsar, only saved his life by a timely flight. In Nóvgorod and Pskof the populace made themselves masters of the city, and were only put down when troops arrived and laid regular siege to those places. In the south-east of Russia, Sténka Rázin, a Cossack of the Don, captured Astrakhán, and established himself on the lower Volga, whence he ravaged the whole of south-eastern Russia. The nobles and boyárs were killed, but the peasantry willingly ranged themselves under his banners, and Moscow was in imminent danger. Sténka Rázin was put down, captured and executed, but his name was always a watchword, and lives till now in popular songs. He was a popular hero, embodying the discontent of the common people, rather than a brigand chief—a Russian Robin Hood.

Most serious, however, in its ultimate consequences was the rise of Dissent in the Russian Church. Actuated by a spirit of reform which was in itself laudable, the Patriarch Nikon undertook the correction of all the printed and manuscript copies of the liturgy. Careful comparisons were made with the formularies and service books of the Eastern Church as accepted at Constantinople, and with the early copies existing in the libraries of the Russian monasteries; and, finally, by a decree of an Ecclesiastical Council, the corrected books were ordered to be the only ones used, and the destruction was commanded of all others. This measure excited the greatest hostility on the part of some of the ignorant clergy as well as of those who were heretical, but who had concealed their heresy under the incorrectness of the books which they used. Still more strong was the feeling among the mass of the people, especially in remote districts, who had a sincere, even if sometimes a superstitious, attachment to the forms and ceremonies to which they and their fathers had been accustomed. It seems certainly a matter of surprise that passions should be so excited and people be found willing to suffer martyrdom for such puerile questions as to whether the name of Jesus should be pronounced 'Isus' or ' Yisus'; whether, in a certain portion of the morning service the word ' hallelujah' should be re-peated twice or three times; and whether the sign of the cross should be made with the two fore fingers extended, or with the two fore fingers and the thumb conjoined as denoting the Trinity. But it will not seem so strange when we consider the Evangelical clergy of the Church of England in their fierce and violent hatred to the ' eastward position,' or to preaching in a surplice instead of a black gown. However fallacious or erroneous the doctrines or ceremonies may have been, the Russian people held to them, and the attempt at reform caused an explosion in the form of religious rebellion of popular wrath and discontent which had long been simmering. While the one-sided development of religious life in Russia, in which devotion to outward forms had obscured the spirit of Christianity, was at the bottom of this great movement, yet the strength of Dissent lay in its democracy, both civil and religious, and in its being a protest against autocracy both in Church and State. Fanatical as were the early Dissenters, they were by no means all ignorant, and included many of the best and worthiest of the traders and the peasantry.

Attempts were made to put down the Dissenters not only by spiritual persuasion but by the force of arms, and some of the most obstinate were executed; but the monastery of Solovétsk, in the White Sea, where the ignorant monks had succeeded in winning over the Streltsi and other soldiers settled there for the protection of the place—for it was also a frontier fortress—held out for eight years against all the forces which the Court of Moscow could send; and in the east of Russia, on the confines of Siberia, the inhabitants of whole villages shut themselves up in their houses and burnt themselves to death, rather than accept a new and, as they considered it, a diabolical religion. The Government had at last an apparent victory, and the revised service books were introduced into the churches; but in obscure convents and distant villages the 'Old Believers,' as they called themselves, still flourished. At the present day nearly one-half of Russia belongs in spirit, if not openly, to the Dissenters, and the reconciliation which is by no means yet complete, between the Dissenters and the official Church has been only accomplished by relaxing the rigour of the laws of persecution.

These riots and rebellions, accompanied as they generally were with clamorous petitions to the Tsar for the punishment of some noble who was charged with the guilt of misgovernment, brought about in the mind of Alexis a mistrust of his subjects. He showed himself more rarely in public, he surrounded himself with guards, approach to the precincts of the palace was forbidden to the multitude, petitions could no longer be presented in person, and it is reported that the Debonair

Tsar, in an excess of terror, once killed a suppliant who came too close to his equipage. Worst of all, that fountain of ills, the secret police, sprang up, and a system of spies and denunciation was soon in full force. The classes and categories of high treason were rigorously defined, and much stress was laid on the length and fulness of the Tsar's title.

An accidental omission of a single word or letter from this long and cumbrous official title—which was frequently repeated several times in the course of a document—was considered as an act of personal disrespect to the prince, almost equal to high treason, and was punished far more severely than many heinous crimes.[1] Then began, too, an endless dispute with the representatives of foreign countries, either in Moscow or when Russian missions were received at foreign courts, on the proper recognition of the Tsar's title, on the exact words to be employed therein, and on the most accurate translation thereof, together with complaints of diminution of title. An excuse was found for a war with Poland in 'diminution' and errors in the Tsar's title in papers signed by Polish officials.

The foreign policy of the reign of Alexis was not a successful one. The Tsar was at first victorious in his wars against Poland and Sweden, and succeeded in reconquering all those provinces inhabited by a Russian population which in former years had formed part of the Russian principalities or of the Tsardom of Moscovy. A wrong policy was pursued, reverses

---

[1] The shortest title of the Tsar that could possibly be used. and which it was necessary to repeat every time that the Tsar's name was used in a document, petition, or discourse, was : ' The Great Lord, Tsar, and Grand Duke, Alexis Michaílovitch, of all Great and Little and White Russia, Autocrat.' The complete title, as amplified in 1667, was: ' By the grace of God, Great Lord, Tsar, and Grand Duke Alexis Michaílovitch, of all Great and Little and White Russia, Autocrat ; of Moscow, Kíef, Vladímir, Nóvgorod ; Tsar of Kasan, Tsar of Astrakhan, Tsar of Siberia, Lord of Pskof and Grand Duke of Lithuania, Smolensk, Tver, Volynia, Podolia, Yugoria, Perm, Viatka, Bulgaria, and others ; Lord and Grand Duke of Nóvgorod of the Lower Land of Tchernígof, Riazán, Polótsk, Rostóf, Yarosláv, Bieloózero, Udoria, Obdoria, Condinia, Vitébsk, Mstisláv, and of all the northern region ; ruler and Lord of the Iverian Land, of the Kartalinian and Georgian Tsars, and of the Kabardinian Land, of the Circassian and Mountaineer Princes, and of many other realms and lands, Eastern, Western, and Northern, Hereditary Possessor, Successor, Lord and Ruler.'

followed, and an ignominious peace was the result. The only permanent advantage was the limited protectorate established over that thoroughly Russian and orthodox population of adventurers inhabiting the banks of the Dnieper known as the Cossacks of the Ukraine, who, under the leadership of Bogdán Khmelnítzky, had thrown off Polish supremacy and applied for the aid of their brethren of Moscow.

I.

SECOND MARRIAGE OF THE TSAR ALEXIS—BIRTH OF PETER.

WHEN the Tsar Alexis was still in the prime of manhood—and it should be remembered that he was just two months older than Charles the Second of England—he lost his wife, the Princess Marie Ilínitchna Miloslávsky. During a married life of barely twenty-one years, she had given birth to thirteen children, several of whom had died in their infancy; and she herself expired in childbed on the 12th of March, 1669. Three months later, Simeon, the fourth son, died; and half a year afterward, at the age of sixteen, Alexis, the eldest son and heir to the throne. Of the two sons still living, Theodore was very infirm and sickly; and Joánn, or Iván, was almost blind, had a defect of speech, and lacked little of being an idiot. Under the circumstances it seemed highly probable to every one that the Tsar would marry again, and the parents of all marriageable girls were busy preparing them for the customary and traditional inspection of candidates for the hand of the Tsar. All, however, were doomed to disappointment.

Alexis frequently visited his chief minister and tried friend, Artémon Serghéievitch Matvéief, who spared nothing to make his house attractive and pleasant to the Tsar, providing concerts and other amusements, and having tragedies, histories, and even comedies performed in his private theatre. This minister, who had served in the foreign regiments, leaned toward all that came from Western Europe, and, although he kept the same open house, had adopted different manners from most of the Muscovite aristocracy and officials. The females of the family, dressed in what were called German clothes, did not scruple to appear at table or in the presence of visitors. Indeed the wife

of Matvéief was a Hamilton, one of a Scotch family settled at
Moscow. There were no daughters, but Matvéief had living
with him a ward, the daughter of an old comrade, Cyril Narýshkin, a chamberlain and a landed proprietor of the remote
district of Tarus, one of a noble but little known family of
Tartar origin, several members of which had died in arms for

their country. There was a family
tie, for Theodore Narýshkin, the
brother of Cyril, had also married
a Hamilton, the niece of Matvéief's wife, under whose charge
Natalia Narýshkin was receiving
her education at Moscow—a tall,
shapely, black-eyed, black-haired
girl. One evening, when the Tsar
was at Matvéief's house, the wife
and the pretty ward of the Prime
Minister came into the room, bringing, as usual, the cups of *vodka*,
the caviare, the smoked fish, and
the other whets to the appetite
which are taken before the Rus-

Tsaritsa Natalia, Mother of Peter the Great.

sian dinner or supper. The widowed Tsar, in the depth of his
grief and gloom, was struck by the pretty face, and still more by
the modest smile—neither forward nor too much abashed—and
by the sensible answers he received to his questions. He ate with
more than usual heartiness, and seemed to enjoy the evening, and
on going away said to Matvéief that he would find a bridegroom
1670.   for his pretty ward. Notice had already been served for
        the inspection and review, on the 11th of February, of
the young girls, either in Moscow or the distant provinces, whose
position and beauty rendered them suitable to be the Tsar's
bride, and word was now sent to Natalia Narýshkin to appear
among the others. According to custom, all the maidens then
present assembled again for inspection on the 28th of April.
Report soon bruited it about that Natalia Narýshkin was the
chosen one. This caused an unpleasant sensation in the Kremlin. The daughters of the Tsar—several of them older than
Natalia Narýshkin—objected to so young a stepmother. They

objected, too, for a more serious reason, as her relations, according to accepted usage, would immediately come into court favour, while their own, the Miloslávskys, would lose their positions, and perhaps be sent into exile. There was jealousy on the part of many families of much higher position in the social and political world than the Naryshkins, each one desiring to obtain for his own friends and adherents the places which would evidently be vacated by the Miloslávskys. The Miloslávskys themselves would have preferred a bride belonging to some family which they could easily influence, and thus, perhaps, keep themselves in power. The opposition to the choice of the Tsar was carried to such a length that there were fears of a repetition of the scenes which caused the ruin of the first bride of the Tsar Michael, and of the one first chosen for Alexis himself. In 1616, the Sóltykofs, at that time the ruling family at court, had so much disliked Marie Khlópof, whom the young Tsar Michael was about to marry, that they had drugged her till she was ill, representing her as incurably diseased, and caused her to be exiled with all her family to Siberia, where she remained for seven years, till the fall of the Sóltykofs, when she was allowed to reside at Nizhni-Nóvgorod. The Princess Marie Dolgorúky, the second bride of Michael, had been suddenly taken ill and had died on the day appointed for the marriage. In 1647, two years after he had ascended the throne, Alexis had resolved to marry, and out of two hundred young girls chose Euphemia Vsévolozhsky. When she was attired for the first time in the royal robes, the ladies-in-waiting twisted her hair so tightly that she swooned in the Tsar's presence. The court physicians were induced to declare that she was afflicted with epilepsy, and Euphemia and all her relatives were exiled to Tiumén in Siberia.

There was evidently danger for Natalia Naryshkin.

Only four days after the second inspection two anonymous letters were found on the porches of the palace, in which accusations were made against Matvéief of sorcery and witchcraft, and of using magic herbs to attract the mind of the Tsar toward his ward. There was a strict investigation, accompanied, as was then customary, with torture, and the contemplated marriage was put off for nine months; but it was finally celebrated on

the 1st of February, 1671, with all the customary pomp, dinners, feasts, and public rejoicing, of which the Tsar Alexis was
so fond.

In spite of the intrigues and dissatisfaction of the elder
daughters of the Tsar and of their relatives, the Miloslávskys,
everything was pleasant on the surface; and all the young people of the court amused themselves as usual during the summer
in the villas and palaces in the neighbourhood of Moscow. The
Tsar was devoted to his wife, was never for a moment without
her, and even took her to his park of Sokólniki, where he indulged in his favourite pastime of hawking. To the delight of
the people, and of all who feared what might happen from the
feeble health of the two remaining sons of the Tsar, a report
was spread, during the winter, that the Tsaritsa was pregnant—
a report which was shortly after officially confirmed; and at
about one o'clock on the morning of Thursday, June 9, 1672
(May 30, and the festival of St. Isaac of Dalmatia according to
the Russian calendar) a son was born who was christened Peter,
and who subsequently became known as Peter the Great.

Messengers were immediately sent to the Metropolitan—for
the Patriarch was dead, and his successor had not yet been
elected—to the other clergy, and to the chief monas-
1672. teries, both at Moscow and Sérghia-Tróïtsa, to all the
officials, and to all the higher nobility in Moscow. At five
o'clock in the morning the great bell of the tower of Iván
Velíki announced the birth of a prince and gave the summons
to prayer. The Tsar Alexis was exceedingly fond of ceremonial display, and spent much of his time in arranging the details
of the great court ceremonies, the receptions of ambassadors,
and the solemn religious state processions. In consequence of
the great delight he felt at the birth of his son, additions were
made to the customary ceremonial. A procession, headed by
the Metropolitan and clergy in robes of cloth-of-gold, with banners and crosses and swinging censers, left the palace of the
Krémlin and went slowly round the great square to the cathedral of the Assumption. After the clergy marched in due order
the higher officials of the government, the nobility according to
their several ranks, and the colonels of the army; then all the
members of the royal family—the princesses, beneath their

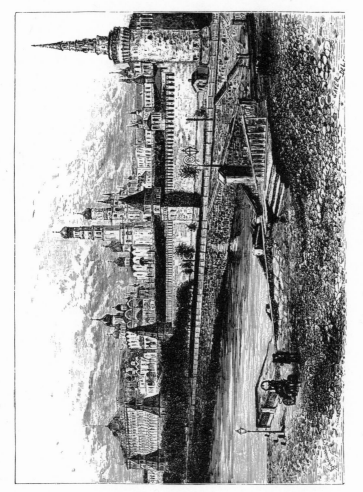

THE KREMLIN—MOSCOW.

closed canopies, being accompanied by the wives and the daughters of the great nobles; and then citizens of Moscow acting as deputations from the merchants and from the various classes and guilds. After prayers and a solemn thanksgiving service, the Metropolitan and clergy felicitated the Tsar upon the birth of

The Great Bell of the Tower of Iván Velíki.

his son; and then Prince Nicholas of Georgia, advancing with the princes of Siberia and Kasímof, who were living at Moscow under the protection of the Tsar, presented the congratulations of the nobles and the citizens, and pronounced an address prepared for the occasion. From the cathedral of the Assumption the procession passed to the cathedral of St. Michael the Archangel, then to the Miracle monastery and to the monastery of the Ascension, and finally to the cathedral of the Annunciation, the nearest to the palace, where mass was celebrated. On returning to the palace the Tsar held a reception in the banqueting hall, and raised the father of the Tsaritsa, Cyril Naryshkin, and the Prime Minister Matvéief, from privy councillors to the dignity of *okólnitchy*, the highest official rank but one, and only inferior to that of a *boyár*.[1] An uncle of the Tsaritsa, Theodore Naryshkin, was promoted, with others, to the rank of privy councillor. Then, in the ante-room, the usual refreshments on the birth of a child were given to the guests, the Tsar with his own hands passing about *vodka* and foreign wines to the nobles and officials, while boyárs, specially assigned to this duty, distributed fruit and wines to the army officers who stood without the palace. The only deviation from the customary feast was that the distribution of confectionery, usual on these occasions, was postponed to another time.

It was customary to give a large state banquet soon after the birth of a prince, but the fast of St. Peter beginning on Monday, and Saturday night being also the fast before the festival of All Saints, which the Russians celebrate on the day we call Trinity Sunday, it was not only impossible to prepare a banquet of the usual kind in two days, but it was also difficult for the guests to come provided with the customary birth presents. A small private supper was nevertheless given in the Golden Hall on the Sunday to the boyárs alone, it being understood that there were to be no personal invitations and no precedence at table.

The Tsar having decided to give the name of Peter to the new-born child, the christening was fixed, after the fasting pe-

---

[1] The titles of *Boyárin* and *Okólnitchy*, given to the two highest classes of the old Muscovite officials, are even more untranslatable than Pasha and Bey. They were purely personal and not hereditary titles; they conferred a rank in the state, but brought no special duties with them. They ceased to exist in the reign of Peter the Great. Other official titles, such as *Dúmnoï Diak*, *Spálny*, etc., which have likewise been abrogated, I have made a shift to translate so as to give an idea of their functions. Just as lately in Roumania, so in olden Russia, the word boyárs was used by the common people as comprehending all the nobility and officials.

riod was over, for the Feast of SS. Peter and Paul, the 29th of
June (old style), that is, according to our calendar, the 9th of
July. The christening took place before mass, in the Miracle
monastery, in the refectory of St. Alexis, the miracle-worker.
The ceremony was performed by the Tsar's confessor, Andréi
Savínovitch, priest of the cathedral of the Annunciation, and the
child was held at the font by Theodore Naryshkin, the elder
brother of the Tsaritsa, who handed it to the Princess Irene, one
of the daughters of the Tsar Michael and the sister of Alexis.
The child was borne to the church in a cradle placed on wheels,
while the priest most venerated for his sanctity—Nikíta—sprinkled the path with holy water. On the next day, the 10th of
July, which was Sunday, the clergy, with their holy pictures,
their crosses, and their gifts, the boyárs and nobles, the delegates from the merchants, and other citizens, both from Moscow
and from the neighbouring towns and villages, all with the customary birth-gifts, met in the palace for morning service, after
which the table was spread in the banqueting-hall. Banquets
on occasions of birth differed from those given on other great
occasions in the palace, especially in the variety of the confectionery and wines. The expense and account-books which have
come down to us show that on this occasion the tables were
fairly loaded with large pieces of sugar-work, which included
immense representations of the Muscovite arms; eagles, swans,
and other birds, even larger than life ; a model of the Krémlin,
with people going in and out, and also a large fortress, with cannon. At the same time the Tsaritsa gave a banquet to the
wives and daughters of the boyárs in her private apartments.
Each of the guests at these two banquets received on departing
a large plate filled with sweets of various kinds, the quantity,
however, proportioned accurately to the rank of the guest.
Smaller plates of sweets were sent to those notable persons who
were not able to be present at the christening feast. Other
banquets followed during four days.

One of the first ceremonies after the birth of a Russian prince
was what was called 'taking his measure'—that is, painting the
image of his patron saint on a board of either cypress or linden
wood, of the length and breadth of the child. The measure of
Peter was taken on the third day after his birth, and the most

skilful artist of the time—Simeon Ushakóf—was ordered to paint a picture representing the Holy Trinity, together with the Apostle Peter, on a board of cypress wood nineteen and a quarter inches long and five and a quarter inches broad. This artist, however, was taken ill and died before he had finished the picture, which was completed by another, Theodore Kozlóf. This 'birth-measure' of Peter, as it is called, was carefully preserved, and now hangs over his tomb in the Cathedral of SS. Peter and Paul, in the Fortress at St. Petersburg.

A governess was found for Peter, first in the person of the Princess Juliana Golítsyn, and subsequently in the boyár's wife, Matréna Leóntief; and a nurse, who was obliged to be ' a good and clean woman, with sweet and healthy milk,' in Neon-íla Lvof.

Besides the nurse and his governess, a prince in those days had a special staff of dwarfs, to be companions and at the same time servants. He had also his own apartments. Peter and his nurse were at first placed in some small rooms in the upper and wooden part of the palace, the walls of which were hung with common cloth. But only a year from his birth—in August, 1673—we find orders for one of the rooms to be hung with leather stamped with silver, and a year later new apartments were prepared, the walls of which were· hung with fine red cloth, and the furniture covered with red and crimson, embroidered with yellow and blue. In 1676 the walls and part of the ceiling were decorated with paintings. In his earliest years Peter enjoyed all the luxury which at that time surrounded a prince, and from which, later on, he so readily broke away. The curious books of accounts mention numerous articles ordered for him in the first four or five years of his life: cradles, covered with gold-embroidered Turkish velvet, sheets and pillows of white silk, coverlets of gold and silver stuffs; caftans, coats, caps, stockings and shoes of velvet, silk and satin, embroidered with gold and pearls; buttons and tassels of pearls and emeralds; a chest for his clothes, covered with dark-blue velvet and ornamented with mother-of-pearl; and a miniature carriage, drawn by ponies, in which he was taken out to drive. Nor were playthings of all kinds wanting; toy horses, miniature clavichords and musical instruments of various kinds, dolls, wooden figures, hobby-horses, toy carriages and carts, and a swing. The most common toys, however, were miniature bows and arrows, pikes, spears, wooden guns, banners, and all sorts of military equipments. But as military things were destined to play such an important part in Peter's military education, we shall leave this subject for a time.

Physically, Peter developed rapidly. He was able to walk when six months old, and being active, bright, and intelligent, he took an interest in all that was going on around him. Being the pet of his parents, he constantly accompanied them in their excursions and visits in the neighbourhood of Moscow. In May, 1675, Matvéief presented him with a small carriage of foreign workmanship, drawn by four small ponies, in which he was driven and guided by the court dwarfs, and began to take a part in the court and public processions. An eye-witness, Adolph Lyseck, an Austrian Secretary of Embassy, in describing the court procession to the Tróïtsa monastery in September, 1675, says :—

'Immediately after the carriage of the Tsar there appeared from another gate of the palace the carriage of the Tsaritsa. In front went the chamberlains with two hundred runners, after which twelve large snow-white horses, covered with silk housings, drew the carriage of the Tsaritsa. Then followed the small carriage of the youngest prince, all glittering with gold, drawn by four dwarf ponies. At the side of it rode four dwarfs on ponies, and another one behind.'

Lyseck in another place speaks of his official presentation to the Tsar Alexis at the palace of Kolómensky :—

'The door on one side suddenly opened, and Peter, three years old, a curly-headed boy, was seen for a moment holding his mother's hand and looking at the reception. This was to be the great astonishment of the court.'

The favourite resort of the court at that time was the palace of Preobrazhénsky. Here Matvéief had caused a small theatre to be built in one of the large halls, and a company of German actors gave comedies, assisted by various boys and young people from the court and the children from the Mestchánsky—a quarter of Moscow inhabited principally by Poles from the western provinces. The first play performed was 'Judith'; another

time the story of Esther was represented, in which the spectators
thought they saw references to contemporary events : Ahasu-
erus and Esther portraying the Tsar and the Tsaritsa, Mordecai
being Matvéief, and the wicked Haman one of the Miloslávskys.   We find mention also of the histories of ' Joseph,' and
' Tobit,' and finally even plays on historical subjects not scrip-
tural, such as the invasion of Tamerlane.   Usually, after the
comedy, German musicians gave a concert, or jugglers performed feats of legerdemain.   The comedies sometimes lasted
five or six hours consecutively, and the feasting went on until
morning.[1]

---

[1] The authorities for the preceding chapter are, chiefly, Ustriálof, *History
of the Reign of Peter the Great*, vol. i., St. Petersburg, 1858; Pogódin, *The
First Seventeen Years of the Life of Peter the Great*, Moscow, 1875 ; Soloviéf,
History of Russia, vol. xiii., Moscow, 1870; Esipof, *Collection of Extracts from
the Archives with regard to Peter the Great*, Moscow, 1872 ; Zabiélin, *Essays
on Russian Antiquity and History*, Moscow, 1873 ; Zabiélin, *Home Life of the
Russian Tsars and Tsaritsas*, Moscow, 1862–69 ; Tumánsky, *Collection of Me-
moirs, etc., Relative to Peter the Great*, St. Petersburg, 1787 ; *Palace Archives*,
St. Petersburg, 1852 ; Astrof, *The Childhood of Peter the Great*, in *Russian
Archives* for 1875.   (All the above in Russian.)

II.

LIFE AT COURT.

When the Tsar was in Moscow, life at court must have been very uniform and sometimes monotonous. Alexis usually rose at four o'clock, and after making his toilet with the assistance of his chamberlains and gentlemen of the bed-chamber, went immediately into his oratory, where the priest and the deacon of the palace chapel awaited him. Here he remained in prayer for fifteen or twenty minutes. After this the deacon read extracts from devotional books suited to the day, the lesson being most frequently a portion of the sermons of St. John Chrysostom. When the Tsar kissed the holy picture he was sprinkled by the priests with holy water which had been brought from some church or monastery, and had been consecrated on the festival of the saint to which that church was dedicated. After these early devotions the Tsar sent one of his chamberlains to the Tsaritsa to wish her good-morning and inquire after her health, and soon after went in person to visit her. The Tsar and the Tsaritsa then went together to one of the palace chapels and heard matins and a short early mass.

Meanwhile the nobles and courtiers had been collecting in the palace since an early hour, and were awaiting in an anteroom the entry of the Tsar from his private apartments. As soon as Alexis appeared they all bowed many times and presented petitions and reports. Some of the officials bowed to the ground as many as thirty times in gratitude for favours received. After some conversation about affairs of state, the Tsar, accompanied by all the nobles, went at nine o'clock to his chapel to hear mass, which at ordinary times lasted about two hours. At convenient intervals during the service the Tsar received reports from the various departments and officials, gave

answers, and consulted the boyárs about public matters, very
much as though he were in the council-chamber. On great festival days, instead of hearing mass in the palace chapel, the
Tsar and his court went to one of the large cathedrals, or to
some church or monastery in which the festival was particularly celebrated. In this case there was a solemn procession, in
which Alexis displayed all his accustomed magnificence. Although the Tsar had the habit of discussing state business during divine service, there was scarcely any one in the country so
pious as he. Doctor Collins, an Englishman, who was the
Tsar's physician for nine years, says that during Lent he would
stand in the church for five and six hours at a time, and make
as many as a thousand prostrations—on great holidays even
fifteen hundred.

After mass the Tsar and his nobles returned to the recep-
tion-room, where he continued to receive reports, which were
read by one of the secretaries, who also made suggestions to
him relating to the proper answers. During the time that business was being conducted none of the nobles in the reception-
room dared sit down. Everyone, except the Tsar, remained
standing, although the boyárs frequently went out into the
halls, or even outside into the courtyard, in order to sit down
and rest themselves. At the regular official meetings of the
council, however, the boyárs and all the officials sat down in
their proper places, one after the other, according to their rank,
those high in position being nearest the Tsar.

The business of state was usually finished by twelve o'clock,
when the nobles retired, and the Tsar went to his dinner, to
which he occasionally invited some of the more distinguished
boyárs, though generally he ate alone. He was served by
nobles of high position, who had the title of carvers, butlers,
cup-bearers, and table-companions. Every dish which was
brought to him was carefully guarded by special officials from
the time it left the cook's hands until it was placed on the table.
In the same way the wines and beer were tasted several times
before they reached the Tsar; and the cup-bearer, who held
the pitcher of wine constantly in his hands, tasted it afresh
every time he poured out for the Tsar. The private table of
Alexis was usually very plain. He ate the simplest dishes;

IVAN THE TERRIBLE IN OLD AGE.

the bread was the common Russian rice bread; he drank only a little wine or light beer, or sometimes a little cinnamon water, or had a few drops of oil of cinnamon in his beer, for cinnamon, Doctor Collins tells us, was the *aroma imperiale*. This, however, was nothing in comparison with his simplicity during the fasts. Dr. Collins says :

'In the great fasts he eats but three meals a week—viz. on Thursday, Saturday, Sunday ; for the rest, he takes a piece of brown bread and salt, a pickled mushroom or cucumber, and drinks a cup of small beer. He eats fish but twice in the great Lent, and observes it seven weeks altogether, besides Maslinets week, wherein they eat milk and eggs. Out of the fast he observes Mondays, Wednesdays, and Fridays, and will not then eat anything that comes of flesh. In fine, no monk is more observant of canonical hours than he is of fasts. We may reckon the fasts almost eight months in twelve, with the six weeks' fast before Christmas, and two other small fasts.'

On festivals, however, as many as seventy dishes were served at the Tsar's table, and nearly all these were given away, according to custom, as presents to the boyárs. Sometimes, as a mark of special honour, the Tsar would select his favourite dish for some particular friend.

After dinner the Tsar took a nap, which lasted about three hours, until vespers. The nobles again assembled in the palace for vespers, and during the intervals of the service the affairs of the state were again the subject of conversation and consultation, which sometimes continued, in the form of an irregular council, after service, although as a general rule the time until supper was spent by the Tsar with his family, or with those who were most intimate with him.

All the latter part of the day was given up to amusement, which at that time often consisted in hearing books read aloud. Most of these books were of an ecclesiastical character, and related either to sacred or church history, to religious dogmas, or to the lives of the saints. The Tsars were frequently among the most learned men of their age in theology and church history, and the most notable example in this respect was Iván the Terrible. Alexis was very fond, too, of having some one to read to him passages from the old chronicles of the Empire and extracts from the reports of his ambassadors abroad, and had translated for him the *courants*, or newspapers, then published in Western Europe. Besides these he loved stories of travel and of life in foreign parts and in remote regions of Russia, and kept in the palace, under the name of pilgrims and beadsmen, a number of old men who had wandered far and seen much, and who had the gift of telling in lively style what they had seen and passed through. The dryness of official history was in this way relieved by anecdotes and sketches taken from life. The Tsar had great respect for these beadsmen, and when one of them died he was buried with a considerable amount of pomp and ceremony in the church of the Trinity hostelry, the Tsar himself attending the funeral. Alexis was also fond of various games—draughts, backgammon, and especially chess; and frequently had spectacles of various kinds, such as wrestling matches and other contests, in the hall specially devoted to that purpose. During the winter he occasionally visited a bear fight. He was fond, too, of inspecting the work of jewellers, armourers, and other handicraftsmen, which was brought to the palace. Of out-door sports he especially affected hawking, and when he went to Sokólniki, one of his favourite resorts for this kind of amusement, the whole order of things was changed. In general, during his visits to the country he paid less attention to the affairs of the state, was less strict in his religious exercises, and devoted far more of his time to amusement.

The Muscovite ideal of woman, founded on the teachings and traditions of Byzantine theology, was purely a monastic one. The virtues of the cloister, faith, prayer, charity, obedience, and industry, were the highest virtues of a woman, and the life of the cloister was best suited to preserve her purity. Socially, woman was not an independent being; she was an inferior creation, dependent on her husband, for except as a wife her existence was scarcely recognized. Of this theoretical position of woman abundant proof is given in all the early didactic literature of Russia, and especially in the 'Domostróï,' that curious manual of household economy written in the time of Iván the Terrible. The wife should be blindly obedient in all things, and for her faults should be severely whipped, though not in anger. Her duty was to keep the house, to look after

THE TEREM, OR WOMEN'S APARTMENT.

the food and clothing, and to see to the comfort of her husband; to bear children, but not to educate them. Severity was inculcated, and to play with one's children was esteemed a sin —a snare of the devil. The wife was bound to stay chiefly at home, and to be acquainted with nothing but her household work. To all questions on outside matters she was to answer that she did not know. It was believed that an element of evil lurked in the female sex, and even the most innocent sport between little boys and girls, or social intercourse between young men and women, was severely reprehended. The 'Domostrói,' and even Pososhkóf, as late as the eighteenth century, recommended a father to take his cudgel and break the ribs of his son, whom he found jesting with a girl. Traces of this feeling with regard to women are still found in current proverbs. 'A woman's hair is long, her understanding is short,' runs one proverb; 'The wits of a woman are like the wildness of beasts,' says another; while a third says: 'As a horse by the bit, so must a woman be governed by threats.' The collections of popular stories and anecdotes are full of instances of the innate wickedness and devilishness of the female sex, with references to all the weak or wicked women of sacred and profane history. In the 'Great Mirror,' compiled in the seventeenth century, we even find the obstinacy of women exemplified by the well-known anecdote of the drowning woman still making with her fingers the sign of 'scissors.'

Although this was the theoretical position of woman in Russian society, practically in small households, where women were important factors, there were great divergencies from the strict rules of the 'Domostrói.' In the higher ranks of life the women were more carefully guarded and restrained, and in the family of the Tsar the seclusion in the *Terém*, or women's apartments, was almost complete. This was in part due to a superstitious belief in witchcraft, the evil eye, and charms that might affect the life, health, or fertility of the royal race. Neither the Tsaritsa nor the princesses ever appeared openly in public; they never went out except in a closed litter or carriage; in church they stood behind a veil—made, it is true, sometimes of gauze—and they usually timed their visits to the churches and monasteries for the evening or the early morning,

and on these occasions no one was admitted except the immediate
attendants of the court. Von Meyerberg, Imperial ambassador
at Moscow in 1663, writes, that out of a thousand courtiers,
there will hardly be found one who can boast that he has seen
the Tsaritsa, or any of the sisters or daughters of the Tsar.
Even their physicians are not allowed to see them. When it is
necessary to call a doctor for the Tsaritsa, the windows are all
darkened, and he is obliged to feel her pulse through a piece of
gauze, so as not to touch her bare hand! Even chance en-
counters were severely punished. In 1674, two chamberlains,
Dashkóf and Buturlín, on suddenly turning a corner in one of
the interior courts of the palace, met the carriage of the Tsaritsa
Natalia, who was going to prayers at a convent. Their col-
leagues succeeded in getting out of the way. Dashkóf and Buturlín were arrested, examined, and deprived of their offices,
but as the encounter was proved to be purely fortuitous and
unavoidable, they were in a few days restored to their rank.
And yet, this was during the reign of Alexis, who was far less
strict than his predecessors.

The Tsar Basil had married a Polish princess, Helena Glín-
ska, and during her lifetime—especially during the minority of
her son, Iván the Terrible—Polish and Western usages crept
into the court. The so-called False Dimítri was eminently liberal-minded, and disposed to accept foreign habits, and had he
reigned longer, a much freer life would doubtless have prevailed
at the Court of Moscow; but he was murdered very soon after
his marriage with the Polish Marie Mníshek. Then, with
the re-establishment of a national dynasty—in the Románofs
—came a reaction in an ultra-national sense. It could hardly
be otherwise; the father of the Tsar Michael was the Patriarch,
and his mother, who had great influence over the young Tsar
and long kept him in leading-strings, was a nun, both having
been forced into monastic life during the Troublous Times.
The ascetic type of woman prevailed. Of this type the wife of
the boyár Morózof, the great minister of the early part of the
reign of Alexis, was a model and pattern. In the latter part of
this reign foreign customs began again to edge in, owing in part
to the annexation of Kíef and Little Russia, and to the influx
of teachers educated after Polish and Western standards, to the

greater intercourse with the West of Europe, and in part to the' increasing influence of the 'German Suburb' or foreign colony at Moscow. Of this last we shall have occasion to speak again.

At this time there were a dozen princesses living in the palace—the sisters, the aunts, and the six daughters of the Tsar Alexis. All were unmarried. It was beneath the dignity of the Tsar to bestow his daughter's hand upon a subject, and differences of religion and ignorance of the languages and manners of other countries prevented marriages with foreign princes. Since the Tartar invasion only two attempts had been made to marry a Russian princess to a foreigner. Boris Godunóf wished to marry his daughter Xénia to the Danish Prince John, brother of King Christian IV., but the bridegroom died of a fever soon after his arrival in Russia in 1602. The marriage of Irene, the daughter of the Tsar Michael, with the Danish Prince Woldemar, a natural son of Christian IV., was never consummated on account of the refusal of Woldemar to change his religion, although it had been expressly stipulated in the marriage contract that he should not be obliged to do so. The prince was kept a prisoner in Moscow until the death of the Tsar, when he was allowed to return to Denmark. It is an indirect evidence of the manners of the princesses, that the Russian envoy at Copenhagen, in recounting the good qualities of Irene, praised her particularly for never getting drunk.

All these princesses of the family of Alexis had been brought up in the old style and with the old prejudices. None, except Sophia—who had shared the lessons of her brother Theodore, under the learned Polish monk Simeon Polótsky—had more than the rudiments of an education, or knew any language but their own. When the Tsaritsa Natalia Narýshkin, who had been brought up by the wife of Matvéief, a Scotchwoman, and had seen something of society, entered the palace, it gave a shock, and her words and acts were criticised and disapproved. She was received much as a young Catholic stepmother would be by a large household composed of spinsters brought up with the strictest Presbyterian notions. One of her very first acts—to raise the corner of her carriage curtain so as to see the crowd —provoked such a storm in the household that she was obliged for a long time to be very rigid in her conformity to the palace etiquette. But as time went on the observance of old forms became more lax. The Tsaritsa shared the amusements of the Tsar. In going to and from the country, and even once in a state procession, she rode in an uncovered carriage with the Tsar and one or two of the children. She saw the plays in the palace theatre from a latticed box, and witnessed ceremonies and festivities from the corner of some convenient gallery. Lyseck says that the reception of his ambassador took place at Kolómensky solely that Tsaritsa Natalia might see it more easily, and that the procession was made to go slowly past the window where she sat, that she might have more time to observe it. She went openly to church, together with the Tsar, on occasion of the visit of the Patriarchs Paisius and Macarius; and in 1675, at the procession of Holy Thursday, when the Patriarch rode through the Krémlin on an ass, which the Tsar led by the bridle, he turned and blessed the Tsaritsa and the princesses, who were posted at the windows of the banqueting-hall.

The household of the Tsar was organised like that of any great noble, though on a larger scale. Of the women's part the Tsaritsa was nominally the head. She had to attend to her own wardrobe, which took no little time, and oversee that of her husband and her children, and had under her direction a large establishment of sewing women. She must receive petitions and attend to cases of charity. She must provide husbands and dowries for the many young girls about her court, and then keep a constant look-out for their interests and those of their families. She had, too, her private estates, the accounts of which she audited, and the revenues of which she collected and expended. What little time was left from household cares and religious duties could be spent in talk, in listening to stories and songs, in laughing at the jests of the court fools, in looking at the amusements of the girls in the play-hall, or in embroidering towels and napkins, robes for the Tsar and princes, and altar-cloths and vestments for the church.[1]

---

[1] See Zabiélin, *Home Life of the Russian Tsars and Tsaritsas* (Russian), Moscow, 1862, 1869; Samuel Collins, *The Present State of Russia*, London, 1671; Meyerberg, *Voyage en Moscovie*, Leyden, 1688; A. Brückner, *Zur Geschichte der didaktischen Literatur in Russland*, and *Die Frauenfrage in Russland*, in the *Russische Revue*, for 1876 and 1879; the *Domostróï* (Russian), St. Petersburg, 1867.

A PEASANT GIRL IN ANCIENT RUSSIAN DRESS.

III.

DEATH OF ALEXIS.—GREAT CHANGES.—PETER'S CHILDHOOD.

THE eldest Tsarévitch, Theodore, had in the earlier part of 1674 been declared to be of full age, and had therefore been recognised as heir to the throne, and the Tsar had presented him as such both to his subjects and to the foreigners at Moscow. His health, however, was so delicate that few expected that he would ultimately reach the throne. The only other living son by the first marriage, Joánn, or Iván,[1] seemed from his infirmities incapable of reigning; and nearly every one believed that the future successor of Alexis would be Peter. Matvéief in all probability was convinced of this; and as the Tsar Alexis at this time was only forty-seven, and was in robust health, he allowed events to take their natural course, making no effort to grasp at the succession for his *protégé*. Suddenly, in February, 1676, the Tsar died. On Epiphany, 1676, 1676. according to custom, he had taken part with all the usual ceremony in the procession for the blessing of the river Moskvá. On the name's-day of his sister Tatiana, he had gone to mass and presented the boyárs with the usual name's-day pasties, filled then as now with fish. On January 27 there had been at the palace a representation of a comedy, followed by a concert, but the Tsar, feeling unwell, retired during the performance and went to bed. His illness did not seem in the least dangerous, but still increased, and ten days after—February 8—he died, after having given his formal benediction to Theodore, who was at that time fourteen years old. In all probability it needed no particular efforts on the part of the daughters of Alexis to bring their father to consecrate the

---

[1] Iván is the popular, Joánn the solemn and official form of the name.

birthright of his eldest son by his blessing. The right of succession to the throne was not strictly fixed by law, but in all Russian families the eldest son succeeded to the father as head of the household, and Theodore, moreover, had the advantage of possession, having been previously formally and publicly proclaimed the heir. The hopes of Matvéief and the Narýshkins rested not so much on the fitness of Peter, for his brilliant qualities were not yet developed, and he had little more than good health to recommend him, as on the debility of Theodore and Iván, who, they thought, would both die long before the

Tsar Theodore (Half-Brother of Peter).

Tsar, their father. The story that Matvéief endeavoured by a *coup d'état* to set aside Theodore in favour of Peter, is a rumour reported by a badly-informed Polish diplomat, devoid of foundation and disproved by events.

After the burial of Alexis and the coronation of Theodore, everything about the court was changed. The Narýshkins went into retirement, and the Miloslávskys came again into power. At first this had but slight effect on public affairs, but a few months later the minister Matvéief, who was the most dangerous rival and antagonist of the Miloslávskys, was suddenly banished, and appointed governor of Verkhoturié, in the northernmost part of Siberia. Matvéief, however, had not succeeded in sailing up the Volga to Léshef, the place where the great Siberian road leaves the river, when he was overtaken with the news that he was accused of an intention to overthrow the Tsar, of dealing with evil spirits, and of the study of magic and witchcraft, by means of a black book filled with ciphers (which in the end turned out to be an algebra for the use of his son). He was judged almost as soon as accused, was deprived of all his property and honours, and was exiled as a state criminal, to live in the wild and distant place of Pustozérsk, in the province of Archangel. At the same time two of the Tsaritsa's brothers, Iván and Athanasius Narýshkin, were sent into exile; others of her friends were removed from Moscow, and she and her children—for a daughter, Natalia, named after her mother, had been born in 1673, while a second daughter, Theodora, had died in her infancy—were placed in a most disagreeable and uncomfortable position. They were sent away from the palace of the Krémlin to live at Preobrazhénsky, a favourite villa of the Tsar Alexis, amid fields and groves, on the river Yaúza, about three miles from the centre of Moscow. What, however, at first seemed a misfortune, turned out to be an advantage. The freer life of the country, even though accompanied by a narrow income and many unpleasant circumstances, was better for the development of Peter than the formal life at Moscow would have been. Natalia felt at first that there was danger of Peter becoming a second Dimítri of Úglitch—that unfortunate son of Iván the Terrible, who was murdered in the reign of his brother, Theodore, by order of Borís Godunóf; but this Theodore was of a mild disposition, and at this time the life of a prince was still held sacred.

The education given to the Russian upper classes at this period seldom consisted of anything more than reading, writing, and singing by note, with some ideas of history, geography, and of the productions of the earth, conveyed by means of picture-books: but instruction in grammar, in mathematics—even in arithmetic—or in the higher branches of learning, was exceedingly rare, except among the clergy. A high school, at which Greek and Latin were taught was in existence at Kíef, but Kíef had only just been re-conquered from the Poles, and was not then definitively part of Russia. Although the influence which this school exercised was gradually felt at Moscow, the Moscow school, on a similar plan, was not started until the reign of Theodore. Even the princes of the royal house received scarcely anything more than this elementary education. Theodore had been exceptionally brought up by the learned monk, Simeon Polótsky, and could speak Polish and Latin. So also could his sister Sophia. The example of the court and the

adoption of Polish manners and usages began to affect the aristocracy, and several families at that time had Polish teachers
for their children. But so restricted was this influence that, at
a time when every Polish and Hungarian gentleman conversed
familiarly in Latin, Prince Basil Golítsyn was, according to
De Neuville, an exception among Russian statesmen. The son
of Matvéief, who had been accompanied in his exile by his
teacher, had few equals in attainments among Peter's comrades.

It is probable that such an elementary education was all
Peter would have received had circumstances not interrupted
his earlier studies and changed the bent of his mind. A pic-
ture-book was ordered to be prepared by one of the Moscow
artists for him when he was only a year old; an alphabet or
primer was given him on December 6, 1675, while his father
was still alive, and the next day prayers were said for his success in his studies, in the church of St. Nicholas Gostún, as was
customary in Russia at that time when a child first began to be
taught.   Peter had preceded by a few days the period fixed by
usage for beginning a boy's education—the feast of the prophet
Nahum.

Soon after Theodore ascended the throne, he appointed as
teacher for Peter, on the recommendation of the privy-councillor, Theodore Sokóvin, a scribe from the Bureau of Petitions,
Nikíta Moíséievitch Zótof, a man enjoying a high reputation
for his learning and morality. The Psalter, the Gospels, the
Hours were the books from which, like other boys of his age,
Peter was taught. Besides learning to read, he acquired much
by heart, and was able, even at a later period of his life, to re-
cite many passages from the Scriptures. Apparently he learned
to write late, for the first copy-books of which we find mention
were not given out until 1680, when he was already seven years
old, and his handwriting was always extremely bad. At the
same time he learned singing by note—an acquirement which
in later years frequently afforded him amusement, when in
country churches he would enter the chancel and join the choir.

Zótof, like a skilful teacher, interspersed his instructions with
amusement, and by a plentiful supply of picture-books, most
of which were specially written and illuminated for Peter, and
by what were then called 'Frank leaves'—that is, German and

Italian engravings and wood-cuts—succeeded gradually in giving his pupil a general knowledge of Russian history, of the deeds of the heroes of early times, of the reigns and wars of the previous Tsars, and some notions of the course of events in antiquity as well as in later Europe, besides a rude idea of natural history.

In this way, between study and play, Peter's life passed on quietly and uneventfully for the six years of the reign of Theodore, the greater part of which was spent at Preobrazhénsky. Although away from the immediate intrigues of the court, yet rumours and agitations reached her country abode, and the Tsaritsa Natalia could never be sure what was in store for her and her children.

Peter doubtless often heard from his mother much sad talk of what she thought their wrongs and their uncomfortable position, much criticism of people in power; many regrets for her protector, Matvéief, with longings for what seemed to her impossible—his return. Boys of Peter's age are quick and intelligent. They keep their ears and eyes open, and they are ever ready with questions. No doubt Peter asked many, and they were answered. The impressions which were then made on him were deep, and would have sufficed greatly to influence his subsequent life, even without the events that followed.[1]

---

[1] See Soloviéf, xiii., ch. 2; Ustriálof, i., ch. 1; Pogódin, pp. 15–29; Esipof; Astrof; Matvéief's *Memoirs; History of the Causeless Imprisonment of the Boyár Matvéief.*

IV.

AFTER Theodore ascended the throne, the chief personage
in the state, who had almost supreme power, and who took
upon himself the supervision of all the departments of government, was Iván Michaílovitch Miloslávsky, a cousin of Theodore's mother. He was supported by the whole of the family
influence, and had been recalled from Astrakhán, where, nominally governor, he had been practically an exile. His insolent
manners made him many enemies, even outside the Narýshkin
party, which was naturally disposed against him. The Miloslávskys were not among the number of the old and distinguished families. Dr. Collins says : ' Eliah, the present emper-
our's father-in-law, was of so mean account, that within this
twenty years he drew wine to some English men, and his
daughter gather'd mushrooms and sold them in the market.'
The Registers of Services show no entry that the family had
ever benefited the state or taken part in public affairs until the
marriage of Alexis. During their twenty years' lease of power
the Miloslávskys had been arrogant and self-willed. They had
not conciliated the old nobility, and now the descendants of
Rúrik were almost in open opposition. Among the discontented
were Bogdán Hítrovo, Master of the Ordnance, who had been
much in the confidence of the Tsar Alexis, and his friend,
Prince Yúry Dolgorúky, a powerful nobleman and chief of the
Streltsi, or National Guard, neither of whom had been taken
into the councils of the new sovereign.

One way which this party took of weakening the power of
the Miloslávskys was by getting young men devoted to their
interests into place at court, and especially into positions of con-

fidence near the Tsar, thinking that they could thus gradually obtain an influence over him which could be used for their benefit. They particularly put forward in this way Iván Yazýkof and the two brothers Likhatchéf. Whatever the original feelings of these young men may have been toward their supporters, they soon acquired such power over the good-natured but weak-minded Tsar that they resolved to employ it rather for their own benefit thán for that of those who had raised them to place. In order to increase their influence they determined to marry the Tsar into some family connected with or devoted to their interest, and chose Agatha Grushétsky, a niece of the privy-councillor Simeon Zborófsky, a nobleman of Polish origin. They managed to give the Tsar a sight of the young lady during a church procession, and Theodore, who was then only eighteen, was so pleased with her appearance that he resolved to marry her. At this there was a great outcry on the part of his sisters, who were jealous of new members coming into the family, and there was opposition by Iván Miloslávsky, who felt his influence on the wane.

A report was therefore presented to Theodore containing grave accusations against her and her mother. The falsity of these was immediately shown by Yazýkof and the Likhatchéfs, and Miloslávsky was prohibited from appearing at court; although after the marriage, which took place on July 28, 1680, this prohibition was removed at the request of the Tsaritsa. Yet he lost all power and influence. Yazýkof was promoted to the grade of *okólnitchy*, and received the position of Master of the Ordnance in place of his old patron Hítrovo, while the Likhatchéfs became chamberlains. The power thus 1681. obtained lasted but a short time, for the Tsaritsa died in childbed on July 24, 1681, and was followed in a few days by her new-born son.

This event was a terrible blow to the favourites, for the health of Theodore was so delicate, that in case of his death they would find themselves face to face with the Miloslávsky party and the princesses, sisters of Theodore, and would run great danger of exile if not of death. They had alienated their own supporters, Hítrovo and Dolgorúky and their friends, and therefore had no resource except to try to make up to the Narýshkin party and the adherents of Peter. With this view, and in spite of opinions of the physicians as to his health, they proceeded to counsel Theodore to marry again. This time they proposed to him Martha Apráxin, the god-daughter of the ex-minister Matvéief, a girl of fourteen years. The first meeting that favoured this idea took place in December of that year; and the chosen bride (as no doubt she had been instructed) immediately asked the Tsar to alleviate the fate of her god-father Matvéief, who, up to this time, had vainly written petitions showing his innocence. The sentence was quashed; the property and estates of Mat-

Tsarevitch Joann, or Iván (Half-Brother of Peter).

véief were returned to him, and in addition, he was given the village of Landékh, and was commanded to wait for further orders at the town of Lukh, near Kostromá, on the Volga.

But these orders were not to come from Theodore, who had become feebler from day to day, and who died 1682. two months and a half after his second marriage, on May 7, 1682. The death of Theodore left two possible candidates for the throne : Iván, the elder brother, the son of the Tsar Alexis by his first wife, Marie Miloslávsky, blind, lame, and half idiotic ; and the son of Natalia Naryshkin, the strong, healthy, and clever Peter. Although there was no law regulating the succession to the throne, except that it should be hereditary in the Románof family, yet primogeniture was consecrated by usage. Theodore had appointed no other successor, and Iván had therefore the greater right to the throne. But the accession of Iván would necessitate a continued regency, and that regency would naturally be influenced by his uncle and cousins, the Miloslávskys. The Miloslávsky family was not popular among the aristocracy, and this very fact disposed many of the nobles to take the side of Peter. To be sure, even under Peter the public affairs would be for a long time in the hands of Matvéief; but Matvéief was a man who had never offended the great nobles, either by his manners toward them, or by the introduction of any reforms trenching upon their privileges. He employed them, as far as he could; at all events, he respected their rank, and so few of them at that time were fit to take part in public affairs that this was all they cared for. Only two great magnates took the side of Iván—Prince Vasiliévitch Golítsyn and Prince Iván Andréievitch Havánsky. Golítsyn had been brought into great antagonism to the aristocracy by the part he had played in the reform movement under Theodore, of which we shall speak presently; but there is also some reason to believe that he was already in such intimate personal relations with the Princess Sophia, of whom he was afterward the acknowledged lover, that he saw through her means, in case of the election of Iván, the possibility of his rising to the highest power and influence in the state. Prince Havánsky, an empty and addle-pated man, of no special ability, prided himself on his descent from King Gédimin of Lithuania, and had a great opinion of his own personal importance. Without any claim to important public positions, his life had been passed in continual surprises that the high places of state were, one after the other, filled by some other than Prince Havánsky. He had been deprived of command at Pskof—the only important position he had ever held—for cruelty, immorality, and notorious incompetency, and the Tsar Alexis had said to him, ' Though I picked you out and put you into service, everybody calls you a fool.' Without ideas, he talked incessantly, bustled noisily about with no definite object, and was such a braggart and boaster that he acquired the popular nickname of *Tararúi*, expressive at once of the inconstancy of the weather-cock and the exultation of the barn-yard fowl. As from Matvéief and the Narýshkins he had nothing to hope for himself, and consequently for Russia, he opposed Peter and took the side of Iván. The sisters of Theodore and the Miloslávsky party had, therefore, little support to expect for their candidate in the council which would decide the election of the Tsar, for, under the circumstances, it was felt that nothing less than a ratification by the representatives of all

Russia, as in the case of the election of Michael, would fix the crown on Peter's head without the liability to further disputes. But as the Miloslávskys had not been sparing of the step-mother and her children in the moment of their triumph, dur-ing the early part of the reign of Theodore, they had to fear the worst, and therefore had to do something in self-defence. By a plentiful use of money and promises, they won over a number of ' young men '—that is, persons without high position, but who, nevertheless, could exercise considerable influence— some courtiers, others delegates of the Streltsi, or National Guard, among whom there was a great deal of discontent. Their plans, however, were not yet matured when Theodore died. Many of the aristocratic party, which used the name of Peter for its watchword, ascertaining 'the movements of the Miloslávskys, feared that the election would result in bloodshed, and came to the palace with coats of mail under their gowns. This time, however, there was no trouble.

When all, according to custom, had given a farewell kiss to the hand of the dead Theodore, and had paid their salutations to Princes Iván and Peter, the Patriarch, the archbishops, and the abbots of the chief monasteries came into the ante-room. The Patriarch, who was himself a boyár, belonging to the Sa-bélief family, put to the assembled nobles the question: ' Which of the two Princes shall be Tsar ?' The nobles at once replied that this should be decided by the people of all the ranks of the Muscovite state. Now delegates from the whole country, two from each district, were in Moscow, having come on the summons of Theodore, in order at a session of the States-General to decide on a fundamental reform of the tax system. No pains, however, were taken to collect these delegates, and the nobles meant by their words merely their adherents, who had collected in the Great Square of the Krémlin, adjoining the palace. The Tsar Shúïsky had been overturned because he had been elected by Moscow alone, and therefore, the States-General had been convened when Michael Románof was chosen. The ' Muscovite State' in the present case meant, practically, a Moscow crowd.

The Patriarch and the archbishops then proceeded to the balcony overlooking the Grand Square of the Krémlin, in front

of the church of the Saviour, and the question was again put:
' To which of the two Princes do you give the rule ? ' There
were loud cries everywhere of ' Peter Alexéivitch,' there were
some cries of 'Iván Alexéivitch,' but these were soon drowned.
The matter was thus decided by the crowd of people of all
ranks; and the Patriarch returned into the palace, and gave
his blessing to Peter as Tsar. The name of only one person
who shouted for Iván is known—Maxim Sumbúlof—and an
anecdote is told of his subsequent meeting with Peter. Once,
when at mass at the Miracle monastery, Peter noticed that one
monk did not go up to receive the *antidoron*, or morsels of
holy bread distributed at the end of the mass. Peter asked
who he was, and was told it was Sumbúlof. He then called
the monk, and asked him why he did not receive the *antidoron*.
The monk answered: ' I did not dare to go by you, Lord, and
raise my eyes to you.' The Tsar bade him go for the *antidoron*, and subsequently calling him again asked: ' Why did I not
suit you in the election for Tsar ? ' Sumbúlof replied: ' Judas
sold Christ for thirty pieces of silver, although he was his
disciple; and I, Lord, was never your disciple. Is it strange,
then, that I—a petty nobleman—should sell you to become a
boyár ? '

All this was in the spring of 1682, when the Whigs were
conspiring against Charles the Second, three years before the
Revocation of the Edict of Nantes, and a year after Strasburg
and Alsace had been annexed by Louis XIV., the same year
that William Penn was colonising Pennsylvania and La Salle
exploring Louisiana.

The election was decided ; Peter was Tsar, and by custom,
the step-mother, as head of the family, was the regent. What
could the princesses and the Miloslávsky party do ? Pretence
was useless ; open opposition was the expression almost of
despair. On the day of the funeral of Theodore, the Princess
Sophia, contrary to all etiquette, insisted on accompanying the
body to the church. Remonstrances were in vain. She not
only went, disregarding the Byzantine prescriptions which kept
the princesses unseen behind a canopy, showing herself openly
to the people, but she was also loud in the expression of her
grief, which was certainly sincere and not feigned. At last,

long before the ceremonies had terminated, the widowed step-
mother, Natalia, left the church, leading her son Peter. This
excited remark, not only among the populace, but still more on
the part of the Princess Tatiana, the eldest member of the
family, the sister of the Tsar Alexis and the aunt of Theodore,
highly respected for her charity and goodness, who sent at noon
a message to Natalia, saying: 'You're a fine relation—could
you not wait till the end of the funeral.' Natalia excused herself on the ground that Peter was so young that it would have
been injurious to his health to have remained in church so long
without eating. Her cousin, Iván Narýshkin, who had just
returned from exile, and was constantly causing trouble by his
thoughtless remarks, said: 'Let him that is dead lie there.
His Majesty the Tsar is not dead, but still lives.' On returning from the funeral Sophia wept bitterly, and turning to the
people cried out: 'You see how our brother the Tsar Theodore
has suddenly gone from this world. His ill-wishers and
enemies have poisoned him. Have pity on us orphans. We
have no father nor mother nor brother. Our eldest brother
Iván has not been elected Tsar, and if we are to blame before
you and the boyárs, let us go live in other lands which are
ruled over by Christian Kings.' These words naturally produced a deep impression.[1]

[1] Solóvief, vol. xiii. ; Ustriálof, ch. 1; Pogódin; Esipof; Astrof; Mat-
véief's *Memoirs ; Causeless Imprisonment of the Boyár Matvéief ;* Medvédief's
Memoirs ; Collins ; Zamyslófsky, *The Reign of Theodore Alexéievitch* (Russian),
St. Petersburg, 1871.

V.

NEED OF REFORM.—ABOLITION OF PRECEDENCE.—GRIEVANCES
OF THE STRELTSI.—RETURN OF MATVÉIEF.

So much for court intrigues. Struggles between courtiers
for place and influence have always been carried on, and are
often not devoid of political and historical importance. Court
intrigues are, however, not everything. In cases where court
intrigue seems to have shaped the destiny of a nation, there
will usually be found some causes of popular discontent—some
struggle in the mass of the nation, which either takes advantage of the intrigue of courtiers to make itself felt, or by means
of which courtiers succeed in their ends. So it was here.
Whatever might be the mutual feelings of the rival families
and of the rival place-holders who surrounded Theodore, and
who placed Peter on the throne, they are only of importance
on account of the popular fermentation which they assisted in
bringing to light.

The need of reform had long been felt everywhere—in the
Church, in civil life, in education, in the administration, especially of justice and of the finances, and more than anywhere
else, in the army. The defects of the army had caused the
defeat of Russia both by Swedes and Poles, and the Tsar Alexis
readily accepted officers, men, and arms from abroad. Russia
was beginning a period of transition, and a period of transition
is always a period of discontent. She had arrived at that state
when all thinking men saw very plainly that the old order of
things had been outlived and must soon come to an end. With
new ideas new systems must be introduced from Western
Europe, and no one knew exactly how changes would take
place, or how far they would go. Feeble as the Tsar Theodore
was physically, he entered fully into the reformatory spirit,

and his short reign was distinguished by many sincere effort to improve the condition of his country. He wished to re-or-ganise the army, and he had a design of establishing an academy in Moscow for the better education of the people, and for the support of the Church. He also formed a project which seemed far in advance of the times, for completely separating the military and civil offices. His early death left many of his plans inchoate, but one great reform he was able to carry out—namely, the abolition of *precedence*, which had long been a curse, and had greatly retarded the proper administration of public affairs. According to this system of precedence, every noble kept strict account of all services which he or his ancestors had rendered to the state, and of the positions and offices which they had held. He felt that he could not take a position less distinguished than any of those which his ancestors had previously occupied—that he could not hold a subordinate office, or take a lower place at the table, or in the Council House, without derogating from his rank, or lowering and dishonouring himself and his family, in his own estimation and that of others. For this reason it was almost impossible to put capable men into positions which the public welfare required them to fill, because incapable men of higher social rank refused to serve under them. So detrimental was this system—which by the practice of so many years had become an inveterate custom—that the loss of several campaigns, growing entirely out of struggle for place, sometimes compelled the Tsars to declare, at the beginning of a war, that it would be conducted 'without precedence'—that is, that the offices and positions held during the campaign should not count in the books of precedence. This method of avoiding the custom had come into vogue as early as the time of Iván the Terrible, and during the reigns of Michael and Alexis nearly all the campaigns had been carried on 'without precedence.' This of course led people to think that the Tsar might at some time issue a ukase entirely abolishing precedence, and accustomed the minds of the nobility to the possibility of such a reform. The campaign against the Turks in 1681, in spite of the great numbers of men under arms, and the large sums expended, had not resulted as had been wished. The Tsar Theodore therefore appointed a commission, presided over by Prince

TSAR THEODORE BURNING THE BOOKS OF PRECEDENCE.

Basil Golítsyn, to consider the subject of the re-organisation of the army on the Western basis. The commission made a report on that subject, and as a preliminary to the system which they wished to introduce, proposed the total abolition of precedence. On January 22, 1682, Theodore called a special council of the boyárs, to which he invited the Patriarch, the archbishops, and delegates from the chief monasteries. At this council the Tsar urged the abolition of precedence as an absolute necessity for the welfare of the state, stating, in the language of that time, that 'precedence was an institution invented by the devil, for the purpose of destroying Christian love, and of increasing the hatred of brother to brother;' and he called attention to his father's efforts, as well as his own, for the suppression of this custom, and put the question to the assembly whether the petition of this commission should be accepted, and whether, in future, all ranks and offices should be without precedence, or, as hitherto, with precedence. The Patriarch, in the name of the archbishops and of the Church, followed with a violent attack on the system, and the assembly voted that the Tsar should accede to the petition, and to the opinions of the Holy Patriarch and the archbishops, and should order that 'henceforward all ranks should be without precedence, because formerly, in many military exploits, and embassies, and affairs of all kinds, much harm, disorganisation, ruin, and advantage to the enemy had been wrought by this, and that it was a system opposed to God, intended to cause confusion and great hatred.' After that the Tsar ordered the official service books to be brought into his presence—the books in which, for many centuries, the official services of every noble family, and of all its members had been carefully noted down. He ordered, at the same time, that all who had such books of their own, either original or copies, should surrender them to the Government. These books were then delivered to an official, who took them into the court-yard, and in a furnace prepared for the occasion burned them in the presence of the Tsar and the nobles.

A reform like this, however useful, could not be effected without exciting some discontent and opposition on the part of the nobility. The only matter of surprise is that it excited so little at the time. Everyone, however, who had any patriotism, or any sense of public duty, felt that it was a necessity. They had been willing to sacrifice their feeling about rank on occasions when the Tsar had specially commanded that the ser-

vice should be without precedence ; they were now willing to sacrifice it entirely. At the same time, if an occasion arose—if there were a time when precedence was not waived—they would risk every- thing rather than allow their fam- ily to be dishonoured. But, while consenting to the measure, the great nobles had bitter feelings against the authors of it, and es- pecially against Prince Basil Golít- syn. Taken with other things, this helped to make them unite their forces, and, as has been said, they supported Peter.

The Streltsi of 1613.

Reference has been made to the want of organisation in the army. The military forces of Russia at this time consisted of the armed peasants, who were brought into the field by their lords and masters, after special summons, at the beginning of every campaign —an undisciplined and unwieldy mob; a few regiments of ' soldiers,' officered by foreigners and drilled in European tactics; and the *Strel- tsi* (literally, archers), a sort of na- tional guard founded by Iván the Terrible. The Streltsi, composed of twenty-two regiments named after their colonels, of about a thousand men each, served ex- clusively under Russian officers, and were governed by the old rules

The Streltsi of a Little Later Date.

of Russian tactics, though subjected to regular discipline. They were concentrated in Moscow, and a few other towns, where they lived in quarters by themselves. They were subject to no taxes and were allowed certain privileges, such as being permitted to have their own mills and shops, and to trade on their own account when they were not actually engaged in military duties. They were for the most part married, their duties were hereditary, and their sons, as soon as they became old enough, entered into their fathers' regiments. In spite of their privileged position, the Streltsi were fair representatives of the mass of the Russian people, among whom they lived and married and had daily intercourse, and from whom they received accession to their ranks. Still, not only had their discipline become weaker by their exceptional position, but much disorder and corruption had crept into their organisation, and there were many complaints that their commanders withheld from them a portion of their pay, that they cheated them in their equipments, and that they compelled them to work as their servants and slaves, and thus prevented them from carrying on their own trade and supporting their families.

In the winter before the death of Theodore, and about the time of the abolition of precedence, the Streltsi of the Pýzhof Regiment made a formal complaint that their colonel was retaining half their pay, and subjecting them to further oppression. Yazýkof, to whom was given the duty of investigating the matter, decided against the Streltsi and took the side of the colonel—for a favourable answer to the petitioners might have offended Prince Dolgorúky, the head of the Department of the Streltsi, an old magnate, whose goodwill it was at that time most necessary to keep—and ordered the more prominent of the petitioners to be punished, so as to teach the Streltsi in future not to complain, but to be obedient to the constituted authorities. Three days before the death of Theodore, the Streltsi accused another colonel, Simeon Griboyédof, of extortion, of cruel treatment, of withholding their pay, occupying their land, compelling them under pain of flogging to work for him, and especially of forcing them to work during the Easter festivities on a country house he was building near Moscow. To prevent what happened before, they this time sent a delegate with the petition to Prince Dolgorúky himself at the department. Dolgorúky, to whom it was reported that the petition had been brought by a drunken and foul-mouthed soldier, ordered the delegate to be whipped. But as he was being taken to suffer his punishment before the eyes of his comrades, he said : 'Brothers, why do you give me up ? I gave the petition by your orders, and for you.' The Streltsi thereupon attacked the guard and rescued their delegate. This affair excited their anger, and in all the regiments complaints began to be louder and more persistent. Finally the Government yielded, or appeared to yield, and an order was given that Griboyédof should be removed and sent to Siberia, and that his property should be confiscated. He was imprisoned for a day and then reinstated. The Streltsi then became frightened, and fearing the fate of the first petitioners, began to take measures for their own safety. The death of Theodore, however, put for a moment a stop to all proceedings, and the Streltsi quietly took the oath of allegiance to Peter. The men of one regiment only refused at first to take the oath, but they were soon won over by the boyárs who were sent to talk with them, and kissed the cross.

The Miloslávsky party, in their efforts for self-defence, naturally took advantage of the discontent of the Streltsi. Iván Miloslávsky gave himself out as ill and received no guests, but he easily found aid in his nephew and even among the Streltsi. Disquieting rumours were spread. Much talk was made about the burdens that would be laid upon the Streltsi by the Naryshkins when they came into power, and it was whispered about that the boyárs, with the help of the German doctors, had poisoned the Tsar Theodore, that they had unjustly elected Peter, passing over the claims of Iván, his elder brother, in order that they might rule under his name, and that they had openly threatened many of the Streltsi with death for their previous complaints. The absence of Matvéief was favourable to any plans for working on the Streltsi against the Naryshkins. He was so much loved by the Streltsi, that, had he been present, he could easily have counteracted such schemes by promising justice. Some regiments assumed a hostile attitude, while others wavered, and one—the Súkharef regiment—refused to listen to these intrigues and remained faithful. In others the officers who endeavoured to restore order and bring the men to some

sense of their obedience to the crown were insulted and attacked.
On May 9, the Streltsi presented petitions against twelve of
their colonels and officers for acts of violence, unjust imposts
and other illegalities, and demanded immediate satisfaction,
threatening, in case it were not granted them, to take the law
into their own hands and recover their losses out of the property of the officers. The new Government had no counsellors
on whom to rely. Among all the nobles of old and venerated
names who made up the aristocratic party, and who had gath-
ered round Peter—Odóiefsky, Tcherkássky, Dolgorúky, Répnin, Troekúrof, Ramodanófsky, Sheremétief, Shein, Kurákin,
Lýkof, Urúsof—there was not one who seemed capable of ad-
ministering a department, and cer-
tainly not of appeasing a storm
like this when tact as well as good
sense was required. There were
no men of experience in the new
Government. The Narýshkins
were young and untried. Yazýkof,
Likhatchéf and Miloslávsky refused to interfere, as it was none of
their business to help out the new
Government; and to increase the
alarm, Matvéief was still far away.
The settlement of the matter was
at last confided to the Patriarch,
who endeavoured to arrange matters with the Streltsi and to satisfy

Officers of the Streltsi.

them with the promise that all would be set right. The Streltsi,
however, demanded that the colonels should be given up to them.
The boyárs were so much frightened that they were inclined to
consent to this demand; but the Patriarch sent the metropolitans and archbishops to the Streltsi, in the hope of persuading
them to thank the Tsar for his promise, and to abandon the
idea of themselves punishing their commanders. Next day
all the colonels were removed from their offices and put into
prison, and an order was given to confiscate all their property,
and pay all the claims of the Streltsi. On the 12th, Simeon
Griboyédof and Alexander Karandéyef, two of the colonels, were

whipped with the knout, and twelve others with rods. Before the execution began, the accusations were read over, and the Streltsi, who stood about, were allowed to fix the measure of punishment, sometimes exclaiming 'harder,' and sometimes 'enough.' Yiélding to a demand which was probably intended as a test of weakness, the Government forbade Yazýkof and the Likhatchéf and several of their immediate supporters to come to court or to appear before the 'Shining Eyes' of the Sovereign. On May 14, the Streltsi presented a new petition against their colonels, demanding the recovery from them of the losses which they had sustained, and the next day the colonels were submitted to the *pravezh*—that is, they were publicly tortured or beaten, until they consented to pay the amount claimed. This semi-judicial proceeding lasted for eight days, until every farthing which had been claimed was made up; and the colonels were then allowed to retire to their houses in the country. As the Streltsi had now been satisfied, and their claims, just and unjust, had been granted, the Government hoped to have a little quiet; and in order to act upon public opinion, resolved that on May 17 there should be a public procession of the Tsar and the court officials to the Cathedrals of the Krémlin. At the same time there was to be a reception at the Palace of the nobility of the province of Smolénsk, of foreigners and of officials. This was very well in its way, but at the same time the great mistake was made of conferring the rank of 'boyár' and 'armourer' on the eldest brother of the Tsaritsa, Iván Narýshkin, a young man only twenty-three years old. Other relations of the Tsaritsa also received increase of rank. These new favours of the Narýshkins displeased not only the Miloslávsky party, but the Streltsi, with whom they were unpopular. It was said that the Narýshkins were trying to get the power on their own side in order to use it for their own personal ends; and it was rumoured that Iván Narýshkin had tried on the Imperial Crown with the remark that it looked better on him than on anybody else, and that he had rudely pushed aside the Princess Sophia, who had remonstrated with him. It was said, too—for the most absurd reports will circulate in an ignorant community—that the Narýshkins wished to destroy all the descendants of the Tsars, and themselves take possession of the throne.

Meanwhile Matvéief, who had been restored to all his ranks and titles on the first day of the accession of Peter, and was then on his estate only two days' journey from town, had received numerous messages recalling him to Moscow, and urging him to hasten. Nevertheless he lingered. He received daily accounts of what was going on at the capital, for even before Theodore's death, many of his old enemies, seeing which way the wind was blowing, and what were the chances of the future, had made conciliatory advances. According to his son's account, seven faithful Streltsi went out to meet him, warned him of the disaffection against the Government and the Naryshkins, and of the threats which had been uttered against him, and advised him not to go on to Moscow. He probably lingered to see if the storm would not blow over, but thinking that, as once he had been such a favourite with the Streltsi that they had even brought with their own hands stones from the graves of their fathers to build his house, he would be able to complete the pacification, he set out for Moscow. After stopping a day to rest at the Tróïtsa monastery and receiving the blessing of the Archimandrite, he was met at the village of Bratóvstchina by a state carriage and by Athanasius Naryshkin, who had been sent to greet him in the name of the Tsar and of the Tsaritsa. Late in the evening of May 21, the old man returned to his house after six years of exile passed amidst the greatest privations. The next day he had an interview with the Tsaritsa ; and had the pleasure of embracing her son, the Tsar Peter. The family and the adherents of the Tsar now thought that all would be right, that the old man with his long experience and good sense, and the general love felt toward him, would be able to overcome all difficulties and to establish order. For three days the house of Matvéief was filled with visitors of all classes and conditions of Moscow. Every one came to congratulate him, even the members of the Miloslávsky party, except Iván Miloslávsky himself, who still gave himself out to be ill. All who came brought presents of one kind or another ; 'sweet money on the sharp knife,' as his son expressed it. So many gifts of all descriptions, especially of provisions, were brought to his court-yard, that there was no longer any room for them in the cellars and store-houses. With tears of joy streaming down his face, the old man received all who came; inwardly he must have experienced feel-ings of triumph at being received in this way in Moscow, after his unjust exile.

Baron van Keller, writing a few days earlier, says: 'The discontent of the Streltsi continues. The Dutch merchants have been much frightened, but the Streltsi have done no harm except to those who have given them cause for dissatisfaction. As a proof that their complaints and griefs are not unfounded, His Tsarish Majesty has shown them much goodness, but has entirely disapproved of their manner of acting, as too vehe-ment and irregular, resembling the proceedings of the neigh-bours the Turkish Janissaries, who likewise have wished to be their own judges, and have caused great confusion and loss. . . . . When the tempest is over Regents will be chosen. . . . . Meanwhile all public affairs are at a stand-still. . . . . Great calamities are feared, and not without cause, for the might of the Streltsi is great and redoubtable, and no resistance can be opposed to them. Their grievances should be corrected so as to avoid bad consequences.'[1]

---

[1] Reports of Dutch Residents at Moscow in the Archives at the Hague; Ustriálof, ch. ii.; Solóvief, vol. xiii.; Pogódin; Matvéief's *Memoirs;* Medvé-dief's *Memoirs;* N. Aristof, *The Moscow Troubles in the Reign of Sophia,* (Russian), Warsaw, 1871.

Flag of the Streltsi of Moscow.

VI.

THE RIOT OF THE STRELTSI, 1682.

On May 25, the Streltsi, armed from head to foot with swords, halberds and muskets, began to collect at a very early hour in their churches in the most opposite quarters of the city, as if waiting for some watchword. Soon a watchword came. About nine o'clock in the morning a man rode hurriedly through the streets, crying out: 'The Naryshkins have murdered the Tsarévitch Iván! To the Krémlin! The Naryshkins wish to kill all the royal family! To arms! Punish the traitors! Save the Tsar!' A general alarm was at once sounded. Drums were beaten, bells rung, and the regimental cannon were brought out. The Streltsi, with their broad banners embroidered with pictures of the Virgin, advanced from all sides toward the Krémlin, as if to attack an enemy, compelling their colonels to lead them on. The peaceable citizens who met them were astonished at this onset; but to their inquiries as to its cause the answer returned was: 'We are going to destroy the traitors and murderers of the family of the Tsar.' No doubt the majority of them sincerely believed that the Tsar was really in danger, that the Naryshkins were desirous of mounting the throne, and that they were patriots going to save their country, and to rescue their ruler from the traitors and the hated boyárs. As they advanced they cut off the long handles of their spears, so as to manage them more easily. Meanwhile the boyárs were quietly sitting in the public offices and in the palace, without the slightest idea of what was passing in the city, or, after finishing the morning's official duties, they were strolling about previous to their midday dinner. Matvéief, on coming out upon the staircase leading to the bed-chamber porch, saw Prince Theodore Urúsof hastily running toward him, with scarcely breath enough to cry out that the Streltsi had risen, and that all the regiments, fully armed and with beating drums, were advancing towards the Krémlin. Matvéief, astonished, immediately returned to the palace with Urúsof, to inform the Tsaritsa Natalia. The words were scarcely out of his mouth before three messengers came in, one after another, each with worse news than the preceding. The Streltsi were already in the old town and near the Krémlin walls. Orders were immediately given to close the Krémlin gates and to prepare whatever means of defence there might be, and the Patriarch was hastily sent for. The officer of the guard, however, came with the intelligence that it was impossible to shut the gates, as the Streltsi had already passed them and were now in the Krémlin. All the carriages of the boyárs had been driven back to the Iván place, and the drivers were some wounded and some killed, while the horses were either cut to pieces or removed from the vehicles. No one could get into the Krémlin or out of it, and the frightened boyárs took refuge, one after another, in the banqueting-hall of the palace.

The Streltsi surrounded the palace, and stopped before the red staircase. Amid the din, the cries and the uproar it was barely possible to distinguish the words: 'Where's the Tsarévitch Iván? Give us the Naryshkins and Matvéief! Death to the traitors!' A brief council having been held in the banqueting-hall, it was decided to send some boyárs out to the Streltsi, to demand of them what they wanted. Prince Tcherkásky, Prince Havánsky, Prince Golítsyn and Sheremétief then went out and asked the Streltsi why they had come to the palace in this riotous way. 'We wish to punish the traitors,' was their reply; 'they have killed the Tsarévitch. They will destroy all the royal family. Give up to us the Naryshkins and the other traitors.' When the boyárs brought back this answer, the Tsaritsa was advised by her father, Matvéief, and others to go out on the red staircase and show to the Streltsi both the Tsar Peter and the Tsarévitch Iván. Trembling with terror, she took by the hands her son and her step-son, and—accompanied by the Patriarch, the boyárs, and the other officials— went out upon the red staircase. 'Here is the Tsar, Peter Alexéievitch; here is the Tsarévitch, Iván Alexéievitch,' the boyárs cried out in loud voices, as they came out with the Tsar-

THE TSARITSA BEFORE THE RIOTERS.

itsa and pointed the children out to the Streltsi. 'By God's
mercy they are safe and well. There are no traitors in the royal
palace. Be quiet; you have been deceived.' The Streltsi
placed ladders against the rails, and some of them climbed up
to the platform where the Tsar's family stood, in order the more
closely to examine them. Peter stood still and looked at them,
face to face, without blanching or showing the least sign of fear.
On coming to the Tsarévitch Iván, the Streltsi asked him if he
really were Iván Alexéie-
vitch. 'Yes,' answered the
youth, in an almost inaudible
voice. ' Again the question
was repeated. 'Are you
really he?' 'Yes, I am he,'
was the reply. The Patriarch then wished to descend
the staircase and talk with
the rioters; but the cry came
up from below, 'We have no
need of your advice; we know
what to do,' and many men
forced their way up past him.
The Tsaritsa, seeing their
rudeness and fearing the consequences, took the children
back into the palace.

Matvéief.

Matvéief, who had for-
merly been a favourite com-
mander of the Streltsi, went down outside of the wicket and
spoke to them in a confident yet propitiatory tone, reminding
them of their former faithful services, especially during the time of
the Kolómensky riots,[1] and of their good reputation which they
were now destroying by their proceedings, and explaining to
them that they were anxious without reason by believing false
reports. He told them that there was no cause for their alarm

---

[1] There were very serious riots during the reign of Alexis, in 1662, origi-
nating in the misery and discontent produced by the debasement of the currency. The rioters marched out from Moscow to the country-house of the
Tsar at Kolómensky.

about the royal family, which, as they had just seen with their own eyes, was in perfect safety. He advised them to beg pardon for the disturbance which they had made, which had been caused by their excessive loyalty, and he would persuade the Tsar to overlook it and restore them to favour. These sensible, good-natured words wrought a deep impression. The men in the front grew quiet; and it was evident that they had begun to reflect. Further off were still heard voices in discussion and conversation, as though a better feeling were taking possession of the multitude. It gradually became calmer.

Matvéief hastened back into the palace to allay the fears of the Tsaritsa, when, unfortunately, Prince Michael Dolgorúky, the second in command of the Department of the Streltsi, came out and, relying on the words of Matvéief, and thinking that all irritation was over, wished to put himself forward and to show his powers of command. In his rudest and roughest tones he ordered the Streltsi to go home immediately, and to attend to their own business. All the good impression which Matvéief's words had produced was immediately dispelled. The opponents of the Narýshkins, who had been rendered silent by the changed disposition of the multitude, again began to raise their voices; and some of the Streltsi, who were more drunken or riotous than the rest, seized Dolgorúky by his long gown, threw him down from the platform into the square, asking the crowd at the same time whether such was their will, while the men below caught him on their spears, exclaiming ' Yes, yes,' cut him to pieces.

This first act of bloodshed was the signal for more. Lowering their spears, the Streltsi rushed into the rooms of the palace, which some had already succeeded in entering from another side, in order to seize upon Matvéief, who was in the ante-room of the banqueting-hall, with the Tsaritsa and her son. The Streltsi moved toward him; the Tsaritsa wished to protect him with her own person, but in vain. Prince Tcherkásky tried to get him away, and had his coat torn off in the struggle. At last, in spite of the Tsaritsa, the Streltsi pulled Matvéief away, dragged him to the red staircase, and with exultant cries, threw him down into the square, where he was instantly cut to pieces by those below.

The Streltsi then burst again into the palace, and went through all the rooms, seeking for those they called traitors. The boyárs hid themselves where they could. The Patriarch was scarcely able to escape into the Cathedral of the Assumption, while the Tsaritsa Natalia and her son took refuge in the banqueting-hall.

The Streltsi ran through all the inner rooms of the palace, looked into the store-rooms, under the beds, into the chapels, thrust their spears under the altars, and left no place without a visit. From a distance they saw Theodore Sóltykof going into one of the chapels. Some one cried out: 'There goes Iván Naryshkin,' and the unlucky man was so frightened that he could not pronounce a single word, or even tell his name. He was at once killed, and his body thrown below. When it was ascertained who it was, and that he was not a Naryshkin, the Streltsi sent the body to old Sóltykof, and excused themselves by saying that his son had been killed by mistake. 'God's will be done,' said the old man, who had even the presence of mind to give the messengers something to eat and drink. After they had left the house, in trying to console his weeping daughter-in-law, he quoted a Russian proverb to the effect that 'their turn will come next.' A servant who had overheard this, and who had a grudge against his master, immediately rushed out, and told the Streltsi that his master had threatened them. They returned and murdered him on the spot.

In the Church of the Resurrection the Streltsi met one of the court dwarfs, named Homyák. 'Tell me where the Naryshkins, the Tsaritsa's brothers, are hid?' they asked. He pointed to the altar, and they pulled out Athanasius Naryshkin, dragged him by the hair to the chancel steps, and there cut him to pieces. His younger brothers, his father, and his other relatives, as well as Matvéief's son, whose description of these events we chiefly follow, took refuge in the apartments of the little Princess Natalia, Peter's sister, which apparently were not searched.

On the portico between the banqueting-hall and the Cathedral of the Annunciation the Streltsi killed the privy-councillor and director of foreign affairs, Lárion Ivánof, who had been one of those sent to negotiate with them, his son Basil, and two

lieutenant-colonels.   Between the Patriarch's palace and the
Miracle Monastery, opposite the Department of Foreign Affairs, the Streltsi caught the old boyár Ramodanófsky, seized
him by the beard and dragged him to the Office of Expeditions.
There they raised him up on the points of their spears, and
then threw him to the ground and cut him to pieces, because, as
they said, he had been too severe with them in the expedition
to Tchigirín.

The dead bodies, with the spears still sticking in them,
were dragged along by the feet to the gates of the Krémlin,
amidst cries of 'Here goes the Boyár Artemon Serghéievitch
Matvéief!'   'This is the Boyár Prince Gregory Gregórie-
vitch Ramodanófsky!'   'Here goes a privy-councillor—make
room for them!'   When the bodies had been dragged to the
Lobnóe place, where the tribune used at popular assemblies
stood, they were hacked into small pieces, amidst cries of 'They
loved to exalt themselves; this is their reward.'   The crowd
that stood around was obliged to express its satisfaction, because everybody who was silent was accused of being a traitor,
and as such was beaten.

Peter Narýshkin, who knew nothing of what was going on,
was found in a house on the other side of the river Moskvá,
and was tortured and killed.   Great efforts were made to find
Doctor Daniel von Gaden, a Jew by birth, whom the Streltsi
believed to have poisoned the Tsar Theodore.   The rioters went
to his house, which was near the Pogány pond, and arrested his
wife.   They also searched the house of his partner, Doctor Jan
Gutmensch, but as they found no one, they went away.   A
new crew came, and succeeded in finding a frightened man, who
had hidden himself in the garret, and took him to the Krémlin
together with Von Gaden's wife, threatening to keep them
until the Doctor was found, and in case of his not being discovered, to kill them both.

Partly from anger against the boyárs, and partly from genuine sympathy, the Streltsi took up the cause of the serfs.   Many
of them had been serfs themselves, and knew the oppressions
to which they were subject.   They wished not only to set the
serfs free and 'restore right and justice to the land,' but also to
gain adherents to their own cause.   With this aim they attacked

the Departments of Justice and of Serfage, broke open the
chests of papers and scattered them through the streets; and
then, going afterward to the houses of the chief boyárs, declared
to the serfs that they were free.   This action produced little
effect; they were joined by few of the common people, who
were slow to move and were frightened, rather than excited,
by the events of the day.   The Streltsi were a mob, but still a
mob of soldiers.   As in many similar cases, a few nobles were
betrayed and given up by their servants.   A few others owed
their safety to the devotion of their faithful slaves.

     That night strong guards were left at the gates of the Krém-
lin with strict orders to let no one in or out.   Pickets were also
stationed at the gates of the
Kitái Gorod and the White
Town.   On their way home
parties of Streltsi entered
various houses and demanded refreshments.   If any one
dared refuse them they beat
the masters and servants,
and excited general terror.
But such conduct excited the
reprobation of the leaders.

     Early the next day, the
26th, the Streltsi came again,
fully armed, and, with beating drums advancing to the
gilded lattice near the apartment of the Tsar, demanded
with loud cries the surrender

The Patriarch Níkon.

of Iván Naryshkin, the Councillor Kirílof, and the two doctors,
Daniel the Jew and Jan Gutmensch.   The princesses endeavoured to save the lives of these people, but they were obliged to
surrender Kirílof and Doctor Gutmensch, although they succeeded in concealing the wife of Doctor Daniel von Gaden in
the room of the young Tsaritsa Martha, the widow of Theodore.
The others were killed.

     The Streltsi then went to the residence of the Patriarch and
threatened with spears and halberds not only the servants but

the Patriarch himself, demanding the surrender of the traitors concealed there; looked through the cellars and outhouses; turned topsy-turvy boxes and beds, and not finding anyone, again came to the Patriarch and repeated their demands. The Patriarch, who had put on his robes, replied that there were no traitors in his house, but that he himself was ready to die.

One band went to the house of the Danish resident, Butenant von Rosenbusch, because they had heard from some one that Doctor von Gaden and his son were sheltered there. 'In the night between Monday and Tuesday,' Rosenbusch himself relates, 'a sharp search was made for a doctor named Daniel von Gaden. At break of day the Okólnitchy Kirílo Ossipóvitch Khlópof and more than one hundred Streltsi came into my courtyard, saying that they had information that the doctor and his son were concealed in my house, and telling me that if he were there I must give him up; and that if I should conceal him, and he should be found in my house it would cost me my life and that of my whole family, and that all my property would be confiscated. I swore, therefore, by all that was holy, that I knew nothing about him, and had not even seen him for a long time. Thereupon he said that he had orders in any case to search my house, which I was obliged to let him do, because my protestation that I was a servant of the king, and that not I but my most gracious king would be affronted, was not taken into consideration; but they went on and searched through everything, chests and boxes—all I had to open for them; and they looked through every corner of my house. Meanwhile came news that the doctor's son had been caught in disguise in the street that very night, so that the Okólnitchy need no longer look for him, but should track out the doctor with all haste. As they could find nothing in my house they ceased their search and went away; but in an hour afterward a captain and about fifty Streltsi returned, and said that they had orders to take me with them to the palace that I might be confronted with the son of the doctor, who had said that his father had been concealed by me. They immediately seized on me and wished to take me off, undressed as I was, without my hose and without my underclothing. I begged most humbly that they would first let me dress myself and ride my horse into the town. My wife

also fell on her knees before them, begging them with tears.
So at last they permitted me to dress myself in the court-yard,
for they would not allow me to stir a step from them.   But
when my horse was brought and I wished to mount it they
would not allow me, saying I could go as well on foot; but at
last, after many prayers, I obtained this.   Thereupon I took
leave of my wife with tears in my eyes; but when I came out
into the street the bountiful God gave me the happy thought
to keep still a little, and then, calling the captain of the Streltsi
close to me, I said: "God be praised! I am not guilty, no never;
I have a clear conscience and do not doubt that as soon as I go
to the castle you will let me go.   Then if you will accompany
me home again I will treat you to as much brandy and beer as
you like, but since the streets are full of your comrades who do
not know anything about me you must take care that none of
your men who meet me do me any harm.   Say that I am an
ambassador who has been called to the court."   This the captain
and his Streltsi promised to do, and they kept their word.

'Whenever a body of Streltsi met us they cried out: "Get
out of the way! An ambassador is going to talk with His Tsarish Majesty," whereupon the Streltsi immediately made way.
When I was near the palace in the great square of the Bazaar,
I saw to my right a colonel named Dókturof led off by the
Streltsi to be killed, and on both sides of the road through
which I had to pass, many dead bodies lay terribly mutilated,
whereupon I was very much frightened.   And what terrified
me most was that some of the Streltsi coming from the Krémlin, when they saw me all cried out: "That is Doctor Daniel.
Give him here, the traitor and magician!"   My Streltsi had
enough to do to keep them back, continually calling out: "Keep
back! It is not Doctor Daniel, but an ambassador who must
speak with the Tsar," so that when I came to the Krémlin gate
it was immediately opened and instantly shut behind me again.
After I had ridden on a little I met several Streltsi dragging
along the naked dead body of the doctor's son.   Then my captain said to me, though he did not leave my side: "This is the
doctor's son; with whom, then, can you be confronted?"   I
thereupon was silent a little.   When I came to the great square,
which was full of armed Streltsi, they began to beat their drums

and sound the alarm bells, which was their sign to kill some one. But Almighty God gave me great courage, and my Streltsi cried out: "Keep still! This is an ambassador who must speak with his Majesty." Space was made for me to ride on as far as the stone staircase, where the lately widowed Tsaritsa and the Princess Sophia Alexéievna were standing with several gentlemen. I wanted, indeed, to go farther, but my Streltsi could make no space, for the square was so full of people that one could have walked on their heads. Then the boyár Prince Iván Andréievitch Havánsky came down and asked the Streltsi: "Is it your pleasure that the oldest Tsaritsa Natalia Naryshkin shall no longer remain at court?" They all cried out: "Yes, that is our pleasure." But as Havánsky turned round he looked into my face, was much astonished, and asked me: "Andréi Ivánovitch"—for that is my name in Russian—"how did you get here?" I pointed to my Streltsi and said: "They brought me here," and then stepped nearer to him until I was two steps from the Tsaritsa and the Princess, to whom Havánsky said something in a voice too low for me to hear, but which was probably nothing bad, for the Princess waved her hand to me to go away. Prince Iván Andréievitch called out to my Streltsi: "Take this man home again, and guard him as you would your eyes," and then made a flattering speech about me. As soon as I got out of the sight of those high personages the Streltsi who accompanied me said: "Andréi Ivánovitch, cover thy head. Thou hast now perfectly established thy innocence." As I came to the great staircase, the Streltsi who stood about there thought that I, like others, should be thrown down, and when they saw my Streltsi take me past the staircase, they all pressed near and asked why I was there and why I was let go, and some still had an idea that I was Doctor Daniel. But my Streltsi kept their word and cried out that I was an ambassador and had spoken with the Princess, and that they should let me have my horse and go my way; but the crowd was so great that I could not get my horse at once, but at last, after pressing a long time through the crowd, I got it and rode home, all the Streltsi accompanying me, joined by many others. Some ran on as fast as they could to bring my wife news that I had been found innocent and let free, for I was obliged to go slowly and quietly, and make no uneasy countenance. When I came home I was received by all my people as one escaped from death's claws. To the Streltsi, who had now increased to over two hundred, I immediately had given as much brandy and beer as they could drink. Three of the highest came into my room and said: "Now give us some money." I answered "yes," and thought twenty rubles would be sufficient; whereupon they laughed scornfully, and demanded from me a thousand rubles. At this I was horrified; whereupon they said: "Andréi Ivánovitch, content us well, or we will leave no life in thy house. Dost thou not know that we have the power? everything must tremble before us; and no harm can come to us for that." I said: "You gentlemen were ordered to bring me home without harm; and now will you yourselves murder me? Therefore do what you will; it is impossible for me to get so much money." Then they cut down half; and at last I agreed with those three persons to give every one of their men half a ruble each. When they went out the other Streltsi would not agree to this, and said that they must each have a ruble. The three men, however, said: "We have agreed with the landlord for half a ruble, and cannot take our words back; you must, therefore, be contented." Whereupon they all kept still. I then had the money counted out, and wrapped each half ruble separately in a paper, and had the Streltsi counted, when we found them to be 287 men strong. They then sat in a circle all about my court-yard, and the money was given out to them by two men, and after they had all once more taken a drink and had thanked me most heartily, they went away. When they were out of the court-yard, I fell on my knees, together with my family, and thanked God for his gracious preservation and assistance, for according to all appearances if I had gone out without my clothes and on foot I should not have come out of their hands alive. If a single man of the Streltsi who accompanied me had lifted his finger to mark me out I should have been killed. The same day another party came to look for the doctor, but they were somewhat more civil than the first time; and in the night (or early on the Wednesday morning) still another party of Streltsi came and searched through my house. They also were civil enough, but they terrified us a great deal, because we felt there would be no end of it until the doctor was found, for the Streltsi were immoderately embittered against him. When at daybreak the news came that the doctor had been found, all we neighbours were right glad, although we knew he was innocent; yet he could not have escaped, and we were saved from much anxiety. That same day I asked the boyár Prince Basil Go-lítsyn (who had taken charge of the Department of Foreign Affairs, instead of Lárion Ivánof) to give me some Streltsi as a guard, which was done; and on Thursday five Streltsi were put in my house, and changed every day.'

The old Narýshkin, the father of the Tsaritsa, with his sons, several other relatives, and the son of Matvéief, a youth of seventeen, concealed themselves at first in the dark closets in the bedroom of the little Princess Natalia, but were afterwards taken to the further room of the Tsaritsa Martha, which had no windows, and was next to the court of the Patriarch's palace. Here Iván Narýshkin, who was particularly sought after by the Streltsi, cut off his long hair, and then an old bedchamber-woman, Klush—who was the only one who knew exactly where they were concealed—took them out in the morning into a dark store-room on the ground floor, covered up the windows with pillows, and wished to shut them in there, but Matvéief said ' No ; if you fasten the door, the Streltsi will suspect something, will break it open and find us and kill us.' The room was therefore made perfectly dark, and the door was left open a few inches, while the refugees crowded together in a dark corner behind it. ' We had scarcely got there,' says young Matvéief, ' before several Streltsi passed and looked quickly round. Some of them peered in through the open door, struck their spears into the pillows, saying spitefully : " It is plain our men have already been here." '

That day the Streltsi captured Iván Yazýkof on the Nikíts-kaya street as he was hurrying to a church to conceal himself. He was met by a servant who knew him. Yazýkof pulled off a valuable ring from his finger and giving it to him begged him not to tell anybody. The rascal promised not to do so ; but immediately called some Streltsi, who ran up, looked through the church and found Yazýkof, dragged him with jeers to the Red Place and killed him.

On the third day, May 27, the Streltsi again came to the Krémlin, and to the beating of drums stationed themselves about the palace, while some of them climbed straight up to the balcony and insisted on the surrender of Iván Naryshkin. They threatened all the servitors of the palace with death if they did not find him, and declared that they would not leave the Krémlin until they had possession of him. They even threatened the life of the Tsaritsa Natalia and of the other members of the Tsar's family. At last it became evident that nothing could be done, and the Princess So-

Iván Naryshkin.

phia went to Natalia and said : 'There is no way of getting out of it; to save the lives of all of us you must give up your brother.' Natalia, after useless protests, then brought out Iván Naryshkin and conducted him into the Church of the Saviour beyond the Wicket. Here he received the Holy Communion and prepared himself for death. Sophia handed him an image of the Virgin and said, 'Perhaps when the Streltsi see this holy picture they will let him go.' All in the palace were so terrified that it seemed to them that Iván Naryshkin was lingering too long. Even the old Prince Jacob Odóiefsky, a kindly but timorous old man, went up to the Tsaritsa and said : 'How long, O lady, you are keeping your brother. For you must give him up. Go on quickly, Iván Kirílovitch, and don't let us all be killed for your sake.' The Tsaritsa led him as far as the Golden Wicket, where the Streltsi stood. They immediately seized on him and began to indulge in all sorts of abuse and insult before her eyes. He was dragged by the feet down the staircase through the square to the Constantine torture-room. Though most fearfully tortured, Na-rýshkin shut his teeth and uttered not a word. Here was also brought Dr. Daniel von Gaden, who was caught in the dress of a beggar, wearing bark sandals, and with a wallet over his shoulders. He had escaped from the town and had passed two days in the woods, but had become so famished that he had returned to the German quarter to get some food from an acquaintance, when he was recognised and arrested. Von Gaden, in the midst of his tortures, begged for three days more, in which he promised to name those who deserved death more than he. His words were written down, while others cried out: 'What is the use of listening to him? Tear up the paper,' and dragged him, together with Narýshkin, from the torture-room to the Red Place. They were both lifted up on the points of spears; afterward their hands and feet were cut off, and their bodies chopped into small pieces and trampled into the mud. With these two deaths the murders came to an end. The Streltsi went from the Red Place to the palace of the Krémlin and cried: 'We are now content. Let your Tsarish Majesty do with the other traitors as may seem good. We are ready to lay down our heads for the Tsar, for the Tsaritsa, for the Tsarévitch and the Tsarévnas.'

That very day permission was granted for the burial of the bodies, many of which had been lying in the Red Place since the first day of the riot; and the faithful black servant of old Matvéief went out with a sheet and collected the mutilated remains of his master, and carried them on pillows to the parish church of St. Nicholas, where they were buried.

On May 28, deputies of the Streltsi regiments came unarmed to the palace and petitioned the Tsar to order his grandfather, Cyril Narýshkin, to be tonsured as a monk. The old man was immediately taken across the Krémlin to the Miracle Monastery, and after taking monastic vows under the name of Cyprian was carried off in a small cart to the monastery of St. Cyril on the White Lake. His younger sons, Leo, Martemian and Theodore, succeeded in escaping from Moscow in common grey peasant clothing under the care of some of their faithful servants, and concealed themselves in distant places, as did some of their relatives. Through the kindness of a dwarf named

Komar who was much attached to Peter, young Matvéief was disguised as a groom, and boldly went out with the dwarf down the chief staircase. There the dwarf mounted his horse, which Matvéief led, and they went through the Krémlin and the White Town to the Smolensk Gate, where the strong guard fortunately did not recognise him. He was handed over to the care of the priest of the Church of the Descent of the Holy Spirit, with an order from the Tsaritsa Natalia to conceal him. The priest passed him on to a groom, a relative of his, where he lived in peasant clothing for some time under the name of Kondrat, and then wandered from one place to another until quiet was restored. Three days after this, on May 30, the Streltsi petitioned again that the Tsar should exile the brothers, Likhatchéf, the rest of the Naryshkins and young Matvéief, and some other adherents of Peter. This decree was immediately issued.[1]

---

[1] Solóvief, vols. xiii. xiv. and app. ; Ustriálof, I. ch. ii. and app., with report of Rosenbusch ; Aristof ; Matvéief's *Memoirs ;* A. Brückner, *Peter der Grosse*, Berlin, 1879 ; Reports of Residents, in Dutch Archives.

VII.

WHEN once the fury of a mob has been excited by the sight
of blood, it will commit deeds which at first all would have
looked on with abhorrence ; and it is rare that a riot, beginning
from whatever cause, does not end in conflagration, pillage, and
robbery. Singularly enough, it was not so with the riot of the
Streltsi. The soldiery satisfied their desire for revenge by killing the men whom they had had cause to dislike in their campaigns, or whom they believed to be injurious to the State.
They pillaged the Department of Serfage, in order to set free
the peasants and gain themselves supporters, but they carefully
abstained from the indiscriminate pillage of private houses.
That they entered drinking-houses and ate and drank without
payment was what might naturally be expected under the circumstances. Rosenbusch and all the eye-witnesses explicitly
state that the Streltsi gave strict orders that no pillage should
be allowed, and kept watch that no persons pretending to be
Streltsi should attack and rob the people, either in the town or
in the environs. About forty persons, some of them Streltsi,
and some poor peasants, were executed for having stolen goods
in their possession, though the value of some articles did not
exceed four kopeks (about eight cents).

Not feeling yet satisfied with the indemnity for the losses
of pay and subsistence, caused by the cheating and robbery of
their officers, the Streltsi, as soon as the murders were over,
and before even the bodies were buried, petitioned the Government to grant them a sum of two hundred and forty thousand
rubles ($495,000) as back pay, and also to confiscate the prop-

erty of those officers and magnates who had been killed in the riot, and distribute it among them.

Frightened as the inmates of the palace were, they were unable to admit demands like these, and they finally succeeded, by a liberal supply of drink, in compromising at the rate of ten rubles ($20) to each man, and by putting up at auction the personal property of those killed, when the Streltsi were enabled to buy what was for sale without much competition. The money to pay the Streltsi had to be raised by a general tax, and for the necessities of the moment much of the silver plate of the palace was melted down and coined into money. Van Keller wrote:—' The new Government is trying to content the Streltsi and the soldiers, but a great amount of money is necessary, and additional taxes and contributions are put upon everybody. This ought to be a good lesson to those vile gain-seekers, and extortioners of gifts and presents.'

The Princess Sophia, Sister of Peter.

A new Government had, indeed, been formed by circumstances and of itself, without apparently any orders from Peter or his mother, but called out by the necessities of the moment. We see by the relation of Rosenbusch, the Danish Resident, that in the latter part of the riot, the Princess Sophia had been brought prominently forward, and had endeavoured to pacify the rioters. This was not strange, for she surpassed all the other princesses in natural abilities as well as in strength of mind and character. She had received an education more masculine than feminine, having shared the studies of her brother Theodore. She had been much with her brother during the last months of his life, had been at his bedside during his illness, and had in this way gradually and involuntarily come to be acquainted with affairs of state, and to be the medium by which the orders of the Tsar had been transmitted. It was in Theodore's sick-chamber that she first knew Prince Basil Golítsyn, and it was there she began to judge of the characters of officials and statesmen. She alone preserved her presence of mind throughout the riots, and it was but natural that all should turn to her for advice or orders. New officials stepped into the places and began to perform the duties of those who had been killed, without at first any rightful authority, although they were afterwards confirmed in their offices. In this way Prince Basil Golítsyn took charge of the Department of Foreign Affairs, Prince Havánsky of the Department of the Streltsi, and Prince Iván Miloslávsky of several other departments.

The feeling that there was a certain illegality in the election of Peter, to the exclusion of his elder brother, Iván, was strong among the Streltsi, and was doubtless greatly increased by the partisans of the Miloslávskys, whose own interests would have been advanced by the accession of Iván. They did not, however, demand the actual deposition of Peter, for he was the son of a Tsar, and had himself been proclaimed Tsar by the Patriarch. They proposed to make Iván Tsar also. On June 3, Prince Havánsky reported to the Princesses that the Streltsi had sent a deputation to say that they, and all classes of the Muscovite State, desired that both brothers, Peter and Iván, should reign together, threatening, if this were refused, to come again to the Krémlin with their arms, and prepared for attack. The chief nobles and officials who could be found were hastily called together, but as they were unwilling to take the responsibility of deciding the matter, a special council was summoned in the palace, to which were invited not only the officials, but also the Patriarch, the archbishops and the leading clergy, and deputies of the Muscovite State. Such deputies happened to be in Moscow at that time, having been called there by Theodore, shortly before his death, for the purpose of equalising taxation; but whether these men took part in the council, or only deputies from the city of Moscow, is a matter of question.

The threat that the Streltsi might make another attack

brought nearly all the nobles to the Assembly, and the proposition of a double reign was urged as in the highest degree advantageous ; for it was maintained that when one Tsar went to the wars, the other could stay at home to govern the country.   Examples in history were not wanting, and members of the council cited in the discussions the cases of Pharaoh and Joseph, Arcadius and Honorius, Basil and Constantine.   Under the threat of the Streltsi, discussion was hardly free, and the partisans of Peter had suffered too much to make strong opposition.   It was, therefore, soon decided that both the brothers should reign together. The great bell was rung, prayers were said in the Cathedral of the Assumption, and solemn petitions put up for the long life of the most Orthodox Tsars, Iván Alexéievitch and Peter Alexéievitch.   It was with difficulty that Iván could be induced by his sisters to take even a nominal part in the Government. He alleged the defects of his sight and speech, and said that he cared more for a quiet and peaceable life than for the world's government, but he would assist his younger brother in council and action.   By the terms of the proclamation in the Cathedral, the name of Iván was mentioned first, as the elder brother, and he was in this way given precedence over Peter; but in consequence of a row into which the Streltsi had got with partisans of Peter, among the populace, who laughed at the idea of Iván really being Tsar, the leaders of the Streltsi felt it necessary to express more clearly the relations between the brothers, and a deputation came to the palace begging that Iván should be the first Tsar, and Peter the second, and obedient to his elder brother.   Two days later, on June 5, there came another deputation of Streltsi, demanding that on account of the youth and inexperience of both the Tsars, the Government should be carried on by the Princess Sophia, as Regent.   When this proposition was discussed in the council, an historical example was again adduced ; for had not Pulcheria been Regent during the youth of her brother, Theodosius ?   Sophia was, therefore, asked to take up the reins of government.   She at first refused, but on being sufficiently pressed consented.   A decree announcing the joint accession of Iván and Peter and the regency of Sophia during their infancy, was issued the same day and sent to the different provinces of the Empire.

Meanwhile, to conciliate and to acquire a greater influence over them, the Government had given to the Streltsi the honorary appellation of the 'Palace Guard.' They had been complimented for their loyalty and fidelity by Sophia herself, and had been feasted in the courts and corridors of the palace at the rate of two regiments a day. The Princess Sophia herself had even handed round cups of *vodka* to the men. But in spite of these feasts and honours, the Streltsi did not feel quite easy in conscience. Although they had made a change in the Government, yet it was carried on by the same sort of people as before. Certain boyárs had been killed, but their places had been taken by others in all respects like them. The enthusiasm with which the movement had started gradually died out. The Streltsi recognised their own incapacity for governing, and despaired of any permanent good from their efforts. They knew that they had acted in a manner contrary to law and discipline—that they were in fact rebels. They had offended the boyár class, not only by their riot and murders, but by their action in favour of the serfs; and at last—for discipline had in the end proved too strong for them—they had placed themselves in a position of antagonism to the serfs. On the very day, when, in consequence of the action of the Streltsi, Sophia was proclaimed Regent, many of the serfs had united in a petition for their freedom, complaining of the measures which the boyárs, their late masters, had taken against them. This petition was rejected with contempt by the Government, and the Streltsi were ordered to hunt out and catch the runaway serfs, to torture, imprison, and punish them, and to restore them to their masters. More than this, the Streltsi were induced to declare that they had no sympathy with the serfs, and would not assist them against their masters. About the time of Pentecost, there were numerous conflicts between the Streltsi and the fugitive serfs. There were night alarms, and the bells of the churches were rung even in the German suburb. Many of the surfs who resisted being cut down mercilessly by the Streltsi, the others became frightened, and began gradually to return to their masters.

While the Streltsi felt safe in Moscow, where the population, if not sympathetic, was at least afraid of them, they knew

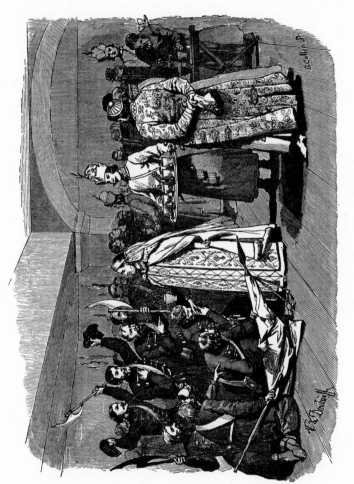

SOPHIA FEASTING THE STRELTSI.

that it would be comparatively easy for the boyárs to raise an army of their adherents in the more distant provinces, lead them to Moscow and obtain the upper hand.   To secure themselves as much as possible against such an event, they presented to the Government, through Alexis Yúdin (one of their leaders, and the right hand of Prince Havánsky), a petition, which was at the same time a justification, purporting to be not only from the Streltsi themselves, but also from all the burghers of Moscow.   In this they attempted to explain and defend their conduct during the riots.   They asserted that they had taken up arms on May 25 to protect the family of the Tsar from great harm; that they had punished Prince Yúry and Prince Michael Dolgorúky, for insults which they had long given to them, and for the harm which they had wrought in depriving them of their pay, and in other great injustice.   They had killed Lárion Ivánof, because he had joined with the Dolgorúkys, and had threatened to hang them all.   They had killed Prince Ramodanófsky, believing him to be guilty of treachery in delivering up Tchigirín to the Turks and the Tartars.   They had killed Yazýkof, because he had taken the side of their colonels, had put great assessments upon them, and had taken bribes.   They had killed the boyár Matvéief and Dr. Daniel von Gaden, because they had poisoned the Tsar Theodore with herbs, and had wished to poison the present Tsar, which Dr. Daniel had confessed when tortured.   They had killed Iván and Athanásius Narýshkin, because they had tried on the Imperial crown, and had plotted all sorts of evil against the Tsar Iván, just as they had done before against the Tsar Theodore Alexéievitch, for which they had been exiled.   They therefore asked permission to erect on the Red Place a column, on which should be inscribed the names of these evildoers, and the crimes for which they were killed; and desired that a document, with red seals, should be given to all the regiments of the Streltsi, to the soldiers, and to all the people of the suburbs, that none of the boyárs or councillors should revile them, or kill them as rioters or traitors, and that no one should be sent without reason into exile, or beaten or punished because they had served with fidelity.   The Government consented: it dared not refuse.   Zickler and Ózerof were ordered to carry out the demands of the Streltsi, and a monument with the proposed inscription was erected on the Red Place.

The erection of this monument does not seem to have impressed contemporaries as it does us. The Dutch Resident in speaking of it says : ' A high pyramid is to be erected, giving the faults of those who were killed, and the justification of the massacres. This is a good lesson and warning to the bribe-takers who have caused so much disorder.'

Order seemed now to be restored ; thanks were solemnly given in the churches for the end of the riots, and the Tsars made a pilgrimage in state to one of the neighbouring convents.[1]

---

[1] Ustriálof, I. ii. ; Soloviéf, vol. xiv.; Matvéief's *Memoirs ;* Reports of Dutch Residents; Aristof; Brückner.

The Baton of Prince Golítsyn.

Cathedral of the Assumption, Moscow, where the Tsars were Crowned.

VIII.

THE DISSENTERS DEMAND DISCUSSION.—CORONATION OF THE TSARS.—1682.

It has already been remarked that the siege and capture of the Solovétsky Monastery and the rigorous persecution of the Dissenters increased the dissatisfaction of the people without having great effect in putting down dissent.[1] It produced a rupture between all the old-believers and the Government, which, from its using force to put down the true religion, made itself

---

[1] See p. 6.

unlawful in their eyes. The Dissenters played a great part in
the insurrection of Stenka Rázin, and in all the popular movements of the time. The administrative centralisation of Russia
had at first touched only the higher ranks of life, both lay and
clerical ; but gradually it began to subordinate to itself the common people, the villagers, and the parochial clergy. In the
concealed, but no less real, struggle against centralisation, the
autocracy obtained everywhere the preponderance ; but discontent remained in the lower classes. As far as concerned their
religious ideas, this discontent, added to the dislike of the new
dogmas and rites, was increased by the arrogant tone which the
superior clergy took toward the village priests and toward the
mass of the common people ; a feeling frequently expressed in
the writings of the dissenters. It was increased, too, by the
dislike the Russians felt to the foreigners settled in Russia, and
to the foreign influences that were daily becoming deeper and
wider—influences not only of the Germans, both Protestant and
Catholic, who had entered the army, and whose families lived
in the German suburb of Moscow, but also those Polish influences which came from the schools of Kíef, and were strengthened and spread by the monks and clergy, who had received
their education in Poland and Kíef. There was even a prejudice against the Greek clergy from Constantinople, who were
thought to be less tainted with Latinism and Romish doctrines,
but were accused of being more eager to amass their rubles than
to keep the purity of the faith. The common people, in their
dislike of novelty, hated the Polish influences that made themselves felt at court and in the administration ; and the Dissenters, like the Streltsi, laid all the blame on the boyárs. They
thought as Kópytof, a Dissenter exiled to the furthest part of
Siberia, said : ' All in Moscow is according to the will of the
boyárs. What the boyárs wish, that they do.'

Such convictions led the Dissenters to think that the apparent triumph of the popular principles which had been proclaimed in the riot of the Streltsi would be advantageous to the
cause of what they considered true religion ; that there would
be a revolution in the habits and maxims of the Government,
and a return to old Russian ideas and practices in religion as well
as in politics.

THE DISSENTERS EXHORTING THE PEOPLE FROM THE RED STAIRCASE.

Many of the Streltsi were Dissenters, and in some regiments this belief predominated ; and it was known that the Prince Havánsky, their new chief, was a great adherent of the old believers, and had for a long time protected one of their leaders, the Protopope Habbakuk, or Avvákum. The third day after the end of the riot in the Krémlin, the Streltsi of the Titóf Regiment, which contained a particularly large number of Dissenters, began to consider what measure they might take for restoring the old belief. They resolved to write a petition in the name of their comrades and of the inhabitants of the suburbs, requesting the Government to 'restore the use of the old books which were printed in the time of the orthodox princes and Tsars, and the five Russian Patriarchs, and to cease loving the Latin-Romish faith, devised according to man's will, but not according to God's.' After much searching they found a man to write such a petition—a monk named Sergius, greatly respected, 'a firm adamant, skilled in learning.' When the petition had been drawn up, and was read in the assembly of the Streltsi, they wept with astonishment to see how many fearful heresies had crept into the new books. They had not the ability to go into details, but were firmly convinced that the true faith was being persecuted. 'Don't give us up, O brethren, to be persecuted as before. Do not allow us to be tortured and burned,' cried Sergius to the assembly.

' O father, we are ready to shed our blood for the old piety,' answered a lieutenant-colonel.

All promised with one voice to stand up for the orthodox faith, if necessary, even to death. One of the demands in this petition was, that a public discussion on the disputed points of the faith should be held either on the Red Place or in the square between the Cathedrals. This discussion the Dissenters insisted upon because, firmly believing the truth of their doctrines, they felt sure of an easy victory, and were convinced that they could readily get over to their side all the people present. Prince Havánsky, when informed by the Streltsi that the petition was ready, was much pleased, and asked whether there was anyone who would be able to enforce the arguments of the Dissenting side. On being informed that there was an old monk ' skilful in disputations and firm in the faith,' Havánsky requested them to come to his house, and fixed a time for the interview.

The Dissenters were very warmly received by Havánsky's servants, but were obliged to wait three hours until the Prince could dismiss some guests who were with him. At last he came in, and, seeing the monk about whom he had heard so much, bowed to the ground and asked : ' For what hast thou come to me, reverend father ? ' Sergius replied that he had brought a petition, with an account of the heresies in the new books. ' I myself am a sinner,' replied Havánsky. ' I much wish that all

should, as of old, worship in the holy Church unanimously and without difference; but, although I am a sinner, I undoubtedly keep to the old piety. I read the old books, and I sign myself with the sign of the cross, made by two fingers.' Havánsky then recited the creed, with the addition, thought indispensable by the Dissenters, of ' and in the real life-giving Holy Ghost,' and continued : ' Thus I believe, and thus I teach, and I pray God to be merciful to the Christian people, and not to allow Christian lands to be utterly ruined by the present new Níkonian belief.' According to custom, he ended his discourse with texts. The petition was then read, but Havánsky did not receive such a favourable impression of the ' firm ada-

Orthodox Sign of the Cross, in Benediction.

mant ' as his supporters desired. ' I see, O father,' he said, ' that you are a peaceful and quiet monk, not talkative, not eloquent. You are not the man for such a great act. We must set against them a man of many words, who can reply to them.' Other Dissenters then suggested to Havánsky the famous Níkita, of Suzdál, as a fit man for the time—a priest who, after having been a leading Dissenter, had formally recanted, but had now gone back again to Dissent. His adversaries had given him the nickname of ' Bladder-head.' Havánsky was delighted with the suggestion, for he had a high opinion of Níkita's abilities, and thought that none of the orthodox could successfully oppose

him in dispute. ' I am glad to help you, brethren,' he said,
and do not at all imagine that, as of old, you will be punished,
or hanged, or cut to pieces, or burned.'

The Dissenters then demanded a public discussion at the
Lobnóë Place in the presence of the Tsars and of all the people,
and, if not there, at least in the Krémlin at the Red Staircase,
and insisted that this discussion should take place without fail
on the following Friday, July 3 ; for Friday, by old custom,
had been specially set apart for religious assemblies. Havánsky replied that Friday would be impossible, because Sunday,
the 5th, was appointed for the coronation of the Tsars. This
was exactly what the Dissenters wished
for, as they said : ' We desire that our lords
should be crowned in the true orthodox
faith, and not according to the Romish-
Latin belief.' Havánsky assured them
that the two Tsars should be crowned according to the old rites and usages existing
since the time of Iván Vasiliévitch. But
the Dissenters wished not alone the old
rites. They said : ' The Tsars will commune
during the Liturgy, and the Patriarch will
officiate according to the new rite, and at
the coronation he will urge the Tsars to
defend the new faith.' Havánsky could
not refute this, and said : ' Well, be it as
you will. Let the assembly be for Friday.'
The Dissenters departed contented.

Orthodox Sign of the Cross,
in Prayer.

At early dawn of Friday, July 3, the deputies of the
Streltsi came to Havánsky and inquired at what time he desired
the fathers to come to the conference. Havánsky replied, ' In
two hours.' Two hours later the fathers appeared in the Krémlin in a triumphal procession. Nikíta carried the holy cross,
made according to the old rite, with three bars. Sergius, the
writer of the petition, bore the Gospels, and Sabatius, a monk,
who had just arrived from the Volokolámsky Hermitages,
carried a picture of the ' Last Judgment.' Crowds of people,
surprised at this unusual procession, collected in the streets, and
asked one another in whispers what it all meant ; and as they

followed the procession, recited in low tones, 'Lord, have mercy upon us! Lord, have mercy upon us!'

On their arrival at the Krémlin, the Dissenters' procession stopped at the Red Staircase, and sent word of their arrival to Prince Havánsky. They were taken, according to custom, into the Hall of Replies, where Havánsky put on an air of ignorance, and went through the usual formula of asking the purpose of their coming. At the same time he made obeisance to the Gospel and to the cross. Nikíta replied; 'We have come to petition with regard to the old orthodox faith, that the Patriarch and the archbishops may be ordered to officiate according

Dissenting Sign of the Cross.

to the old rite. If the Patriarch refuse to do this, let him answer in what respect the old books are bad, and why he has persecuted the adherents of the old rite.' He promised, for himself and his adherents, to show many heresies in the new books. Havánsky replied to Nikíta, as he had formerly done to Sergius: 'I myself am a sinner, but I believe according to the old books.' He took the petition and went up to the chamber of the Tsars. Returning in a little time, he said that, at the request of the Patriarch, the Tsars had put off the discussion of the petition until Wednesday, as it was an important matter, which needed much time, as the books must be compared, and he advised them to come on Wednesday, after dinner. Nikíta, however, did not forget that the coronation was arranged for Sunday, and immediately asked: 'How will the Tsars be crowned?' 'According to the old rite,' answered Havánsky. Nikíta insisted that the Patriarch should officiate at the liturgy, as of old, with seven wafers, and that the cross upon these wafers should be the real and true cross, and not a Latin one. To get rid of him, Havánsky answered: 'Bring me some wafers baked with the impress of the old cross. I myself will take them to the Patriarch, and order him to serve according to the old rite; and you, Father Nikíta, go home.'

Next day, two other refugee Dissenters arrived—Father

Dorothéus and Father Gabriel. There was great joy among the Dissenters, who felt sure of a speedy triumph. Nikíta requested a certain widow of his acquaintance to prepare the wafers in the old style.

Although Nikíta started out early on Sunday morning with his wafers carefully packed in a wallet, when he arrived at the Krémlin, he found the crowd so great in the square about the Cathedral that it was impossible for him to reach even the barriers. Much against his will, he was obliged to return, and coming sadly into the assembly of the faithful, placed the wafers on the table, saying : 'Pardon me, O holy fathers ! The people would not allow me to approach the Cathedral, and I have brought back the wafers.' They were, therefore, after service, distributed among the faithful at benediction.

Double Throne used at Peter's Coronation.

Meanwhile the coronation had taken place. On the evening of July 4, 1682, there was a grand vesper service in all the churches, and especially in the Cathedral of the Assumption, where it was celebrated by the Patriarch Joachim, attended by all the superior clergy. During the night a square platform, raised on twelve steps, was erected in the middle of the Cathedral, immediately under the dome, and covered with crimson cloth. From this platform to the chancel, the pavement was spread with red cloth, on which two strips of scarlet velvet

were laid for the Tsars, and a strip of blue for the Patriarch.
On each side were raised seats covered with Persian carpets and
cloth-of-gold, for the clergy. On the centre platform a double
throne was erected. There had not been time to make entirely
fresh regalia for the double coronation, and the silver-gilt throne
of handsome workmanship made for the Tsar Alexis was divided by a bar in the middle, so that it could be used by the two
boys. A seat was placed behind, so that the monitor of Peter,
through the hole in the back, could whisper to him the necessary responses. The crown, sceptre, and globe, originally presents from Constantine Monomachus, Emperor of the East, to the
Grand Duke Vladímir of Kíef, had been imitated in smaller
size, and at less expense, for the use of Peter. The old historic
ones, with which all the Tsars had been crowned, were reserved
for Iván. This was the last time they were ever used. The
successors of Peter were Emperors, not Tsars; and the crown
and pectoral cross of Monomachus, the visible symbols of the
relations of the Muscovite Tsars to the Emperors of Constantinople, are now mere curiosities in the Imperial treasury at Moscow. On the left side of this throne was a third throne, for the
Patriarch, the spiritual emperor. This, too, was used for the
last time. The power of the clergy was to be diminished, and
the rule of the Patriarch to be broken.

In the chancel were placed six reading-desks, two lower than
the rest, covered with satin embroidered with jewels, on which
were to be placed the crown·and sceptre and pectoral cross of
Monomachus, containing a relic of the true cross.

At the first dawn of day, on July 6, the bells began to ring
joyfully and there was a great procession of the clergy from all
the churches. At five o'clock the two boy Tsars went to the
Palace Chapel for matins, and then in procession to the banqueting-hall. Here, in honour of the day, they promoted to the
rank of boyár Prince Andréi Havánsky, Michael Plestchéief,
and Matthew Miloslávsky. Lárion Miloslávsky and Zméief were
made okólnitchi, and Hítrovo and Pushétchnikof appointed
privy-councillors. The Tsars wore long robes of cloth-of-
gold covered with lace and fringes, broad sleeves, and caps set
with precious stones. Not only were their robes cut from the
same piece, but the candles they held were of the same length,
that there might seem to be no inequality. Select boyárs were

then sent to the treasury to fetch the cross, the crowns, the sceptres, and the other regalia, which were brought in by priests, and then carried to the Cathedral of the Assumption, where they were received by the Patriarch and the superior clergy on gold dishes, and placed on the lecterns prepared for them. On entering the banqueting-hall the boyárs informed the Tsars that all was ready, and then a long procession—beginning with the inferior officials, rising to the highest boyárs,

Orb of Monomachus.   Crown of Monomachus.
  Orb of Peter.   Crown of Peter.

then to the Tsars, and gradually diminishing again to the petty officials and nobles—went slowly down the Red Staircase, from the banqueting-hall to the Cathedral of the Assumption, over a path made on the pavement by crimson cloth, which was sprinkled by priests with holy water, through the dense masses of the populace which filled the whole square. At the entrance of the Cathedral, the Tsars were met by the Patriarch who wished them long life and held out the cross for them to

kiss.   After kissing the great pictures on the altar-screen, especially the Virgin painted by St. Luke, the Tsars took their
places on the platform.   Standing here amid the throng of
their subjects in this old cathedral, the gilded walls and pillars of
which, lighted up by flickering candles, displayed the rude pictures of saints and martyrs ; under the great central dome,
from which looks down the gigantic image of our Saviour, with
hands upraised in the act of blessing, the Tsars, after reciting
the story of their accession to the throne, demanded of the
Patriarch the rite of consecration and coronation.   The Patriarch in reply, asked to what faith they belonged.   They answered: ' To the holy orthodox Russian faith,' and set forth in
a long speech the good which they expected to do to their
people.   Then, after hymns and prayers, and swinging of censers, the Patriarch placed on their heads the crown of Monomachus, threw over their shoulders the coronation vestments,
placed on their breasts the pectoral cross, gave the sceptres and
globes into their hands, and then, when all had again taken their
seats, ascended the pulpit and preached a sermon upon the
mutual duties of Tsar and people.   Then followed the mass,
during which the Tsars, in sign of their being priests as well as
kings, went within the chancel behind the altar-screen, and administered to themselves the Eucharist with their own hands.
When the service was over, the Tsars again kissed the true cross,
the relics and the holy pictures, and with the nobles went in
procession to the Cathedral of the Archangel Michael, where they
paid reverence to the tombs of their ancestors, the Tsars who are
buried there, and especially to that of the Tsarévitch Dimítri,
who had already been canonised, and of whose death recent
events must have often made them think.   Thence they went to
the Cathedral of the Annunciation, then to the banqueting-hall
of the palace, where they received congratulations.   Two days
later occurred the great official banquet of the coronation.[1]

---

[1] Soloviéf, vol. xiv.; Ustriálof, I. iii.; Pogódin; Aristof; Medvédief's
Memoirs ; Savva Románof, *History of the Faith and the Petitions of the
Streltsi* (Russian), reprinted in Tikhowravof's Collection, Moscow, 1863;
Avvákum, *Autobiography* (Russian), St. Petersburg, 1861 : A. Stchápof, *The
Country and Dissent* (Russian), St. Petersburg, 1862; A. Stchápof, *Russian
Dissent* (Russian) Kazan, 1859 ; Complete Collection of Russian Laws; Tu-
mansky's Collection.

IX.

THE RIOTOUS DISPUTATION OF THE DISSENTERS, AND ITS ENDING. 1682.

A WEEK was passed in waiting, though it was made useful by meetings for prayer and public preaching in the remoter quarters of Moscow. On July 13, the Dissenters and the delegates of the Streltsi resolved again to demand the solemn dispute which had been promised them by Havánsky, and for that purpose went to the Krémlin. Havánsky, who had heard that the Streltsi were not entirely agreed upon the matter, asked, in the name of the Tsar, if all the regiments were united in their desire to restore the old belief. The delegates replied that all the regiments and the people of the suburbs would joyfully stand up for the old orthodox Christian faith. Havánsky repeated the question twice, and again the delegates replied: 'We are ready not only to rise, but even to die for the faith of Christ.' When Havánsky had reported this answer to the Princess Sophia, he went with the delegates to the Patriarch, and after a lively exchange of words and arguments the Patriarch agreed to a solemn disputation on Wednesday, July 15, the next day but one. This having been decided upon, Havánsky and the delegates advanced to the Patriarch and received his blessing; but Paul, one of the leading Dissenters, declined it unless the Patriarch should bless him according to the old rite. This was refused, and Paul went away without the benediction. Havánsky kissed him on the forehead, exclaiming: 'I did not really know you, my dear fellow, until now.'

Meanwhile the Dissenters lost no time. Their leaders went everywhere throughout the town, preaching in the streets, and calling upon the inhabitants to rise for the old orthodox faith. On Wednesday, July 15, Nikíta, after performing service with the Titóf regiment, went with his adherents to the Krémlin, accompanied, as before, by delegates of the Streltsi, and a crowd of people. They drew near the Cathedral of St. Michael the Archangel, close to the Red Staircase, set up their reading-desks, placed upon them old images and books, and lighted their candles. Nikíta stood upon a bench, and began in a loud voice to preach to the people.

The Patriarch was at this time celebrating the liturgy and praying for the appeasement of the riot. As soon as he learned that the crowd had arrived, he sent priests out to exhort them, and distributed among them printed copies of the recantation which Nikíta had signed in the time of the Tsar Alexis, and by which he had promised in future to abstain from the errors of Dissent. The Streltsi tore up the copies of the recantation, seized the priest and handed him over to the Dissenters, whom they had taken under their protection. The Dissenters went on reading the pamphlets written by the Solovétsky monks about the true method of signing the cross, while all around listened with silence and respect, and many wept.

As soon as the service in the Cathedral was ended, the crowd demanded that the Patriarch should come out into the Place. Havánsky insisted at the palace that the Patriarch should be ordered to go out to quiet the people, but that neither the Princess Sophia nor the Tsaritsas should be present at the assembly, as the crowd was too great, and they might be in danger. Sophia decided that the conference should take place in the banqueting-hall, and, in spite of the efforts of Havánsky, insisted upon being present, together with the Tsaritsa Natalia and her aunt Tatiana.

The Patriarch was then advised, as a matter of precaution, to come to the palace with all the archbishops by the back entrance; but to send the old parchment manuscripts and books from the Patriarchal Sacristy by the priests up the Red Staircase. The crowd expressed great satisfaction as they saw the books being carried past them to the palace. 'Now,' they said, 'the truth will evidently be made clear.' The leaders of the Dissenters for a long time refused to enter the banqueting-hall, saying that they would not be safe, and that they would be in danger of being arrested. Havánsky gave them his solemn as-

surance that no harm should attend them. Still there was hesitation until Nikíta told Prince Havánsky that he believed him,
and then they agreed to go. Once again Havánsky tried to
frighteñ Sophia, and induce her not to be present in the banqueting-hall. The Patriarch steadfastly refused to go there
without her, and Sophia said decisively that she would not
abandon the Patriarch. Havánsky then sent word to the Dissenters to enter.

The Dissenters started with their crosses, their gospels, their
images, desks and candles, chanting hymns as they went.

In an anteroom they met the priests who were carrying the
ancient books and parchments into the banqueting-hall ; there
was much scuffling and pushing, and some blows were exchanged. Havánsky, hearing the disturbance, angrily turned
out the priests, who had come there by orders of the Patriarch,
and admitted only the Dissenters and as many of the crowd as
could force their way into the hall with them.

The Dissenters had come to declaim against what was new,
and to insist upon the re-establishment of old and time-hon-
oured rites and practices. Yet, strangely enough, they accepted without comment a novelty far greater than that which
they had come to inveigh against, for, on the throne not the
Tsar, but the Princess Sophia sat, together with her aunt Tatiana ; and in arm-chairs below were the Tsaritsa Natalia and the
Princess Mary. The young Tsars were not present, but in all
probability looked on the scene from one of the small windows
below the ceiling which were made for such purposes.

Bowing to the Princess, the Dissenters stationed their reading-desks before the throne, arranged their images and books,
and lighted their candles, exactly as they had done in the open
air. Sophia turned to them, with half-concealed anger, and
asked :

‘ Why have you come so boldly into the Tsar’s palace, as if
to infidels and heathen, and what do you want of us ? How
dare you go about the town and the Krémlin preaching your
Dissenting heresy, and exciting the common people ? ’

‘ We have come to the Tsars, our Lords,’ said Nikíta, “ to
petition about the amendment of the orthodox faith, that divine
service may be performed according to the old rites, as was or-

dered in the time of the Tsar Michael Feódorovitch, and of the Patriarch Philarét.'

The Patriarch then turned to them, and repeated what he had already said to them in his own house:

'It is not for you common people to manage Church matters. You ought to be advised by the Holy Church, and by the archbishops, whose duty it is to judge of these things. Our faith is that of the old orthodoxy of the Greek rite; we have only corrected the service-books grammatically from Greek manuscripts, parchments and books.'

'We have not come to talk about grammar,' answered Nikíta, 'but about the dogmas of the Church;' and he boldly began to enumerate his arguments, beginning with the question, 'why the archbishop should carry his cross in his left hand, and his candle in his right hand.'

Athanásius, the archbishop of Holmogóry, began to explain, when Nikíta advanced, as if to seize him by the collar, saying:

'Why dost thou, who art the foot, place thyself above the head? I am not talking to thee, but to the Patriarch.'

'Do you see what Nikíta is doing?' cried out Sophia, turning to those about her. 'He wants to fight, even before us. If we were not here, he would certainly have killed the Patriarch long ago.'

'No, lady, I did not beat him; I only waved him off, so that he should not speak before the Patriarch.'

'How do you, Nikíta, dare to talk to the Patriarch?' Sophia continued. 'Is it not enough for you to be in the presence of our "piercing eyes"? You made a recantation to our father of blessed memory, and to the most holy Patriarch, with a great curse upon yourself, never to petition against the faith, and now again you have set about the same business.'

'I do not deny,' replied Nikíta, 'that I did sign a recantation through the power of the sword; but to the petition, which I gave to the assembly, not one of the archbishops dared answer. Simeon Polótsky aimed his book—"The Staff" at me; but in that book he did not touch a fifth of what I said. If you will allow me to read my answer against that "Staff," I will refute it.'

'Hold your tongue,' said the Princess, angrily. 'You have

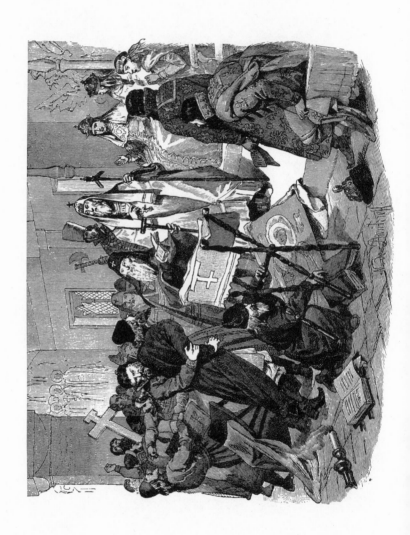

no business to talk with us or even to be in our presence;' and she ordered the petition to be read.

When they came to the place where it was stated that the heretical monk, Arsénius, had, together with Níkon, wrongly influenced the mind of the Tsar Alexis Michaílovitch, and that since that time true piety had ceased in Russia, Sophia could no longer contain herself; angrily interrupting the reading, and starting from her throne, she said :

'We will no longer endure such talk. If Arsénius and the Patriarch Níkon were heretics, then our father and brother were also heretics, and it is plain, then, that the Tsars are not Tsars, that the Patriarch is not the Patriarch, and that the archbishops are not archbishops. We will no longer hear such outrageous things. Sooner than that, we will leave the Empire.'

With these words she left her place and moved away from the throne. The boyárs and the delegates of the Streltsi immediately begged her to return to her place, and swore that they were ready to lay down their lives for the Imperial house; but there were some voices that called out :—

'It has long been time, lady, for you to go to a monastery. You have troubled· the Empire quite enough. Tsars will be good enough for us. Without you the place will not be empty.'

A cry such as this could scarcely weaken the impression made upon the Streltsi delegates by the words of Sophia.

'It is all because the people are afraid of you,' said the Princess to them. 'It was from hope in you that these riotous Dissenters have come hither so boldly. What are you thinking about ? Is it right for such brutes to come to us with rioting, and cry at us, and give us discomfort ? Are you, who were true servants of our grandfather, our father, and our brother, really joined to the Dissenters ? You call yourselves our true servants. Why, then, do you allow such misconduct ? If we are going to be in such slavery that we and the Tsars can no longer live here, we will go to another town, and we will tell the people what we have suffered.'

Nothing could affect the Streltsi more than the threat that the Tsars would leave Moscow. While they knew well enough that the riots and murders of May had excited the feelings of the boyárs and upper classes, they also knew that the common people obeyed them only because they feared them ; and if the Tsars should leave Moscow and collect an army in the country, there would be no hope for them.   The delegates therefore answered :—

'We are ready to serve our lords with truth and fidelity, and to lay down our lives for you and the orthodox faith, and to act according to your commands.'

Sophia then returned to her place and the reading of the petition continued.   She could not always restrain herself from interrupting and arguing with the Dissenting monks.   After the petition had been finished the Patriarch took in one hand the gospel written by the Metropolitan Alexis, and in the other the decretal of the Patriarch Jeremiah, with the creed, just as it was written in the newly corrected books.   'Here are the old books,' said the Patriarch.   'We follow them fully.'   But the strongest impression of all was made by one priest who advanced with a book printed in the time of the Patriarch Philarét, and said :—'Here is one of your dear books of Philarét, which allows meat to be eaten on Holy Thursday and Holy Saturday.'   Nikíta, who had kept silence after the outburst of Sophia, could only mutter : ' It is printed by such rascals as you.'

It was, however, impossible—much as the Patriarch and the archbishops might argue—to overcome the Dissenters, who steadfastly reiterated their statements, without listening to arguments of any kind.   Havánsky walked up and down the hall, but made no attempt to preserve order.   Meanwhile, it was getting late, and it was time for vespers, which neither party was willing to omit.   Besides that, all were faint and weary, having eaten nothing since morning, and Sophia was glad of a pretext for closing this unruly assembly.   She declared that, on account of the approach of vesper time, it was impossible to carry on the conference any longer, and that an Imperial decree about the matter would be issued afterward.   The Princess retired to an inner room of the palace, together with the Patriarch and the archbishops.

The Dissenters ran in a crowd down the Red Staircase, and, lifting up their hands, with two fingers, cried : 'This is the

way we should cross ourselves; this is the way.' On all sides
were heard cries from the people : 'How did the matter end?'
'Why, our side beat them,' was shouted in return. 'We argued down all the archbishops and overcame them. This is
the way to pray; this is the way to cross yourselves.' They
then hastened to the Lobnóë Place, followed by the crowd.
There they began again to explain the Solovétsky pamphlets ;
and then, after chanting a hymn, and raising their hands again
with a two-fingered cross, they set out for the Yaúza suburb,
many of them so tired that they fell swooning on the road. At
the quarters of the Titóf regiment, they were met by ringing of
bells, and after performing a triumphal service in the Church
of the Saviour they went home.

Sophia saw there was no use of trying to convince the Dissenters by argument, and took measures of another kind. She
called the delegates of the Streltsi together, and begged them
not to desert the Tsars for these old monks, recalled their faithful services to the dynasty, and succeeded in persuading them—
some by promises, others by money, and others again by rewards and favours. More than this, the Streltsi were invited
to the palace, in detachments of a hundred at a time, and were
feasted with beer, mead, and wine. The Streltsi were not all
Dissenters, and but few of them had the slightest conception
of the matter in question. As before, on May 15, they had
murdered Matvéief and the rest in support of the dynasty, so
now they had believed the Holy Church to be in danger. It
was therefore comparatively easy for Sophia to persuade them.
When the Dissenters came to complain to them of their desertion, they began to beat and revile them, and call them dis-
turbers of the people. Some of the leading Dissenters were
seized and delivered up to the authorities. There were no
great formalities of trial, and sentence was soon passed. Nikíta
was beheaded a week afterward, on July 21, on the Red Place ;
while his companions, whose punishment was mitigated through
the interference of Havánsky, were imprisoned in various monasteries. The adherents of the Dissenters, in Moscow, were
obliged to conceal their feelings.

The reign of Sophia was a grievous time for the Dissenters.
They were prosecuted and suppressed, and often driven into

open conflict with the troops sent against them. The State,
with its material force, with its sword, had taken the place of
the Church, with its spiritual force, in punishing heresy. After
the siege of the Solovétsky Monastery, many Dissenters had
given up praying for the Tsar; now, as an effect of the persecu-
cutions of Sophia, they began to consider the Tsar as Antichrist,
a feeling which increased during the rule of Peter.

The Dissenters were mistaken in putting themselves forward so soon as representatives of the popular feelings and aspirations; the nation was disunited and divided, and no hearty
support was accorded to them. But this was one of the last of
the many struggles of the Russian people against autocracy and
centralisation, and the boldness and courage of Sophia, while ward-
ing off a present danger, made at the same time a clearer field for
the development of the Imperial power by her brother Peter.[1]

---

[1] See note at the end of the preceding chapter.

The Cross of Peter.

X.

ALTHOUGH the Dissenters had been put down, and the difficulties of the Church had been turned rather than settled, there still remained Havánsky to deal with. He had acquired such influence and authority—he had made himself so prominent of late, especially in the dispute of the Dissenters—he was a man of such arrogant and braggart disposition, that no dependence could be placed upon him. He might at any time use his influence with the Streltsi to become dangerous to the Government, and more especially to Iván Miloslávsky, the leading figure of the new administration, of whom he was a personal enemy. It is not necessary to infer that Havánsky had actually any thought of overturning the Government, or, relying on his royal descent from King Gédimin of Lithuania, of placing the crown on his own head. But there were persistent rumours that he was desirous of marrying his eldest son to one of the daughters of the Tsar Alexis, and the slightest words which he spoke were repeated at court with exaggerations and variations.

Meanwhile the town was far from quiet; the Streltsi continued still to have their own way, to be riotous and disobedient, and there were constant rumours of coming disturbances —at one time that the boyárs were collecting an army to annihilate the Streltsi, and at another that the Streltsi were about to rise to murder the boyárs. On July 12 a crowd of Streltsi came with a demand that the boyárs should be delivered up to them, for threatening to make away with them and torture them. Enquiries were made into the foundation of such rumours, and it was found that the converted Tartar prince, Matthew, had said something of this kind. On being subjected to torture, Matthew confessed that, dissatisfied with the smallness of his pension and the little honour he received, he had spread this report, hoping to gain something by the disturbance. The Tartar prince was drawn and quartered. Bizáef, a man from Yaroslav, who had spread false reports of a similar nature against Veshniakóf, a nobleman of Moscow, and his son, a former colonel, was arrested and executed. The old Veshniakóf died from the torture, for to get at the truth in such cases torture was impartially applied to all parties alike. An old colonel, Yánof, a very honourable and worthy man, was taken by the Streltsi, who were displeased with him for his alleged severity in times gone by, subjected to severe torture, and afterward put to death on the Red Place, in front of the recently erected monument.

The new commander-in-chief, Havánsky, and his son, looked through their fingers at all these murders and cruelties, and took no steps to prevent them; on the contrary, they always took the side of the Streltsi, under the convenient pretext that it would be dangerous to excite them. On August 26, Havánsky brought to the palace a petition of the Streltsi that, for the benefit of those men who were brought from the districts belonging to the court, there should be collected equipment money to the amount of 25 rubles (about $50) a man, making altogether an amount of more than 100,000 rubles (about $200,000) which they demanded. The boyárs, in council, resisted this unlawful demand. Havánsky indignantly left the council, and it was reported to the Government that on going back to the Streltsi he had said:

'Children, the boyárs are threatening even me on your account because I wished well to you. I can do nothing more for you; you will take such measures now as you think best.'

Whether Havánsky said this or not, it was quite sufficient that he was reported to have said it. His refusal to carry out orders and his general conduct had become insupportable. Sophia felt herself almost in slavery to him and to the Streltsi; while Iván Miloslávsky, who had even been demanded for execution by the Streltsi at Havánsky's suggestion, kept increasing the anger and indignation of Sophia by all the means in his power. Miloslávsky had been in such fear of late that he had been little in Moscow, and, to use the words of a contemporary, 'was creeping like an underground mole,' and was concealing himself in his villas in the neighbourhood of the capital. A plan was therefore formed for the ruin of Havánsky. This plan was nothing else, indeed, than the execution of the threat which Sophia had made at the time of the Dissenter riot— namely, that she would leave Moscow, and inform the people of Russia of such great disturbance and insubordination. It was, however, necessary to blind the eyes of Havánsky, in order that he might not see the danger and consequently take measures of precaution. His own self-confidence rendered this all the easier.

On July 29 it was the custom to have a religious procession, in which the Tsar always took part, from the Cathedral of the Assumption to the Donskóy Monastery, a few miles out of Moscow, in commemoration of the preservation of the capital from the attack of the Crim Tartars, in the reign of Theodore Ivánovitch. A rumour was set afloat that the Streltsi intended to profit by this occasion to seize the persons of the Tsars and kill them. Consequently, neither the Tsars nor any other member of their family took part in the procession. The next day— the 30th—Sophia, the Tsars, and the Imperial family went to the villa of Kolómenskoe, which had been the favourite residence of the Tsar Alexis.

All the members of the Imperial family who were not in the secret were naturally much disturbed by this sudden move, and the whole population of the capital was agitated by the departure of the court, and feared lest some new calamity was about to fall on them. Other people also began to leave Moscow ; the Dutch merchants made preparations for going to Archangel, with such of their goods as they could transport; the Dutch Resident asked Prince Havánsky for a guard to protect his house. The Streltsi, also, were much alarmed. They feared that the absence of the court from Moscow foreboded no good. A few days after, on August 2, a deputation of the Streltsi arrived at Kolómenskoe, to express their regret that the Tsars had left Moscow. 'It has been stated to our Lords,' they represented, 'that we, the Palace Guard, have become riotous, and have evil designs on the boyárs and the people near the sovereigns, and that secret correspondence is going on between the regiments; that we are wanting to go to the Krémlin with arms, as we did before, and this is the reason, we hear, that the Tsars have deigned to leave Moscow. But there is no design or plot at all in any of the regiments, nor will there be; and we beg our Lords not to believe such lying words, and to deign to go back to Moscow.'

The answer was simply: 'Your Lords know nothing about any plots of yours. They have gone from Moscow according to their Imperial will and pleasure. Even before this, there were frequent excursions by the Imperial family to the village of Kolómenskoe.' The deputies were sent away with this reply.

The Streltsi quieted down, because they saw that the court remained at Kolómenskoe, for there was no intention of going elsewhere until a proper occasion arose, in order not to excite distrust. Havánsky came to court, in part to see what was going on, and in part to try to frighten Sophia by showing that she needed the support of the Streltsi, and, consequently, his assistance. He stated before the boyárs that various noblemen of Nóvgorod had been to him and said that their comrades intended to come to Moscow, ostensibly to petition about their pay, and that they would kill the inhabitants without distinction. Sophia replied: 'Information of that kind should be stated publicly in Moscow, in the council-chamber, and to the people of all ranks, and letters with the great seal will be sent to Nóvgorod for more exact information.' This disturbed Havánsky, who used all efforts to prevent the public announcement of the fact and to keep back the letters from Nóvgorod.

Taking as an excuse the name's-day of the Tsar Iván—September 28—Sophia ordered Havánsky to send to Kolómenskoe the Streménoy, or 'Stirrup,' regiment—a regiment particularly devoted to the Tsars. Havánsky feared letting this regiment out of his hands. Knowing that Sophia had great influence with it, and dreading lest that influence should be extended over the other regiments, he refused to obey the order, on the ground that he had previously ordered the regiment—although without the Tsars' permission—to go to Kíef. It was not until after the order had been repeated several times that Havánsky yielded.

The Russian year at that time began on September 1 (Old Style, that is, on September 11 by the Gregorian calendar), for it was an article of belief in the Church that the world was created at the beginning of the autumn, and it had been the custom in Moscow to celebrate the first day of the year with great solemnity. The court, nevertheless, did not return for this festival, although orders were given to Havánsky to take part in the service at the cathedral. He did not go; and, to the astonishment of all Moscow, there was only one man of the higher nobility present, and the Patriarch was very angry that the ceremony was attended with so little of the usual pomp. There were even few of the common people there, for everyone was afraid. Rumours had been assiduously circulated that on this or some other festival there would be another Streltsi riot; and the Streltsi themselves were no less frightened, for rumours were running amongst them that on this or some other festival an attack would be made on them by the people and the boyárs, after they had gone on guard, and that their wives and children would be killed. The carriage of Havánsky was constantly attended by a guard of fifty men, and he had as constantly a large company of men in his courtyard—a thing which previously had been unknown with the Streltsi commanders.[1]

On the next day, September 12, the court, under the pretext of pilgrimage to various monasteries, slowly made a circuit of Moscow, gradually getting further and further away from it; going first to the Sparrow Hills; then to the monastery of St. Savva, near Zvenígorod, for the festival of St. Savva on September 16; and then through Pávlovsky and Khliébovo to Vozdvízhenskoe, for the festival of that village—the Elevation of the Cross—on

---

[1] To us, who live under regular and settled governments, such fears seem exaggerated and ridiculous. They are not impossible or unusual in a different state of society. In Constantinople, from 1876 to 1878, scarcely a week passed without rumours of this kind. Now it was a general massacre of Christians by the Mohammedans fixed for the Bairam, and then postponed to another feast, when all preparations were made for resistance, and the communications of the foreign embassies in Pera with their ships of war in harbour were carefully studied; now, it was a rising of the Greeks or the Armenians for Christmas, or New Year's Day, or Easter, which excited no less alarm among the Mussulmans of Stambul. The fear, as it proved, was vain, but the alarm was real. This is not the only case when the Russia of two hundred years ago recalls the Turkey of to-day.

September 24 (September 14, Old Style). In this village Sophia considered herself safe, for it was only about two hours' journey from the strongly-fortified monastery of Tróïtsa. Here Sophia commanded the court to remain for several days, to celebrate her own name's-day on the 27th. Orders were therefore sent to Moscow for all the nobility and high officials to come to Vozdvízhenskoe, partly for matters of state, partly for the celebration of the name's-day of the Princess, and partly to receive the son of the Hetman of the Cossacks, whose arrival Havánsky had announced. Havánsky and his son were also invited, and it is probable that Sophia resolved to make use of the excellent occasion which the arrival of the Hetman's son brought about. At the same time, letters were sent—of course without Havánsky's knowledge—to Vladímir, Súzdal and other neighbouring towns, calling upon the nobility and people in service to come to protect the Tsars, who were threatened with death through the treachery of Havánsky.

On the 27th—the festival of St. Sophia—a large number of people of all ranks had collected in Vozdvízhenskoe. After mass and a collation, at which the Tsars and their sisters were present, there was a council of boyárs. The Privy Councillor Shaklovíty made a report of the crimes attributed to Prince Havánsky and to his son, and read a long anonymous letter, found, it was said, at Kolómenskoe, in which Prince Havánsky, his son, and their adherents were accused of plots against the lives of the Tsars and the boyárs, and in which it was alleged that they themselves desired to ascend the Muscovite throne. In all probability this letter was untrue, and may, indeed, have been invented, although such anonymous letters were frequent in those days, but it served the purpose, and the assembly, without hearing further proof, or allowing an opportunity for defence, condemned Havánsky and his son Andrew, as well as several of their adherents.

Information had been obtained that Prince Havánsky, who, together with his son, had left Moscow the day before, was encamped among the peasants' barns near the village of Púshkino, and that young Havánsky was in his villa at Bratóvstchina on the river Kliázma. Prince Lýkof, with a considerable force, was sent down the Moscow road, and succeeded in surprising

and arresting both the Havánskys and bringing them, together
with the few Streltsi who were with them, to Vozdvízhenskoe,
where every arrangement had been made for the execution. As
soon as the arrival of the Havánskys was known, orders were
given to stop them in front of the gates of the house in which
the Tsars were staying; while the boyárs and other officials
went out and sat on benches and chairs brought for them. The
accusation was read by Shaklovíty. In this many acts of insubordination and illegal conduct were mentioned, and they
were accused, among other things, of having incited the first
riot of the Streltsi. Prince Havánsky immediately made a
protest, and offered, if time were given him, to show who were
the real promoters of this riot. He declared his innocence of
all the points of accusation, and said that if his son were guilty
he would be the first to curse him and to deliver him over to
justice. Miloslávsky immediately reported this to Sophia, and
urged her to execute them at once, and she consented, for both
—and he especially—feared a revolution would be brought about
by Havánsky. A severe order came from Sophia to listen to
nothing on the part of Havánsky, and to carry justice immediately into effect. No executioner could be found, but finally a
soldier of the Streménoy regiment beheaded Iván Havánsky.
His son kissed the breathless body of his father, and then laid
his head upon the block. Odýntsof, who had taken part in the
first Streltsi rioting, and Yúdin, who had assisted in the riot of
the Dissenters, were also executed.

The same day a rescript in the name of the Government
was sent to Moscow to the Streltsi, informing them of the execution of their commander Havánsky and his son, but at the
same time stating that there was no anger or dissatisfaction
with the Streltsi, and ordering them to serve with the same
fidelity as previously. But another son of Prince Havánsky,
Prince Iván, had succeeded in escaping to Moscow, and, arriving there that very night, told the Streltsi that his father had
been captured in the village of Púshkino by the boyárs' people,
and had been punished without the orders of the Tsars, and
that it was the intention of the boyárs to march to Moscow and
to burn all the houses of the Streltsi, and for that reason it
would be well for them to fortify themselves in Moscow. The

counsel was immediately followed. The Streltsi seized their arms, occupied the Krémlin, took from the arsenal the cannon, lead and powder, placed a strong guard everywhere, and put the city in a state of siege, allowing no one to enter or depart from it. There were cries that it was necessary to attack the boyárs, and people went in crowds to the Patriarch, who endeavoured to persuade them to remain calm and not to resort to force. They threatened to kill him for what they considered to be siding with the boyárs; but it all ended in threats, for fear was the prevailing feeling. The Butýrki soldiers, who had taken part in the Streltsi riot, were also frightened. Some of their men had got lost in the Marína wood, and they felt it necessary to get some cannon and protect themselves; and fearing the advance of the boyárs, of which there were rumours, they sent their wives and children into the town for safety.

Meanwhile, the movements of the Streltsi were immediately reported at the court, and couriers were sent out on all sides to call together in the Tróïtsa Monastery all men fit for service, fully armed. To this monastery the court immediately repaired, and the place was put into a condition of defence, the chief command being given to the most faithful follower of Sophia, Prince Basil Golítsyn.

On September 29, Andrew, the Archimandrite of the Miracle Monastery, came to Tróïtsa with a message from the Patriarch that the Streltsi petitioned the Tsars to return to Moscow, where they would suffer no harm, and begged them not to be angry with them, as they had no evil designs. The Government at once replied that it only remained for the Streltsi to show themselves obedient as before, and cease to terrify the whole town of Moscow; and as for Havánsky, who had been punished for his treachery, not to meddle with that matter, as punishment and mercy were left by God to the rulers.

The arrival at Tróïtsa of adherents from all sides enabled the court to act decisively. The boyár Michael Golovín was sent to govern Moscow, and by his actions showed the Streltsi that they no longer inspired fear. This had a good effect, and on October 2d the Streltsi sent a delegation to Golovín, praying that they might be allowed to send a certain number from each regiment to Tróïtsa, to give their submission, as they did not dare to do so without an order to that effect. An order was immediately given that twenty men from each regiment might go to Tróïtsa. Two days later the Streltsi petitioned the Patriarch to send an archbishop with them to Tróïtsa, as they were afraid to go alone. The Patriarch sent with them Hilárion, the Metropolitan of Súzdal; but even this did not entirely quiet them. Many went back to Moscow; the remainder were presented to Sophia, who met them with a severe reprimand for their misconduct, and showed them the considerable army which had been collected to punish them. The Streltsi gave a written submission, in which they alleged that they were ready to obey, that those regiments assigned to Kíef and other towns would proceed at once, that they would restore to the arsenal everything which had been taken, and would be most obedient and faithful servants. This, however, was not enough. The Regent promised the pardon of the Streltsi and soldiers only on conditions which expressed, in very exact terms, the obedience which would be required of them. The Streltsi consented. Prince Iván Havánsky, the younger, was taken to Tróïtsa and sentenced to death; although, when his head was on the block, his punishment was commuted to exile.

On Sunday, October 18, the Patriarch, after the service in the Cathedral of the Assumption, which was filled with Streltsi, placed on the reading-desks the Gospel and a precious relic— the arm of St. Andrew, the first missionary to Russia, and patron of the country. The new articles for the Streltsi were read, and those present kissed both the Gospel and the relic as a sign of their implicit obedience. The court remained at Tróïtsa, guarded by the levies of the nobility, and naturally the Streltsi were brought to agree to a final concession. On November 7, they presented a petition asking to be allowed to pull down the stone column which had been erected on the Red Place in commemoration of the events of May. The permission was of course given. The column was destroyed to its foundation on November 12, the iron plates, with the inscription, were torn off and burnt, and even the foundation was dug up out of the ground. The rescripts given to the Streltsi after the May riots were returned, and new ones given in their stead. All the troubles of the spring and summer were now ascribed to Prince Havánsky and the Dissenter Colonel Alexis Yúdin; and it was forbidden to call the Streltsi traitors or rebels.

Four days after this, on November 16, the court returned to Moscow, surrounded by the troops of the nobility, who acted as guards instead of the Streltsi. The Department of the Streltsi—for now they were no longer to be called the 'Palace Guard'—was placed, temporarily in the hands of the okólnit-chy Zméief, and a month afterwards was given to the councillor Theodore Shaklovíty.

The new commander soon showed his firmness, and by his

Guards of State at Receptions and Processions.

vigorous measures succeeded in rapidly getting the Streltsi under control. He took occasion of various infringements of discipline to rearrange all the regiments and to transfer the worst and most riotous of the Streltsi to the cities of the Ukraine. In this way he restored quiet to the town without exciting any great bad feeling on the part of the Streltsi, for he was conciliatory as well as adroit and firm. The most important of his measures were formed into a new code for the government of the troops, and inserted in the laws as an act to punish riotous conduct and inflammatory language. It took a longer time to put down the disturbances in the remoter provinces, which had been set going by news of the success of the Streltsi, and by seditious letters from Moscow. It was of the more importance to restore order to the country as speedily as possible, because the Poles had taken occasion of the riots at Moscow to cause disturbances in the border provinces, with the hope of getting them into their possession. Strict orders were therefore sent everywhere to governors to arrest and punish all runaway Streltsi, to restore to their masters all fugitive serfs, and to punish severely robbery and marauding. Various old laws which had been abolished or moderated in the time of Theodore were restored in all their severity. The fingers

of thieves were to be cut off, and the third offence was punishable
with death. Later on this was mitigated, in so far that, for the
first offence the criminals lost their ears and not their fingers.
Most difficulty was found in appeasing the always unruly country
of the Don Cossacks, and in putting down the bands of marauders which started from that region, and which constantly threatened to bring about a new revolution, equalling in proportion
that of the famous Sténka Rázin. The perseverance of Sophia
and the firmness of her ministers at last brought about a tolera-
ble pacification of the whole country.

The youth of Peter, the loneliness and friendless condition
of his mother, and the imbecility of Iván, left Sophia mistress
of the situation. Her right to rule had been recognised by the
decree which inserted her name as Regent, and, on the whole,
she ruled well for seven years, and with advantage to Russia.
At first she made no appearance in public as a member of the
Government, although she transacted business with the higher
officials and sometimes received foreign embassies. She was,
however, so little in public view that the diplomatists of that
time rarely speak of her in their despatches, but always of
Prince Golítsyn as the real ruler of Muscovy. Her name appeared in public decrees only as 'The Most Orthodox Princess,
the Sister of Their Majesties,' until the end of 1685, when, for
the first time, she is mentioned as Autocrat on an equality with
her brothers, and it was not until two years later that a formal
decree was issued to this effect, punishing certain persons who
had drawn up papers without inserting the word Autocrat after
her name.

The greatest figure during Sophia's reign is Prince Basil
Golítsyn, whom we have already had occasion to mention several times. He was born in 1643, of one of the great Russian
families descended from the rulers of Lithuania, had served
with distinction in the campaign against the Turks at Tchigirín, and as we already know, had taken the leading part in the
abolition of precedence. During the May riots he had been
given the direction of foreign affairs by the temporary Government, and, after the Government of Sophia had become regularly established, he received by a decree the title of Keeper of
the Great Seal, or Chancellor. His more immediate duties,

however, always remained those of Minister of Foreign Affairs. Of his character as a statesman it will be more easy to judge when we have considered the chief events of Sophia's reign, and especially the new relations which Russia then entered into with foreign powers. As a man, Golítsyn had received a good education, and was imbued with Western culture and Western ideas. By his dignity, his ready courtesy, and, above all, by his wealth and magnificence, he produced a great impression on all the foreign ambassadors with whom he came into contact, with whom he could talk in Latin without the aid of an interpreter; and Baron van Keller, and especially Neuville,—an agent sent to Moscow by the Marquis de Bethune, the French ambassador in Poland,—were particularly under his charm. Neuville speaks of the splendour of his house and the urbanity of his manners—so different from those of the other Russians whom he met, calls him a veritable *grand seigneur*, and says that on entering the house of Prince Golítsyn he thought he was in the palace of some great Italian prince. He was much struck, too, by the circumstance that Golítsyn, instead of pressing him to drink, as was the Russian habit, advised him on the contrary not to take the small glass of *vodka* brought in on the arrival of guests, as it could not be pleasant to a foreigner. Golítsyn sought the society of foreigners, dined and supped at the houses of the foreign envoys, as well as of the chief officers in the German suburb; was in intimate relations with General Gordon; and, among other things, protected the young Swiss, Lefort, who was destined afterward to hold a position rivalling his own. If we may judge from the ideas and plans of Golítsyn, as recounted by Neuville, for the development of trade in Siberia, for the reform of the military organisation of the country and of the internal legislation, as well as for a possible emancipation of the serfs, all of which remained merely as projects— for the state of things during the government of Sophia left no chance to carry them out—we must consider him as one of the most liberal-minded men of that epoch, and fully fitted to sympathise with and carry out the reforms of Theodore, and even of Peter. When Golítsyn was condemned and banished, in 1689, a full inventory of all the property in his house was taken, which still exists in the archives of the Ministry of Justice.

From this we can form some idea of his magnificence as well as of his tastes. Besides costly furniture and tapestry hangings, equipages, busts, painted glass, carvings in wood and ivory, mathematical and physical instruments, a tellurium in gold and silver, portraits of the Tsars as well as of the princes of Western Europe, crystal, precious stones, and silver plate and musical instruments, there were silver mountings for horse trappings and harness to the value of what would now be eight thousand pounds, and an immense sum in silver coin. In his library there were books in several different languages, many historical works, and, what is most interesting, a manuscript of an encyclopædical work on statesmanship and political economy, with a special reference to Russia, written by the learned Serbian, Yury Krýzhanitch, in his exile at Tobolsk, which now serves as most precious material for estimating the character of the time just before Peter. In it are developed all the ideas of reform then current among the few, some of which were carried into effect by Peter.

Prince Iván Miloslávsky took a prominent part in the councils of Sophia until his death, which occurred soon after. But the man on whom she and Golítsyn relied more than the rest for the execution of their designs was Theodore Shaklovíty, the new commander of the Streltsi. He was, by origin, from Little Russia, apparently without more than the rudiments of an education, but adroit, decided, and devoted. He was ready to carry out any order of his sovereign, no matter what. The command of his superior was for him a sufficient reason, and, at the same time, his devotion was such that he was willing to engage in plots and intrigues on a mere hint, in order to advance the interests of his master.

The councils of Sophia were completed on their spiritual side by the monk Sylvester Medvédief, a countryman of Shaklovíty, who had originally been a brilliant young civilian, and at one time had been attached to a great embassy to Curland. He preferred, however, to give up civil life, and to enter the Church. He was a zealous disciple of Simeon Polótsky, the tutor of the Tsar Theodore and the Princess Sophia, and, as such, was thought to be tainted with Romish heresies. His contemporaries considered him the most learned man in

Russia, and he wrote several theological works, one of them called 'Manna,' in which he carried on a heated controversy with the Patriarch Joachim, on a question which then greatly divided both clergy and laymen in Russia—namely, the actual moment when Transubstantiation began during the celebration of the Eucharist. For us, he chiefly lives in his short but interesting memoirs of the early part of Sophia's reign and of the troubles of 1682.[1]

[1] Ustriálof, I. iv. ; Soloviéf, vols. xiii., xiv. ; Pogódin ; Medvédief's *Memoirs ;* Aristof ; Kostomárof, *Russian History in the Lives of its Actors* (Russian), St. Petersburg ; Brückner, *Peter der Grosse ;* Brückner, *Fürst W. Golítsyn* in the *Russische Revue,* 1878 ; M. Posselt, *Franz Lefort, sein Leben und seine Zeit,* Frankfurt, 1866 ; Kryzhanitch, *The Russian State* (Russian), Moscow, 1859 ; Neuville, *Relation curieuse et nouvelle de Moscovie,* Paris, 1698 ; Papers in the Russian and Dutch Archives ; Complete Collection of Russian Laws, 954.

XI.

DURING the early period of Sophia's regency, Peter was left very much to himself. But as his name was used in all public documents he was required to sign many of them, and he seems to have performed this part of his duty with punctuality and accuracy. He had also to go to Moscow, on occasions of cere-mony, to take part in the reception of foreign ambassadors, and to be present at state banquets, and at the ceremonies and processions on religious festivals. The Polish envoy, in his re-port on affairs at Moscow, stated that Sophia was exceedingly fond of her brother Peter, and was endeavouring to put the state in good condition in order to hand the Government over to him when he became old enough. The sincerity of her attachment to Peter we may be allowed to doubt, but she at least manifested no open ill-will to him, and, indeed, there are several entries in the books of the court of her favourable dis-position to him. Thus, in July, 1684, she presented him with some diamond clasps, buttons and stars. With his brother Iván, Peter was always on the best of terms, and especially so after the Government had become settled. Van Keller, writing in 1683 of Peter's residence in the country, says: 'The natural love and intelligence between the two Lords is even better than before. God will it long continue so.'

So much was Peter's mind set on military objects, and on playing at soldiers, that even a day or two after the first riot of the Streltsi, we hear of his sending down to the arsenal for drums, banners and arms. The troubles of the Dissenters and of Prince Havánsky naturally kept him from indulging the full bent of his inclinations in the country, and for the rest of the

year he was detained in Moscow by official duties. Early in
1683, however, we find him ordering uniforms, banners, and
wooden cannon, all of which were immediately furnished by
the authorities, and as soon as he was able to go into the country, to Preobrazhénsky and to the Sparrow Hills, messengers
came almost daily to the Krémlin for lead, powder and shot.
On his eleventh birthday—in 1683—he was allowed for the
first time to have some real guns, with which he fired salutes,
under the direction of a German artilleryman named Simon
Sommer, who had recently come from foreign part, and was a
captain in the regiment of General Shépelof. After this he
was allowed small brass and iron cannon ; and that he might
indulge his taste for music as well as for military pastime,
musicians—especially drummer-boys—were selected for him
from the different regiments. About that time—July, 1683—a
German traveller, named Engelbert Kämpfer, passed through
Moscow on his way to Astrakhán, and, in his diary, which still
exists in manuscript in the British Museum, tells of his reception at the Russian court, as acting secretary for the Swedish
Envoy, Fabricius :—

' Here we got off our horses, and, handing our swords to a
servant, walked up some steps and passed through a building
magnificent with gilded vaults, and then through an open stone
passage, again to the left, and through an anteroom in the audience hall, the floor of which was covered with Turkish carpets,
where we came to the " piercing eyes " of their Tsarish Majesties. Both their Majesties sat, not in the middle, but somewhat to the right side of the hall, next to the middle column,
and sat on a silver throne like a bishop's chair, somewhat raised
and covered with red cloth, as was most of the hall. Over the
throne hung a holy picture. The Tsars wore, over their coats,
robes of silver cloth woven with red and white flowers, and, instead of sceptres, had long golden staves bent at the end like
bishops' croziers, on which, as on the breast-plate of their robes,
their breasts and their caps, glittered white, green and other
precious stones. The elder drew his cap down over his eyes
several times, and, with looks cast down on the floor, sat almost
immovable. The younger had a frank and open face, and his
young blood rose to his cheeks as often as anyone spoke to him.

He constantly looked about, and his great beauty and his lively manner—which sometimes brought the Muscovite magnates into confusion—struck all of us so much that had he been an ordinary youth and no imperial personage we would gladly have laughed and talked with him.   The elder was seventeen, and the younger sixteen years old.   When the Swedish Envoy gave his letters of credence, both Tsars rose from their places, slightly bared their heads and asked about the king's health, but Iván, the elder, somewhat hindered the proceedings through not understanding what was going on, and gave his hand to be kissed at the wrong time.   Peter was so eager that he did not give the secretaries the usual time for raising him and his brother from their seats and touching their heads : he jumped up at once, put his own hand to his hat and began quickly to ask the usual question : " Is his royal Majesty, Carolus of Sweden, in good health ? "   He had to be pulled back until the elder brother had a chance of speaking.'

It was evident that Peter must have been a large, healthy boy, if when he was only eleven he appeared to Kämpfer and the Swedish mission to be sixteen.

It is interesting to compare with this the account of Johann Eberhard Hövel, who in the next year, 1684, came on a mission from the Emperor Leopold I.   Peter was at that time ill with the measles—an illness which excited considerable alarm among his partisans—and was unable to receive.   Hövel, therefore, saw no one but the Tsar Iván.   He says that when the health of the Emperor was asked about, the Tsar was so weak from long standing that he had to be supported by his two chamberlains, who held up his arms, and he spoke with a very weak and inarticulate voice.   General Gordon, who was received a few days later, January 22, had tried to put off his reception in order to see both the Tsars at once ; but as he was obliged to leave soon for his command at Kíef, was received only by Iván and Sophia.   According to his account, Iván was sickly and weak, and always looked toward the ground.   He said nothing himself, and all the questions were put through Prince Golítsyn.   This was just after the marriage of Iván with Praskóvia Sóltykof, of a distinguished family.   This marriage Hövel, as well as many other people, considered to be a plot on the part of

Sophia to obtain heirs from the elder brother, and thus get rid of the claims of Peter, whom he calls ' a youth of great expectancy, prudence, and vigour.' Considering, however, that Iván, in spite of the infirmities of his eyes, his tongue and his mind, was in fairly good health, it was the most natural thing in the world that his friends should desire him to marry. Later in the same year, in June, Laurent Rinhuber, a doctor of medicine, coming from Saxony, was received at court, and was granted an audience by the Tsars. He says : ' Then I kissed the right hand of Peter, who, with a half-laughing mouth, gave me a friendly and gracious look and immediately held out to me his hand ; while the hands of the Tsar Iván had to be supported. He is a remarkably good-looking boy, in whom nature has shown her power ; and has so many advantages of nature that being the son of a king is the least of his good qualities. He has a beauty which gains the heart of all who see him, and a mind which, even in his early years, did not find its like.'

In the autumn of the same year, 1684, Peter had another attack of illness, which was more severe than the measles and which caused great alarm. His recovery excited universal joy, more especially in the foreign quarter of Moscow. There were many banquets and feasts in honour of his convalescence, and Prince Boris Golítsyn, the cousin of the Chancellor and the chief adviser of Peter, together with other Russians of that party, dined with the Dutch minister, and caroused till a late hour. A year later, in September, 1685, Van Keller writes :—

' The young Tsar has now entered his thirteenth year : nature develops herself with advantage and good fortune in his whole personality ; his stature is great and his mien is fine ; he grows visibly, and advances as much in intelligence and understanding as he gains the affection and love of all. He has such a strong preference for military pursuits that when he comes of age we may surely expect from him brave actions and heroic deeds, and we may hope that some day the attacks of the Crim Tartars will be somewhat better restrained than at present. This was the noble aim always set before the ancestors of the young Tsar.'

The military exercises of Peter brought him into constant contact with German officers at Moscow, for all the best officers

PETER PLAYING AT WAR.

and even soldiers were foreigners, and it was necessary to draw
on the German suburb for the officers and instructors for the
new regiment which was organised, at the end of 1683, for
Peter's amusement. The first man who was enrolled as a
soldier in the regiment was Sergius Bukhvástof, one of the
grooms of the palace, and Peter was so much struck with his
readiness, and so much pleased with the formation of this regiment, that long afterward he ordered the Italian artist Rastrelli,
then a favourite in St. Petersburg, to cast a life-size statue of
him as the first Russian soldier. Other volunteers soon presented themselves, and Peter himself enlisted as bombardier,
for which duty he had an especial fancy, and then passed
through the various grades until he became colonel and chief
of the regiment. Among the other volunteers were Yekím
Vorónin and Gregory Lúkin—at whose deaths, during the
siege of Azof, Peter grieved greatly, ' as he and they had been
brought up together'—and Alexander Menshikóf, the future
favourite. This was the beginning of the celebrated Preobrazhénsky Regiment, even now the first regiment of the
Imperial guard, and of which the Emperor is always the chief.
The name Preobrazhénsky was given to it first because it was
formed and quartered at the palace and village of Preobrazhénsky, or the Transfiguration, which, in turn, took their name
from the village church. Peter and his friends called this regiment, and others which were afterwards formed, 'the guards,'
but the common name for them at Moscow was the Potiéshnie
Koniúkhi—i.e. 'Amusements Grooms,' or 'Troops for Sport.'
    The number of volunteers for this regiment increased so
rapidly that the village of Preobrazhénsky could not hold them
all, and it was necessary to quarter some of the soldiers in the
adjoining village of Seménofsky, where another regiment called
the Seménofsky Regiment grew up. All the young nobles who
desired to gain Peter's good graces followed his example by
enrolling themselves in one of these regiments. Thus, Prince
M. M. Golítsyn, the future Field Marshal, began his service as
drummer in the Seménofsky Regiment, and Iván Ivánovitch
Buturlín served up to the rank of major in the Preobrazhénsky Regiment.
    Peter entered upon his military exercises with such zest that

they ceased to be mere child's play. He himself performed every exercise, giving himself no rest night or day. He stood his watch in turn, took his share of the duties of the camp, slept in the same tent with his comrades, and partook of their fare. There was no distinction made between the Tsar and the least of his subjects. When his volunteers became proficient in their discipline, he used to lead them on long marches in the neighbourhood of his country home, and went at times even as far as the Trinity Monastery at Kaliazín. As his followers were armed, these marches were in the nature of campaigns, and the troops, such as they were, were under strict military discipline, and were regularly encamped at night with the usual military precautions. In 1685, when Peter was thirteen years old, he resolved on something further, and, in order to practise the assault and defence of fortifications, began to construct a small fortress on the banks of the Yaúza, at Preobrazhénsky, the remains of which are still visible on the edge of the Sokól-niki wood. This fort, probably at the suggestion of one of the German officers, was called Pressburg. It was built with a considerable amount of care, timber was drawn for the purpose from Moscow, and its construction took the greater part of the year. Peter named it with great ceremony, leading a procession from Moscow which included most of the court officials and nobles. All this, as has been said, brought Peter into very close relations with the foreign suburb, and the foreigners in Moscow were fond of social amusements, always accompanied, according to their habits, with beer, wine, and tobacco. Peter, who was precocious, both physically and mentally, took his full share in these entertainments and on the return feasts he gave it may be imagined that there was no stint of drink. With such society Peter gained not only a knowledge of men and of the world, but his inquiring mind led him to be curious about many subjects which rarely before had troubled the head of a Russian Prince. Without regard to rank or position, he was always glad to make the acquaintance of those from whom he could learn anything, and was especially attracted by all that was mechanically curious.

Frequently, for amusement, he used to hammer and forge at the blacksmith's shop. He had already become expert with the lathe, and we have documentary evidence to prove that he had practically learnt the mechanical operation of printing as well as the binding of books. We can believe that the Electress Charlotte Sophia did not exaggerate when, in 1697, in describing her interview with Peter, she said that he 'already knew excellently well fourteen trades.'

All this was a school for Peter; but do not let us be led astray by the word school. Peter's military education was such as he chose to give himself, and entirely for his own amusement. There was nothing in it similar to the regular course of military training practised in a cadet school. Peter was only too glad to escape from the nursery and house to the amusements of the street and the fields. Although we know that in the Russia of that day the intellectual development of a youth did not at all keep pace with his physical growth, and that when a lad was grown to the stature of a man, he immediately assumed the duties and responsibilities of a man, though in mind he might be still a child; yet there was generally the semblance of discipline. The way in which Peter seems to have slipped through the hands of his instructors, tutors and guardians shows not only his strong self-will, but the disorganisation of his party, and the carelessness of his family. Such a training may have been useful, and, indeed, it was useful to Peter; at all events it was better than nothing; but in no sense of the term can it be considered education. This Peter himself, in later life, admitted, and the Empress Elizabeth tells how, when she was bending over her books and exercises, her father regretted that he had not been obliged or enabled to do the same.

One more word with regard to Peter's military amusements. They were, as we have said, mere amusements, and had not the regularity or the plan which subsequent chroniclers and anecdote-writers ascribe to them. In playing at soldiers, Peter followed his natural inclination, and had in his head no plan whatever for reorganising or putting on a better footing the military forces of his country. The reorganisation of the Russian army, indeed, grew out of the campaigns and exercises at Preobrazhénsky; but it was not until real war began that Peter saw of what service these exercises had been to him and to others, and found that the boy-soldiers could easily be made the nucleus of an army.

The year 1688 was an important one for Peter. In January he was induced by his sister Sophia to take part for the first time in a council of state, and thus made his public appearance in political life in something more than a mere formal way. But his mind was at that time too full of his military exercises for him to care for state affairs, and, after visiting all the public offices on the day of commemoration of the death of his father, when he gave money to some prisoners and set others free, he went back again to the country, to his troops. Later on, his intellect began to awaken, and he seriously applied himself to study; and then, too, his thoughts were first turned to navigation and things naval, which soon became the ruling passion of his life. He told the story himself, long afterwards, in his preface to the 'Maritime Regulations.'

He had heard somewhere that abroad, in foreign parts, people had an instrument by which distances could be measured without moving from the spot. When Prince Jacob Dolgorúky was about to start on his mission to France, and came to take his leave, Peter told him of this wonderful instrument, and begged him to procure him one abroad. Dolgorúky told him he himself had once had one, which was given him as a present, but it had been stolen, and that he would certainly not forget to bring one home. On Dolgorúky's return in May, 1688, the first question of Peter was whether he had fulfilled his promise; and great was the excitement as the box was opened and a parcel containing an astrolabe and a sextant was eagerly unwrapped; but, alas! when they were brought out no one knew the use of them. Dolgorúky scratched his head, and said that he had brought the instrument, as directed, but it had never occurred to him to ask how it was used. In vain Peter sought for some one who knew its use. At last his new doctor, Zacharias von der Hulst, told him that in the German suburb he knew of a man with a notion of mechanics—Franz Timmermann, a Dutch merchant, who had long ago settled in Moscow, and who had a certain amount of education. Timmermann was brought next day. He looked at the instrument, and, after a long inspection, finally said he could show how it should be used. Immediately he measured the distance to a neighbouring house. A man was at once sent to pace it, and found the measurement correct.

TIMMERMAN EXPLAINING TO PETER THE USE OF THE ASTROLABE.

Peter was delighted, and asked to be instructed in the use of the new instrument. Timmermann said: 'With pleasure; but you must first learn arithmetic and geometry.' Peter had once begun studying arithmetic, but was deficient in its full knowledge. He did not even know how to subtract or divide. He now set to work with a will, and spent his leisure time, both day and night, over his copybooks. These are still preserved at St. Petersburg, and we find there many problems, written in the hand of Timmermann, with Peter's efforts at solution. The writing is careless, and faults of grammar abound; but the ardour and resolution with which Peter worked are evident on every page. Geometry led to geography and fortification. The old globe of his schoolroom was sent for repairs, and he had, besides, the one in metal presented to his father, which still is shown in the treasury at Moscow.

From this time Timmermann became one of Peter's constant companions, for he was a man from whom something new could always be learned. A few weeks later, in June, 1688, as Peter was wandering about one of his country estates near the village of Ismaílovo, he pointed to an old building in the flax-yard and asked one of his attendants what it was. 'A storehouse,' replied the man, 'where all the rubbish was put that was left after the death of Nikíta Ivánovitch Románof, who used to live here.' This Nikíta was an own cousin of the Tsar Michael Románof, and in that way the estate had descended to Peter. With the natural curiosity of a boy, Peter had the doors opened, went in, and looked about. There, in one corner, turned bottom upward, lay a boat, yet not in any way like those flat-bottomed, square-sterned boats which he had seen on the Moskvá or the Yaúza.

'What is that?' he asked.

'That is an English boat,' said Timmermann.

'What is it good for? Is it better than our boats?' asked Peter.

'If you had sails to it, it would go not only with the wind, but against the wind,' replied Timmermann.

'How against the wind? Is it possible? Can that be possible?'

Peter wished to try it at once. But, after Timmermann

had looked at the boat on all sides, it was found to be too rotten for use; it would need to be repaired and tarred, and, beside that, a mast and sails would have to be made. Timmermann at last thought he could find a man capable of doing this,
and sent to Ismaílovo a certain Carsten Brandt, who had been
brought from Holland about 1660 by the Tsar Alexis, for the
purpose of constructing vessels on the Caspian Sea. After the
troubles of Astrakhán, when his vessel, the ' Eagle,' had been
burnt by Sténka Rázin, Brandt had returned to Moscow, and
had remained there, making a living as a joiner. The old man
looked over the boat, caulked it, put in the mast and arranged
the sail, and then launched it on the river Yaúza. There, before Peter's eyes, he began to sail up and down the river, turning now to the right and then to the left. Peter's excitement
was intense. He called out to him to stop, jumped in, and
began himself to manage the boat under Brandt's directions.
' And mighty pleasant it was to me,' he writes in the preface
to his ' Maritime Regulations,' where he describes the beginning of the Russian navy. It was hard for the boat to turn,
for the river was narrow and the water was too shallow. Peter
eagerly asked where a broader piece of water could be found,
and was told of the Prosyány Pool. The boat was dragged
overland to the Prosyány Pool. It went better, but still not
to his satisfaction.[1] At last Peter found that about fifty miles
beyond the Tróïtsa Monastery there was a good large lake,
where he would have plenty of room to sail—Lake Plestchéief,
near Pereyaslávl. It was not, however, so easy for Peter to
get there. It was not customary for the Tsars or members of
their family to make journeys without some recognised object,
and what should a boy of this age do so far away, and alone ?
An idea struck Peter. It was then June, and there was a great
festival at the Tróïtsa Monastery. He asked his mother's permission to go to Tróïtsa for the festival, and as soon as the
religious service was over he drove as fast as he could to Lake
Plestchéief. The country was at that time delightful. The
low hills were covered with the fresh green of the birches,

---

[1] The story of Peter's terror of water, and of the efforts he made in order
to accustom himself to it, is due to the imagination of an anecdote-monger,
and is without foundation. See Ustriálof, II. 332 pp.

PETER FINDING THE GRANDFATHER OF THE RUSSIAN FLEET.

mixed with the more sturdy lindens and the pines black by contrast. The faint smell of the lilies of the valley came up from the meadows on the lake shore. Peter did not notice this. His mind was too intent upon navigation; he saw only that the lake was broad enough, for it stretched out of sight. But he sooned learned that there was no boat there, and he knew that it was too far to bring the little English boat which he had found at Ismaílovo. Anxiously he asked Brandt whether it were not possible to build some boats there.

'Yes, sire,' said Brandt, 'but we shall require many things.'

'Ah, well! that is of no consequence,' said Peter. 'We can have anything.'

And he hastened back to Moscow with his head full of visions of shipbuilding. He scarcely knew how to manage it, for to engage in such a work at Lake Plestchéief would require his living there for some time, and he knew that it would be hard to bring his mother to consent to this. At last he extorted this consent, but he was obliged to wait at Moscow for his name's-day, when there was a Te Deum at the Cathedral, after which the boyárs and grandees paid their respects at the palace and received cups of *vodka* from Peter and goblets of wine from the hands of his mother. He hastened off the next day—July 10—together with Carsten Brandt and a shipbuilder named Kort, an old comrade whom Brandt had succeeded in finding at Moscow. Timmermann, probably, also accompanied him. Fast as Peter and his comrades worked together—for he had remained with them in the woods—there was so much to do in the preparation of timber, in the construction of huts to live in, and of a dock from which to launch the boats, that it came time for Peter to return long before any boat was ready, and there was no sign that any could be got ready before winter set in. The Tsaritsa Natalia had grown anxious for her son. He had been away nearly a month, and political affairs were taking a serious turn. Much to his regret, therefore, Peter came back to Moscow for his mother's name's-day, on September 6, leaving his faithful Dutchmen strict injunctions to do their utmost to have the boats ready by the following spring.

The place chosen by Peter for his shipbuilding, was on the east side of Lake Plestchéief, at the mouth of the river Trúbezh. The only traditions still remaining of Peter's visit are the site of a church dedicated to the Virgin at the Ships, and the decaying remains of some piles under water, which apparently formed the wharf or landing-stage. Lake Plestchéief, nowadays, is famous for nothing but an excellent and much-sought-for variety of fresh-water herring.

The boat which Peter found at Ismaílovo is thought by many to have been constructed in Russia by Dutch carpenters, in 1688, during the reign of the Tsar Alexis, at a place called Dédinovo, at the confluence of the rivers Moskvá and Oká. By others it is thought to be a boat sent by Queen Elizabeth to the Tsar Iván the Terrible. Ever since Peter's time it has borne the name of the ' Grandsire of the Russian fleet,' and is preserved with the greatest care in a small brick building near the Cathedral of Sts. Peter and Paul, within the fortress at St. Petersburg. In 1870, on the celebration of the 200th anniversary of Peter's birth, it was one of the chief objects of interest in the great parade at St. Petersburg; and again, in 1872, it was conveyed with much pomp and solemnity to Moscow, where, for a time, it formed a part of the Polytechnic Exposition.[1]

---

[1] Pogódin, pp. 99–142; Ustriálof, II. i. ; Soloviéf, vol. xiii. ; Posselt, *Lefort ;* Adelung, *Uebersicht der Reisenden in Russland,* ii. pp. 371 ff. ; Adelung's *Meyerburg,* pp. 349 ff., St. Petersburg, 1827; Gordon's *Diary ;* Russian Laws, ii. ; Reports of Dutch Residents ; Esipof; Astrof; Maritime Regulations.

PETER LAUNCHING THE GRANDFATHER OF THE RUSSIAN FLEET.

XII.

ON account of another festival, the name's-day feast of the Tsaritsa Natalia was postponed for a day. After a religious service in the cathedral, the nobility and the delegates of the regiments of Streltsi and soldiers were admitted to the palace to express their good wishes, and were entertained at dinner, before which they each received a glass of *vodka* from the hand of the Tsaritsa. This shows that, however heated might be the feelings of the respective parties surrounding Sophia and her brother, the formal respect due to the widow of the Tsar Alexis was still preserved.

There was no use in Peter's returning to his boats now that winter was so near, even had his mother and his friends been willing to allow him to go. He therefore again turned his attention to his soldiers, who had so long been out of his mind, and from the demands which he made upon General Gordon and others for drummers, fifers, and drilled recruits—demands which were with difficulty granted, both by Gordon and Golítsyn—he was evidently preparing manœuvres of considerable importance. Just at that time a second campaign was decreed against the Turks and Tartars, and the Streltsi and regular soldiers were all ordered to the front, in order to reach winter-quarters near the frontier, and manœuvres on any large scale at Preobrazhénsky were therefore given up. The previous campaign of Golítsyn against the Tartars had turned out so badly that there was discontent at the declaration of a new one. There was dissatisfaction in Moscow with the rule of Sophia and her favourite, and Peter's partisans were evidently of opinion that it was time for him to take upon himself the burdens of the government, and that they were strong enough to assist him. That there was high feeling between the parties at court is shown by many little entries in Gordon's diary, though, usually, he was careful not to mention anything which might in any way compromise himself. But he says, for instance, that he dined with General Tabort, where he met Prince Basil Golítsyn and many of *that party ;* and a fortnight later he tells us that he rode back from Ismaílovo with Leontius Neplúief, with whom he talked at length about the *secret plots and plans.* Peter himself added a little to the flame of party feeling by unthinkingly getting into conversation with an

Mohammed IV., Sultan of Turkey.

army scribe, who happened to be drunk, and asking him many details about the pay and condition of the troops. This act was viewed with displeasure by the Government.

Besides the preparations for the campaign, Golítsyn and Sophia were much troubled by the position of affairs abroad. There was fear lest France, by attacking Austria, might compel the Emperor to make a separate peace with the Turks, and the question came up, what it was necessary to do in such a conjuncture. It was thought that the recent capture of Belgrade by the Austrians might induce them more readily to compromise with the Sultan, and messengers were therefore sent both to Vienna and Warsaw to stir up the Emperor, and, in any case, to obtain for Russia as good terms as possible. A great deal of interest, too, was taken at this time in the affairs of England, for William of Orange had just landed at Torbay, and James II. had fled. But a short time before this last piece of news, which took two months in coming, and was communicated in official despatches to the Dutch Minister and in private letters to General Gordon, the latter had had a conversation with Prince Basil Golítsyn at dinner, in which Golítsyn had said ; 'With the father and brother of your King we could get along very well, but with the present King it is perfectly impossible to come to an understanding ; he is so immeasurably proud.' Gordon pretended to understand this as complaining that no envoy was sent to Russia, and answered: 'The King, as I believe, on account of the troubles in his own States, has not leisure enough to think of things that are so far off.' But Golítsyn said, further: 'The English cannot do without Russian products, such as hides, hemp, potash, tallow, and timber for masts ;' upon which Gordon gave, as he says, an answer of a double sense, implying that he agreed with the Prince. Gordon, who was a zealous Catholic, lost no opportunity of defending King James, and for his steadfast adherence to the Stuart cause gained encomiums even from the Dutch Minister, at a dinner given by him on King William's birthday.

To add to the troubles of the Government, and the prevailing discontent, Moscow was plagued with fires. As in most Russian towns of the present day, the houses at Moscow were built of logs, the interstices being stuffed with tow, the roofs, too, being generally of wood. The day following the name's-day of the Tsaritsa Natalia a fire broke out in the house set apart for the entertainment of foreign ambassadors, just outside the Krémlin, which spread to the north-east with great rapidity, overleaped the walls of the Kitai-gorod and the White Town, crossed the river Yaúza into the quarter of the Streltsi, and the suburb called the Ragóshkaya, and destroyed over 10,000 houses. Besides several smaller and almost daily fires, there was one on September 16 in the Krémlin, which burnt down all the priest-houses of the cathedrals and the roofs of the Department of Foreign Affairs and the Department of Kazan. On the night of the 20th, the stables of the Patriarch and the palace of the Tsars narrowly escaped destruction. On the 27th, there was a fire at Preobrazhénsky, in the neighbourhood of the palace, which consumed the house of Prince Boris Golítsyn. On October 11 a fire broke out near the Ilínsky Gate, which extended as far as the Ustrétinka, far beyond the White Wall, and burnt a whole quarter of the town, including many public buildings.   This last fire created such embarrassment for the Government that when, four days afterward, Gordon went to town to ask for a hundred roubles of his pay for that year, he was told that he could not receive it, because the treasury was exhausted, so much money having been advanced to all sorts of people who had suffered by the great fire, in order to enable them to rebuild their houses.

Peter had grown so tall and strong that there had long been a feeling among his party that it was time for him to marry.   To this not even Sophia offered any opposition;—above all things the succession to the throne must be secured.   The marriage of Iván, which she had brought about, had produced daughters only.   One of these, indeed, subsequently ascended the Russian throne as the Empress Anne, but at that time, in spite of the fact that the Regent

Eudoxia Lopúkhin, First Wife of Peter the Great.

was a woman, and even that her name was inserted in public acts as Autocrat, it was still thought desirable to have male heirs.   Even as long ago as the end of 1685, when Prince Archil of Georgia came to Moscow, and was received with great pomp, there were rumours that Peter would soon marry his beautiful daughter.   In December, 1687, Prince Basil Golítsyn spent a few days with Peter in the country, which was thought to be a very good omen, and again there was talk of Peter's marrying—this time a relative or friend of Golítsyn.   A month later, there was more talk of this marriage project, but the lady was not named.

Now the plan was a more serious one.   The usual prepara-

tions were made for collecting at court young girls of noble
family, and out of these there was chosen Eudoxia, or Avdótia,
Lopúkhin, the daughter of the Okólnitchy, Hilary Abrámovitch
Lopúkhin, who, on the marriage, according to custom, changed
his name and received that of Theodore.   The Lopúkhins were
a very good old Russian family, descended from the Princes of
Tmútarakán, and several of them had risen to the dignity of
boyár.   In this generation they were likewise connected with the
Ramodanófsky, Golítsyn, Troekúrof, and Kurákin families, and
thus with the prominent members of the aristocratic party.
The bride, who was three years older than Peter,[1] is said to have
been pretty, quiet and modest, brought up in the old Russian
way.   We do not know whether she was selected by Peter himself for her good looks, or whether his choice was directed by
his mother and his family.   It was probably thought that a good,
quiet, stay-at-home wife would be likely to keep him at home,
would put a stop to those long excursions for military manœuvres
and for boat-building, and, above all, would bring to an end some
little heart-affairs in the German quarter.

In this his family were partly mistaken.   The marriage was
celebrated on February 6, 1689, and two months were scarcely
over before Peter, seeing the approach of spring, could no
longer resist his inclinations, and started off again for his boat-
building on Lake Plestchéief.

On his arrival at Pereyaslávl on April 13 he found two
boats nearly finished, and, as if to welcome him, the ice broke
up, affording soon the opportunity of sailing on the lake.   He
immediately set to work with his carpenters to complete the
boats, and on the very day of his arrival wrote to his mother:

'To my most beloved, and while bodily life endures my
dearest little mother, Lady Tsaritsa and Grand-Duchess Natalia
Kirílovna.   Thy little son, now here at work, Petrúshka,
I ask thy blessing and desire to hear about thy health, and
we, through thy prayers, are all well, and the lake is all
got clear from the ice to-day, and all the boats, except the big
ship, are finished, only we are waiting for ropes, and therefore
I beg your kindness that these ropes, seven hundred fathoms

---

[1] She was born July 30, 1669.

long; be sent from the Artillery Department without delaying, for the work is waiting for them, and our sojourn here is being prolonged. For this I ask your blessing. From Pereyaslávl, April 20 (O. S.), 1689.'

Instead of sending the cables, his mother wrote to him to come back at once, as on May 7 there would be the requiem mass in commemoration of his brother, the Tsar Theodore, and it would be impolitic as well as indecent for him not to be present. Heart-broken at the thought of leaving his boats when they were so nearly ready, he was at first inclined to refuse, and wrote:

'To my most beloved and dearest mother, Lady Tsaritsa Natalia Kirílovna, thy unworthy son, Petrúshka, I desire greatly to know about thy health; and as to what thou hast done in ordering me to go to Moscow, I am ready, only, hey! hey! there is work here, and the man you sent me has seen it himself, and will explain more clearly; and we, through thy prayers, are in perfect health. About my coming I have written more extendedly to Leo Kirílovitch, and he will report to thee, O lady. Therefore, I must humbly surrender myself to your will. Amen.'

The Tsaritsa insisted, as did also his newly-married wife, who writes:

'Joy to my lord, the Tsar Peter Alexéivitch. Mayst thou be well, my light, for many years. We beg thy mercy. Come to us, O Lord, without delay, and I, through the kindness of thy mother, am alive. Thy little wife, Dúnka,[1] petitions this.'

There was no resisting longer; he had to go. His mother and his wife kept him a whole month at Moscow, but again he got away, and went back to Pereyaslávl, where he found that the shipbuilder, Kort, had died the day before. He set to work himself, and at last the boats were finished, and he wrote to his mother:

'To my dearest mother, I, the unworthy Petrúshka, asking thy blessing, petition. For thy message by the Doctor and Gabriel, I rejoice, just as Noah did once over the olive-branch. Through thy prayers we are all in good health, and the boats

---

[1] Dúnia, Duniásha, Dúnka, are diminutives of Avdótia.

have succeeded all mighty well. For this may the Lord grant thee health, both in soul and body, just as I wish.'

Some time after, Peter's mother sent the boyár Tíkhon Stréshnef to see how he was getting on. Peter sent back by him a few words to his mother, written, like all the preceding, on a scrap of dirty paper, with a trembling hand, evidently still tired with the saw and hatchet :—

'Hey! I wish to hear about thy health, and beg thy blessing. We are all well : and about the boats, I say again that they are mighty good, and Tíkhon Nikítitch will tell you about all this himself. Thy unworthy. *Petrus.*'

The Latin signature, although the rest is in Russian, shows strongly Peter's inclination to things foreign. In his stay at the lake and his daily intercourse with the carpenters, he had also made great progress in learning Dutch.

Another requiem was to be said at Moscow. Etiquette required Peter's presence, and political affairs were taking such a turn that the Tsaritsa insisted on his coming back. Again he abandoned his boats, and went hastily to Moscow, though not so quickly but that he was four days too late for the ceremony. The members of the aristocratic party now made such strong representations that he was persuaded to remain in Moscow, at first for a short time, and then longer, until the situation of affairs had become such that an open rupture between the aristocratic party and Sophia was unavoidable. Before describing the manner in which this was brought about, it is necessary to say something about the condition of public affairs in the Empire.[1]

---

[1] Pogódin, 143–149; Ustriálof, II. i. v.; Soloviéf, xiv.; Gordon's *Diary;* Dolgorúky, *Genealogy.*

XIII.

THE administration of internal affairs in Russia by Sophia's
Government need not long detain us. The reforms projected
by Theodore were all abandoned, and the deputies from the
provinces, called to Moscow by him, were immediately sent
home. There was so much to do in order to remove the traces
of the riots and disturbances of 1682 that there was no time
left for reform. The most important laws on the statute book
are those relating to the return to their masters of runaway
peasants, to the disputes connected with the boundaries of estates, and to the punishment of robbery and marauding. Besides this, the Dissenters were everywhere relentlessly persecuted and suppressed. There is a sad old Russian proverb that
'when wolves fight, sheep lose their wool.' So, while the nobles and grandees were quarrelling with each other—all of them
too strong to be put down by the central Government—the
peasantry and poor wretches who had no strong protection were
suffering. They perhaps might have complained to Moscow;
but there is another proverb that 'in Moscow business is not
done for nothing;' and people sometimes suffered for their
complaints. The Government did what it could, and some
malefactors were punished; but a special decree had to be issued that a man could be punished if he sent his children or
his serfs to commit a murder. Later on, as order began to be
restored, punishments were somewhat mitigated, and some care
began to be taken of the suffering common people. Wives
were no longer to be buried alive for the murder of their husbands, but merely to have their heads cut off. The punishment
of death was, in certain cases, commuted to imprisonment for

life, with hard labour, after severe whipping with the knout. While peasants who had run away and joined the Streltsi regiments were to be sent back, serf-women who had married soldiers were allowed to remain free, but were to be heavily fined. Persons who had been temporarily enslaved for debt were to be no longer left entirely at the mercy of their creditors, but were to work out the debt at the rate of five rubles a year for a man, and two and a half for a woman, and the creditors were no longer allowed to kill or maim them. It was also forbidden to exact debts from the wives and children of debtors who had died leaving no property.

Many edicts were issued with regard to the convenience of the inhabitants of Moscow itself, in respect to Sunday trading, to indiscriminate peddling and hawking in the streets, to putting up booths in unauthorised places, for the better prevention of fires, and the like. People were forbidden to stop and talk in the middle of the roadway, and were ordered to keep to the right side. It was forbidden to drive at full speed through the streets in a manner which is still frequently seen both in Moscow and St. Petersburg, and is always adopted by the heads of the police department—that is, with a trotting horse drawing the vehicle and a galloping horse harnessed loosely at the side. It was forbidden to beat the crowd right and left to make one's passage through it. It was forbidden to fire guns or pistols in the houses or out of the windows. It was forbidden to throw filth and manure into the streets. An edict beginning like the following might seem strange, were it not that the strictest regulations had to be made to keep order within the palace itself :—

' Chamberlains, lords in waiting, nobles of Moscow, and gentlemen of the guard ! At present your servants station themselves in the Krémlin with their horses in places not allowed, without any order, cry out, make noise and confusion, and come to fisticuffs, and do not allow passers-by to go on their road, but crowd against them, knock them down, trample them under foot and whistle over them ; and as soon as the captains of the watch and the Streltsi try to send them away from the places where they have no right, and prevent them from crying out and from ill-doing, these servants of yours swear at and abuse the captains and Streltsi, and threaten to beat them.'

The foreign relations of Russia at this period demand a little longer explanation.

In the early times, the dominion of Russia extended to the Gulf of Finland, and the greater part of the territory now included in the province of St. Petersburg was Russian. Extending along the shore of the Gulf, from the mouth of the river Naróva on the southern to that of the Séstra on the northern side, it included most of the territory watered by the 'Vuóksa, the Néva, the Izhóre, the Tósna, and the Lugá, and formed one of the old Fifths of Great Nóvgorod, under the name of the Vódska Fifth of the land of Izhóre. In this district were some of the very earliest Russian settlements, such as Karélia, Ládoga, and the fortress of Ivángorod, constructed opposite Nárva, at the mouth of the Naróva, by Iván III. In early times there were many contests with the Swedes, and one of the most famous victories in early Russian history is that gained, in 1242, by the Grand Duke Alexander Yaroslávitch against the Swedes on the banks of the Néva, which gave him the surname of *Nevsky*, and which led to his being made a saint in the Russian calendar. By the treaty of Oriékhovo, in the beginning of the fourteenth century, the boundaries between Russian and Swedish Finland were the rivers Séstra and Vuóksa. In spite of subsequent wars with Sweden, this boundary remained unchanged until the Troublous Times, in the beginning of the seventeenth century, when, in order to secure his predominance over his rivals, the Tsar Basil Shúïsky called the Swedes to his assistance, and, as a recompense for a corps of five thousand men, ceded the town and territory of Karélia, or Kéxholm, on the western shore of Lake Ládoga. The Swedish troops at first rendered considerable assistance to the Russians against the pretender; but when the Russians had been defeated in a decisive battle with the Poles at Klúshino, they abandoned their allies, went over to the enemy, and seized the town of Nóvgorod. They easily took possession of the Vódska Fifth, and all the efforts of the newly-elected Tsar, Michael Románof, to drive them out were futile. Peace was finally brought about, at Stólbovo, in 1617, through the mediation of Dutch and English ambassadors, one of whom was Sir John Merrick. England and Holland were desirous of retaining Northern Russia for their

trade, and were unwilling to see it pass into Swedish hands.
British interests were at stake here. Michael had to yield to
circumstances. He received back Nóvgorod, Ládoga, and other
districts; but was obliged to give up to the Swedes the fortresses
of Ivángorod and Oréshek—now Schlüsselburg—and the whole
course of the Néva, and pay, in addition, 20,000 rubles, or what
would be at the present time more than $200,000. What was
perhaps still harder, the Tsar had to give up one of his titles,
and allow the Swedish king to style himself ruler of the land of
Izhóre.

In the reign of Alexis, efforts were made to gain access to
the Baltic, from which the Russians had been cut off, by taking
the town of Riga, which belonged to the Swedes. Embarrassed, however, by a war with Poland, Alexis was unable properly
to support this war. His troops were unsuccessful, and he was
compelled, by the treaty of Kárdis, to reaffirm all the conditions
of the hated treaty of Stólbovo. It was the custom at that time
for a Tsar, on ascending the throne, to confirm all the treaties
executed by his predecessors. Theodore refused to confirm the
treaty of Kárdis, without some concessions. He had his griev-
ance against the Swedes—that they had in official documents
refused to speak of the Tsar as Tsar, but had called him simply
Grand Duke of Muscovy, and the subject of title was one about
which all the Russian rulers were very sensitive. Besides that,
the Orthodox Church had been subjected to persecution in the
lands under Swedish rule. The ambassadors of Theodore therefore demanded that, as a recompense for these insults, the land
of Izhóre, which had been unjustly seized by the Swedes during
the reign of his grandfather, should be returned to Russia. To
such a proposition King Charles XI. refused to listen. Negotiations continued at intervals, and Theodore died without the
treaty of Kárdis being reaffirmed.

The policy of Sophia was in direct opposition to that of the
two previous reigns, and was a far more healthy one. Both
Alexis and Theodore had revolted at the idea of acquiescing in
the permanent alienation of any portion of Russian territory.
Their patriotism and their love of national honour made them
feel that every effort should be used to recover to Russia those
provinces which had been torn from it. They, therefore, were

unwilling either to make treaties recognising the Swedish claims or to keep them when they were made. It is not to be supposed that Sophia or her counsellors were less patriotic than their predecessors, but they felt the necessity of reorganising the Empire, of improving its internal condition, and of establishing good government on a firm basis, before attempting to recover the lost provinces. In fact, Sophia acted much as the French Government has acted since the war of 1870. She desired to devote herself to internal administration, and to the formation of an army, before engaging in a struggle with her neighbours. As soon, therefore, as Iván had been proclaimed Tsar, the Government hastened to put an end to any designs of its neighbours, who had already got wind of the rioting of the Streltsi, and the troubles consequent on the death of Theodore. Couriers were sent to Stockholm, Warsaw, Vienna, and even to Copenhagen, the Hague, London, and Constantinople, to announce the death of Theodore, the accession of the new sovereigns Iván and Peter, and the speedy arrival of plenipotentiaries for the purpose of affirming existing treaties. Immediately afterward, in October, 1683, an embassy was sent to Stockholm, consisting of the Okólnitchy and Lord-Lieutenant of Tcheboksáry, Iván Prontchístchef, the Chamberlain and Lord-Lieutenant of Borófsk, Peter Prontchístchef, and the Secretary Basil Bobínin, with a letter from the Tsars completely affirming the Treaty of Kárdis, and practically giving up all claims to the ancient possessions of Russia on the Gulf of Finland. Charles XI., as may easily be believed, received this embassy with great pleasure, and with all due ceremony he took the oath on the Holy Gospel to fulfil the treaty exactly and honourably. He dismissed the ambassadors with the usual presents, and entrusted to them an autograph letter to the Tsars, stating that he would not delay sending his plenipotentaries to Moscow to renew the peace in the usual form by the oaths of their Tsarish Majesties. The Russian ambassadors returned to Moscow, in January, 1684, and three months later the Swedish ambassadors arrived—the President of the Royal Council, Conrad Gildenstjern, the Councillor of the Royal Chancery, Jonas Klingstedt, and the Livonian nobleman, Otto Stackelberg. The nobles living on their country estates for 150 miles about Moscow were ordered to meet the

embassy, and the Regent appointed a commission to discuss
matters, under the presidency of Prince Basil Golítsyn, including among others the Okólnitchy Buturlín, and the Privy-
Councillor Ukraíntsef. Apparently as a matter of form, the
commission thought it necessary to make certain representations
to the Swedes which were entirely unexpected by them. These
consisted chiefly in complaints about matters of etiquette, in
which it was said the Swedish Government had not acted properly; that they had purposely refused to the Tsars the title of
Tsarish Majesty, and had spoken of them in the Treaty of
Westphalia simply as Grand Dukes of Muscovy, and that they
had permitted the publication of various libels and pasquils, as
well as false reports about occurrences in the Russian Empire,
especially with regard to the rebellion of Sténka Rázin. The
Swedes answered these complaints with very little trouble, expressed their perfect willingness to call the Tsars by any name
they pleased; and at a second conference, a week later, managed
to raise on their side some points of disagreement, such as that
the name of the King of Sweden had been written ' Carlus,' and
not 'Carolus,' expressing, at the same time, a desire that the
Russians should enter into an alliance with Poland and the
German Empire against the Turks, that the boundaries between
Sweden and Russia should be exactly defined, and that, in
future, resident ministers should be kept at the Swedish court,
to avoid disputes. At this meeting the Russians said nothing
more about their former complaints, agreed to the Swedish demands, with the exception of that concerning the treaty of alliance with Poland, and finally expressed the readiness of the
Tsars to take the customary oath in confirmation of the Treaty
of Kárdis.

After the protocol had been duly signed, the ambassadors
were invited to the Palace to be witnesses of the solemn confirmation of the treaty by the oaths of the two Tsars. They
were driven in the Imperial carriages to the ambassadorial office,
where, in the Chamber of Responses, they were received by
Prince Golítsyn. Afterward they were conducted by Privy-
Councillor Ukraíntsef, between lines of Streltsi, up the Red
Staircase, and then, passing through files of guards armed with
partisans and halberds, were introduced into the banqueting-

hall, where the boy Tsars, clad in all the paraphernalia of roy-
alty, sat on their double throne, supported on either side by
rhinds or guards of honour, handsome and stately youths of
noble blood, clad in white satin and cloth-of-silver, and carrying
halberds.   The boyárs and state officials sat on benches along
the wall.   The Tsars, through Prince Golítsyn, asked the usual
questions about the healths of the ambassadors, for which they
returned thanks, and then sat down on a bench placed opposite
the throne.   Some moments after, the Tsars personally asked
about the King's health, and, on a sign from Prince Golítsyn,
read a speech, in which they declared their unchangeable intention of carrying out all the articles of the treaty.   After the
speech they ordered the ambassadors to come near to them, and
the priests to bring the Gospels, while Prince Golítsyn placed
on the desk under the Gospel the protocols confirming the treaty.
The Tsars then rose from their places, took off their crowns,
which they gave to great nobles to hold, advanced to the desk
and said that, before the Holy Gospel, they promised sacredly
to keep to the conditions of the treaty according to the protocols.   In conclusion they kissed the Gospels, and Prince Golítsyn
handed the paper to the ambassadors and allowed them to depart.

The same day the ambassadors had a farewell audience of
the Princess Sophia, who received them in the Golden Hall.
On coming out of the banqueting-hall, they advanced down the
private staircase to the Palace Square, then through lines of the
Streménoy regiment, armed with gilded pikes, passed the guards
carrying halberds, to the Golden Entrance, where the suite stopped, while the ambassadors advanced.   At the door they were
met by two chamberlains, who announced to them that the
great lady, the noble Tsarévna, the Grand Duchess Sophia Alexéievna, Imperial Highness of all Great and Little and White Russia, was in readiness to meet them.   The ambassadors bowed, and
entered the room.   The Princess Regent sat on a throne ornamented with diamonds—a present from the Shah of Persia to
her father, Alexis.   She wore a crown of pearls, and a robe of
silver cloth embroidered with gold, edged and lined with sables,
and covered with folds of fine lace.   On each side of her, at a
little distance, stood two widows of boyárs, and further off two

A GROUP OF BOYARS—KREMLIN IN THE BACKGROUND.

female dwarfs. Around the room stood chamberlains and a few boyárs. Prince Basil Golítsyn and Iván Miloslávsky stood near the Princess Regent. The ambassadors were announced by Ukraíntsef, and gave the salutation from the King and Queen, and the Queen Dowager. The Princess, rising, asked about their health in these words : ' The most powerful Lord Carolus, King of Sweden, and her Royal Highness, his mother, the Lady Hedwig Elenora, and his consort, the Lady Ulrica Elenora, are they well ? ' After listening to the usual reply, she beckoned the ambassadors to approach her, and after they had kissed her hand she asked about their health. The ambassadors thanked her, and sat down on a bench. Then the gentlemen of the ambassadorial suite were called up and admitted to hand-kissing. Finally, the Princess requested the ambassadors to congratulate the King and Queen, and dismissed them, sending them subsequently a dinner from her own table.[1]

---

[1] Russian Laws, ii.; Soloviéf, xiv. ; Ustriálof, I. v. ; Aristof.

XIV.

Much more important to settle than the dispute with Sweden was the dispute with Poland, and complicated with this was the question of Little Russia, which brought, in its turn, the question of war with the Turks. The Tsar Alexis, as we remember, in accepting the suzerainty over Little Russia, broke with the Poles; and his first successes made him desirous of restoring to his empire all those parts of Russia which entered into the principality of Lithuania. He conquered them rapidly, one after another, declared their union with Russia, and took the title of Grand Duke of White Russia, of Lithuania, and of Podolia and Volynia. The obstinate struggles between the Poles and Russia lasted twelve years, and, in spite of the domestic difficulties of both nations, would probably have lasted longer, had not the Ottoman Porte interfered, in the hope of gaining possession of Little Russia. Both countries were threatened by this attempt of the Sultan, whose might then terrified all Europe, and they hastened to make peace. But as it was impossible to agree on all points, they made, at Andrússova, in 1667, a truce for twelve years, on condition that at stated intervals envoys should be sent to the frontier to endeavour to negotiate a permanent and substantial peace; and that if these overtures failed, recourse should be had to the mediation of the Christian powers. By this truce the Russian Tsar gave up his claim to Lithuania, White Russia, Volynia, and Podolia, and all the territory on the western side of the Dniéper, with the exception of the ancient town of Kíef, which, in view of the progress of the Turks, he was allowed to retain for two years, in order to save its sacred shrine from Mussulman profanation,

binding himself to return it to Poland at the end of that
period. In return for this concession the rights of the Tsar
were made good to Smolénsk and its surrounding district, the
region of Séversk, and the Ukraine east of the Dniéper. The
country of the Zaporóghi Cossacks, or 'beyond the cataracts' (of
the Dniéper), which served as a mutual barrier against the Turks
and Tartars, was declared common property. Besides this,
Alexis promised to send an army of 25,000 men for the defence
of Poland against the Turks, promised to attempt the subjuga-
tion of the Crimea, and to pay about 200,000 rubles to indem-
nify the Polish nobility for their property in the district ceded
to Russia. It was also agreed that neither side should make a
separate peace with the Turkish Sultan, or with the Crimean
Khan. The first commission which met in consequence of this
treaty, in 1669, was unable to effect a peace, and could only
agree in confirming in every point and particular the Truce of
Andrússova. But the Russians found it difficult to decide to
give up Kíef, as they were obliged to do at this time, and
brought various complaints against Poland, for which they
wished satisfaction and indemnity. Rather, however, than engage in a new war, both sides agreed simply to put off all the
questions until the meeting of the next commission in 1674.
The meeting of 1674 was fruitless, as was also that of the
final commission which sat in Moscow in 1678, in the reign of
the Tsar Theodore. The plenipotentiaries could once more
agree only to leave matters *in statu quo* until the end of the
latest term fixed by the Truce of Andrússova, June, 1693—that
is, for fifteen years longer. Nevertheless, the Tsar, alarmed
by the threat of the Polish ambassadors, and fearing to break
off all relations, returned to the King the districts of Nevl,
Sebézh, and Velízh, which had been granted to Russia by the
Treaty of Andrússova, and paid the indemnity of 200,000
rubles, as agreed upon. All other questions were postponed
until a new commission had been appointed, to meet in two
years from that time with mediators. This commission never
met. Matters got more complicated, partly because, in spite of
the treaties, first Poland, and then Russia, concluded a separate
peace with the Turks.

As soon as Iván and Peter were crowned, their Government

sent an embassy to Warsaw to confirm the treaty of Andrússova and receive the usual oath for its fulfilment. As soon as King Jan Sobieski heard of this embassy, he sent to Warsaw to ask if the ambassadors had full power to treat on the points in dispute, which had been left by the Commission of 1678, especially with regard to the surrender of Kíef and the sending of a corps of twenty-five thousand men for use against the Turks. The ambassadors had come without full powers to this effect, and the King in consequence refused to take the oath to the treaty, and sent a special messenger to Moscow to insist upon some arrangement being made. Mean-while Sobieski persuaded the Polish Diet to agree to the conclusion of a treaty of alliance with the German Empire ; for the rebellion of Emmeric Tekeli had caused an invasion of the Turks, and the overthrow of Austria would be, in Sobieski's opinion, of the utmost danger to Poland. The treaty of alliance

Jan Sobieski, King of Poland.

was concluded in May, 1683, both sovereigns agreeing to the use of their influence to induce other Christian princes to join the alliance, and especially the Tsars of Muscovy. For this purpose Sobieski proposed to Russia to send new plenipotentiaries to the old meeting-place of Andrússova, in order to conclude a lasting alliance. The Russians consented to the commission, and negotiations began in January, 1684, at Andrússova. The Commissioners—thirty-nine in number—met, but could not decide anything. The Poles refused to give up their claim to Kíef, and the Russians could not give their consent to assist them against the Turks. Even the victory of Sobieski over the Turks before

Vienna, in September, 1683, could not persuade the Government of Sophia that war was better than peace, although it made it waver. The importance of this victory, and of the deliverance of Vienna from the Turks, was not under-estimated at Moscow, where it was celebrated by Te Deums in the churches and the ringing of bells. Prince Golítsyn had asked the opinion of General Gordon, who had seen twenty years' service in Russia, most of it against the Poles and the Tartars. Gordon, in a carefully-written paper, considered the advantages and disadvantages, both of peace and war, and finally concluded in favour of war, and an alliance with Poland. Golítsyn, however, was too undecided, or had too little confidence in the good intentions of Poland and Austria for him to resolve on an alliance, and the Commission of Andrússova, as has been already said, had no result.

In the spring of 1684 the Republic of Venice entered, with Austria and Poland, into a Holy Alliance against the Turks, of which Pope Innocent XI. was formally pronounced the patron. All parties agreed to bring their influence to bear on Russia to join them. Although this new crusade against the Turks was the great object of the foreign policy of Innocent XI., and is regarded as one of the great glories of his pontificate, yet this was not the first time that Rome had used all its influence at Moscow for the furtherance of this object. The predecessors of Innocent, Clement IX. and Clement X., had this matter warmly at heart, and did their best to excite the Russians to join their neighbours against Turkey. The despatches to the Vatican of the nuncios at Warsaw and Vienna are full of information as to the negotiations. In 1668, Clement XI. even began a correspondence—which was kept up for years—with the Shah of Persia, in which he warmly and affectionately urged that Mussulman monarch to join the Christian league against Constantinople. Meanwhile, France and Sweden were intriguing at Constantinople against Austria and the Emperor, and stirring up rebellion in Hungary. The dry texts of despatches and documents are, in this case, wonderfully instructive, for they prove that the first wars of Russia against Turkey were caused, not by Muscovite ambition, but by the constant urging of the Pope and the Catholic powers.

In pursuance of the agreement with Poland and Venice, in the spring of 1684, the imperial ambassadors, Baron Blumberg and Baron Scherowski, had brought, besides their formal letters, a personal one from the Emperor to Golítsyn, requesting him to use his influence for the alliance.   Golítsyn thanked the Em-

Pope Innocent XI.

peror for his great condescension and kindness, and promised to use all his powers for the benefit of Christianity, but, at the same time, declared to the ambassadors that Russia would enter into no engagement of the kind desired until permanent peace had been concluded with Poland.[1]

---

[1] A curious and very rare pamphlet, printed in 1684, entitled *Beschreibung des Schau- und lesewürdigen Moscowitischen Einzugs und Tractements, etc.*, gives an account of the embassy of Baron Blumberg, and, in addition, a copy

Meanwhile, although Austria and Venice were successful in their efforts against Turkey, good fortune seemed to abandon Sobieski. In the summer of 1684, he was engaged in an unsuccessful siege of Kamenétz, in Podolia, and afterward, in 1685, not being himself able to accompany the army, on account of illness, he sent the Hetman Jablonowski into Moldavia, hoping, by occupying that province, to cut Podolia off from Turkey and force Kamenétz to surrender. Jablonowski crossed the Dniester and advanced into Moldavia, but was signally defeated by the Turks, and obliged to retreat with great loss. These failures caused the Polish king to renew the negotiations for an alliance with Russia, and in January, 1686, there arrived in Moscow from Poland the most splendid embassy which that city had ever witnessed. There were four ambassadors, at the head of which were the Voievode Grimultowski and Prince Oginski, the Chancellor of Lithuania, with a suite of about a thousand men and fifteen hundred horses. The ambassadors were splendidly received; they were met everywhere by the Russian nobility and their retainers; they were escorted into Moscow and through the crowded streets by the Streltsi, and by the famous 'winged guard,' or *Zhiltsi;* they were feasted and entertained. But the Russian negotiators, under the guidance of Prince Golítsyn, disputed for seven long weeks over the conditions of the peace. The Poles agreed to give up Kíef, but would not consent to the surrender of the adjoining territory, demanded too great a sum as indemnity, and were unable to come to an understanding with regard to the promise of military assistance to be furnished by Russia to Poland. The ambassadors finally declared the negotiations broken off, and took their formal leave of the Tsars and Sophia; yet they did not depart, but requested a renewal of negotiations. By this time, the in-

---

of the speech which he made to the Tsars on his final audience, in which he describes Turkey as the ' sick man '—a term supposed to have been invented by the Russian diplomacy of a quarter of a century ago. ' Now,' he says, ' is the most suitable time for obtaining the desired end. Sweden is in a condition of perfect peace; Poland, in consequence of the truce which has been concluded, is quiet and without danger to you; the diseased and dying Ottoman Empire and its complete powerlessness—for it is only a body condemned to death, which must very speedily turn to a corpse—are the auguries for a complete solution of the question,' &c., &c.

terchange of views was carried on entirely by writing, and finally an arrangement was arrived at by which Poland ceded for ever Kíef to Russia, and the Tsar, agreeing to declare war against the Sultan of Turkey and the Khan of the Crimea, promised immediately to send troops to protect the Polish possessions from Tartar invasion, and in the next year to send an expedition against the Crimea itself. Both powers agreed not to conclude a separate peace with the Sultan. Besides this, it was arranged that Russia, as an indemnity for Kíef, should pay Poland 146,000 rubles ($280,000). A considerable amount of territory was given up on the western bank of the Dniéper, together with Kíef; and Tchigirín and the other ruined towns on the lower course of the Dniéper were not to be rebuilt. Persons of the Orthodox faith in the Polish dominions were to be subjected to no kind of persecution on the part of the Catholics and Uniates, and were to be allowed the free exercise of their religion ; while in Russia Catholics were to be allowed to hold divine service in their houses, although they could build no churches. The boyár Boris Sheremétief, and the Okolnitchy Tchaadáef were sent to Lemberg to obtain the oath and the signature of King Jan Sobieski to the treaty, but were obliged to wait two months for him. That year the King had himself headed an invasion of Moldavia, and had occupied Jassy, but being surrounded by hosts of Tartars, and his troops being stricken with disease and almost famished, he had been obliged to retreat. Saddened by his military disasters, Sobieski was still more grieved over the cession of Kíef ; and although he received the ambassadors with due honours, and gave his solemn oath to the treaty, yet tears ran from his eyes as he pronounced it. He could not even conceal his vexation in a letter which he wrote to the Tsars of Russia, complaining of their inaction.

Sophia and her Government considered this treaty to be the greatest act of their regency. In the proclamation announcing it to the people, she said that Russia had never concluded such an advantageous and splendid peace. In one sense this was true. The acknowledgment by Poland of the right of Russia to Kíef was very satisfactory to the pride of Russia, and fraught with great advantage. It was an advantage, too, to be on terms of solid amity with such an uneasy neighbour as Poland. The

SOBIESKY CONSENTING TO THE CESSION OF KIEF.

disadvantages caused by the ensuing declaration of war against Turkey were not mentioned in the proclamation; and, although they were great, they were, in point of fact, outweighed by the advantages of the treaty.

At the same time that the political union of Kíef to Russia was thus assured, a religious union of the inhabitants of the western provinces and of the Ukraine to the provincial throne of Moscow was also provided for. Originally Kíef had been subjected to the metropolis of Moscow, but, in the fifteenth century, in order more completely to separate the inhabitants of these provinces from their co-religionists in Russia, the Prince of Lithuania succeeded in establishing at Kíef an independent Metropolitan, consecrated by the Patriarch of Constantinople. When the Cossacks of Bogdán Khmelnítzky accepted the Russian suzerainty, it was stated in the treaty that the Metropolitan of Kíef should be under the jurisdiction of the Patriarch of Moscow; but neither the Metropolitan of Kíef at that time nor his successor were willing to accept the diplomas from the Tsars without the permission of the Patriarch of Constantinople, lest they should bring upon themselves the curse of the Eastern Church, and continued to style themselves Exarchs of the Patriarch of Constantinople. Owing to these difficulties, since 1676 there had been no Metropolitan, and the spiritual affairs of the country were under the supervision of Lazarus Baránovitch, the aged Archbishop of Tchernígof, who admitted the supremacy of the Patriarch of Moscow. Negotiations for the election of a new Metropolitan, and his subjection to the Patriarch of Moscow, began in 1683 with Samóilovitch, the Hetman of the Cossacks of the Ukraine, who entered warmly into the project and succeeded in bringing affairs to a conclusion. Much as he opposed the treaty of alliance with Poland, he was strongly in favour of the union with Moscow of the Metropolis of Kíef, for he felt that this union would bind the inhabitants of Little Russia still more closely to Great Russia, sever their connection with Poland, and at the same time give the Russian Government, through the Metropolitan, a certain amount of influence over all the Orthodox Christians residing in the Polish dominions. He made, however, several reservations and conditions, the chief of which were—that all the ancient rights and liberties of the provinces should remain untouched; that the Metropolitan of Kíef should occupy the first rank among the Metropolitans of Russia; that he should still have the title of Exarch of Constantinople; that the Patriarch of Constantinople should properly cede the province to the Patriarch of Moscow, in order that there might be no schism or confusion in the minds of the Little Russians; that the Patriarch should not interfere or meddle in the affairs of the province; that the printing of books should be allowed at the Lavra of Kíef; and that a school for free sciences in the Latin and Greek languages should be allowed in the Brátsky Monastery, as before. These demands were all allowed, with the exception of that asking for the Metropolitan the title of Exarch of the Patriarch of Constantinople, as this was thought to be contradictory and useless. Orders for the election of a Metropolitan of Kíef were then issued, and although at first there was some difficulty in persuading the clergy that they could safely venture on the election without running the risk of the curse of the Patriarch of Constantinople, as his permission had not yet been obtained —and, indeed, had not even been asked—yet, under the skilful guidance of Lazarus Baránovitch, the assemblage elected as Metropolitan Prince Gideon Sviátopolk-Tchetvertínsky, the Archbishop of Lutzk, who had been obliged to leave Poland on account of the oppression which he suffered at the hands of the Catholics and Uniates, and had taken refuge in the Monastery of Batúrin, the capital of Little Russia and the residence of the Hetman. Prince Gideon—for the title of prince, in conformity to the Polish custom, had been left to him—went to Moscow, and was duly consecrated, on November 8, 1685, by Joachim, the Patriarch of Moscow, although no answer had yet been received from Constantinople. The Archbishop of Tchernígof, and Yasínsky, the Archimandrite of the Lavra of Kíef, refused to acknowledge Gideon as their superior, as they had for many years been subject only to the supremacy of the Patriarch of Moscow. A compromise was made, and their claims to be independent of the new Metropolitan were allowed during the lives of the actual incumbents.

At the end of 1684, a Greek, Zachariah of Sophia, had been sent to the Patriarch Jacob of Constantinople, to obtain his consent to a change in the supremacy of the Metropolis, but the Patriarch had replied that the times were so troublous with the Church in Turkey that it was impossible to do anything. The Grand Vizier was on the point of death, and no one knew who would take his place. After the consecration of Gideon, a Government secretary, Nikíta Alexéief, was sent to Adrianople, where the Sultan was then living, partly to complain to the Sultan about his calling the people from the eastern to the western bank of the Dniéper, and partly to arrange with the Patriarch about the Metropolis of Kíef. Alexéief, and Lisítsa, who were sent by the Hetman, received information from the Patriarch that it was impossible for him to do anything until he had the consent of the Grand Vizier, as it would be necessary to call together the Metropolitans, some of whom disliked him and would be sure to report to the Grand Vizier that he was in treaty with the Muscovites, and he would then be at once executed. Alexéief then tried to get an interview with Dositheus, the Patriarch of Jerusalem, who was at that time in Adrianople, making collections of money, but Dositheus refused to see Alexéief until he had had an interview with the Grand Vizier. Alexéief, after seeing the Grand Vizier, was permitted to see the Patriarch of Jerusalem, but could not succeed in making him agree to the Russian proposals. He at first positively refused, basing his objections partly on rules of Church discipline and partly on the want of respect that had been manifested by the election and consecration of the Metropolitan without the consent of the Eastern Church; said that it was a division of the Church; that he would never consent to it, and would oppose it by every means in his power. Alexéief tried to explain that the distance of Little Russia from Constantinople made the relations with that Patriarch a matter of difficulty, and that, as Little Russia was now united with Great Russia, the good of all the Christians there demanded religious union. He was, however, able to effect nothing with Dositheus, who said it was impossible to do anything without the Grand Vizier. Alexéief was not inclined to have the Mussulmans mixed up in the matter. Having learned that the Patriarch of Constantinople had been overthrown by an intrigue, and that Dionysius, the previous Patriarch, had again ascended the throne, and was about going to the Porte to receive his *berat*, he went to the Grand Vizier, and explained to him the desire of the Tsars with regard to the Metropolis of Kíef. The Turks, who were threatened by war on three sides and wished to keep the peace with Moscow, were willing not only to satisfy the Russian complaints with regard to the emigration of the people from the eastern to the western bank of the Dniéper, but to free the Russian prisoners; and the Grand Vizier promised to send for the Patriarch on his arrival, and order him to comply with the wishes of the Tsars. Alexéief then returned to Dositheus, the Patriarch of Jerusalem, and found a total change in his sentiments. Dositheus said he had succeeded in finding a rule—which, it appeared, had escaped his memory—by which an archbishop could pass over a portion of his eparchy to another archbishop, and promised to advise the Patriarch Dionysius to comply with the Russian requests. Furthermore, he himself wrote to the Tsars, and he gave the Patriarch of Moscow his blessing, not together with the Patriarch of Constantinople, but alone. Dionysius, the new Patriarch of Constantinople, made not the slightest objection, and promised that as soon as he returned to Constantinople and had assembled his Metropolitans, he would give all the necessary documents. The Grand Vizier told Alexéief that he had heard of the efforts of the Poles to induce Russia to enter into an alliance with them, begged him to express to the Tsars the hope and wish of the Sultan that this would not be done, and that they would always remain, as before, in the increased love and friendship of the Sultan; and, furthermore, allowed Alexéief to rebuild in Constantinople the church of St. John the Baptist, which had recently been burnt down. This Alexéief had asked as an act of kindness to the Patriarch of Constantinople, for, according to Turkish law, while service could be freely carried on in the existing Christian churches, no new ones were allowed to be built, nor were old ones accidentally destroyed or ruined allowed to be rebuilt; mosques were erected in their place. On arriving at Constantinople, Alexéief received all the necessary documents from the Patriarch, presented the Patriarch of Constantinople with 200 ducats and three 'forties' of sables, and the Patriarch of Jerusalem with 200 ducats, and was requested by them to ask the Tsars for presents for all the archbishops who had signed the document, as similar presents had been given when the Metropolitan of Moscow took the title of Patriarch.[1]

---

[1] This history of the re-union of Kíef reminds one strongly of the recent history of the formation of an independent Bulgarian Church. Soloviéf, xiv. ; Ustriálof, I. vi., vii. ; Theiner, *Monuments Historiques*, Rome, 1859.

XV.

RUSSIA accepted in all seriousness and lost no time in carrying out one part of the treaty of Eternal Peace with Poland, in endeavouring to induce the Christian powers of Europe to join them in a struggle against the Turks. Boris Sheremétief and Iván Tchaadáef, who took the treaty to King John Sobieski for his ratification, headed an embassy to Vienna, to prevail upon the Emperor Leopold to join the Russian-Polish alliance. In the negotiations which took place at Vienna, the Russian ambassadors set forth their treaty with Poland, their ancient friendship with Austria, the campaign which they had made against the Tartars in the previous year, which, without bringing any particular benefit to themselves, had kept the Tartars from Poland, and had left the hands of the Austrians and Venetians free, and which had, in reality, been in part the cause of their successes against the Turks. For this they now asked nothing more than that the Emperor should become a member of their league, that the title of 'Majesty,' and not 'Serenity,' should be given to the Tsars by the Imperial Court, and that the ambassadors should receive their letters of farewell from the hand of His Majesty, and not from the Chancellor. On being ásked what princes they intended to invite to join this league, they replied: 'The greatest among the Christians: the King of France, the King of England, the King of Denmark, the Elector of Brandenburg; and they also intended to send an embassy to the King of France and to the Duke of Baden.' One of the Austrian negotiators replied that the Russians might do this if they thought it best, but that His Imperial Majesty had sufficient allies to ruin the Turk: the Holy Father, the King of Spain, the King of Sweden, the King of Poland, the Republics of Venice and Holland, the Electors of Saxony and Bavaria, and, in a word, all the Empire, which was capable enough of destroying the Ottoman if they went at it in good faith and with vigour. To the application for the title of 'Majesty,' and the threat to sever friendly relations until it should be given, they were told to say nothing more about it, or they would be sent away, but that the Emperor would grant the other points, would receive from their hands the letters from the Tsars, and would give them letters from his own hand, on condition that the Tsars would grant in their domains entire liberty to the Catholic religion. To this the Russian ambassadors replied that they had no instructions on this point; that it was as much as their heads were worth to listen to any propositions which would change the established order of things in Muscovy; that there could be no public exercise of other religions, but that Mass could be said in private houses, and private schools could be established, and that the Tsars would protect the Catholic religion as well as all others as soon as quiet should be re-established. The Austrians said that if this was so, the Emperor would give them a reply by his own hand. At the last conference there was another of the interminable disputes about title, and the Austrian Commissioners blamed the ambassadors for having, in the letter of credence, translated the Russian word for 'autocrat' by the Latin word *imperator*, and not *dominator*, as they claimed it should be. After a full explanation of the three titles of the Russian Tsar, the great, the medium, and the small, the Austrians agreed to what they considered a considerable concession in granting that letters and decrees given by the chanceries and signed by the secretaries should give the Tsars the title of Majesty, but that in letters signed by his own hand the Emperor would not confer this title, as he gave it to no one. So great was the fear of the ambassadors at having overstepped their powers that at this conference they gave back the protocols and note which they had received, signed by the Secretary of the Chancellor, saying that they did not wish them ; whereupon they were told that the substance of the negotiations would be inserted in the letter of re-credence. They begged that no details should be mentioned in this letter, as it was not customary, and especially urged that nothing should be said on the head of religion, as it might do them harm at home. Nevertheless, they were forced to take a protocol signed by the Secretary, under the threat of being sent back without any letter of reply. The tenor of this was that, as the Russians had desired that they should be treated like the other Christian princes, His Imperial Majesty wished the Tsars, in future, when they sent embassies, to pay their expenses, offering to do the same when he despatched embassies to Russia. The Austrians, it seemed, claimed that their last ambassador, Baron Scherowski, did not receive carts for the transportation of the presents to the Tsars, and had been obliged to keep at his own expense those which he had hired in Poland.

This was the first attempt to put Russian embassies on a footing with those of other powers. Up to that time they had been treated in the Oriental manner—that is, the expenses of foreign embassies sent to Russia had been defrayed by the Russian Government, and, in a similar way, the cost of Russian embassies abroad had been paid by the powers to whom they were sent. The total expenses of the Russian embassy to Vienna were about one hundred thousand florins, including the presents ; but the presents to the ambassadors were reduced from thirty thousand florins, as originally proposed, to fourteen thousand florins, with presents amounting to two thousand florins more for the secretaries. The reason of this was, that it was reported to the Imperial Government that the Tsars had sent as presents furs to the amount of thirty thousand florins, while those the ambassadors had actually given were worth only five or six thousand florins. The conduct, too, of the ambassadors and of their numerous suite—many of whom were frequently drunk and made disturbances in the street—and the numerous complaints brought against them, made the Austrian Government anxious to get rid of them as soon as possible. After finishing their negotiations and having an interview with Prince Lubomirsky, the Grand Marshal of Poland, who had just come from Rome, they were invited to the Imperial hunt at Aspern, and received by the Empress, who had just recovered from her confinement, and were then granted a farewell audience by the Emperor. In a letter which the Emperor handed them he said that he had learned with much joy of the resolution of the Tsars to make

THE RUSSIAN AMBASSADORS AND THE FRENCH POLICE OFFICIALS.

war against the common enemy of the Christian name, as well
as of their treaty with Poland; that there was no need to make
any special treaty between Austria and Russia:—'For,' he
added, 'the treaty that your Serenities have just concluded with
Poland is also sufficient to keep us in the same alliance, and
when we shall come to the treaty of peace with the Turks we
will inform you through the King of Poland or by letter. With
regard to the title of "Majesty," the ambassadors to your Serenities will inform you that it is not in the power of our Imperial
Majesty to give it, since there has been no example that we
have given it to any other power. Nevertheless, to show your
Serenities our fraternal friendship and cordiality, we have willed
that our ministers and officers should give you the title of
"Majesty," and we have received at the audience of leave your
ambassadors, and given our letters from our Imperial hand,
which we shall do in future to all the ambassadors and envoys
who shall come from your Serenities. This is on the condition,
however, that your Serenities shall take under your protection
the Catholic and Roman religion which we profess, and, although
we have spoken about it to your ambassadors in several conferences, they have always protested their unwillingness to hear of
it. Nevertheless, we find ourselves obliged to say to your Serenities that what we shall do in this matter according to our Imperial good pleasure shall be of no value in case your Serenities
are unwilling to protect the Catholic and Roman religion—a
case which, we think, will never arise, on account of your great
and fraternal friendship.'

Vólkof, one of the mission, went from Vienna to Venice
with similar instructions. Through the kindness of the Austrian
Government, he was provided with letters of introduction from
the Emperor to the Chevalier Cornaro.

The same year, Prince Jacob Dolgorúky and Prince Jacob
Myshétsky were sent on an embassy to Holland, France and
Spain.

The choice of ambassadors seems to have been unfortunate,
for none of them spoke any other language than Russian, and
they were unacquainted with the ways or even the manners of
diplomacy. In Holland they were well received, and sent from
there a courier to announce their arrival at Paris. Owing to

ignorance of usage, the courier refused to deliver the letter with
which he was charged to anyone but the King in person. As
he could not be persuaded to communicate it to the Minister of
Foreign Affairs, his request for an audience was refused, and
he was sent back without the actual contents of the letter being
known. News, however, of the approaching embassy had been
received by the Court of Versailles from its agents in Holland.
When the Russian ambassadors reached Dunkirk, they were
met by M. de Torff, a gentleman in ordinary of the King's
household, who was sent to compliment them, and to ascertain
the object of their mission. They promised De Torff that they
would fully explain the objects of their mission to Monseigneur
de Croissy, the Secretary for Foreign Affairs, before demanding audience of the King, and promised further that they would
in all respects conform to the royal wishes. Not satisfied with
verbal promises, De Torff insisted that they should put them
in writing, and, at their dictation, he wrote a letter to that effect,
which was signed by them, and which he sent to Versailles.
On the return of the courier the embassy set out for Paris (on
July 22), in carriages sent from the court. All their luggage
was sealed at the Custom House, and was not to be opened
until they reached Paris. It was fully explained to the ambassadors that there it would be examined and passed, and that
in the meantime the royal seals must not be touched. In spite
of this, and of their promise to comply with the royal wishes,
they broke the seals of their luggage at St. Denis, where
they exposed for sale the articles they brought with them.
'Their house was thronged with merchants, and they made a
public commerce of their stuffs and furs, forgetting, so to speak,
their dignity as ambassadors, that they might act as retail merchants, preferring their profit and private interests to the honour of their masters.' De Torff managed to put a stop to this
proceeding, and the ambassadors formally entered Paris in a
great procession, on August 9, and three days afterwards had
their first audience of the King at Versailles. In Paris there
was another difficulty. The ambassadors refused to allow their
luggage to be examined by the customs officers; locksmiths
were brought, and a police official, sent by the provost, undertook to search the luggage. He was reviled and insulted, and

one of the ambassadors actually drew a knife upon him. The affair was at once reported to the King, who sent to the ambassadors the presents he had intended for the Tsars, and ordered them to leave the country at once ; but the ambassadors refused to accept the presents without an audience of the King. Louis XIV., indignant at this, sent back to the ambassadors the presents they had brought him from the Tsars, and again ordered them to leave. They refused to budge, and De Torff was obliged to take all the furniture out of the house in which they were living, and forbid them anything to eat. Next day the ambassadors were brought by hunger and discomfort to a sense of their position, and begged De Torff to intercede for them ; for they feared, they said, that if the King should refuse the presents, or if they should go away without an audience of leave, they would lose their heads on their return to Moscow. They even consented to allow their luggage to be examined, and to conduct negotiations with the Minister of Foreign Affairs and not with the King personally, which they had previously refused to do. Not receiving a favourable answer, they started, and it was not until they had reached St. Denis, where De Torff made a little delay—though he sent on the luggage to show that no long stay must be thought of—that the affair was arranged. The luggage was at last examined, the ambassadors had a political interview with Monseigneur de Croissy, in which they explained the object of their mission, and two days afterwards had a parting audience of King Louis XIV., dined at court, and were shown the gardens and fountains of Versailles. By this time they had become so pleased with France that they did not wish to leave on the day fixed, and used every pretext to prolong their stay. They finally departed from St. Denis on September 10, and reached Havre, with the speed of those times, in four days. Here, after a few days' detention from bad weather, they were put on board a French man-of-war, which was to take them to Spain, for, on account of the difficulties they had caused, permission was refused them to go overland. Before they sailed, De Torff made a request, in the name of the King, that thenceforth the Tsars should pay the expenses of their own embassies. The King promised to do the same. To please the ambassadors, the request was put into writing.

This proposal, like the similar one made at Vienna, aimed at the assimilation of Russian embassies to those of European powers, and at the abolition of the Oriental method of mutual entertainment. No more Russian embassies came to France for a long time, and the matter seems to have been so far forgotten that no specific instructions on this subject were given to the French agents in Moscow. At last M. de Baluze, the French minister at Moscow, writes to the King in August, 1704, complaining that the hundred rubles (about four hundred French livres) which he received weekly from the Tsar's treasury, was not regularly paid, and saying that he thought he had a right to this money, as Russian embassies to France were paid for by the King. In the preliminary examination given to all despatches at the Foreign Office, the Minister of Foreign Affairs has run his pencil though this passage, with the remark 'skip,' addressed to the Secretary whose duty it was to read it aloud to the King.

With regard to the commerce which the embassy appeared to have carried on in St. Denis and Paris, it must be said that, owing to the very bad financial system prevailing in Russia, the salary of ambassadors was chiefly paid in furs, which they were to dispose of as they could, and unless they were allowed to sell them they might be unprovided with current funds. The history of this embassy is as important as it is curious, because the ambassadors, on their return, presented false reports to the Tsars as to the treatment which they had undergone. Those reports produced a strong impression at Moscow, and brought about great coolness, almost hostility, in the relations between the two countries. It was some time before the reason of this was ascertained at Paris. When it became known, a memorandum, giving a true account of what had passed, was sent to the French Residents in Poland and Germany.

The sum and substance of the conference at St. Denis was this : The ambassadors began by saying that Russia had made a league with Poland against the Turks, and they had come on behalf of their masters to His Majesty, as the greatest Prince in the world, to beg him to enter into this league, and to join his arms with theirs for the glory of the Christian name. De Croissy replied that His Majesty had much friendship for the Tsars, and had always approved and still approved of their

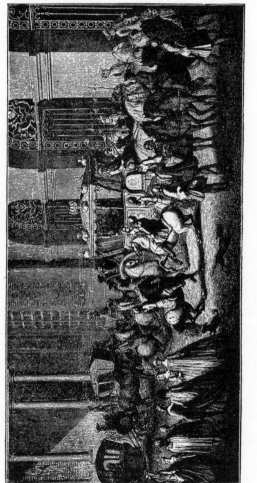

RECEPTION OF A RUSSIAN EMBASSY AT VERSAILLES.

turning their arms against the Turks; that he had also heard with pleasure of the treaty of alliance which they had concluded with Poland ; that he had made known on several occasions the sincerity of his intention for the glory of the Christian name ; that in reality he ought to go to war against the Emperor of Germany on his sister-in-law's account, in view of the oppression she had suffered in the Palatinate, but that he abstained because he did not wish to trouble the prosperity of the Christian arms. He could not declare war against Turkey without reason, for he had recently renewed the capitulations, and, besides, a war would injure the commerce of his subjects in the East, and, on account of the great distance, would be too expensive. The ambassadors replied that the Tsars had also been at peace with the Turks when they declared war against them, and that, in acting for the glory of Jesus Christ, one ought not to have regard for treaties; that they had not hesitated on that score to attack the Turk. As far as commerce was concerned, that could be carried on equally well, and possibly much better, with the successors of the Turks—the Christian nations of the East. But still, if the King would not enter the league, they hoped at least he would not trouble the prosperity of their arms by a declaration of war. De Croissy answered: ' The King has no wish to disturb the Christians in their enterprise. Tell the Tsars that, so long as the allied princes do not give to His Majesty legitimate cause for complaint, he will always be very glad to see them continue to employ their arms in putting down the Infidels.' The ambassadors then set forth to the minister the great advantage which would accrue to France by entering into commerce with the Russians by way of Archangel, and promised French traders all the advantages then enjoyed by the English and the Dutch. This De Croissy said he would take into consideration, and then suggested that, as the King of France sent missionaries to China, and learned that caravans for Pekin left Tobolsk, the capital of Siberia, every six months, he would be glad if the Tsars would permit the passage through Siberia, with these caravans, of Jesuits and other missionaries, as the last-named journey was much easier than that by the sea. The ambassadors said they had no power to consent to this, but thought that no difficulty would be raised.

At that time there was prevalent at Moscow a sort of suspicion of everything French, and sensible as the Dutch Resident was, he was afflicted with this disease, and saw everywhere French intrigues.   It was plain to him that the Danish Resident, Von Horn, was acting in the interests, if not in the pay, of Louis XIV.   He calls him, in one of his despatches, 'a better Turk than Christian'; and in another he says: 'He makes such a show, and spends so much money, that it must necessarily come out of some other purse than his own.'   He even discovered a Frenchman in the Danish suite.   He believed, and apparently succeeded in making the Russians believe, that Von Horn had come to Moscow for the purpose of putting a stop to a good understanding between Sweden and Russia.   It also seemed plain to the Dutch Resident that the French had intrigued at Constantinople to incite the Turks to make war on Austria and invade Hungary, and that they intrigued, both at Warsaw and at Vienna, to prevent the triple alliance.   It was for the interest of France that Austria and the Empire should be humbled, and for that purpose it seemed to him natural that France should not desire Russia to enter into an alliance with Austria, or Sweden to be on friendly terms with its neighbour.

The negotiations, therefore, at Moscow were not always easy matters, and from time to time persons came there who were really nothing but adventurers, but to whom a fictitious importance was given, either from their own braggart airs or from the suspicion that they were French spies.   Among these was a man calling himself sometimes M. de Sanis, sometimes Comte de Sanis, sometimes Sheikh Alibeg, but always a relative of the Shah of Persia, and a brother-in-law of the renowned traveller Tavernier.   He made out that he had been baptised, and therefore could not at once go back to Persia, but at the same time he would set forth his great importance in that country, and wrote, or pretended to write, frequent letters to the Shah—at least some drafts of letters were subsequently found among his effects.   He came with a certain amount of money, he spent more, and borrowed besides.   He gave entertainments at which the grandees and the most notable foreign residents appeared; he was on good terms with the Danish Resident, and it was plain to all right-thinking Dutch and English that he was nothing less than a French spy. In hopes, perhaps, to worm out some secrets, they even lent him money. One night, however, he disappeared, leaving nothing but debts and cast-off clothing; he succeeded somehow in spiriting himself across the frontier, and was never heard of after, except through a small pamphlet published at Geneva in 1685, which purported to give his veracious history.

The prejudice against France lingered on for a long time, even until the visit of Peter to the Court of Versailles in 1716, and it was, perhaps, as much due to this prejudice as to any better reason that the Government of Sophia, on the proposition of the Envoy from Brandenburg, gave full and free permission to all Protestants driven out of France by the revocation of the Edict of Nantes to settle in Russia, to establish themselves there, and to enter the public service.[1]

---

[1] Archives of the Ministry of Foreign Affairs at Paris—Russie; Reports of Dutch Residents at Moscow in the Archives at the Hague.

Peter's Travelling Sledge.

XVI.

EVEN before the conclusion of the permanent peace with Poland, Russia had been brought into hostile relations with Turkey, through the intrigues of Doroshénko, the chief of the Zaporovian Cossacks on the lower Dniéper. Wishing to secure the independence of his band, Doroshénko had played, by turns, into the hands of Russia and Poland, and had even finally given in his submission to the Turks. He had extended his domain to the western side of the Dniéper, and had established his capital at Tchigirín, or Cehryn, a small fortified town on the river Tiasmín, near the Dniéper, and on the very frontiers of Turkey. Although the Turks insisted upon their supremacy, they rendered him no assistance, and Doroshénko, to insure himself against the Turks, swore allegiance to the Russian Tsar —an allegiance that was considered so lax that the Government felt it necessary to occupy Tchigirín with troops and send Doroshénko to private life in Little Russia. Up to this time there never had been any hostilities between the Russians and the Turks, for the capture of the town of Azof, in the reign of the Tsar Michael, had been effected by the Cossacks of the Don, and their proceedings, after careful consideration at a meeting of the States General, were disapproved, and the town was returned to the Turks. The relations between Russia and Turkey had been so friendly that the Russian ambassadors at Constantinople were always treated with greater consideration than those of other powers, and they more generally succeeded in accomplishing their ends. Russia was at that time virtually an Oriental power; its envoys understood the feelings and ways of Orientals, and its relations with the Turks were, therefore, simpler and more easily managed than those of the Western

nations. The occasional incursions of the Crim Tartars into
the Russian border provinces had produced disputes and dis-
agreements, but these were readily settled. The troubles caused
by the Cossacks of the Ukraine, since their separation from
Poland and their first oath of allegiance to Russia, had lasted so
long, and had been the cause of so many forays of the Tartars, that
it was almost in an imperceptible manner that the friendly relations of Russia and Turkey became so far cooled as to produce an open war. On the representation of the Tartar Khan
that Doroshénko had gone over to the Russians, the Sultan
drew forth from the Seven Towers, in which he was imprisoned,
Yúry Khmelnítsky, the son of old Bogdán, a fugitive Cossack
Hetman, and proclaimed him Hetman and Prince of Little
Russia. He declared his claim to the whole of the Ukraine
and Little Russia, and his intention of taking possession of
the country by force of arms. The efforts of the Russians
to ward off the war were futile, as they could not consent
to deliver up the whole of the Ukraine to the Turks. War
with Turkey seemed to the Russians of that day a much more
dangerous and terrible thing than it really proved to be. The
Turks were then at the height of their success; they still
held the greater part of Hungary, and their troops had not
yet been defeated before Vienna. In point of fact, the whole
war was reduced to two campaigns against Tchigirín. In
August, 1677, the Seraskier Ibrahim Pasha, together with
Khmelnítsky, appeared before Tchigirín, where they were to
be met by the Tartar Khan. Prince Ramodanófsky had command of the Russian forces, supported by the Hetman Samóilovitch and his Cossacks. The efforts of the Turks and Tartars to prevent the crossing of the Russians failed. The Pasha
of Bosnia, with sixteen thousand troops, was routed, and on
September 7, only three weeks after his first appearance there,
and on the anniversary of the evacuation of Corfu by the Turks,
and the deliverance of Malta, Ibrahim Pasha was obliged to
raise the siege and hastily retire, pursued by the whole garrison
of Tchigirín. The Turks retreated in such haste that in three
days they arrived at the river Bug, although they had taken
thirteen to advance from there to Tchigirín. They lost all their
artillery and all their baggage, and their loss in men was esti-

mated by themselves at 10,000, and by the Russians at only
4,000—a circumstance almost unique in military annals, where
it is a received rule to undervalue your own losses and exaggerate those of the enemy. When the Turks had got out of
reach, the Russians put Tchigirín into a state of defence and
withdrew the great body of their troops to Little Russia, while
they discussed whether it were better to abandon Tchigirín entirely, or to increase its garrison and hold it against the Turks.
The latter alternative was considered preferable, for Samoílovitch
represented that, if the town were destroyed, the Turks could
easily rebuild it, and would then have an open road into the
heart of the Ukraine. As soon as the news of the Turkish
disaster reached Constantinople, great preparations were made
for a new campaign. Taxes were increased, and all persons in
service were ordered to be ready for departure. The Seraskier
Ibrahim Pasha was disgraced, and the Khan of the Crimea,
Selim Ghirei, who was charged with the blame of the defeat,
was deposed. A Russian ambassador, Porosúkof, was sent to
Constantinople to endeavour to make peace, as, in spite of their
defeat, the Turks still insisted on the surrender of Tchigirín and
the lower Dniéper, and the Russians were obliged to continue
their preparations for a new campaign. About the middle of
July, 1678, the Grand Vizier Kara Mustapha Pasha appeared
before Tchigirín, and, after a solemn sacrifice to God, to implore
his protection, the siege was begun. The investment progressed
slowly, and the Turks were in such straits that they were about
to abandon the siege, when, on the advice of Ahmed Pasha,
they resolved to throw themselves between the Russians and
the fortress on the other side of the river, and risk everything
in a battle. They were signally defeated, and retreated with
great loss. Nine days later they resolved to make one more
attack, and while the Russians and Cossacks were celebrating,
with an unusual amount of drunkenness, the feast of St.
Matthew, which fell on a Sunday, they exploded two mines,
which made a breach in the wall, and took the town by assault.
Subsequently they succeeded in repelling a night attack on their
camp by the Russians ; but news having reached the Grand
Vizier that the Russians contemplated another such attack,
he thought it best to retire, and was subsequently worsted in

LIFE IN THE UKRAINE—"THE RETURN FROM THE MARKET."

an encounter with the troops of Ramodanófsky, who followed him up. Although one aim of the Turkish campaign had been accomplished—the destruction of Tchigirín—no part of the Ukraine had been occupied, and barely a quarter of the Turkish army returned with the Grand Vizier to Adrianople.

The Turks made no further campaign, but the Russians were constantly agitated by the prospect of greater sacrifices and greater losses. Negotiations for peace were carried on, and were at last successful in 1680, when, by the advice of the Grand Vizier, these negotiations were continued with the Khan of the Crimea. By the peace thus concluded, which was ratified at Constantinople in 1681, a truce for twenty years was agreed upon with the Tartars and the Turks, the Turkish dominions were allowed to extend to the Dniéper, and even the Zaporovian Cossacks were for the moment given up to them, while Kíef and all the Ukraine was recognised as belonging to Russia. Although the Russians were at first unwilling to consent to the surrender of the Zaporovians, yet the news of the treaty was received with great joy, not only at Moscow, but also through the whole of Little Russia, for it was thought that the relief from dangers of war with Turkey were cheaply bought at the sacrifice of a bare steppe and a troublesome population. In spite of the treaty concluded in the reign of Theodore, the action of Turkey towards Russia was frequently very unfriendly. Contrary to the provisions of the treaty, the towns on the lower Dniéper were allowed to be again inhabited; more than that, the inhabitants of the eastern bank of the river were invited to cross and settle on the other side, and even Tchigirín was colonised by Wallachs. In addition to this, incendiaries were sent across the river to set fire to towns and farm-houses, in hopes that the population would thus be forced to emigrate to the western side.

The Government of Sophia was bound by the Treaty of Eternal Peace with Poland to make war upon the Turks, and was incited besides by the splendid success of the Austrians in recapturing Buda, and by the progress of the Venetians in the Morea, but it intended to direct the Russian arms not so much against the Turks themselves as against their dependents, the

Tartars. The relations with the Tartars had become almost
unendurable. Although the old lines of defensive walls through
the country still existed, they were badly kept up, and in the
early part of the seventeenth century, and even during the reign
of Alexis, in the midst of peace, towns were surprised and their
inhabitants all carried off to slavery. In 1662, the Tartars
captured the town of Putívl, and carried off twenty thousand
prisoners. There was not a harbour in the East, in Greece,
Turkey, Syria or Egypt, where Russian slaves were not to be
seen rowing in the galleys; the Khan of the Crimea sent at one
time to the Sultan eighty Russian boys as a present. The
Serbian Krýzhanitch says that, so great was the crowd everywhere of Russian slaves, that the Turks asked in mockery
whether any inhabitants still remained in Russia. For a while
the Tartars were kept in some kind of order by the yearly payment of large sums, which the Russians called presents, and the
Tartars called tribute; but even during the regency of Sophia
the Tartar incursions were renewed and the inhabitants of
whole villages were carried away, although these forays were on a
much smaller scale than before. In 1682, the Russian Envoy
Tarakánof was seized by order of the Khan, taken into a stable
and beaten with a cudgel, as well as tortured by fire, in order
to extort his consent to the payment of a larger tribute. As a
result of this, the Russians refused to send any more envoys,
and insisted that all negotiations should be carried on at some
place on the frontier. The Government at Moscow was influenced more and more by a feeling of national honour, but it was
remote from the scene of hostilities. The Cossacks of the
Ukraine, who would have to bear the burden of the campaign,
and who would be exposed to reprisals in case of disaster, were
not so inclined to engage in war, either against the Turks
or the Tartars. If war must be, they preferred it against their
old enemies, the Poles. For that reason the Hetman Samoílovitch constantly opposed the alliance with Poland, and de-
precated any campaign against the Tartars. He thought the
Tartars easy to manage—at the expense, to be sure, of a sum
of money—and preferred the comfort and security of his
subjects to the delicate feelings of honour of the regency at
Moscow. Curiously enough, more advice against the war came

from the Patriarch of Constantinople, who, in the name of the
Eastern Christians, begged the Tsars to remain at peace with
Turkey, as in case of war the Sultan would turn all his rage
against them. 'We beg and pray your Tsarish Majesty,' wrote
Dionysius, in January, 1687, 'do not be guilty of shedding
the blood of so many Christians; do not help the French and
extirpate the orthodox Christians. This will be neither pleasing
to God nor praiseworthy to men.'

War, however, had been resolved upon, and, in the autumn
of 1686, the order was given to prepare for a campaign against
the Crimea. In the decree of the Tsars it was declared:—

'The campaign is undertaken to free the Russian land from
unendurable insults and humiliations. From no place do the
Tartars carry away so many prisoners as from Russia; they
sell Christians like cattle, and insult the orthodox faith. But
this is little. The Russian Empire pays the Infidels a yearly
tribute, for which it suffers shame and reproaches from neighbouring states, and even this tribute does not at all protect its
boundaries. The Khan takes money, dishonours Russian envoys, and destroys Russian towns, and the Turkish Sultan has
no control whatever over him.'

An army of 100,000 men was collected at the river Merlo,
under the chief command of Prince Basil Golítsyn, and in May,
1687, he was joined on the Samára by Hetman Samoílovitch
with 50,000 Cossacks. Golítsyn, though a great statesman,
was not a good general, and accepted the command much against
his will. It was forced upon him by his enemies; he himself
would have preferred to remain at Moscow to counteract their
schemes. This was the time when the aristocratic party was
forming itself around Peter, and was using his name in their
opposition to the regency of Sophia. Golítsyn was especially
hated by that party. He had only one faithful adherent in
Moscow on whom he could thoroughly depend, and their
interests were closely bound together. That was Shaklovíty.
Golítsyn had no sooner started on his campaign than he began
to perceive the machinations of his enemies, not only in Moscow, but in the camp. From Moscow he heard that his old
enemy Prince Michael Tcherkásky was rising in power, and
was about to succeed to the place of the boyár Stréshnéf.

Golítsyn wrote to Shaklovíty, as he did constantly during the campaign, telling his griefs, and begging his assistance:—

'We always have sorrow and little joy, not like those who are always joyful and have their own way. In all my affairs my only hope is in thee. Write me, pray, whether there are not any devilish obstacles coming from these people. For God's sake, keep a sleepless eye on Tcherkásky, and don't let him have that place, even if you have to use the influence of the Patriarch or of the Princess against him.'

The reason why Golítsyn talked about using the influence of the Patriarch was because he found that the Patriarch was not entirely well disposed to him, and had taken various vestments from a church which he had built and decorated, and prohibited their use. In the camp, the boyárs were disobedient and quarrelled over their places, and did much to annoy him. At the outset of the campaign, Prince Boris Dolgorúky and Yúry Stcherbátof appeared, dressed in deep black, with all their retainers in mourning, and long black housings spread over their horses. This was not only a personal insult to Golítsyn, but also, owing to the superstition of the time, from which Golítsyn was not entirely free, exercised a powerful influence on the minds of the soldiery, as a presage of ill-luck. This presage was, to a great extent, justified by the results of the campaign. The united army of the Russians and Cossacks advanced southward through the steppe till they reached a place called the Great Meadow, near the little stream of Karat-chakrák, about one hundred and fifty miles from the Isthmus of Perekóp. Not a sign of any kind could be seen of the Tartars, but the Russians were met by a worse enemy—a fire on the steppe which destroyed all the grass and forage for miles around, threatened the loss of the baggage and provision trains, and at the most oppressive period of a southern summer caused the army great suffering from flame and smoke. A timely rain filled the streams, but still there was no forage, and the army was obliged to retreat without even having seen the enemy. Golítsyn encamped at the first suitable locality, proposed to send a force of 30,000 men to the lower Dniéper, and reported to Moscow for further orders. Meanwhile a rumour got into circulation in the camp that the steppe had been set on fire, not by

the Tartars, but by the Cossacks, with the intention of relieving themselves from the burden of the further campaign. This story, in the highest degree improbable, found some credence, when connected with what was called the obstinacy of the Hetman Samoílovitch in originally opposing the war against the Tartars, and with the numerous complaints of oppression against him from his own subjects. The Government, after sending Shaklovíty to investigate the case, decided to remove Samoílovitch. Preparations were secretly made, and, on August 2, he was arrested in the night, relieved of the post of hetman, and sent to Moscow. The ukase dismissing him said nothing about the accusation of setting fire to the steppes, but stated merely that, in order to prevent an outbreak, the interest of Little Russia required the removal of a hetman who had no longer the confidence of the population. This able, energetic, and remarkable man was succeeded as hetman by the famous Mazeppa, then the Secretary General of the Cossack Government. Mazeppa's election, as well as the fall of Samoílovitch, was due in a very great measure to the personal influence of Golítsyn, who disliked Samoílovitch. Mazeppa showed his gratitude, not by words alone, but by a present of 10,000 rubles. This change was detrimental to Russian interests. Samoílovitch had been thoroughly devoted to his people and to the Russian Government, while Mazeppa began a policy of deceit which culminated in his rebellion against Russia during the Swedish invasion. Samoílovitch died in banishment in Siberia, and one of his sons was executed. His whole property was confiscated, and half of it given to Mazeppa.

Golítsyn returned to Moscow late in the evening of September 14, and the next morning was admitted to kiss the hands of the Regent and the two Tsars. Although, according to the Swedish Envoy Kochen, forty or fifty thousand men had been lost in the campaign, yet Golítsyn was hailed as a victorious general, and speedily regained all his former power and prestige. He received a gold chain and three hundred ducats, and gold medals were struck and given to the officers and nobility, while smaller medals, all of them bearing the effigies of Sophia, Iván and Peter, as well as the initial letters of their names, were given to the soldiery. Money and land was bestowed lavishly, as never before after a Russian campaign, and even the troops which came too late were not left without reward. The proclamation of the Regent to the Russian people spoke of the campaign as a splendid victory, recounted the speedy and difficult march, the panic of the Tartar Khan, the horrors of the burning steppes, and the safe retreat. In order to keep up the credit of the Russian arms, equally glowing accounts of the expedition were sent abroad, and printed in Dutch and German, and Baron Van Keller himself saw that an apology for Golítsyn was properly printed in the Dutch newspapers.[1]

------

[1] Ustriálof, vol. i. ch. x. ; Soloviéf, vol. xiv. ; Possel, *Lefort*, vol. i. ; Gordon's Diary ; Brückner, *Fürst W. W. Golizyn* in *Russische Revue*, 1878 ; von Hammer, *Histoire de l'Empire Ottoman.*

Medal Given to Prince Golítsyn for the Crimean Campaign.

XVII.

The Poles were no more lucky than the Russians in the campaign of 1687. They vainly besieged the fortress of Kamenétz, in Podolia, and were obliged to retire in disgust. Their allies, the Austrians and Venetians, were more fortunate. They beat the Turks in Hungary, Dalmatia and the Morea, and took possession of the chief frontier fortresses. It was in this campaign that Morosini took Athens, a conquest glorious to the Venetians, but regretted by posterity. An unfortunate bomb struck the Parthenon, and exploded the Turkish powder stored in it, and reduced this wonderful building to its present state. From the Piræus Morosini took the four marble lions which now decorate the front of the arsenal at Venice. The Turkish defeat and disasters resulted in a military rebellion, which cost the Grand Vizier his life, and the Sultan Mohammed IV. his throne. He was replaced by his elder brother, Suleiman II. Turkey had never been in such straits, and there seemed to the Christian inhabitants every chance of freeing themselves from the Turkish yoke. Dionysius, the former Patriarch of Constantinople, who had been deposed for the fourth time through the intrigues of rival bishops who paid higher bribes to the Divan, but according to his own account for having yielded in the matter of the metropolis of Kíef, wrote to the Tsars from his refuge at Mount Athos, and in the name of the orthodox Christians besought the Russians to turn their arms once more against the Turks.

'All states and powers,' he wrote, ' all pious, orthodox kings and princes have together risen up against Anti-Christ, and are warring with him by land and sea, while your empire sleeps. All pious people—Serbs, Bulgarians, Moldavians, and Walla-

chians—are waiting for your holy rule. Rise; do not sleep;
come to save us.'

The same messenger, Isaiah, Archimandrite of the Monastery
of St. Paul at Mount Athos, brought a letter from Sherban
Cantacuzene, the Hospodar of Wallachia, who also wrote that
all orthodox people begged the Tsars to deliver them from the
hands of the 'Pharaoh in the flesh.' A similar letter came
from Arsenius, the Patriarch of Serbia. The Christians, however, prayed the Russians not so much against the Turks as
against the Latins and Catholics. They feared that if Turkey
were subjugated by the Austrians and Venetians, without the
intervention of Russia, the religious tyranny of the Roman
Church would be worse than the oppression of the Sultan.
The Regent replied to these demonstrations by urging the
Wallachians to send the large Slavonic forces, of which they
had boasted, to assist them in another campaign against the
Tartars, saying that after the Crimea was conquered they would
see to the freedom of the countries of the Danube and the Bal-
kans. Panslavism had already been preached in Moscow, and
especially by the Serb Yúry Krýzhanitch, the first great Slavophile, and it is interesting to see how, even in the earliest time
of difficulty between Turkey and Russia, the Slavonic popula-
tions subject to the Sultan looked to Russia as their natural
friend and protector.

There were many difficulties, however, in the way of a
second campaign. The financial condition of Russia was very
bad, the Russian envoy Póstnik had been unsuccessful in concluding a loan in England—if other reasons were wanting, the
troubles of the last year of James II. were sufficient—and taxes
were already most burdensome. Fears lest Poland and Austria
might conclude a separate peace with the Turks which would be
disadvantageous to Russia; the urgent demands of the Poles for
assistance, and the fact that the Tartar Khan, in spite of strict
orders from the Sultan, had himself taken the offensive and
had ravaged the provinces of Russia and Poland, advancing, in
March, 1688, through Volynia and Podolia nearly to Lemberg,
and carrying off 60,000 of the inhabitants into slavery,—these
were sufficient reasons for a new campaign.

In the autumn of 1688 the new campaign against the

KAMENETZ IN PODOLIA.

Crimea was proclaimed. All preparations were made for starting at an early period in the spring, and for guarding against
the calamities which had frustrated the previous expedition, and
the troops were ordered to be at their rendezvous no later than
February, 1689. This time it was absolutely necessary for
Golítsyn to defeat the Tartars, in order to frustrate the machinations of his political and personal enemies. Hatred to him
went so far that it is said an assassin even attacked him in his
sledge, and was arrested by one of his servants. The assassin
was tortured, but no publicity was given to the affair. Just as
Golítsyn was starting out on the campaign, a coffin was found
in front of the door of his palace, with a warning that if this
campaign were as unfortunate as the preceding one, a coffin
would be made ready for him. An example not only of the
suspicions which Golítsyn entertained of those about him, but
of the superstition in which he, as well as many other eminent
and educated men of that time, believed, was that one of his
servants, Iván Bunakóf, was subjected to torture for having
'taken his trace'—that is, for having taken up the earth where
Golítsyn's foot had left an imprint. Bunakóf explained it by
saying that he took the earth in his handkerchief and tied it
round him to cure the cramp, as this remedy had been recommended to him, and always, when any cramp seized him, he
immediately took up some of the surrounding earth. The explanation was considered insufficient, and the man was punished.

By the end of February, Golítsyn had collected 112,000
men, and set out on his march. A month later he reported
that the expedition was greatly retarded by the snow and the
extreme cold. He was soon joined by Mazeppa, with his Cossacks. About the middle of April, news reached Moscow that,
although there had yet been no fires in the steppe, the Khan
had announced his intention to set fire to it as soon as the Russians approached Perekóp, and orders were sent to Golítsyn to
have the steppe burnt in advance of the Russian troops in order
that they might find fresh grass springing up for them as they
went on. No misadventure of any kind took place; there was
plenty of water, and by the middle of May Golítsyn drew near
to Perekóp and first met the Tartar troops. The nomads, in
great multitudes, attacked the Russians on all sides, and were

beaten off with some difficulty, although they still continued to
harass the Russian advance. We learn from the diary of General Gordon that the troops were engaged in several slight contests of this kind, but that there was no decisive battle. Golítsyn, however, reported to the Government that he had gained
a great victory over the Tartars, and inflicted enormous losses
upon them. On May 30, the Russians reached the famous
Perekóp, a fort protected by a high wall and a deep ditch, running entirely across the isthmus. It had seemed that Perekóp
was to be the end of the campaign, and Golítsyn had apparently
thought that once they arrived there the Tartars would be
frightened, and would immediately surrender. He found, however, that the fort of Perekóp was not to be easily taken, especially by troops that had already been two days without water;
and that, even should Perekóp be taken, the steppes of the
Crimea, being arid plains, destitute of water, and possessing
only a little saltish vegetation, would be even worse than the
places he had already passed through. He therefore sent a
message to the Khan, hoping to get from him a peace advantageous to Russia. The negotiations lingered, and it was impossible for Golítsyn to wait longer. He therefore began his
retreat without having captured Perekóp, and without having
secured peace. That Golítsyn should have returned at all, that
he should have extricated his army from this uncomfortable
position without losing the greater part of it, was interpreted
by the Government at Moscow as a great success, and glowing
bulletins were issued, and great rewards were promised to those
who had taken part in the campaign. For reasons of state it
was necessary to uphold Golítsyn, who was the ablest and
strongest member of the Government. But Sophia had other
excuses—her passionate affection for Golítsyn blinded her to
his defects. She implicitly believed the exaggerated despatches
which he had sent home, in which defeat was skilfully converted into victory, and replied in letters which plainly indicate the
relations which existed between them:

'My Light, Brother Vássenka:—Mayst thou be in good
health, little father, for many years! Through the mercy of
God and the Holy Virgin, and by thy own good sense and good
fortune, thou hast been victorious over the children of Hagar,

and may the Lord give thee in future to overcome our enemies!
And yet, my love, I can scarcely believe that thou art returning
to us; I shall only believe it when I see thee in my embrace.
Thou hast asked me, my love, to pray for you. In truth I am
a sinner before God and unworthy, yet, even though a sinner, I
dare to hope in his mercy. I always petition him to let me see
my love again in joy.'

When Golítsyn had written that he had begun to retire
from Perekóp, Sophia answered:

'This day is mighty joyful to me because the Lord God has
glorified his holy name, as also that of his mother, the Holy
Virgin, for thee, my love. Such a thing was never heard of,
nor did our fathers see such mercy of God. Like the children
of Israel has God led you from the land of Egypt—then by
Moses, his disciple, now by thee, my soul. Praise to our God,
who has thus been merciful to us through thee. Oh! my little
father, how shall I ever pay thee for these, thy countless
labours? Oh! my joy, light of my eyes, how can I believe my
heart that I am going to see thee again, my love! That day
will be great to me when thou, my soul, shalt come to me. If
it were only possible for me, I would place thee before me in a
single day. Thy letters confided to God's care, have all reached
me in safety. Thy letters from Perekóp came on Friday, the
11th. I was going on foot from Vozdvízhenskoe, and had just
arrived at the monastery of the Miracle-Working Sergius, at
the holy gates themselves, when thy letter came about the battles. I do not know how I went in. I read as I walked. What
thou hast written, little father, about sending to the monasteries, that I have fulfilled. I have myself made pilgrimages to
all the monasteries on foot. Thou writest that I should pray
for thee. God, my love, knows how I wish to see thee, my
soul, and I hope, in the mercy of God, that He will allow me
to see thee, my hope. With regard to the troops, do just as
thou hast written. I, my father, am well, through thy prayers,
and we are all well. When God gives me to see thee, my love,
I will tell thee about all I have done and passed through.'

The official thanks sent to Golítsyn were in strong terms,
though in somewhat different form. He himself was most anxious to magnify his victories, and sent messengers direct from

the camp to the King of Poland, informing him of the defeat of 150,000 Tartars, of the flight of the Khan, and of the general panic. Employing a trick which is now so common as not to cause surprise, Golítsyn instructed the Resident at Warsaw to send extracts from his letter to Vienna, Venice, and Rome, and to take measures that accounts of his victory, printed in all parts of Europe, should come back to Moscow.

Not all, however, took such a rosy view of the campaign as did Golítsyn. General Gordon, in a letter to his relative the Earl of Errol, says: 'The 20th wee came befor the Perecop, et lodged as wee marched, where wee were to enter into a treaty with the Tartars, which tooke no effect, our demands being too high, and they not condiscending to any other thing as to establish a peace of the former conditions, so that not being able to exist here for want of water, grass et wood for such numbers as wee had, and finding no advantage by taking the Perekop, the next day wee returned, and from midday till night we were hotly pursued by the Tartars, the danger being great et fear greater, if the Chan with all his forces should persue us, so that I was commanded from the left wing with 7 Regiments of Foot, et some of horse (yet all on Foot), to guard the Rear. They persued us very eagerly 8 dayes together, yet gained but litle, haveing no such great numbers as wee suspected. Nothing troubled us et our horses et draught beasts so much in this march as the want of water, for albeit wee had so many great caskes with water along with yet was farr short of giveing relieffe to all, and had not God Almighty sent us rains more as ordinary in these places, wee had suffered great losses. On the 12th of June, we came to the River Samara, where wee were past danger, yet hold on our march circumspectly untill we came to the R. Merlo.' And Lefort, who took part in the campaign, wrote to his family at Geneva: 'The Muscovites lost 35,000 men—20,000 killed and 15,000 taken prisoners. Besides that, seventy cannon were abandoned, and all the war material.' The remembrance of the loss of these cannon remained for a long time, and Manstein tells us that Münnich, in his campaign in the Crimea in the reign of the Empress Anne, recovered some of the cannon lost by Golítsyn.

Accusations were subsequently brought that Golítsyn had

been bribed by the Tartar Khan to retreat from Perekóp, and there was a story that before Perekóp, the Tartar emissaries brought secretly to Golítsyn's tent two barrels of gold pieces, which turned out afterwards to be nothing but copper money slightly gilded. This story rests on the testimony of deserters and renegades, and scarcely deserves notice, except that it formed part of the charges of high treason subsequently preferred against Golítsyn. It was not, however, so much his imaginary treason as it was his carelessness, his military incapacity, and his self-will in carrying on negotiations without consulting the other superior officers, which caused this disaster to the Russian arms.

Not by any means the best satisfied with the Crimean campaign was Peter. Apart from the severity with which the party of boyárs who surrounded him judged all the acts of the government of Sophia, he himself had been pursuing so vigorously his military studies, and was so deeply impressed with the importance of putting an end to the Tartar domination, that he was a severe critic of Golítsyn's military operations. Golítsyn arrived at Moscow on July 8, was received in great state at the banqueting-hall by Sophia and her brother Iván, and was publicly thanked; but the rewards promised to those who had taken part in the campaign could not then be published, because Peter refused his consent, as he was unwilling that they should receive so much as had been promised without consulting him. It was not until August 5, after much intreaty, and with great difficulty, Peter was induced to allow the rewards of the campaign to be announced. On the next day they were read out to the boyárs and their comrades in the inner rooms of the Palace, and afterwards to the general public on the Broad Staircase. Golítsyn received a large gold cup, a caftan of cloth of gold lined with sables, a large sum of money, and an estate in the district of Suzdál; while the other Russian officers received money, silver cups, stuff for caftans, and part of the estates which they already enjoyed as crown tenants were made hereditary with them. The foreign officers received each a month's wages, sables, cups, and rich stuffs. Commemorative gold medals were given to everyone, and it was ordered that the names of all who died in the campaign should be mentioned in the public prayers in the Cathedral. Etiquette then required that the officers who had been thus distinguished should go to Preobrazhéhsky, to pay their respects to the Tsar Peter, and thank him for his grace. They went, but they were not received; 'at which some were much troubled,' says Gordon, 'but others were not, because they thought it was better to take the bitt and the buffet with it, for everyone saw plainly and knew that the consent of the younger Tsar had not been extorted without the greatest difficulty, and that this merely made him more excited against the generalissimo and the most prominent counsellors of the other party at court; for it was now seen that an open breach was imminent, which would probably result in the greatest bitterness. Meanwhile everything was, as far as possible, held secret in the great houses, but yet not with such silence and skill but that everyone knew what was going on.' [1]

---

[1] Ustriálof, vol. i. ch. x. ; Soloviéf, vol. xiv. ; Posset, *Lefort*, vol. i. ; Gordon's *Diary ;* Brückner, *Golizyn ;* Σ. Δ. Βυζαντίου, Ἡ Κωνσταντινοόπολις, Athens, 1851-69.

XVIII.

THIS unfortunate campaign of Golítsyn was the turning point in the struggle between the aristocratic party and the Government of Sophia. The boyárs had gradually been getting stronger, and had even succeeded in forcing their way into power and preferment. One of the Naryshkins had been made a boyár shortly before. The gravamen of any charge against Sophia was that she had made herself the equal of her brothers, the Tsars, by assuming the title of Autocrat, in commemoration of the peace with Poland. So long as her government had been successful, this assumption might have been permitted, but now that two campaigns had shown the weakness and inefficiency of the regency, now that the aristocratic party was strong enough to take matters into its own hands, this could be used as an accusation against her. This was foreseen by others, if not by Golítsyn himself, and even as early as April Van Keller had written to Holland: 'If the campaign against the Tartars shall be no more successful than the last, there will probably be a general rebellion,' saying, at the same time, that he dared not write much lest his letters should be opened.

Another point of accusation against Sophia, although at this time it was not proved that there was anything criminal in her design, was her desire to have herself crowned as Empress and Autocrat. In point of fact, in August, 1687, Shaklovíty had endeavoured to persuade the Streltsi to petition the Tsars for the coronation of the Regent. This, however, was such an unheard-of thing that the Streltsi received the proposition coldly, and no more was done at that time, but the next year the idea was revived. After the end of the first Crimean campaign, a Russian, or rather, a Polish artist from Tchernígof, named Tarasévitch, engraved a portrait of Sophia, together with her

brothers, and also a portrait of Sophia alone, with crown, sceptre and globe; her full title as Grand Duchess and Autocrat en-
circled the portrait, and about this, in the style of the portraits
of the German Emperors, were placed, instead of the portraits of
the Electors, the symbolic figures of the seven cardinal virtues
of Sophia. The Monk Sylvester Medvédief composed an inscription in verse of twenty-four lines, in which the Princess was
declared to be the equal and superior of the Babylonian Semi-
ramis, of Elizabeth of England, and of the Greek Pulcheria.
Copies of these portraits were printed on satin, silk, and paper,
and were distributed in Moscow. None now exist. One impression was sent to Amsterdam, to the Burgomaster Nicholas Witsen,
with the request that he would have the inscription and titles
translated into Latin and German, and a new portrait engraved
in Holland, for distribution in Europe. Copies of this engrav-
ing reached Russia just before the fall of Sophia, and were
nearly all destroyed by order of Peter, so that now it is the
greatest rarity among Russian historical portraits. Two copies
only are known to exist.

A sketch of Sophia, written by De Neuville in this very
year, 1689, will perhaps assist us in forming a more accurate
idea of her:—

'Her mind and her great ability bear no relation to the de-
formity of her person, as she is immensely fat, with a head as
large as a bushel, hairs on her face and tumours on her legs,
and at least forty years old. But in the same degree that her
stature is broad, short and coarse, her mind is shrewd, unpre-
judiced and full of policy.'

An incident which occurred about the time of the return of
Golítsyn shows, in a measure, the position of affairs at Moscow
about this time. On July 18—the festival of the miraculous appearance of the Picture of the Virgin of Kazán—there was a
procession in which the Tsars usually took part, from the Krémlin
to the Kazán Cathedral, founded by Prince Pozhársky, in commemoration of the delivery of Moscow from the Poles. The Regent Sophia appeared in the Cathedral of the Assumption with
her two brothers, just as she had done in preceding years. On
the conclusion of the liturgy, Peter, in consequence of a remark
of one of his counsellors, approached his sister and ordered her
not to walk in the procession. This was an open declaration of

THE OFFENDING PICTURE OF SOPHIA, WITH THE INSCRIPTION BY
SYLVESTER MEDVEDIEF.

war. To prevent Sophia from appearing in public at a state
ceremony, as she had done during her whole regency, meant to
remove her from the conduct of public business. She accepted
the declaration of hostility, but refused to obey the command.
She took from the Metropolitan the picture of the Virgin, and
walked after the crosses and banners. Peter angrily left the
procession, went for a moment into the Cathedral of St. Michael

Our Lady of Kazán.

the Archangel, and immediately afterwards left Moscow and
went to his villa at Kolómenskoe.

The tension of the two parties was now very great, and, as
always in such cases, private individuals loudly expressed their
grievances, their hopes and their fears. Such irresponsible ut-
terances were naturally exaggerated by rumour, and each party
was convinced that the other was threatening and had an intention of attacking it. Extracts from Gordon's diary give us

some slight idea of the feeling then prevalent. On August 7, he writes: 'Things continue to have a bad look, as they promised to do on Saturday.' On the 9th: 'The heat and bitterness are even greater, and it appears that they will soon break out.' On the 16th he mentions 'rumours unsafe to be uttered.' Both parties naturally took up a defensive position. Whatever might be their suspicions of the motives and intentions of their opponents, it was safer, with the forces at their disposal, to meet an attack than to make one, and at the same time the moral effect was stronger. What excuse could Peter have to attack his elder brother and his sister in the Krémlin, while it would be very difficult to get even the Streltsi to assist in an attack on Preobrazhénsky? They still had too much respect for the person of the Lord's anointed, and remembered too well the consequences of the riots of 1682. In such a situation, as everywhere, both parties were on their guard, and both parties were suspicious. As when Sophia, in August, 1688, went to visit Peter at Preobrazhénsky, on the occasion of the benediction of the river Yaúza, she took with her three hundred Streltsi to guard against any sudden attack of his guards, so now on St. Anne's day, when Peter was expected at the Krémlin to visit his aunt the Princess Anne, at the Ascension Convent, Shaklovíty posted fifty men in a concealed place near the Red Staircase, to be ready for an emergency. The Princess Anne had long been an invalid and was greatly loved and respected by the whole Imperial family, especially by Peter. Peter came from Kolómenskoe, remained several hours with his aunt and went away to Preobrazhénsky, and there was no need of alarm. Nevertheless, it needed but a spark to cause a general explosion, and it was not long before it came.

In order to strengthen her position, Sophia took whatever occasion offered to sound the Streltsi, and to urge them to be faithful to her in case of a conflict. Meeting some Streltsi in the church of the Mantle of the Virgin, she said: 'Can we endure it any longer? Our life is already burdensome through Boris Golítsyn and Leo Naryshkin. They have had the room of our brother, the Lord Ivan Alexéievitch, filled up with firewood and shavings, and they have desired to cut off the head of Prince Basil Golítsyn who has done so much good. He made peace with Poland and had successes on the Don; and it

is for his very successes that they hate him. Do not abandon
us. May we depend upon you? If we are unnecessary, my
brother and I will take refuge in a monastery.'

'Your will be done, O lady,' they replied; and for their
acclamation they received a present of money. It was by
speeches of this kind and frequent gifts, that Sophia attempted
to maintain an authority and influence which she felt to be gradually declining. Prince Basil Golítsyn, who was always averse
to taking decided measures, remained quiet, assisted Sophia
with his advice, but opposed any plans of open attack on the
party of boyárs who surrounded Peter, and thought it best to
await events. Shaklovíty was much more decided. He held
frequent meetings with those Streltsi in whom he had the
greatest confidence, and was unsparing in his denunciations of
the party of Peter. While not absolutely inciting any attempt
against Peter himself, he constantly suggested the possibility
of doing away with Prince Boris Golítsyn and Leo Naryśhkin,
and sending the Tsaritsa Natalia into a convent or otherwise
getting rid of her. In order to encourage his supporters, he
professed the greatest contempt for the boyárs of the opposite
party, calling them all 'withered apples.'

On August 17th, Sophia ordered a small body of Streltsi to
come armed to the Krémlin, in order to accompany her on a
pilgrimage she intended making to the Donskóy Monastery.
They were to be armed because, in a similar pilgrimage which
she had made a few days before to another convent a man had
been killed in the neighborhood shortly before her arrival.
After these arrangements were made, a placard or anonymous
letter was brought to the palace, stating on that very night, the
guards from Preobrazhénsky would make an attack on the
Krémlin. Apparently, no inquiry was made into the origin of
this letter, and it may possibly have been invented by Shaklovíty, or one of his men, for the purpose of giving an excuse for
a larger collection of Streltsi. Still, in the position of affairs,
it is very natural that Sophia was rendered uneasy, even by anonymous letters, and that she took what, under the circumstances,
were very necessary precautions. Shaklovíty thereupon collected many more Streltsi, part of them inside the Krémlin,
others in the old town, and others still in the Lubiánka Place,
outside the wall, in the direction of Preobrazhénsky. Orders

were also given that the gates of the Krémlin should be closed all night, and that in future a rope should be tied to the alarm bell of the Cathedral, so that it could be pulled from the palace, and Shaklovíty, with several officers, came to the Krémlin and slept all night in the banqueting hall. The orders for the assemblage of the Streltsi in the old town, and on the Lubiánka, were not accurately carried out. There was much riding to and fro, and consequently great confusion, as no one knew the exact reasons for their assembling, and Shaklovíty did not consider it necessary to inform them. They were there to wait for orders —that was enough. Some explained that they were there to protect the Krémlin against an attack from Preobrazhénsky, while others thought they were to march that night against the Naryshkin party.

In Preobrazhénsky there was also much excitement in consequence of the rumours brought from Moscow. Many of Peter's adherents had gone thither during the day and many of them had remained there during the night, but no measures of precaution seem to have been taken, and there was no apprehension of an immediate attack. During the night Plestchéief, one of Peter's chamberlains, brought a despatch to the Krémlin. It was on current routine business and had nothing to do with the present circumstances. In the disorder and excitement which prevailed there, especially with numbers of soldiers tired of waiting and eager for the fray to begin, this arrival was wrongly interpreted, and one of the Streltsi named Gládky, seized on Plestchéief, dragged him from his horse, tore away his sabre, beat him, and took him into the palace to Shaklovíty.

Among the Streltsi, and even among the confidants of Shaklovíty, Prince Boris Golítsyn and Leo Naryskin had succeeded in gaining over a number of men to serve them as spies and give information of what passed. With money, with promises, with assurances that Peter would inevitably come into power, and that in the end it would be far more profitable to serve than to oppose him, it was comparatively easy to obtain tools. Seven men, the chief of whom was the Lieutenant-Colonel Lárion Yelisárof, had orders to bring immediate information to Preobrazhénsky of any decisive step. Yelisárof, who had been given by Shaklovíty command of the forces stationed

PETER AWAKENED.

that night on the Lubiánka, met his fellow-conspirators, compelled the sacristan to open the church of St. Theodosius, and
called up a priest, when they all took solemn oath of mutual
fidelity and secrecy. On learning from one of them, who had
been sent to the Krémlin to see what was going on, that Plestchéief had been pulled from his horse and beaten, they apparently believed that the crisis had come, and two of their number, Mélnof and Ladógin rode at full speed to Preobrazhénsky
to give notice of the murderous attack which was being organised against Peter and his mother. They arrived a little after
midnight. Peter was awakened out of a sound sleep and told
to run for his life, as the Streltsi were marching against him.
In his night-dress and barefooted, he ran to the stables, had a
horse quickly saddled and rode off to the nearest woods, where
he directed his companions to bring his clothes as soon as possible. Dressing in the woods, he rode in haste to the neighboring village of Alexéievo, and thence to the monastery of Tróïtsa, where he arrived about six o'clock in the morning, so
weary that he had to be lifted from his horse and put to bed.
Bursting into tears, he told the Abbot of his sad fate and of
the attack his sister was making upon him. His mother, his
wife, and his sister, attended by the boyárs and the guards of
Preobrazhénsky, arrived at Tróïtsa two hours later, and shortly
after came the Súkharef regiment of Streltsi, which was devoted to Peter, and to which Naryshkin and Boris Golítsyn
had immediately sent marching orders.

Meanwhile, if there had been any intention in the Krémlin
—which is very doubtful—of advancing on Preobrazhénsky, it
had been given up, and no one there, except the seven spies of
Peter, knew of the message sent to Preobrazhénsky. Two
hours before daylight, the Princess Sophia went to matins at
the church of Our Lady of Kazán, accompanied by Shaklovíty
and many Streltsi. Yelisárof himself was there, and to a remark made by one of the scribes attending Shaklovíty, that it
was unusual to have so many Streltsi assembled in the Krémlin
at night, replied simply that it was unusual, nothing of the kind
having been done before. After matins, Sophia, turning to the
Streltsi who accompanied her, said: 'Except for my alarms and
my precautions the guards would have murdered all of us.' On
returning from church, Shaklovíty sent a message to Prince

Basil Golítsyn, telling him that the Princess wished to see him. Golítsyn excused himself on the ground of illness and remained at home. Very shortly afterwards, the messengers sent by Shaklovíty to watch on the road to Preobrazhénsky for the movements of Peter's adherents, two of whom had been among those bought up by the Narýshkins, returned as if they had faithfully performed their mission, and reported that Peter had ridden away in the night, barefooted, with nothing on but his shirt, and that none knew whither he had fled. 'He has plainly gone mad,' said Shaklovíty; 'let him run.' When Shaklovíty said this, it was very possible he did not feel the full force of the effect of Peter's escape from his fictitious danger. But it did not require a long reflection to show Sophia and her counsellors that a most decisive step had been taken. Sophia herself had shown the advantages of a refuge at Tróïtsa in the affair with Prince Havánsky. It would be impossible to induce the Streltsi to march against a monastery of such sanctity as Tróïtsa, and against their anointed ruler. Peter would have the support of the country at large, as Sophia had previously had, and would eventually be able to dictate his own terms. The flight to Tróïtsa had been prepared beforehand by Boris Golítsyn and Narýshkin, and everything had been arranged in view of an emergency. It was a great stroke of policy, but it was only saved from being also a comedy by Peter's plain good faith—by his manifest ignorance of the plans of his friends, and by his evident fright when he was told that an attack was imminent. Although the flight had been arranged beforehand—although the information given by Yelisárof and his companions of the expected attack was false—we are not necessarily to suppose that it was arranged for this very night. The plan was that Peter should escape to Tróïtsa whenever the emergency made it necessary; and it was the zeal of Yelisárof and his companions to earn their reward which incited them to send such startling news with such little foundation. The struggle between the two parties could no longer have been avoided, but it might have been a struggle of a very different character.

The next day, August 19, Peter sent a messenger to his brother and sister, inquiring the reason of the great assemblage of Streltsi in the Krémlin. The answer was that the Streltsi

PETER AT THE TROITSA MONASTERY RECEIVING THE DEPUTATIONS OF THE STRELTSI.

were assembled for the simple purpose of accompanying Princess Sophia to the Donskóy Monastery. No other reason could be given, for it was impossible to say that the Streltsi were brought together in apprehension of an attack. It was equally natural that this answer was in the highest degree unsatisfactory, and gave the party of Peter an additional strength, because it seemed to everyone equivocal. Immediately afterwards, Peter sent a request for the presence of Colonel Zickler and fifty Streltsi. After some hesitation, Zickler was sent with fifty men carefully selected from those who had no knowledge of the affairs of the Government. It subsequently became known that this was a little intrigue of Zickler, who had been one of the chief men in the first revolt of the Streltsi in May, 1682, and who, hoping to win favour with Peter, who was strong and whose claims seemed to be in the ascendant, had sent word by a friend to have him called to Tróïtsa. As soon as he arrived, he revealed all that he knew and gave in writing copies of all secret orders which, to his knowledge, had been given to the Streltsi and officers. Immediately afterwards, Yelisárof, Mélnof and others of Peter's spies succeeded in making their way to Tróïtsa, where they gave such information and made such denunciations as they could. Sophia, in particular trouble of mind, resolved to attempt a reconciliation, and sent to Tróïtsa Prince Ivan Troekúrof, whose son was an intimate friend of Peter, charging him to persuade her brother to return to Moscow. This was the only way of ending the quarrel honourably for her and of preserving some semblance of power and dignity. Peter's friends, however, saw that this was inadvisable for them, and that the advantages he possessed by remaining at Tróïtsa he might lose by being at Moscow. Troekúrof returned with news by no means reassuring. Immediately afterwards, there followed written orders from Peter to the colonel of each regiment of the Streltsi and of the regular soldiers, commanding him to make his appearance at Tróïtsa before August 30, accompanied by ten of his men. These orders were the subject of a council at the Krémlin, and ultimately the picked men of each regiment were called together and told not to go to Tróïtsa, nor to meddle in the dispute between Sophia and her brother. The colonels still hesitated and said their going to Tróïtsa would make no difference in the position of affairs. Sophia, hearing of this, came out again and said very decisively to the colonels that, if any one of them attempted to go to the Tróïtsa Monastery, he would immediately lose his head. Prince Golítsyn gave a positive command to General Gordon not to leave Moscow on any order or under any excuse. Next day Peter sent word to Iván and Sophia that he had sent for the officers of the Streltsi, and requested a compliance with his orders. Prince Prosorófsky, the tutor of Iván, together with Peter's confessor, were sent to Tróïtsa with instructions to give reasons why the officers were not allowed to go, and to make another attempt at conciliation. They returned two days after, without having been able to accomplish their mission, and reports were spread through Moscow that the orders for the journey of the colonels to Tróïtsa had been given without the knowledge of the Tsar.

Shaklovíty sent spies to Tróïtsa to ascertain what was going on there. Some were caught; those who returned brought him anything but comforting intelligence. An endeavour was then made to work on the feelings of the wives and families of the Streltsi, that they might induce those men who were at Tróïtsa to return, especially the soldiers of the Súkharef regiment. These tentatives however were vain and more and more people went to Tróïtsa every day. Finally, Sophia persuaded the Patriarch to go to Tróïtsa and try to bring about a reconciliation. The Patriarch Joachim was probably very ready to abandon the camp of those who were really his enemies. Though he had supported the Government of Sophia, he was by his family—the Savéliefs—closely connected with the aristocratic party and had never been in the most cordial relations with Sophia's immediate adherents. He especially hated Sylvester Medvédief, and had reasons for being suspicious of Shaklovíty. As soon as he reached Tróïtsa he was shown the revelations of the spies, and the confessions obtained by torture from the prisoners, in which mention was made of plots not only against the life of Peter, but against his own. This convinced him. He believed without further inquiry, and remained in Tróïtsa, thus openly taking the side of Peter. After a few days' waiting, on September 6, still more urgent letters were sent to Moscow, addressed not only to the Streltsi, but also directly to the people, ordering the immediate appearance at Tróïtsa of the colonels and ten of their men, together with deputies from each class of

the population. Disobedience was punishable with death. In
the disturbed state of the city, agitated by constant rumours,
these letters produced a very great impression. It became apparent that the Tróïtsa party would win. A crowd of Streltsi,
with five colonels, marched to Tróïtsa. They were received by
the Tsar and the Patriarch, who stated to them the results of
the investigation into the alleged plot, urged them to confess
all they knew, and promised them pardon. The Streltsi with
one voice affirmed their allegiance to Peter's Government, dis-
claimed any intention of insubordination, and denied all knowledge of any plot or conspiracy. Two men only accused Shaklovíty of plots against the Tsar.

Finally, Sophia resolved as a last effort at conciliation to go
herself to Tróïtsa and seek a personal explanation with her
brother. Taking with her an image of the Saviour, she set
out from Moscow on September 8, accompanied by Prince Basil
Golítsyn, Shaklovíty, Neplúief and a guard of Streltsi. She
halted about eight miles from Tróïtsa, in the village of Vozdvízhenskoe, where Havánsky had been executed, and was met
by the chamberlain, Iván Buturlín, with the order not to come
to the monastery. 'I shall certainly go,' replied Sophia, angrily,
but afterwards Prince Troekúrof appeared, with a threat from
Peter that, if she should be bold enough to come, she would be
treated as perhaps she might not like. Disappointed and furious with anger, Sophia immediately returned to Moscow, which
she reached on the night of September 11, and two hours before dawn sent for the most faithful of her adherents. Telling
them of the insults she had received, she said: 'They almost
shot me at Vozdvízhenskoe. Many people rode out after me
with arquebuses and bows. It was with difficulty I got away,
and I hastened to Moscow in five hours. The Narýshkins and
the Lopúkhins are making a plot to kill the Tsar Iván Alexéievitch, and are even aiming at my head. I will collect the regiments and will talk to them myself. Obey us, and do not go
to Tróïtsa. I trust in you; in whom should I trust rather than
you, O faithful adherents! Will you also run away? Kiss the
cross first,' and Sophia herself held out the cross for them to
kiss. 'Now, if you run away,' she added, 'the life-giving cross
will not let you go. Whatever letters come from Tróïtsa, do
not read them ; bring them to the palace.'

The same day, Colonel Iván Netcháef came from Tróïtsa to Moscow with letters, both to Iván and to Sophia, containing an official statement of the plot against Peter's life, and with a demand that Shaklovíty, the monk Sylvester Medvédief and other accomplices should be immediately arrested and sent to Tróïtsa for trial. This produced very great confusion in the palace and general disturbance among the people. Sophia asked Netcháef how he dared take upon himself such a commission. He answered that he did not dare to disobey the Tsar. The Princess, in her rage, ordered his head to be struck off at once, a command which would probably have been faithfully fulfilled had an executioner been found at hand. The Streltsi who had escorted Netcháef from Tróïtsa were ordered to present themselves in the court of the palace, together with those other Streltsi who happened to be at the Krémlin. Sophia went out to them and made a long and earnest speech, in the course of which she said:

'Evil-minded people have consented to act as tools. They have used all means to make me and the Tsar Iván quarrel with my younger brother. They have sown discord, jealousy and trouble. They have hired people to talk of a plot against the life of the younger Tsar, and of other people. Out of jealousy of the great services of Theodore Shaklovíty, and of his constant care, day and night, for the safety and prosperity of the empire, they have given him out to be the chief of the conspiracy, as if one existed. To settle the matter and to find out the reason for this accusation, I went myself to Tróïtsa, but was kept back by the advice of the evil councillors whom my brother has about him, and was not allowed to go farther. After being insulted in this way, I was obliged to come home. You all well know how I have managed for these seven years; how I took on myself the regency in the most unquiet times; how I have concluded a famous and true peace with the Christian rulers, our neighbours, and how the enemies of the Christian religion have been brought by my arms into terror and confusion. For your services you have received great reward and I have always shown you my favour. I cannot believe that you will betray me and will believe the inventions of enemies of the general peace and prosperity. It is not the life of Theodore Shaklovíty that they want, but my life and that of my elder brother.'

SOPHIA'S APPEAL TO HER PARTISANS.

She concluded by promising to reward those who should remain faithful, and who should not mix in the matter; and threatened to punish those who should be disobedient and assist in creating confusion. Then the notables of the burghers and of the common people were sent for, and Sophia addressed them in a similar tone. A third time, on the same day, she called them all together and made them ' a long and fine speech,' as Gordon calls it, in the same spirit. As the Patriarch was away and the elder Tsar was not in perfect health, all the preparations for the festival of the New Year, which occurred on this day, the 11th (1st O. S.) of September, were abandoned; vodka was given to the Streltsi; the chief nobles and the foreigners were asked to wait awhile, and about noon received a cup of vodka from the hand of the elder Tsar. Meanwhile, the wrath of Sophia against Netcháef had passed away. She sent for him, pardoned him, and was gracious enough to offer him also a cup of vodka. Some of the Streltsi whose surrender had been demanded by Peter were concealed by their comrades; Shaklovíty found refuge in the palace of Sophia; Medvédief and some others ran away. It was reported, nevertheless, that the Tsar Peter had promised to spare the lives of those persons in case they surrendered.

The next day, Prince Boris Golítsyn, who, as Peter's chief counsellor, had the management of affairs at Tróïtsa, sent a counsel to his relative, Prince Basil Golítsyn, to come to Tróïtsa and ' preoccupate the Tsar's favour.' Basil Golítsyn replied by sending a scribe to his cousin to ask him to be the means of reconciliation between the two parties. The answer was, that the best thing he could do, in any case for himself, was to come as soon as possible to Tróïtsa, being assured of a good reception from Peter. But honour and duty both forbade him to leave the side of Sophia.

In spite of the orders which had come from Tróïtsa to the Streltsi to keep quiet and make no disturbance, and in spite of the requests made to them by Sophia, they began to fret at this long period of commotion, so that Sophia finally gave out that she with her brother Iván would again try to go to Tróïtsa. The Streltsi at Tróïtsa were anxious to return to Moscow, promising to win the others to their side; and many officers of Peter thought it would be better for him to transfer himself to Preobrazhénsky, Alexéievo, or some other village in the immediate neighbourhood of Moscow, where his adherents would be greatly increased without danger to himself. Golítsyn and Naryshkin, however, feared bloodshed, and it was thought better to remain at Tróïtsa. On September 14, there was brought to the German suburb a rescript to all the generals, colonels, and other foreign officers (although no one was mentioned by name), giving a brief statement of the conspiracy of Shaklovíty, Medvédief, and ten Streltsi against the Tsar, the Patriarch, the Tsaritsa Natália and several distinguished boyárs, and announcing that an order had been given for the arrest of the persons implicated, and commanding furthermore all officers into whose hands this rescript should come to appear at Tróïtsa, fully armed and on horseback. This paper was received by Colonel Ridder, who brought it to General Gordon, and the latter called together all the foreign generals and colonels and in their presence unsealed the packet. On consultation, it was resolved to communicate it to Prince Basil Golítsyn. He was much disturbed, but, appearing as calm as he could, said he would report it to the elder Tsar and the Princess, and would send him word how to act. Gordon remarked that they risked their heads in case of disobedience. The boyár replied that he would certainly give an answer by evening, and asked him to let his son-in-law, Colonel Strasburg, wait at the palace for it. Gordon made preparations for immediate departure, and told everyone who asked his advice that, no matter what the order might be, he was resolved to go. The other foreign officers followed his example. They set out that evening and arrived at Tróïtsa the next morning, where they were given an audience of Peter and allowed to kiss his hand. The departure of the foreign officers from Moscow practically decided the contest. Sophia, on receiving information that she would not be allowed to go to Tróïtsa, was very indignant, and did not wish to give her consent to the surrender of Shaklovíty. The Streltsi, who had begun to see the imprudence of their long support of Sophia, came in crowds to the palace and asked that Shaklovíty might be given up, offering to take him to Tróïtsa themselves. The Regent refused absolutely, and again besought them not to meddle in the quarrel between her and her brother. The Streltsi were discontented with this; voices were raised in the crowd, saying; 'You had better finish the matter at once. If you do not give him up, we shall sound the alarm bell.' This cry stupefied Sophia, who saw that it was all over. Those who surrounded her feared violence, and told her that it was in vain to oppose this demand; that in case of a rising many people would be killed, and it would be better to give him up. She reluctantly gave her consent, and Shaklovíty, who up to this time had been concealed in the palace chapel, received the Eucharist and was sent to Tróïtsa that night, September 17, with the Streltsi who had come for him. Those boyárs who had, up to that time, remained in Moscow, all took their leave for Tróïtsa, except Prince Basil Golítsyn, who retired to his villa of Medviédkovo, where the news of the surrender of Shaklovíty greatly disturbed him. Shaklovíty, on his arrival, was straightway put to the torture of the knout. After the first fifteen blows he made a confession, in which, however, he denied that there was any plot whatever against the life of the Tsar Peter, and that any plans had ever been concocted for the murder of the Tsaritsa Natalia, the Narýshkins or the boyárs of Peter's party, although the subject had been mentioned in conversation. The same day, Prince Basil Golítsyn, Neplúief and others of his adherents presented themselves at Tróïtsa. They were not allowed to come within the walls of the monastery but were ordered to remain in the village outside. At nine o'clock in the evening, Golítsyn and his son Alexis were ordered to come to the abode of the Tsar. When they appeared on the staircase they were met by a councillor, who read to them an order depriving them of the rank of boyár, and sending them, with their wives and children, into exile at Kargópol, and confiscating all their property, on the ground that they had reported to the sister of the Tsars without reporting to the Tsars personally; that they had written her name in papers and despatches on an equality with that of the Tsars, and also because Prince Basil Golítsyn, by his conduct in the Crimean expedition of 1689, had caused harm to the Government and burdens to the people.[1]

[1] Solóviéf, xiv. ; Ustriálof, II. ch. ii., iii. ; Pogódin, 160-204; Medvédief's *Memoirs ;* De Neuville ; Posselt, *Lefort ;* Gordon's *Diary ;* Aristof; Reports of Dutch Residents ; De Rovínsky, *Russian Engraved Portraits* (Russian), St. Petersburg, 1872; Brücker, *Golizyn ;* id. *Peter der Grosse.*

XIX.

VICTORY AND VENGEANCE.

THERE had been great disputes among the friends of Peter about Golítsyn. Precedence had still left its traces. Time had not yet sufficiently elapsed for the new system to come into play. The condemnation of Prince Basil Golítsyn for treason would have been a disgrace to the whole family, and Boris Golítsyn was therefore anxious to save his cousin, himself, and his family from such a calamity. But the enemies of Golítsyn did their best by exciting Peter's anger to render his fate harder. After Shaklovíty had been tortured once, and when he was expecting his second trial, he determined to give the Tsar, in writing, an exact account of the whole matter. Prince Boris Golítsyn himself took him paper and pen. Shaklovíty wrote eight or nine sheets, and as it was after midnight when he had finished and the Tsar had gone to bed, Prince Boris took the papers home with him, intending to give them to the Tsar on the following morning. The enemies of Boris Golítsyn, especially the Naryshkins, who carefully followed all his movements, hastened to report to Peter that the Prince had taken away the confession of Shaklovíty, with the intention of taking out all that reflected on his cousin Basil. The Tsar immediately sent to Shaklovíty to ask whether he had written a confession, and ascertained that he had given it to Prince Boris Golítsyn. The latter, however, was luckily informed by a friend of the impending catastrophe, and hastened with the papers to the Tsar, who asked, in a threatening tone, why he had not presented them immediately. Golítsyn replied that it was too late at night, which satisfied Peter, who continued, as before, to keep Golítsyn in his confidence, although the Tsaritsa Natalia and her friends were still hostile to him.

After listening to his sentence, Prince Basil Golítsyn wished to hand to the councillor who read it to him an explanation, in which he had briefly set forth the services he had rendered to the Government during the time he had taken a part in public affairs. He wished to be allowed to write this to the Tsar or to the council, but the councillor did not dare receive it. Golítsyn afterward found some way of having it presented to the Tsar, but it produced no effect. Neplúief was condemned to exile in Pustozérsk (afterward changed to Kola), ostensibly for his harsh treatment of the soldiers under his command, and was deprived of his rank and property. Zméief was ordered to reside on his estate in Kostromá, while Kosogóf and Ukráintsef were retained in their former posts. These noblemen went back to their quarters, when they were advised by some of their friends at court to start immediately for their places of exile.. This they did, but rumours were immediately spread that they had run away, and they were sent for and finally sent off under guard, Golítsyn's enemies still attacked him, and insisted that banishment to Kargópol was too light a punishment, and that he should be sent to Pustozérsk. Finally, the place of his exile was changed to Yarénsk, a wretched village in the province of Archangel, but much better than Pustozérsk, where Matvéief had lived so long. Golítsyn's enemies still insisted that he should undergo examination and torture, and finally an official was sent out to meet him at Yaroslàv. He was again examined, although he escaped torture. He confessed to no complicity in any plot or conspiracy, and stated that he was not in any way an intimate friend of Shaklovíty, but merely an acquaintance. His suite was diminished, he was allowed altogether only fifteen persons, the money, furniture, and clothes with which he started were taken away from him, and orders were given that he should be kept closely guarded on the journey and not permitted to speak to anybody. In Vológda he was met by the Chamberlain, Prince Kropótkin, not, however, with any further orders from the Government, but with a tender message from Sophia, who hoped soon to procure his release, through the intercession of the Tsar Iván, and who sent him a packet of money for the journey. With great difficulty in the wintry weather he reached Yarénsk in

January, but even here he was pursued by new denunciations, had to submit to fresh examinations, and finally was removed, first to Pustozérsk, and later to Pinéga, where, after nearly a quarter of a century of wretched existence—his numerous petitions for mercy being disregarded—he died in 1714.

Shaklovíty and his accomplices were condemned to death. It was reported that Peter was utterly averse to this sentence, and only yielded on the insistence of the Patriarch. When it was known that Shaklovíty was to be punished without undergoing a second torture, many of the officials collected in the monastery and petitioned that Shaklovíty should be again tortured, that he might be forced to declare all his accomplices. The Tsar, however, sent word to them that he himself was satisfied with the confessions of Shaklovíty, and it was not for them to meddle in this affair. The investigation of the plot— so far as we can judge from the fragmentary papers which have come down to us—does not seem to have been very careful. Reliance was chiefly placed on the denunciations of Yelisárof and his band, and on the evidence obtained by torture. The evidence is very contradictory; and, apart from that, very little reliance can be placed on confessions obtained in this way. There was apparently no cross-examination of the denouncers, and in very few cases were they confronted with the accused. Yet, notwithstanding all this, very few persons were found to be actually guilty, and even the extent of their guilt is very doubtful. There does not appear to have been any plot for the murder of Peter, although attempts had been made to excite the Streltsi against Peter's friends, and in private it had been hinted that it would be an advantage if the Tsaritsa Natalia, the Naryshkins, and two or three others of the nobles were out of the way. In no case was the Princess Sophia at all implicated by the testimony, although it is very probable that she knew of what had been going on—that is, of the attempts to excite the Streltsi. She was ambitious; the habit of power had fed the love of it; and she would doubtless have been glad to take advantage of a successful rising, by which she might have contrived to retain for some time to come a certain share of the supreme authority.

On September 21, Shaklovíty, Petróf, and Tchérmny were

beheaded. Major Múromtsef, Colonel Riazántsef, and the private Lavréntief were beaten with the knout, and after having their tongues torn out, were exiled to Siberia. Sylvester Medvédief had escaped from Moscow, and had gone toward the Polish frontier, where he was arrested in the monastery of Biziúk, together with Major Gládky, and sent to Tróïtsa. When tortured, he refused to confess himself guilty of conspiracy, admitted that he had heard proposals against the lives of some of Peter's adherents, but asserted that he had threatened those who spoke in such wise with ruin in this life and hell-fire in the life to come if they should engage in any such attempt; he denied that he had committed any act whatever against the Government, or had any designs against the Patriarch; but he admitted having written an inscription with complimentary verses for the engraved portrait of Sophia. He was degraded from the clergy, and was placed in a monastery under strict surveillance. Here he was induced to retract the views expressed in his book on religion, called ' The Heavenly Manna.' He was subsequently again denounced by Strizhóf, who had been in the confidence of Shaklovíty, and who accused him of having been in league with a Polish sorcerer who had come to Moscow to cure the eyes of the Tsar Iván; that there they had told him of the approaching marriage of Sophia to Prince Basil Golítsyn, and that Medvédief would be made Patriarch instead of Joachim. Medvédief was again subjected to the severe torture of fire and hot irons, and was finally executed in 1691.

After the surrender of Shaklovíty, Peter wrote from Tróïtsa to his brother Iván that the sceptre of the Russian state had been confided to them—two persons—by the solemn decree and ceremony of the church, and that nothing had been said about any third person who should be on equality in the Government, and that, as their sister Sophia had begun to rule of her own will, and had interfered in affairs of state, in a manner disagreeable to them and hard for the people, and as Shaklovíty and his comrades had made criminal attempts against his life and that of his mother, he therefore thought the time had come, as he was now of full age, for himself and his brother to govern the country without the interference of a third person such as his sister, who, to their lasting shame, had even wished to be crowned. He therefore begged his brother to grant him permission to change all unjust judges and to appoint just ones— without specially consulting him in each case—for the good of the state, and ended by asking his paternal and fraternal blessing. The demands of Peter were of course complied with. Nothing was said at that time about the future fate of Sophia, but shortly after an order was given excluding the name of Sophia from all the official documents where it had previously been inserted. Immediately afterward, Peter sent Prince Ivan Troekúrof to his brother to request the removal of his sister Sophia from the palace of the Kremlin to the Novodevítchy convent, where he had appointed her to live in a sort of honourable confinement. Sophia for a long time was unwilling to retire into this convent, and did not remove thither until about the end of September. Well-furnished rooms were prepared for her there, looking out on the Devítchy plain. She had a large number of servants and everything which was necessary for a pleasant and peaceful life. She was not, however, allowed the liberty of going out of the convent, and could see no one but her aunts and her sisters, and these only on the great festivals of the church.

So long as Sophia remained in the Kremlin, Peter refused to return to Moscow, and it was only after she had gone to the convent that he set out from Tróïtsa, passed a week or more in cavalry and infantry manœuvres, under the direction of General Gordon, in the neighbourhood, and finally arrived at Moscow on October 16. He went first to the Cathedral of the Assumption, where he was received by his brother Iván, who rushed to his embrace, and afterward, arrayed in his robes of state and standing at the top of the Red Staircase, showed himself to his people as their lawful ruler.

In the middle of this revolution, when the city was all in confusion and terror, Mazeppa, Hetman of the Cossacks of the Ukraine, arrived at Moscow. By order of the Regency, he was met at the Kalúga gate by a secretary with one of the Tsar's carriages, which, apparently, was somewhat the worse for wear, for Mazeppa, on taking his seat, said: 'Thank the Lord! Through the grace of the Tsar I am now riding in one of the Imperial carriages. But what sort of a carriage is it? (with a

NOVODEVITCHY MONASTERY.

sniff). It is apparently an old German one.' 'In this carriage the extraordinary ambassadors of foreign rulers always ride,' answered the secretary, with dignity. In his further conversa-

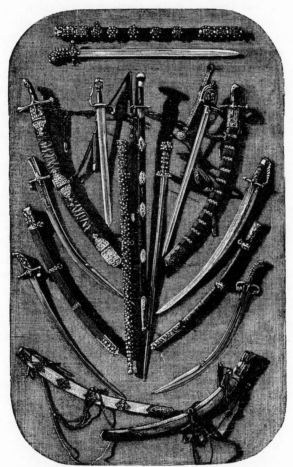

Sabres of Mazeppa, Chief of the Cossacks (in the Museum of Tsarkoe Selo).

tion, and also in the speech which he made on being received at the palace, he spoke of the unheard-of victories which Golítsyn had won in the Crimea, as surpassing those of Darius, the Persian King.

When matters began to go badly for Sophia and Golítsyn, when Shaklovíty had been surrendered, and everyone was going to Tróïtsa, Mazeppa became alarmed about his relations to the new Government, fearing that it might be remembered against him that he had been an ardent partisan of Golítsyn. He too, therefore, hastened to Tróïtsa. Among the advisers of Peter, there were some who thought it better to get rid of Mazeppa, but others more wisely represented that the Hetman had heretofore been changed for misconduct or unpopularity only; that it would be dangerous to introduce a new precedent; and that in any case, in the disturbed state of affairs, it would be difficult to find·a successor to Mazeppa without the expenditure of much money. Mazeppa was therefore well received, and, seeing his good reception, he thought to make sure of the future by breaking completely with his past. He said that Golítsyn had extorted large sums of money from him before being willing to instal him as Hetman, and begged to be remunerated from the property of the traitor. This request was regarded as a sign of complete submission, and all his demands were complied with. He received a charter confirming all the previous rights and liberties of Little Russia; he obtained additional Russian troops for the defence of the Ukraine; he induced the Government to consent to keep the Russian officials and soldiery in better order and under stricter discipline, and with less inconvenience to the Cossacks; and he was also successful in carrying out some plans of vengeance against his personal enemies. Satisfied with this and with the presents of money he received, he returned to the banks of the Dnieper.[1]

---

[1] Ustriálof, II. ch. iii. iv. ; Soloviéf, xiv.; Pogódin ; Medvédief; Brückner, *Golizyn.*

XX.

The only practical result of the downfall of Sophia was that the aristocratic party filled the offices of state and administered the Government. Peter himself left everything in the hands of his counsellors, and for several years took merely a formal part in the administration. He confined himself almost entirely to military exercises and boat-building, and to indulging his mechanical tastes. He had no care for affairs of state, and felt no interest in them. His uncle, the boyár Leo Naryshkin, occupied the most prominent position in the new Government as Director of Foreign Affairs, in which office he was assisted by the councillor Ukraíntsef, a man of great experience and capacity. The other prominent offices were divided among the chief families of the aristocratic party, especially

Prince Boris Golítsyn.

among those most nearly connected with Peter, his mother, and his wife—Urúsof, Ramodanófsky, Troekúrof, Stréshnef, Prozorófsky, Lopúkhin, Golófkin, Lvof, Sheremétief, Dolgorúky, Lýkof—so that the whole cabal was well represented. Prince Boris Golítsyn, in spite of his difficulty with the Naryshkins, retained his old position as Director of the Department of the Palace of Kazán, and four other prominent men who served under Sophia—Répnin, Sokóvnin, Odóiefsky, and Vinius—were kept in their posts. The provincial administration, and even the government of the army, remained almost untouched. The boyár Borís Sheremétief, in spite of the favour with which he had been regarded by the Regency, was maintained as general-in-chief of the army which protected the southern frontier against the Tartars. General Gordon, too, kept his place and his influence. Except that the energy of Sophia, Golítsyn, and Shaklovíty was wanting, the policy of the new ministers differed little from that of their predecessors.

One of the first consequences of the change of administration was an outburst of the popular hatred against foreigners, a hatred which had long been accumulating in the minds of the people, and which had not infrequently manifested itself in various and even violent forms. There was a seemingly ineradicable feeling in the Russian mind that the country suffered from foreigners, that foreign merchants came like a swarm of locusts and ate up all the good things of the land, and that foreign countries were in conspiracy to keep Russia poor. The political economists, Iván Pososhkóf and Yúry Krýzhanitch, sensible men as they were in other respects, shared this feeling, and wished to put a sort of Chinese wall around Russia, so as to keep people from going in or out. They were protectionists in the most positive form. Very few Russians had been abroad, except on Government embassies, and those were diligently occupied in carrying out the prescriptions of a formal etiquette, and were cut off, by their ignorance of foreign languages, from the possibility of understanding western Europe. There was the fear lest contact with the west and with foreigners should corrupt Russia, and above all lead to heresy, especially to Roman Catholicism. The few cases where Russians had gone abroad for purposes of study were not re-assuring. Of all the young men sent abroad by Boris Godunóf, not more than two or three returned, and the son of the celebrated boyár Ordín-Nastchókin, who had been educated by a Polish teacher and had travelled in Poland, finally ran away from his father and his country, and renounced his religion. This possible corruption of Russian

orthodoxy and of Russian manners seemed to weigh the most
heavily on the mind of the Russian Conservatives.   There were
a few men at different epochs who rose superior to this prejudice—Iván the Terrible, Godunóf, the so-called false Demetrius, Theodore, Sophia, Prince Basil Golítsyn, and Peter.   But
the aristocratic party that surrounded Peter was deeply conservative, and, therefore, very prejudiced.   The Patriarch, who
was now one of the leaders of the aristocratic party, had, even
before the last Crimean campaign, protested against the employment of foreign soldiers, and especially of that arch-heretic
General Gordon, and had pre-
dicted disaster to the Russian arms in consequence. His
advice was naturally disregarded, for the foreigners
were the only officers capable
of taking command; but, as
disaster did come, his predic-
tions were by many thought
to be verified.   Prince Basil
Golítsyn, in a way an enlight-
ened man and well-disposed to
foreigners, had to a certain degree, protected the Jesuits.
Such protection was necessary, for, in spite of the tol-
eration at the Court of Moscow toward Calvinists and

General Patrick Gordon.

Lutherans, the Catholics were never allowed for long to have
churches specially set apart for the purpose, although they
were admitted at times to say mass in private houses.   As soon
as Golítsyn was overthrown, a decree was issued for the banishment of the Jesuits within two weeks, and the Imperial Envoy
found it impossible to obtain exceptions, or even much delay.   It
required a long diplomatic correspondence, the urgent demand
of the Emperor Leopold, and all the personal influence of
General Gordon with Peter, to get permission for one priest,
not a Jesuit, to reside in Moscow.

One case of religious persecution had begun months before.

A German fanatic from Breslau, Quirinus Kuhlmann, another German preacher, Nordermann, and a painter, Henin, were accused of teaching and disseminating heretical and blasphemous doctrines. Their case was investigated by the translators of the Foreign Office, and, for better information, referred to the Protestant pastors then living in Moscow, as well as to all the Jesuits then there. Apparently Kuhlmann was a sort of Quaker, but had developed a body of doctrine based on the mystical works of Jacob Böhme. The report of Pastor Meincke was very strong against Kuhlmann, and after the three men accused had been subjected several times to violent tortures without bringing them to yield, they were condemned to death. Kuhlmann and Nordermann were burned alive in the Red Place at Moscow on October 14, four days before Peter came to the capital. Henin avoided a like death by taking poison in prison and committing suicide.

We must remember the time at which this took place. Thomas Aikenhead was executed for heresy at Edinburgh in 1696, witches were burned in England in 1676, and hanged even in 1796. A witch was burned at Wurtzburg in 1749, and nineteen were hanged at Salem, Massachusetts, in 1692.

Not only were the Jesuits expelled, but within a year from the permission given to the exiled Huguenots to settle in Russia, strict orders were sent to the frontier to stop all foreigners and thoroughly examine them as to whence they came and what reason they had for visiting Russia, and to detain them until orders were received from Moscow. Among others kept in this way was Dr. Jacob Pelarino, a Greek physician recommended to the Tsar by the Emperor. Another physician of Peter, Dr. Carbonari, also recommended by the Emperor Leopold, had his letters and papers seized and was strictly forbidden to carry on any further correspondence with Vienna or with the Jesuits, under pain of expulsion. At the same time, orders were given to Andrew Vinius, the Director of Posts, to inspect all letters which passed the Russian frontier either going or coming. This measure regarded especially the exchange of correspondence with persons in Poland. The Polish minister complained greatly that either he did not receive his letters at all, or else that they had been opened. According to Van Keller, this was denied by the Government, but General Gordon wrote to his son in Poland not to date his letters from any place in that country, and always to send them by the way of Riga or Danzig, in order to prevent their being opened or confiscated.

The previous system of exclusion had, in fact, changed very little. James, the second son of General Gordon, had been educated in the Jesuit College at Douai. In 1688 he came to Moscow, but showed an unwillingness to enter the service of the Tsar and went to England, took up arms for King James II., was wounded in a fight with the Dutch and forced to leave the country. He next went to Warsaw with the intention of entering the Polish service, but his father pressed him hard to come back to Russia. One thing only stood in the way—James did not desire to enter the Tsar's service unless he could have the privilege of leaving Russia at the expiration of the term for which he should be engaged. This was an unheard-of thing in Russia, for all foreigners in the Russian service were obliged to remain there until they died, and even General Gordon himself, in spite of his excellent position at court during the whole of the reign of Sophia, although allowed to go abroad for business and sent on special missions, could never get permission to resign. After many requests on Gordon's part, all he could obtain was that if his son came to Russia he would not be compelled to enter the Russian service, and could return, but that if he once took the oath he must remain. Gordon, on this business, was in frequent correspondence with his son during the whole of 1690, and finally advised him to come to Russia, but not to engage himself, and to remain a free man 'until circumstances changed.' By this expression 'until circumstances changed'—General Gordon evidently meant the same thing as he did, when, in a letter, he said: 'If the Tsar Peter should take upon himself the government,' referring to the fact that Peter not only took no part in public affairs, but had little influence with the real rulers of the country, who were nominally his ministers.

On March 10, 1690, Gordon was invited to dine at court at the banquet given in honour of the recent birth of Peter's son, Alexis; but the Patriarch, who now felt himself strong, protested against the presence of foreigners on such an occasion,

and the invitation was withdrawn. On the next day, nevertheless, Peter invited him to a country house, dined with him
there, and rode back to town with him, conversing all the way.
. A few days later, on March 27, the Patriarch Joachim died.
In the form of a testament especially directed to the Tsars, he
left a powerful expression of his hatred toward the foreigners.
He counselled the Tsars to drive out from Russia all heretics
and unbelievers, foreigners and enemies of the orthodox church,
and warned them against adopting foreign customs, habits, and
clothing, begged them to forbid all intercourse of any kind with
heretics, whether Lutherans, Calvinists, or Catholics, and laid
great stress on the danger to the country if, in the blessed land
ruled over by the Tsars, foreigners should hold high places in
the army, and thus rule over orthodox men. He advised the
immediate destruction of the foreign churches, and was especially bitter against the Protestants for their attacks on the
adoration of the Virgin and the saints. He held up the fate
of the Princess Sophia and of Basil Golítsyn as a warning;
they had rejected his advice about the employment of foreigners in the last Crimean campaign. He said, in confirmation
of his complaints: 'I wonder at the counsellors and advisers
of the Tsar who have been on embassies in foreign countries. Have they not seen that in every land there are peculiar rites, customs, and modes of dress, that no merit is allowed
to be in anyone of another faith, and that foreigners are not
permitted to build churches there? Is there anywhere in German lands a church of the orthodox faith? No! not one. And
what here never should have been permitted is now allowed to
heretics. They build for their accursed heretical gatherings
temples of prayer, in which they evilly curse and bark against
orthodox people, as idle worshippers and heathens.'
     Great difficulty was found in choosing a new Patriarch, and
it was five months before the election was made. Peter and
the higher and more educated clergy were in favor of Marcellus,
the Metropolitan of Pskof, 'a learned and civilised person,'
while the Tsaritsa Natalia, the monks, and the lower clergy were
in favour of Adrian, the Metropolitan of Kazán. According to
General Gordon, 'the greatest fault they had to lay to the
charge of Marcellus was that he had too much learning, and so

they feared and said he would favour the Catholics and other
religions, to which purpose the Abbot of the Spasky monastery
had given in a writing to the Queen Dowager, accusing him of
many points, and even of heresy.　But the younger Tsar, continuing firm for him, removed with the elder Tsar and the
whole court to Kolómenskoe.'　At a later date, September 3,
Gordon says : ' The Metropolitan of Kazán, Adrian, was chosen
Patriarch, notwithstanding the Tsar's inclination for Marcellus,
the Metropolitan of Pskof, whom the old boyárs and the gen-
erality of the clergy hated, because of his learning and other
great good qualities, and chose this one because of his ignorance
and simplicity.'　Subsequently, when Peter passed through Livonia, according to Blomberg : ' He told us a story that, when
the Patriarch in Moscow was dead, he designed to fill that place
with a learned man, that had been a traveller, who spoke Latin,
Italian and French ; the Russians petitioned him, in a tumul-
tuous manner, not to set such a man over them, alleging three
reasons : (1) because he spoke barbarous languages; (2) because
his beard was not big enough for a Patriarch ; (3) because his
coachman sat upon the coach-seat and not upon the horses, as
was usual.' '

---

[1] Ustriálof, I. iii. iv. ; Soloviéf, xiv. ; N. Tikhonrávof, *Quirinus Kuhlmann*
(Russian), Moscow, 1867 ; Gordon's *Diary ;* Blomberg, *An Account of Livo-
nia, &c.*, London, 1701 ; Despatches of Dutch residents in archives at the
Hague.

XXI.

ALTHOUGH foreigners came to Russia from the earliest period, yet it was not until the time of Iván III. that they arrived in great numbers. That prince received foreign artists and artisans so well that numbers of Italian architects, engineers, goldworkers, physicians, and mechanics hastened to Moscow. His marriage with the Greek Princess Sophia Palæologos gave rise to new and more frequent relations with Italy, and he several times sent to Rome, Venice, and Milan for physicians and men of technical knowledge. It was in this way that the Cathedral of the Assumption came to be built by Aristotle Fioraventi of Bologna, that of St. Michael the Archangel by Aleviso of Milan, and the banqueting hall of the palace, and the walls and the gates of the Kremlin by other Italian architects. German miners, too, came, or were sent by Matthew Corvinus, King of Hungary, and some of them discovered silver and copper mines in Siberia.

Iván IV., the Terrible, appreciated foreigners, and invited large numbers of them into Russia. But, besides this, it was during his reign in 1558, that an English expedition penetrated into the White Sea, and the trade with England began, which soon took great proportions, and brought to Russia many English merchants. After the conquest of Livonia and portions of the southern shore of the Baltic very many prisoners of war were sent to Moscow, and elsewhere in the interior of Russia, and were never allowed to return to their own country.

Under Iván's son Theodore, and Boris Godunóf, the intercourse with western Europe constantly increased. Favours were given, not only to the English merchants, but also to Dutchmen and Danes, to immigrants from Hamburg and the

Hanse Towns. Godunóf invited soldiers and officers as well as physicians and artisans. His children were educated with great deviations from Russian routine. He even thought of marrying his daughter to a Danish prince, and, when at his country estate, was fond of the society of foreigners. The so-called False Demetrius had very great inclinations toward foreigners. This was very natural, for he had been educated in Poland, and had seen the advantages of western culture. Polish manners prevailed at his court; he was surrounded by a guard of foreign soldiers; he protected all religions, especially the Catholic; he urged Russians to travel abroad, and so willingly received foreigners that a Pole, in writing about the immigration of so many foreigners into Russia, said: 'For centuries long it was hard for the birds even to get into the realm of Muscovy, but now come not only many merchants, but a crowd of grocers and tavern-keepers.' Under the Tsar Theodore, son of Iván the Terrible, there were, according to Fletcher, about 4,300 foreigners in the Russian service, most of them Poles and Little Russians, but still about 150 Dutchmen and Scotchmen. In the reign of Boris Godunóf, the foreign detachment in the army was composed of twenty-five hundred men of all nationalities. Two officers, owing to their conduct during the Troublous Times, and the memoirs which they have left, are well-known—the Livonian, Walter Von Rosen, and the Frenchman Mar-

Arms of the Tsar's Body-Guard—Partisan.

geret. The body-guard of Demetrius was composed of three hundred foreigners, all of them so well paid that they stalked about in silk and satin. Margeret was captain of one division of this body-guard.

In the beginning of the sixteenth century, the Grand Duke Basil established the residence of his foreign body-guard, consisting of Poles, Germans and Lithuanians, on the right bank of the river Moskvá, outside the town, in a place called Naléiki, in order, as Herberstein said, that the Russians might not be contaminated by the bad example of their drunkenness. Later on, this district became inhabited by Streltsi and the common people, and the Livonian prisoners of war were established by Iván the Terrible on the Yaúza, near the Pokróf gate. When Demetrius was so desperately defended by his foreign body-guard, that a Livonian, Wilhelm Fürstenberg, fell at his side, the Russians said: 'See what true dogs these Germans are: let us kill them all;' and during the Troublous Times, the foreigners in Moscow were subject to constant attacks from the Russians. Persecutions were organised against them, as at other times and places against the Jews. There was not a popular commotion in which threats, at least, were not made against them, and during one of the attacks the whole foreign quarter was burnt to the ground. After this, the foreigners lived within the walls, and for a while enjoyed the same privileges as Russian subjects, adopting their dress and their habits. Livonian prisoners of war had, even before the Troublous Times, made their way within the town, and had built a church or two. For some reason they incurred the wrath of the Tsar, were driven from their houses, and their property was plundered. Margeret says of them :

Arms of the Tsar's Body-Guard — Partisan.

'The Lutheran Livonians, who, on the conquest of the greatest part of Livonia, and the removal of the inhabitants of Dorpat and Narva, had been brought as prisoners to Moscow, had succeeded in getting two churches inside the town of Moscow, and celebrated in them their public divine service. At last, on account of their pride and vanity, their churches were torn down by the Tsar's command, all their houses were plundered, and they themselves, without regard to age or sex, and in winter, too, were stripped to nakedness. For this they were themselves thoroughly to blame, for instead of remembering their former misery, when they were brought from their native country, and robbed of their property and had become slaves, and being humble on account of their sufferings, their demeanour was so proud, their conduct and actions so arrogant, and their clothes so costly, that one might have taken them for real princes and princesses. When their women went to church, they wore nothing but satin, and velvet, and damask, and the meanest of them at least taffeta, even if they had nothing else. Their chief gains were from the permission they had to sell brandy and other kinds of drinks, whereby they got not ten per cent., but a hundred per cent., which appears most improbable, but is nevertheless true. But what always distinguished the Livonians marked them here. One could have imagined that they had been brought to Russia to display here their vanity and shamelessness, which on account of the existing laws and justice they could not do in their own country. At last, a place was given to them outside the town to build their houses and a church. Since then, no one of them is allowed to dwell inside the town of Moscow.'

When affairs became more settled under the Tsar Alexis, by a decree of 1652 there was a systematic settling of all foreigners in a suburb outside the town ; the number of the streets and lanes was set down in the registers, the pieces of land, varying from 350 to 1,800 yards square, were set apart for the officers, the physicians, the apothecaries, the artisans and the widows of foreigners who had been in the Russian service. This suburb, which was nicknamed by the Russians Kúkui, now forms the north-eastern portion of the city of Moscow, intersected by the Basmánnaya and Pokrófskaya streets, and still contains the chief Protestant and Catholic churches. It is fairly depicted to us in one of the drawings made by the artist who accompanied Meyerberg's embassy in 1661. As the houses

were of wood, and surrounded by gardens, this suburb had all
the appearances of a large and flourishing village.

Reutenfels, who was in Russia from 1671 to 1673, estimated
the number of foreigners in the country as about 18,000. Most
of them lived in Moscow, but a large number inhabited
Vológda, Archangel and other towns where there was foreign
trade, as well as the mining districts.

The residence of the foreigners in a separate suburb naturally enabled them to keep up the traditions and customs of
Western Europe much more easily than if they had mingled
with the Russians. They wore foreign clothing, read foreign
books, and spoke, at least in their households, their own languages, although they all had some acquaintance with the Russian tongue, which sometimes served as a medium of communication with each other. The habitual use of a few Russian
words, the adoption of a few Russian customs, conformity to
the Russian dress and ways of thinking on some points, was the
most they had advanced toward Russianisation. Rarely did
they change their faith to advance their worldly prospects,
although the children of marriages with Russians were brought
up in the Russian church. In general, they held close to their
own religion and their own modes of education. They kept up
a constant intercourse with their native countries, by new arri-
vals, and by correspondence with their friends. They imported
not only foreign conveniences for their own use, but also received from abroad the journals of the period, books of science
and history, novels and poems. Their interest in the politics of
their own lands was always maintained, and many and warm
were the discussions which were caused by the wars between
France and the Low Countries, and the English Revolution.
In this way, the German suburb was a nucleus of a superior
civilisation.

In thinking of the foreign colony in Moscow at the end of
the seventeenth century, it is impossible not to remember the
English and German colonies in St. Petersburg and Moscow of
the present day. Here they have kept their own religion, their
own language, and, in many cases, their own customs. But still
they have something about them which is Russian. In no respect is the comparison more close than in the relations which

they keep up with the homes of their ancestors. Although most of the English colony of St. Petersburg, for instance, were born in Russia, and some of them are even descended from families who settled there during the time of Peter the Great, or even before, yet frequently the boys are sent to English schools and universities, there are English houses of the same family connected with them in business, and, in cases, one of the family is a member of Parliment. The English colony, especially in St. Petersburg, is on a better footing than it is in most foreign countries. Its members are not living there to escape their debts at home, or to avoid the consequences of disgrace, nor are they there simply for the purpose of making money. Russia has been their home for generations, and they deservedly possess the respect and esteem, not only of their own countrymen, but of the Russians.

The influence of the foreign residents in Russia was especially seen in the material development of the country. The Russians were then, as they are now, quick to learn and ready to imitate. A Pole, Maszkiewicz, in the time of the False Demetrius, remarked that the metal and leather work of the Russians after Oriental designs could scarcely be distinguished from the genuine articles. Foreigners understood this quality of Russian workmen, and frequently endeavoured to keep their trades as a monopoly for themselves. We know that Hans Falck, a foreign manufacturer of bells and metal castings, sent away his Russian workmen when engaged in the delicate processes, in order that they might not learn the secrets of the art. The Government found it necessary, in many cases, to make contracts with foreign artisans that they should teach their trades to a certain number of Russian workmen. It was the Englishman John Merrick, first merchant and subsequently ambassador, who was one of the earliest to teach the Russians that it was better for them to manufacture for themselves than to export the

Arms made for Russians—Arquebuse of Tsar Alexis, made in 1654.

raw materials. He explained to the boyárs how people had been poor in England as long as they had exported raw wool, and had only begun to get rich when the laws protected the woollen manufacturers by insisting on the use of wool at home, and especially on the use of woollen shrouds, and how greatly the riches of England had increased since the country began to sell cloth instead of wool. It was in part through his influence that a manufactory of hemp and tow was established near Holmogóry. In a similar way, paper-mills, glass-factories, powder-mills, saltpetre-works, and iron-works were established by foreigners. A Dane, Peter Marselis, had important and well-known iron-works near Túla, which were so productive that he was able to pay his inspector three thousand rubles a year, and had to pay to his brother-in-law, for his share, twenty thousand rubles.

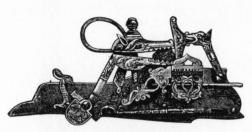

Lock of Arquebuse.

We can see the relative value of this, when we remember that, at that time, two to two and a half quarters of rye could be bought for a ruble, and that, twenty years later, the salary of General Gordon, one of the highest in the Russian service, was only one thousand rubles a year; while the pastor of the Lutheran church in Moscow in 1699 received annually only sixty rubles. Concessions for copper mines were also given to Marselis and other foreigners, and the Stróganofs, who possessed such great and rich mining districts on the frontier of Siberia, constantly sent abroad for physicians, apothecaries, and artisans of all kinds.

It has already been said that the foreigners in Russia were not too well pleased with the ease with which the Russians learned their trades; neither did this please foreign Governments. The famous Duke of Alva said that it was 'inexcusable to provide Russia with cannon and other arms, and to initiate the Russians into the way war was carried on in Western Europe, because, in this way, a dangerous neighbour was being educated.' Sigismund, King of Poland, did his best to hinder the intercourse which sprang up between Moscow and England, and wrote to Queen Elizabeth that ' such commercial relations were dangerous, because Russia would thus receive war material; and it would be still worse if Russia, in this way, could get immigrants who should spread through the country the technical knowledge so necessary there. It was in the interest of Christianity and religion to protest against Russia, the enemy of all free nations, receiving cannon and arms, artists and artisans, and being initiated into the views and purposes of European politics.'

It was natural that, with constant and increasing intercourse with foreigners, the Russians should adopt some of the customs which the strangers had brought with them. For a long time the foreigners were greatly laughed at for eating salads, or grass, as the peasants called it, but this habit gradually spread. In the early part of the seventeenth century, the Dutch introduced the culture of asparagus, and garden roses were first brought by the Dane, Peter Marselis. The use of snuff and of smoking tobacco was speedily acquired, much to the horror of all right-thinking and orthodox people, who saw in this a plain work of the devil; for was it not said in the Bible: ' Not that which goeth into the mouth defileth a man; but that which cometh out of the mouth, this defileth a man.' Many Russian nobles even adopted foreign clothes, and trimmed their hair and beard. Nikíta Románof, the owner of the boat which Peter found at Ismaílovo, wore German clothes while hunting, for which he was sharply reprimanded by the Patriarch; and the conduct of Prince Andrew Koltsóf-Masálsky, in cutting his hair short, in 1675, caused so much displeasure that the Tsar Alexis issued an ukase, forbidding, under heavy penalties, the trimming one's hair or beard, or the wearing of foreign clothes. This decree soon fell into desuetude, and at the time of which we are speaking, foreign clothes and foreign habits were not at all uncommon among the Russians of the higher ranks. Even Peter himself occasionally wore foreign dress, and was severely blamed by the Patriarch for daring to appear in such costume at the death-bed of his mother.

The theatrical performances devised by Matvéief for the Tsar Alexis have already been mentioned, as showing the influ-

ence of foreigners. But it is curious to find that the performances were directed by Johann Gottfried Gregorii, the pastor of
the Lutheran church. He not only wrote some of the plays, but
started a theatrical school, where the school-boys of the German
suburb and the sons of some of the chief inhabitants were
taught acting.

One of the most important steps in civilisation introduced
by foreigners was the letter-post. Postal communications had
previously existed in the interior of the country, but, even for
Government purposes, they were very slow, and nearly all letters were sent by private hand, or by a chance messenger. It
was in 1664 that a decree of the Tsar Alexis gave a Swede
named John privileges for the organisation of an international
letter-post, and in 1667 the first postal convention was made
with Poland. John of Sweden was succeeded by Peter Marselis, the Dane, and he by Andrew Vinius, who first received
the title of Postmaster of His Majesty the Tsar, and was ordered
to conclude postal conventions with the neighbouring States.
The institution of the post-office did not please all Russians as
much as it did the foreigners, and, if we may judge from the
continued existence of a censorship, is still looked upon with a
certain degree of suspicion. The Russian political economist,
Iván Pososhkóf, writing in 1701, complains:

'The Germans have cut a hole through from our land into
their own, and from outside people can now, through this hole,
observe all our political and commercial relations. This hole is
the post. Heaven knows whether it brings advantage to the
Tsar, but the harm which it causes to the realm is incalculable.
Everything that goes on in our land is known to the whole
world. The foreigners all become rich by it, the Russians become poor as beggars. The foreigners always know which of
our goods are cheap and which are dear, which are plentiful and
which are scarce. Thereupon they bargain, and know immediately how much they are obliged to pay for our goods. In
this way trade is unequal. Without the post, both sides would
be ignorant of the prices and the stock of goods on hand, and no
party would be injured. Besides, it is a very bad thing that
people know in other countries everything that happens in ours.
This hole, then, should be shut up—that is, the post should be

THE RURAL POST IN RUSSIA.

put an end to ; and, it seems to me, it would be very sensible not to allow letters to be sent, even through messengers, except with a special permission each time from the proper authorities.' [1]

---

[1] A. Brückner, *Culturhistorische Studien*, Riga, 1878 ; Gordon's *Diary ;* Adelung, *Uebersicht der Reisenden in Russland ;* Ustriálof; *Relations of Foreigners about the False Demetrius* (Russian) ; Margeret, *Estat de l' Empire de Russie*, Paris, 1607 ; Herberstein ; Olearius ; Korb ; Collins ; Pososhkóf, *Works* (Russian), Moscow, 1842.

XXII.

WITH very many inhabitants of the German suburb Peter had already made acquaintance at Preobrazhénsky, and as the German suburb lay on the road from Preobrazhénsky to Moscow, it is not improbable that he occasionally halted, from time to time, to say a word to his friends. But his first continued and frequent relations with the foreign quarter began in 1690, and so soon after the death of the Patriarch that it would seem almost as if, in dining with General Gordon on May 10, in the company of his boyárs and courtiers, he was actuated in some degree by a spirit of opposition to the feeling against foreigners then prevalent at court. Gordon says that 'the Tsar was well content,' and this must indeed have been the case. Peter must have found in the hospitality shown to him by a foreigner something new and agreeable, for, from this time, his visits to the German quarter became so frequent that, at one period, he seems almost to have lived there. For a long time his most intimate and trusted friends were foreigners.

The name of General Gordon has already been often mentioned. He was at this time about fifty-five years old, the foreign officer of the greatest experience and the highest position, and, besides this, a man of wide information, of great intelligence, of agreeable manners, shrewd, practical, even canny, and full of good common sense, a devout Catholic, a staunch royalist, in the highest degree loyal, honest and straightforward. Patrick Gordon was one of the well-known and illustrious family of Gordon; by his mother an Ogilvie, a cousin of the first Duke of Gordon, and connected with the Earl of Errol and the Earl of Aberdeen, he was born on the family estate of Auchluchries, in Aberdeenshire, in 1635. His family were staunchly Catholic

and royalist, and in the heat of the Revolution there was no
chance of his receiving an education at the Scotch universities,
or of his making his way in public life, so that, when he was
only sixteen, he resolved on going abroad. Two years he passed
in the Jesuit college at Braunsberg, but the quiet life of the
school not suiting his adventurous spirit, he ran away, with a
few thalers in his pocket, and a change of clothing and three or
four books in his knapsack. After staying a short time at Kulm
and at Posen, he found his way to Hamburg, where he made
the acquaintance of some Scotch officers in the Swedish service,
and was readily persuaded to join them. This was at a time
when very many foreigners, and especially Scotchmen, were
serving in the armies of other countries. This was the era of
soldiers of fortune, of whom Dugald Dalgetty is the type best
known to us, but of whom more honourable examples could be
found. Whether officers or soldiers, they were hired to fight,
and generally fought well during the term of their contract;
but changing masters from time to time was not considered
wrong nor disgraceful, either by them or by the governments
which they served. Gordon, after being twice wounded, was
twice taken prisoner by the Poles. The first time he escaped,
but on the second occasion, as the band with whom he was
caught was accused of robbing a church, he was condemned to
death. He was saved through the intercession of an old Fran-
ciscan monk, and was then persuaded to quit the Swedes and
enter the Polish army. A few months later, in the same year,
1658, he was captured by the Brandenburgers, allies of the
Swedes, and was again persuaded to join the Swedes. Marauding was considered at that time a necessary part of war, and
Gordon succeeded several times in filling well his pockets, of
which he gives an honest and simple account; but he lost everything in a fire, and once was himself robbed. For a while he
found it better to leave the service, and apparently engaged
with some of his friends in marauding on his own account, and
his band of partisans soon became well known through the
whole region. Again he entered the Swedish service, and again,
in November 1658, was taken prisoner by the Poles, who could
not be persuaded to exchange him, and insisted on his again
joining them. He served for some time with the Poles in Little

Russia, and was present in a warm battle with the Russians, where he was wounded. When Charles II. ascended the English throne, Gordon wished to go home to Scotland, but Lubomirsky, the Crown Marshal of Poland, persuaded him to wait a little time, and promoted him to the rank of captain. His father meanwhile wrote to him that there would be little chance for him at home, and, at the same time, he received pressing offers from both the Russians and the Austrians. He decided in favour of the Austrian service, but the negotiations fell through, and he finally made a contract with the Russians for three years. It was only when he had arrived at Moscow that he found that the contract made with the Russian agent was repudiated, and that he would never be allowed to leave the Russian service. For a long time he refused to take the oath, and insisted on the terms of the contract. He finally had to yield. All his efforts to resign and to leave Russia were fruitless, and, apparently, it was not until 1692, when he was already an intimate friend of the Tsar, that he entirely gave up the idea of ending his days in Scotland. Once settled in Moscow, he found his best chance for promotion lay in marrying, and thus showing his interest in the country. He did good service in the Russian army wherever he was placed—in Little Russia, at Kíef, at the siege of Tchigirín, and in the Crimean expeditions. He had long enjoyed the confidence of the Government, and was in intimate social relations with the chief Russian boyárs. Once, on account of his influential royalist connections, he had been sent to England on a diplomatic mission, to present a letter of the Tsar Alexis to King Charles II. with reference to the privileges of the English merchants, and twice he had been allowed to go to Scotland for personal reasons, but his wife and children were on each occasion kept as hostages for his return.

Gordon's travels had brought him into connection with many great personages of the time. He had known personally Charles II. and James II., and had been presented to Queen Christina after she had left Sweden. Greatly interested in foreign politics, he everywhere had friends and acquaintances, from whom he received news, gossip, wine, scientific instruments and books —whether ' Quarle's Emblems,' or treatises on fortification or pyrotechny. With all his friends, with his relations in Scotland, Lord Melfort at Rome, ambassadors and Jesuits at Vienna, officers in Poland and at Riga, and with merchants everywhere, he kept up a constant correspondence. There was not a post-day that he did not receive many letters, and send off an equal number. Of many of these he kept copies. One day there is an entry in his diary of his despatching twenty-six letters.

His carefully kept diary, in which he set down the occurrences of the day—telling of his doings, the people he had met and talked with, his debts and expenses, the money he had lent, his purchases of wine and beer, his difficulties about his pay— is invaluable to the student of the political as well as of the economical history of Russia.[1]

In September 1690, the Tsar, attended by his suite, dined with General Lefort. This was the first time that Peter had visited a man whose acquaintance he had made not long before, who was soon to become his most intimate friend, and to exercise great influence over him. Franz Lefort was born at Geneva in 1656, of a good family (originally from Italy), which has kept a prominent position in Genevese society and politics until the present time. His father was a well-to-do merchant, and his elder brother, Ami, was one of the syndics of the town. At this time Geneva had become rich, and was developing a certain amount of frivolity and luxury. The old Calvinistic habits were being corrupted by dancing and card-playing. Paris was looked upon as the home of the arts and graces, of culture and of pleasure, and the youths of Geneva took the Parisians as their model. The schools of Geneva were famous, and the Protestant princes and aristocracy of Germany frequently sent their sons to finish their education in this Protestant stronghold. Without neglecting the solid studies they could learn French, and, at a time when the wars made visiting Paris impossible, could learn too French politeness and manners, fencing, dancing and riding, and the exercises of a gentleman, and prepare

---

[1] This diary of General Gordon, which is written in English in six large quarto volumes, is preserved in the archives at St. Petersburg. Unfortunately, some parts are missing, notably from 1667–1677, and from 1678–1684. A German translation, in some places altered, was published by Posselt, 1849–1852, and a few extracts are printed from the original manuscript in ' Passages from the Diary of General Patrick Gordon,' published by the Spalding Club at Aberdeen in 1859.

themselves for holding their little courts in rivalry of Louis XIV.

These princes had sometimes as many as a dozen gentlemen, comrades and retainers, with them, and some of the Lutheran princes brought a style of life not at all in harmony with the strict Puritanical and Calvinistic manners of the place. Much as the solid burghers of Geneva objected to the contamination to which their sons were exposed by mingling with this gay and worldly society, yet they had too much respect for the persons of the princes to take very strong measures, and perhaps, by their too great deference, increased the pretensions of the young men and the admiration they excited. The record books of the consistory are full of complaints against the princes and their followers, but they display at times the other side. The Prince of Hasse-Cassel and the Prince of Curland complained against some clergymen, who, they said, had by their remonstrances prevented a dancing party at the house of Count Dohna (then the owner of the château of Coppet, which was afterward to be known as the residence of Madame de Staël), and had thus deprived them of an evening's enjoyment. The Council recommended that more respect should be paid to people of such position. Between 1670 and 1675, no less than twenty princes of reigning families—in the Palatinate, Würtemburg, Anhalt, Anspach, Brandenburg, Brunswick, Holstein, Saxony, Saxe-Gotha, &c. &c.—were receiving their education at Geneva, to say nothing of the lesser nobility. Lefort, whose instincts had already taught him to rebel against the strict discipline of Calvinism, had, by his amiability and his good manners, become an intimate member of this society. It can easily be understood that late suppers, card-playing, and worldly conversation did not increase any desire for following the sober life of a merchant recommended to him by his family. To get him away from temptation, he was sent as clerk to a merchant in Marseilles, but this in the end did not suit him, and he returned home. Partly from his own feelings, partly from the example of the society which he frequented, he had a great inclination to enter the military service and see a little of war. This, besides being against the laws and policy of Geneva, was looked upon with horror by his family, who did all in their power to

prevent him; but he finally extorted their consent, and went to
Holland to take part in the war then going on in the Low Countries. He was provided with a letter of introduction to the
hereditary Prince of Curland from his brother, whose friend he
had been at Geneva, and served as a volunteer with him, although, through the intrigues of the Curland officers, he never
succeeded in obtaining a commission. Finally, seeing no chance
of promotion, he left the prince, and was persuaded to enter
the Russian service with the rank of captain. Arriving in Russia in 1675, he did not succeed in getting the position he desired, and lived for two years at Moscow as an idler in the German suburb, where he enjoyed the friendship and protection of
some of the more distinguished members of the colony. At one
time, he even acted as a secretary for the Danish Resident, and
intended to leave Russia with him. At last he entered the
Russian service, and, like most other officers who wished to secure their position, married. His wife was a connection of
General Gordon. His personal qualities brought him to the
notice of Prince Basil Golítsyn, who protected and advanced
him. His promotion was to some extent, perhaps, due to the
interest taken in him by the Senate of Geneva, which, on his
suggestion, addressed to Prince Golítsyn a letter in his behalf.
After serving through the two Crimean campaigns, he went to
Tróïtsa, along with the other foreign officers, at the time of the
downfall of Sophia, and was shortly afterward, on the birth of
the Tsarévitch Alexis, promoted to be major-general.

At this time about thirty-five years old, Lefort was in all
the strength of his manhood. He had a good figure, was very
tall—nearly as tall as Peter himself, but a little stouter—had
regular features, a good forehead, and rather large and expressive eyes. He was a perfect master of knightly and cavalier
exercises, could shoot the bow so as to vie with the Tartars of
the Crimea, and was a good dancer. He had received a fair
education and had a good mind, although he was brilliant
rather than solid, and shone more in the *salon* than in the camp
or the council-chamber. His integrity, his adherence to his
Protestant principles and morality, his affection for his family,
and especially for his mother, command our respect. What
endeared him to all his friends was his perfect unselfishness,

frankness and simplicity, his geniality and readiness for amusement, and the winning grace of his manners.

It is not astonishing that the Tsar found Lefort not only a
contrast to the Russians by whom he was surrounded, but also,
in certain ways, to the more solid but less personally attractive
representatives of the foreign colony, such as Van Keller and
Gordon. To Gordon, Peter went for advice, to Lefort for
sympathy.

From this time on, Peter became daily more intimate with
Lefort. He dined with him two or three times a week, and
demanded his presence daily, so that Butenant, Sennebier, and
all who wrote to Geneva, spoke of the high position which
Lefort held, and his nephew, the young Peter Lefort, complained that he was rarely able to talk to his uncle, even about
business, as he was constantly in the company of the Tsar.
The letters written by Lefort to Peter, on the two or three
occasions when they were separated from each other, show
what a merry boon companion he was. At the same time, no
one, except Catherine, was able to give Peter so much sympathy, and so thoroughly to enter into his plans. Lefort alone
had enough influence over him to soothe his passions, and to
prevent the consequences of his sudden outbursts of anger.
While Lefort was in no way greedy or grasping, his material
interests were well looked after by his royal friend. His debts
were paid, a house was built for him, presents of all kinds were
given to him, and he was rapidly raised in grade, first to lieu-
tenant-general, then to full general, commander of the first
regiment, admiral and ambassador. Peter, too, entered into
correspondence with the Senate of Geneva, in order to give
testimony at Lefort's home of the esteem in which he held
him.

In a society which included such men as Lefort and Gordon,
Van Keller, and Butenant Von Rosenbusch—the Dutch and
Danish envoys—and representatives of such good and well-
known names as Leslie, Crawfuird, Menzies, Graham, Bruce,
Drummond, Montgomery, Hamilton and Dalziel, not to men
tion the eminent Dutch merchants, it was natural that Peter
should find many persons whose conversation was interesting
and useful to him. His chief friends, however, among the

COMPANIONS OF PETER.

1. PRINCE GREGORY DOLGORUKY.
2. PRINCE NIKITA REPNINE.
3. PRINCE WILLIAM DOLGORUKY.
4. PRINCE RAMODANOFSKY.
5. COUNT THEODORE APRAXIN.
6. PRINCE IVAN TROUBETSKOY.
7. ANDREW MATVEIEF.
8. PRINCE BORIS KURAKIN.

foreigners were Von Mengden, the colonel, and Adam Weyde, the major of the Preobrazhénsky regiment, in which Peter served as a sergeant, Ysbrandt Ides, who was soon sent on a mission to China, Colonel Chambers, Captain Jacob Bruce and Andrew Crafft, the English translator of the foreign office— with all of whom he was in constant communication, and with whom, during his absences, he frequently exchanged letters. But a surer friend and assistant, and a more constant corre- spondent, was Andrew Vinius, the son of a Dutch merchant, who had established iron-works in Russia during the time of the Tsar Michael. His mother was a Russian. He therefore knew Russian well, and was educated in the Russian religion. He had served at first in the ministry of foreign affairs, but during the latter years of Alexis, had been given charge of the post-office.

Peter's Russian friends were chiefly the comrades and com- panions of his childhood, most of whom held honorary posi- tions at court. Such were Prince Theodore Troekúrof, Theo- dore Plestchéief, Theodore Apráxin, Gabriel Golófkin, Prince Iván Trubetskóy, Prince Boris Kurákin, Prince Nikíta Répnin, Andrew Matvéief, and Artémon Golovín. Most of these showed by their after life that they had been educated in the same school with Peter. To these should be added a few young men who had served in his play-regiments, and who occupied positions in the nature of adjutants, or orderlies, such as Lúkin and Vorónin. There were besides, a few men far older than Peter, who were personally attached to him, and nearly always with him. Such were Prince Boris Golítsyn, the two Dolgorúkys, Iván Buturlín, Prince Theodore Ramo- danófsky, his early teacher Zótof, and Tikhon Stréshnef, the head of the expeditionary department. There is something a little curious in the relation of these older men to Peter. They served him faithfully, and were on occasion put forward as figure-heads, without exercising any real authority. To most of them, also, Peter, in his sportive moments, had given nick- names, and both he and they always used these nicknames in their correspondence. Thus, Zótof was called the 'Prince Pope,' from a masquerade procession in which he officiated in this way, surrounded by a band of bishops, priests and deacons ;

and frequently too, in masquerading attire, he and his troop of singers went about at Christmas-tide to sing carols. The Boyár Iván Buturlín, perhaps the oldest of them all, was given the title of ' The Polish King,' because, in one of the military manœuvres of which we shall speak presently, he had that title as the head of the enemy's army. Prince Ramodanófsky, the other generalissimo, got the nickname of ' Prince Cæsar,' and is nearly always addressed by Peter in his letters as ' Majesty,' or ' Min Her Kenich' (My Lord King). Stréshnef, in the same way, was always called ' Holy Father.'

These, with many more of the younger court officials, Timmermann and a few others, formed the so-called ' company,' which went about everywhere with Peter, and feasted with him in the German suburb, and with the Russian magnates. The ' company' went to many Russian houses, as well as among the Germans. Leo Narýshkin was always glad to see his royal nephew at his lovely villa of Pokrófskoe or Phíli. A splendid church built in 1693, in the choir of which Peter sometimes sang, still attests his magnificence, and the fact that it was here that Prince Kutúzof decided on the abandonment of Moscow to the French in 1812, adds yet more to the interest of the place. Close by is the still lovely Kúntsovo, then inhabited by Peter's grandfather, the old Cyril Narýshkin. Prince Boris Golítsyn, who was much more than the drunkard De Neuville tells us of, frequently showed his hospitality. Sheremétief received them at Kúskovo, and the Sóltykofs, Apráxins, and Matvéiefs were not behindhand.

What especially attracted Peter and his friends to the German suburb was the social life there, so new to them and so different from that in the Russian circles. There was plainly a higher culture; there was more refinement and less coarseness in the amusements. The conversation touched foreign politics and the events of the day, and was not confined to a recapitulation of orgies and to loose talk—for we know only too well what the ordinary talk at Russian banquets was at that time. There was novelty and attraction in the occasional presence of ladies, in the masking, the dancing, the family feasts of all kinds, the weddings, baptisms, and even funerals. In many of these Peter took part. He held Protestant and Catholic children at the

THE STONE JUG.

font, he acted as best man at the marriages of merchants'
daughters, he soon became an accomplished dancer, and was
always very fond of a sort of country-dance known as the
'Grossvater.' When, too, did any Russian lose a chance of practising a foreign language which he could already speak?

Dinner was about noon, and the feast was frequently prolonged till late in the night—sometimes even till the next morning. Naturally, even in German houses at this epoch, there
was excessive drinking. Gordon constantly speaks of it in his
diary, and not unseldom he was kept in his bed for days in consequence of these bouts. He, however, suffered from a constitutional derangement of his digestion. Peter seemed generally
none the worse for it, and Lefort, we know by the account of
Blomberg, could drink a great quantity without showing it.
The consumption of liquors must have been very great, for
when Peter came to dine he frequently brought eighty or ninety
guests with him, and a hundred servants. Lefort, in one of his
letters, speaks of having in the house three thousand thalers'
worth of wine, which would last only for two or three months.
Judging from the prices paid by Gordon for his wine—his
'canary sect,' his 'perniak,' his 'white hochlands wine,' and his
Spanish wine—this would represent now a sum of about $25,-
000. It is not to be supposed that, because so much liquor was
used, the company was constantly intoxicated. Brandy and
whisky were drunk only before or between meals; the greatest
consumption was probably of beer and of the weak Russian
drinks, mead and *kvas.* A dinner with some rich provincial
merchant, or a day with some hospitable landed proprietor in
the south of Russia, would give us typical examples of the heroic meals Peter and his friends enjoyed, with their caviare and
raw herring, their cabbage and beet-root soup, their iced *bat-
vinia* and *okróshka,* the sucking pig stuffed with buckwheat, the
fish pasty, the salted cucumbers and the sweets. The guests did
not sit at the table guzzling the whole day long. There were
intervals for smoking, and the Russians enjoyed the interdicted
tobacco. There were games at bowls and nine-pins, there were
matches in archery and musket practice. Healths were proposed and speeches made, attended with salvos of artillery and
blasts of trumpets. A band of German musicians played at

intervals during the feasts, and in the evening there were exhi-
bitions of fireworks out-of-doors, and there was dancing in-doors.
Lefort, in a letter describing one of these nights, says that half
the company slept while the rest danced.

Such feasts as these, so troublesome and so expensive, were
a burden to any host, and we know that Van Keller, and even
Gordon, were glad to have them over. When Peter had got
into the habit of dining with his friends at Lefort's two or three
times a week, it was impossible for Lefort, with his narrow
means, to support the expense, and the cost was defrayed by
Peter himself. Lefort's house was small, and although a large
addition was made to it, yet it was even then insufficient to accommodate the number of guests, who at times, exceeded two
hundred. Peter therefore built for him, at least nominally, a
new and handsome house, magnificently furnished, with one
banqueting hall large enough to accommodate fifteen hundred
guests. Although Lefort was called the master of the house,
yet it was, in reality, a sort of club-house for Peter's 'company.'
During the absence of Peter, and even of Lefort, it was not
uncommon for those of the 'company' remaining at Moscow to
dine, sup, and pass the night there.

Peter and his friends entered with readiness into the Teutonic custom of masquerading, with which, according to the
ruder habits of that time, were joined much coarse horse-play,
buffoonery, and practical joking. Together with his comrades,
Peter went from house to house during the Christmas holidays,
sang carols, and did not disdain to accept the usual gifts. In
fact, if these were not forthcoming, revenge was taken on the
householder. Korb, the Austrian Secretary—for these sports
were kept up even in 1699—says in his diary :—

'A sumptuous comedy celebrates the time of Our Lord's
nativity. The chief Muscovites, at the Tsar's choice, shine in
various sham ecclesiastical dignities. One represents the Patriarch, others metropolitans, archimandrites, popes, deacons, sub-
deacons, &c. Each, according to whichever denomination of
these the Tsar has given him, has to put on the vestments
that belong to it. The scenic Patriarch, with his sham metropolitans, and the rest in eighty sledges, and to the number of
two hundred, makes the round of the city of Moscow and the

German suburb, ensigned with crosier, mitre, and other insignia of his assumed dignity. They all stop at the houses of the richer Muscovites and German officers, and sing the praises of the new-born Deity, in strains for which the inhabitants have to pay dearly. After they had sung the praises of the new-born Deity at his house, General Lefort recreated them all with pleasanter music, banqueting, and dancing.

'The wealthiest merchant of Muscovy, whose name is Filadílof, gave such offence by having only presented two rubles to the Tsar and his boyárs, who sang the praises of God, new-born, at his house, that the Tsar, with all possible speed, sent off a hundred of the populace to the house of that merchant, with a mandate to forthwith pay to every one of them a ruble each. But Prince Tcherkásky, whom they had nicknamed the richest rustic, was rendered more prudent by what befell his neighbour: in order not to merit the Tsar's anger, he offered a thousand rubles to the mob of singers. It behooved the Germans to make show of equal readiness. Everywhere they keep the table laid ready with cold viands, not to be found unprepared.'

Gordon, during all these years, always mentions at Christmas-tide the companies of carol singers, among whom may be particularly remarked Alexis Menshikóf and his brother. On one occasion he says: 'I paid them two rubles, which was half too much'

Once Peter appeared at Lefort's with a suite of twenty-four dwarfs, all 'of remarkable beauty,' and all on horseback ; and a few days after, Peter and Lefort rode out into the country to exercise this miniature cavalry. In 1695, the court fool, Jacob Turgénief, was married to the wife of a scribe. The wedding took place in a tent erected in the fields between Preobrazhénsky and Seménofsky. There was a great banquet, which lasted three days, and the festivities were accompanied by processions, in which the highest of the Russian nobles appeared in ridiculous costumes, in cars drawn by cows, goats, dogs, and even swine. Turgénief and his wife at one time rode in the best velvet carriage of the court, with such grandees as the Golítsyns, Sheremétiefs, and Trubetskóys following them on foot. In the triumphal entry into Moscow, the newly married pair rode a camel, and Gordon remarks: 'The procession was ex-

traordinary fine.' Although the jesting here was perfectly
good-natured, yet it may have been carried a little too far,
for a few days after poor Turgénief died suddenly in the
night.[1]

---

[1] Gordon's *Diary ;* Posselt, *Lefort ;* Ustriálof, II. iv. ; Brückner, *Peter der Grosse ;* Korb, *Diary of an Austrian Secretary of Legation,* translated by Count MacDonnell, London, 1863.

XXIII.

For fully five years Peter left the government to be carried on by his ministers, who managed affairs in the good, old-fashioned Russian way. During the whole of this time not a single important law was passed, nor a decree made with regard to any matter of public welfare. Peter neither interested himself in the internal affairs of the country nor in the increasing difficulties with Poland, and the need of repressing the incursions of the Tartars. In spite of his years, his size, and his strength, he was nothing but a boy, and acted like a boy. He devoted himself entirely to amusement, to carousing with his 'company,' to indulging his mechanical tastes, to boat-building, and to mimic war. He had no inclination toward the more brutal pastimes so much enjoyed by the old Tsars, but, at the same time, he had no taste for horsemanship or field sports, and did not care for the chase, either with dogs or falcons. Sokólniki, with its hunting-lodge, fell into decay. Its name still recalls the falconers of old, but the May-day festival now held there, with the outspread tents, which bear the appellation of 'the German camp,' takes us back to Peter and the German suburb.

During the 'Butter-Week' or carnival of 1690, Peter gave on the banks of the river Présna, in honour of the birth of his son Alexis, a display of fireworks, made in part by himself—the first at that time seen in Moscow, for previously he had confined his experiments to Preobrazhénsky. These displays were not always unattended with danger. A five-pound rocket, instead of bursting in the air, came down on the head of a gentleman, and killed him on the spot; at another time, an explosion of the material wounded Franz Timmermann and Captain

Strasburg, son-in-law of General Gordon, and killed three work-men. As soon as the river Moskvá had got clear of ice, Peter organised a flotilla of small row-boats, and going aboard of his yacht (the same which he had found at Ismaílovo), sailed with a company of boyárs and courtiers down the river as far as the monastery of St. Nicholas of Ugrétch, and spent some days feasting in the neighbourhood. He no sooner returned to Moscow than he prepared for some military manœuvres, and stormed the palace at Seménofsky. Hand-grenades and fire-pots were freely used, but even when slightly charged or made of pasteboard these were dangerous missiles, and by the burst-ing of one of them the Tsar and several of his officers were injured. Peter's wounds were probably not light, for he ceased

Model of a Ship Built by Peter. From the Marine Museum, St. Petersburg.

his amusements, and appeared rarely in public from June until September, when other mock combats were fought between the guards and various regiments of Streltsi. In one of these Gen-eral Gordon was wounded in the thigh, and had his face so severely burnt that he was kept a week in bed.

The following summer was passed in much the same way. At the opening of navigation, a new yacht, built by Peter's own unassisted hands, was launched on the Moskvá, and again there was a merry excursion to the monastery of Ugrétch, in spite of stormy weather. Military exercises then continued all the sum-mer at Preobrazhénsky, and a grand sham battle was ordered. This was postponed for two months on account of the serious illness of the Tsaritsa Natalia, and took place only in the month of October. Two armies were engaged; the Russian, consisting

THE PROCESSION IN HONOR OF THE PERSIAN AMBASSADORS.

chiefly of Peter's play troops, or guards, commanded by Prince
Theodore Ramodanófsky, to whom was given the title of the
Generalissimo Frederick, was matched against the Streltsi under Generalissimo Buturlín. The fight lasted five days, and
resulted in the victory of the Russian army, though not without disaster, for Prince Iván Dolgorúky died, as Gordon says,
'of a shot got nine days before, in the right arm, at the field
ballet military.'

Tired of his soldiers, Peter again turned to his boats, and at
the end of November 1691, went to Lake Plestchéief, where he
had not been for more than two years. He remained there a
fortnight, in a small palace built for him on the shore of the
lake, a mile and a half from Pereyaslávl. It was a small, one-
story, wooden house, with windows of mica, engraved with different ornaments, the doors covered for warmth with white felt,
and on the roof a two-headed eagle, surmounted by a gilt crown.
During the course of the next year he visited the lake four
times, on two occasions staying more than a month. He occupied himself with building a ship, as he had been ordered to
do by ' His Majesty ' the generalissimo, Prince Ramodanófsky,
and worked so zealously that he was unwilling to return to
Moscow for the reception of the Persian ambassador, and it
was necessary for Leo Naryshkin and Prince Boris Golítsyn to
go expressly to Pereyaslávl to show him the importance of returning for the reception, in order not to offend the Shah. Two
days after, he went back to his work, and invited the ' company' to the launch. Only one thing remained to complete his
satisfaction, and that was the presence of his family. His
mother, sister, and wife finally went to Pereyaslávl in August
1692, with the whole court, and remained there a month, apparently with great enjoyment. Troops came up from Moscow, and the whole time was spent in banquets, in parties on
the water, and in military and naval manœuvres. The Tsaritsa
Natalia even celebrated her name's-day there, and did not return to Moscow until September, ill and fatigued with this un-
accustomed life.

Her illness soon passed over, but Peter was seized with a
violent attack, from his too hard work and his over indulgence
in dissipation. In November, he was taken down with a dysen-

tery which kept him in bed for six weeks. At one time his
life was despaired of. It is reported that his favourites were
aghast, as they felt confident that in case of his death Sophia
would again ascend the throne, and that nothing but exile or
the scaffold awaited them ; and it is said that Prince Boris
Golítsyn, Apráxin, and Plestchéief had horses ready, in order,
in case of emergency, to flee from Moscow. Toward Christmas,
Peter began to mend, and by the middle of February 1693, although still not entirely recovered, was able to go about the
city, and, in the quality of best man, invite guests to the marriage of a German gold-worker. In the same capacity, he took
upon himself the ordering of the marriage feast and plied the
company well with drink, although he himself drank little.
Apparently from this illness date the fits of melancholy, the
convulsive movements of the muscles, and the sudden outbursts
of passionate anger with which Peter was so sadly afflicted.

During the carnival, the Tsar again gave an exhibition of
fireworks on the banks of the Présna. After a thrice-repeated
salute of fifty-six guns, a flag of white flame appeared, bearing on
it in Dutch letters the monogram of the generalissimo, Prince
Ramodanófsky, and afterward was seen a fiery Hercules tear-
ing apart the jaws of a lion. The fireworks were followed by
a supper, which lasted till three hours after midnight. The
Tsaritsa was so pleased with the fiery Hercules that she presented her son—the master fire-worker—with the full uniform
of a sergeant of the Preobrazhénsky regiment.

As soon as the carnival was over, Peter went again to Pereyaslávl, where he stayed at work during the whole of Lent,
and in May went there again, and sailed for two weeks on the
lake. This was his last visit, for he soon went to a larger field
of operations, on the White Sea, and visited Pereyaslávl only
in passing from Moscow to Archangel, and again before the
Azof campaign, to get the artillery material stowed there.
After that, he was not there again for twenty-five years—until
1722, when on his road to Persia. He then lamented over
the rotten and neglected ships, and gave strict instructions that
the remnants of them should be carefully preserved. These
orders were not obeyed, and of the whole flotilla on Lake
Plestchéief there now exists only one small boat, which was

preserved by the peasants, and since 1803 has been kept in a special building, under the direction of the local nobility, guarded by retired sailors. There remains nothing else but the name of the Church of Our Lady at the Ships, and a festival on the sixth Sunday after Easter, in commemoration of Peter's launch, when all the clergy of Pereyaslávl, attended by throng of people, sail on a barge to the middle of the lake, and bless the waters.

The revival of Peter's interest in boat-building and navigation was probably due in part to the conversations which he had heard among his foreign friends. He had dined with the Dutch Resident, Van Keller, in June 1691, and both from him and from the Dutch merchants whom he was constantly meeting he heard expressions of joy that the commercial intercourse between Archangel and Holland, which had been interrupted for two years by the French cruisers, had at last been renewed. All the goods had been detained at Archangel, and there had been a general stagnation of trade; but now that the Dutch had sent a convoy into the North Sea, several merchant vessels had safely reached their destination. Together with this news, came the intelligence that the richly laden Dutch fleet from Smyrna had also arrived at Amsterdam, without mishap. About the same time, Peter had received from Nicholas Witsen, the Burgomaster of Amsterdam—who had been in Russia years before, and had written a very remarkable book, the 'Description of North and East Tartary,'—a letter, urging the importance of the trade with China and Persia, and suggesting means for its advancment. It was in consequence of this letter that Ysbrandt Ides was sent on a mission to China, and this, together with the talk about the Dutch trade, had doubtless given Peter some new ideas of the importance to the country of commerce, and of its protection by ships of war. In the despatches which Van Keller wrote about Peter's occupations on Lake Plestchéief, he remarks : ' The Tsar seems to take into consideration commerce as well as war.' Subsequently he mentions the proposed sham-fight, but says that the people of Moscow augured no good of it. After reporting that he had informed Peter of the great victory which King William and the English fleet had obtained over the French at La Hogue, he says that Peter desired to see the original despatch, and had it translated; 'Whereupon it followed that his Tsarish Majesty, leaping up and shouting for joy, ordered his new ships to fire a salute.' In another despatch, he wrote that this young hero often expressed the great desire that possessed him to take part in the campaign against the French under King William, or to give him assistance by sea.[1]

---

[1] Soloviéf, xiv. ; Ustriálof, II. v. ; Brückner, *Peter der Grosse;* Gordon's *Diary;* Posselt, *Lefort;* Kochen's Despatches in *Russian Antiquity* (Russian), for 1878 ; Reports of Dutch residents in archives at the Hague.

XXIV.

No doubt the English victory at La Hogue, and the revival of the trade with Holland, had much to do with Peter's visit to Archangel. He himself, writing long afterward, when he was, perhaps unconsciously, inclined to magnify the importance of his early doings, says, in the preface to the Maritime Regulations:

'For some years I had the fill of my desires on Lake Pereyaslávl, but finally it got too narrow for me. I then went to the Kúbensky Lake, but that was too shallow. I then decided to see the open sea, and began often to beg the permission of my mother to go to Archangel. She forbade me such a dangerous journey, but seeing my great desire and my unchangeable longing, allowed it in spite of herself.'

Although the Tsaritsa Natalia allowed her son to visit Archangel and the White Sea, she exacted a promise from him that he would not go out upon the sea, and would look at it only from the shore.

Peter set out from Moscow on July 11, 1693, with a suite of over a hundred persons, including Lefort and many of the 'company,' his physician, Dr. Van der Hulst, a priest, eight singers, two dwarfs, forty Streltsi, and ten of his guards.

The journey from Moscow to Archangel was, till a few years since, performed in much the same way as it was by Peter. A railway is now substituted for the carriage-road to Vológda, but from that town one must go by water down the Súkhon and the Dvína. With the high water of spring, it is easy enough, but the rivers were then so low that Peter's huge painted barge was two weeks on the way before it arrived at the wharf of Holmogóry, to the ringing of the cathedral bells.

Holmogóry was then the administrative centre for the north of
Russia, and it was necessary to do the usual courtesies to the
Voievóde and the Archbishop, before the Tsar could pass the long
and narrow town of Archangel, stretching along the right bank
of the Dvína, with its clean German suburb and its port of
Solombála, crowded then, as now, with merchants, and take up
his residence beyond the city, in a house prepared for him on
the Moses Island.   The salt smell of the sea was grateful and
exciting, and the day after his arrival he went on board the
little yacht 'St. Peter,' which had been built for him, and, in
spite of the promise to his mother, anxiously waited for a
favourable wind to carry him to sea.   A proposed visit to the
Solovétsky monastery was postponed to another year, for
various English and Dutch vessels were about sailing, and he
was anxious to visit them, and to convoy them on their way.   In
about a week, on August 16, a fair wind arose, the ships set out,
and Peter sailed on merrily in his yacht; he had gone two
hundred miles from Archangel, and was near the Polar Ocean,
before he realised that it was full time to return.   On arriving
at Archangel, five days afterward, his first care was to write to
his mother, that he had been to sea and had safely returned.
Meanwhile she had written to him, urging his return.   In reply
to this letter, he said:

'Thou hast written, O lady! that I have saddened thee by
not writing of my arrival.   But even now I have no time to
write in detail, because I am expecting some ships, and as soon
as they come—when no one knows, but they are expected soon,
as they are more than three weeks from Amsterdam—I shall
come to thee immediately, travelling day and night.   But I beg
thy mercy for one thing : why dost thou trouble thyself about
me?   Thou hast deigned to write that thou hast given me into
the care of the Virgin.   When thou hast such a guardian for
me, why dost thou grieve ?'

This letter was preceded to Moscow by the news that Peter
had gone on a sea journey.   Everyone was alarmed at an event,
the like of which had never happened before in Russia, and
magnified the dangers to which the Tsar had been, or might
be, exposed.   Natalia wrote again to her son, urging his return,
expressing joy at his not being shipwrecked, and reminding him

that he had promised not to go to sea. She even had a letter written in the name of his little son Alexis, then only three years old, begging him to come back. To this he replied:

'By thy letter I see, Oh! Oh! that thou hast been mightily grieved, and why? If thou art grieved, what delight have I? I beg thee make my wretched self happy by not grieving about me, for in very truth I cannot endure it.'

Again, on September 18, he writes:

'Thou hast deigned to write to me, O my delight! to say that I should write to thee oftener. Even now I write by every post, and my only fault is that I do not come myself. And thou also tellest me not to get ill by too quick a journey. But I, thank God! shall try not to get ill, except by coming too quickly. But thou makest me ill by thy grief, and the Hamburg ships have not yet arrived.'

It was not merely curiosity to see the Hamburg ships that kept Peter at Archangel. Ever since the discovery of the White Sea by Richard Chancellor, in 1553, and the privileges given to the English factory by Iván the Terrible, and Philip and Mary, Archangel had become the great emporium for Russian commerce with the West. The business of Nóvgorod had been greatly injured by the loss of its independence and the misfortunes which befell the town, and its trade was now chiefly transferred to Archangel. During the summer months, that town, conveniently situated at the mouth of the river Dvína, presented a spectacle of great commercial activity. At the time of the annual fair of the Assumption, as many as a hundred ships, from England, Holland, Hamburg, and Bremen, could be seen in the river, with cargoes of various descriptions of foreign goods, while huge Russian barges brought hemp, grain, potash, tar, tallow, Russian leather, isinglass and caviare down the Dvína. For caviare there was a great market in Italy, and several cargoes were sent every year to Leghorn. The foreign merchants who lived in Moscow, Yarosláv, and Vológda went to Archangel with the opening of the navigation every spring, and stayed there until winter. Twenty-four large houses were occupied by foreign families and the agents of foreign merchants. Depôts for all the goods sent to Archangel, both Russian and foreign, had been built by the foreigners Marselis and Scharff, at the command of the Tsar Alexis, and were protected by a high stone wall and towers. Trade had now revived, and, in the summer of 1693, ships were constantly arriving, and Archangel was alive with business. On the wharfs and at the exchange, Peter could meet merchants of every nationality, and see cargoes of almost every kind. It was a grief to him that among all these ships there were none belonging to Russians, nor any sailing under the Russian flag. The efforts of the Russians to export their own produce had never been successful. At Nóvgorod there had been a league among all the merchants of the Hanse Towns to prevent the competition of Russian merchants, and to buy Russian goods only at Nóvgorod. At a later time, an enterprising merchant of Yarosláv, Anthony Láptef, took a cargo of furs to Amsterdam, but, in consequence of a cabal against him, he could not sell a single skin, and was obliged to carry his furs back to Archangel, where they were at once bought, at a good price, by the Dutch merchants who owned the vessel which brought them home.

Peter resolved to do something for Russian trade, and gave orders to Apráxin, whom he named Governor of Archangel, to fit out two vessels at the only Russian shipyard, that of the brothers Bazhénin, on the little river Vavtchúga, near Holmogóry. These were to take cargoes of Russian goods, and to sail under the Russian flag. He hesitated where to send them. In England and Holland he feared the opposition of the native merchants, and in France he was afraid that due respect might not be given to the Russian flag. It was at last resolved to send them to France, but as they finally sailed under the Dutch, and not under the Russian flag, one of them was confiscated by the French, and was the subject of long dispute.

Archangel proved so interesting that Peter decided to return there in the subsequent year, and to take a trip on the Northern Ocean. He even had vague ideas of coasting along Siberia until he came to China, but the North-east passage was not to be effected until our own day. For any purpose of this kind, his little yacht 'St. Peter' was too small, and he, therefore, with his own hands, laid the keel of a large vessel at Archangel, and ordered another full-rigged forty-four-gun frigate to be bought in Holland. The Burgomaster of Amsterdam, Nicholas Witsen, through Lefort and Vinius, was entrusted with the purchase.

While at Archangel, besides the time which he gave to the study of commerce and ship-building, Peter found leisure for inspecting various industries, and for practising both at the forge and at the lathe. A chandelier made of walrus teeth, turned by him, hangs now over his tomb in the Cathedral of St. Peter and St. Paul, at St. Petersburg, and carved work in bone and wood, and iron bars forged by him at this time, are shown in many places. Besides the social pleasures, the balls and dinners, in which he indulged at Archangel as much as at Moscow, he frequently attended the neighbouring church of the Prophet Elijah, where he himself read the epistle, sang with the choir, and made great friends with the Archbishop Athanasius, a learned and sensible man, with whom, after dinner, he conversed about affairs of state, the boyárs, the peasants who were there for work, the construction of houses and the foundation of factories, as well as of ship-building and navigation.

After the short summer was over, the Hamburg ships having long since arrived, Peter started on his homeward journey, and after stopping for a short time at the saw-mills and wharfs of the brothers Bazhénin, on the Vavtchúga, arrived at Moscow on October 11. It was too late in the season at that time to think of any military manœuvres, and Peter had settled down to his usual round of carouses and merry-making, when suddenly, on February 4, 1694, after an illness of only five days, the Tsaritsa Natalia died, at the age of forty-two.

For some reason or other, Peter preferred not to be present at his mother's death-bed. A dispute with the Patriarch had probably something to do with it. It is said that when Peter had been suddenly called from Preobrazhénsky to the Krémlin, to his mother's bedside, he appeared in the foreign clothes which he wore for riding, and that the Patriarch remonstrated with him. Peter angrily replied that, as the head of the church, he should have weightier things to attend to, than to meddle with the business of tailors. General Gordon says:

' His Majesty had promised to come to me to a farewell supper and ball. I went to the palace two hours before daybreak,

but did not find His Majesty, on account of the evident danger
in which his mother was.   He had taken leave of her, and had
gone back to his house at Preobrazhénsky, whither I hastened,
and found him in the highest degree melancholy and dejected.
Toward eight o'clock came the news that the Tsaritsa was dead.'

   Peter's grief was great and sincere.   For several days he
scarcely saw any one without bursting into a fit of weeping.
He had tenderly loved his mother, and had been much under
her influence, although she had opposed his desire for novelty
and his inclination toward foreigners.   Her place in his affections was, to a great extent, taken by his sister Natalia, who,
without understanding his objects, at least sympathized with
him.   She was of the younger generation, not so averse to
what was new or what came from abroad, was readily influenced
by her brother, and, like a good and faithful sister, loved and
admired him, and was always ready to believe that whatever
he did was the best thing possible.   As to his wife Eudoxia, it
is difficult to say much.   She had been brought up in the old-
fashioned Russian way, and had received almost no education.
She had a bitter dislike to all that was foreign, and to the
friends by whom Peter was surrounded.   This was perhaps
natural : she disliked the men, who, as she thought, alienated
her husband from her.   The marriage had not been one of
love ; Peter had married simply to obey his mother, and found
the society of his wife so uncongenial that he spent very little
time with her.   Two children had been the result of the marriage—one, Alexis, born in March, 1690, was destined to inherit something of his mother's nature and to be a difficulty
and a grief to his father, and to cause the saddest episode of
his life ; the second, Alexander, born in October, 1691, lived
but seven months.   Peter had already, in the German suburb,
made an acquaintance that was destined to influence his future
life, and to destroy the peace of his family.   This was Anna
Mons, the daughter of a German jeweller, with whom Peter's
relations had daily grown more intimate, and in whose society
he passed much of his leisure time.

   A few days after his mother's death, Peter began again to
visit the house of Lefort, but though he conversed freely with
his friends about the matters which interested him most, and an

extra glass was drunk, no ladies were present, and there was no
firing of cannon, no music nor dancing.   The next day he wrote
to Apráxin, at Archangel :

'I dumbly tell my misfortune and my last sorrow, about
which neither my hand nor my heart can write in detail without
remembering what the Apostle Paul says about not grieving for
such things, and the voice of Esdras, " Call me again the day that
is past."   I forget all this as much as possible, as being above
my reasoning and mind, for thus it has pleased the Almighty
God, and all things are according to the will of their Creator.
Amen!   Therefore, like Noah, resting awhile from my grief,
and leaving aside that which can never return, I write about the
living.'

The rest of the letter was taken up with directions about the
construction of the small ship which he had begun, and the
preparation of clothing for the sailors.   He evidently desired to
go to Archangel that winter, but he felt the propriety of being
present at the requiem on the fortieth day after his mother's
death.   Little by little other things interfered, and the journey
was put off.

Another letter written by Peter to Apráxin shows him in
better spirits, willing to see the humorous side of things, and
ready to make little jokes about Ramodanófsky and Buturlín,
who were old Russians and opposed to all Peter's novelties,
but who still loved him, and yielded with the best grace they
could :—

'Thy letter was handed to me by Michael Kuroyédof, and,
after reflecting, I reported about it all to my Lord and Admiral,
who, having heard my report, ordered me to write as follows.
First : that the great lord is a man mighty bold for war, as well
as on the watery way, as thou thyself knowest, and for that reason he does not wish to delay here longer than the last days of
April.   Second: that his Imperial brother, through love and
even desire of this journey, like the Athenians seeking new
things, has bound him to go, and does not wish to stay behind
himself.   Third : The rear-admiral will be Peter Ivánovitch
Gordon.   I think there will be nearly three hundred people of
different ranks; and who, and what rank, and where, that I will

write to thee presently.   Hasten up with everything as quickly as you can, especially with the ship.   Therefore I and my companions, who are working on the masts, send many respects. Keep well.   PITER.'

About this time, a large amount of powder and a thousand muskets were sent to Archangel, while twenty-four cannon, intended for one of the new ships, were ordered to wait at Vológda until the arrival of the Tsar.   In informing Apráxin of this, Peter sends his salutations to the two workmen whom he had sent on, Niklas and Jan, and begs him not to forget the beer. About the same time, or even earlier, General Gordon wrote to his friend and business agent Meverell, at London, to send to Archangel a good ship with a 'jovial captain,' and a good supply of powder; and in writing to his son-in-law, at Archangel, recommends him also to brew a quantity of beer.

All preparations being made, the Tsar, on May 11, set out for Archangel, '*pour prendre ses divertissements et même plus que l'année passée*,' as Lefort wrote to his brother Ami ; having with him many more of his 'company' than he had taken the year before.   It required twenty-two barges to convey them down the Dvína, and the 'caravan,' with Ramodanófsky as admiral, Buturlín as vice-admiral, and Gordon as rear-admiral, accompanied by a plentiful display of signals and the firing of cannon, accomplished its journey in ten days, arriving at Archangel on May 28.   It is hardly necessary to say that the title of admiral was purely as sportive a one as that of generalissimo, or of commodore of a fleet of row-boats ; it implied nothing as to the present or future existence of a Russian naval force, nor did it give any rank in the state.   The Tsar himself was known as the 'skipper.'

Peter established himself in the same house on the Moses Island where he had been the preceding year.   His first care was to go to the church of the Prophet Elijah, and to thank God for his safe arrival ; his second to inspect the ship building at the wharf of Solombála, which fortunately was completed, and on the 30th was triumphantly launched, the Tsar himself knocking away the first prop.   But, as the frigate ordered in Holland had not arrived, it was impossible as yet to go to sea,

and the Tsar utilised the delay by making the trip to the Solovétsky monastery which he had postponed the year before. For
this, on his birthday, he embarked on his small yacht, the 'St.
Peter,' taking with him the Archbishop Athanasius, some of the
boyárs attached to his person, and a few soldiers. He started
out on the night of June 10, but was kept at the mouth of the
Dvína by a calm. The wind freshened the next day, and soon
turned to a gale. When he had arrived at the mouth of the
Únskaya Gulf, about eighty miles from Archangel, the tempest
was so great that the little ship was in the utmost danger. The
sails were carried away, the waves dashed over the deck, and
even the experienced sailors who managed the yacht gave up in
despair, and believed they must go to the bottom. All fell on
their knees and began to pray, while the archbishop administered the last sacrament. Peter alone stood firm at the rudder,
with unmoved countenance, although, like the rest, he received
the communion from the hands of the archbishop. His presence of mind finally had its effect on the frightened mariners,
and one of them, Antíp Timoféief, one of the Streltsi from the
Sọlovétsky monastery who had been engaged as a pilot, went to
the Tsar, and told him that their only hope of safety lay in running into the Únskaya Gulf, as otherwise they would infallibly
go to pieces on the rocks. With his assistance, the yacht was
steered past the reefs through a very narrow passage, and on
June 12, about noon, anchored near the Pertomínsky monastery.
The whole company went to the monastery church and gave
thanks for their miraculous preservation, while Peter granted
additional revenues and privileges to the brotherhood of monks,
and rewarded the pilot Antíp with a large sum of money. In
memory of his preservation, Peter fashioned, with his own
hands, a wooden cross about ten feet high, with an inscription
in Dutch, '*Dat kruys maken kaptein Piter van a. cht.* 1694,'
carried it on his shoulders and erected it on the spot where he
had landed.

The storm lasted three days longer, but on the 16th Peter
again set sail, and arrived the next day safely at the monastery,
where he remained three days in prayer and fasting, and in
veneration of the relics of its founders, St. Sabatius and St. Zosimus. The monks must have been astonished at the devotion

shown by the son of that Tsar who had besieged them for nine long years because they had refused to accept the 'innovations' of the Patriarch Nikon. They must have been convinced that, after all, they were right. At all events, they were pleased with the generosity of Peter, who gave one thousand rubles and additional privileges to the monastery, besides gifts to individual monks. The safe return of the Tsar was feasted at Archangel, not only by his friends, who had been greatly alarmed, but by the captains of two English vessels then in port, and he himself wrote brief accounts of his journey, first of all to his brother Iván, to whom he said that he had at last fulfilled his vow of adoring the relics of the holy hermits Sabatius and Zosimus, but mentioned not a word of the danger he had run. From his wife, to whom he had written nothing, Peter received two letters, complaining of his neglect. Apparently he sent no answer.

A month later, the new vessel which he had launched on his arrival was ready for sea, and with great rejoicing was christened the ' St. Paul.' About the same time, Peter's heart was gladdened by the receipt of a letter from his friend Vinius, at Moscow, saying that the frigate bought by Witsen in Amsterdam had sailed six weeks before, under the command of Captain Flamm, and ought by that time to be due in Archangel. Vinius spoke also of many fires which had taken place at Moscow, one of which had burned down four thousand houses. Previous information of this had been received in letters from Lieutenant-Colonel Von Mengden and Major Adam Weyde:—

' In Moscow there have been many fires, and of these fires the people said that, if you had been here, you would not have allowed them to be so great.'

In replying to Vinius, Peter expressed his joy at the sailing of the vessel, then spoke of the launching of the one built at Archangel, which, he said, ' is completely finished, and has been christened the " Apostle Paul," and sufficiently fumigated with the incense of Mars. At this fumigation, Bacchus was also sufficiently honoured.' But how impudent is your Vulcan; he is not satisfied with you who are on dry land, and even here, in

---

[1] A Swedish galliot, which arrived from Bordeaux, after a five weeks' voyage, on July 7, with four hundred casks of wine, probably supplied the libations for Bacchus.

the realm of Neptune, he has shown his effrontery;' and went
on to tell how all the ships at Archangel would have been burnt,
through a fire catching on a barge laden with grain, had it not
been for the great exertion of himself and his men.   Finally,
on July 21, the forty-four gun frigate, 'Santa Profeetie,' so
impatiently expected from Holland, arrived, under the command of Captain Jan Flamm, with a crew of forty sailors.   She
had been five weeks and four days on the journey.   Peter hastened to the mouth of the river to meet her, and finally, at four
o'clock, she cast anchor at Solombála.   In the midst of the feast,
Peter sat down and wrote to Vinius a brief letter :—

    ' MIN HER : I have nothing else to write now, except that
what I have so long desired has to-day come about.   Jan
Flamm has arrived all right, with forty-four cannon and forty
soldiers, on his ship.   Congratulate all of us.   I shall write you
more fully by the next post, but now I am beside myself with
joy, and cannot write at length.   Besides, it is impossible, for
Bacchus is alway honoured in such cases, and with his leaves
he dulls the eyes of those who wish to write at length.

                'The City, July 21.
                    SchiPer Fonshi
                    Psantus ProFet
                    ities.'

    The frigate needed a few repairs, but these were soon made,
and in a week Peter was ready to start on his cruise.   The
'Apostle Paul,' with Vice-Admiral Buturlín, took the lead,
followed by four German ships returning home with Russian
cargoes.   Then came the new frigate, the 'Holy Prophecy,'
with the admiral and the Tsar, followed by four English ships
returning with their cargoes.   The yacht 'St. Peter,' with General Gordon as rear-admiral, followed.   The movements of the
fleet were to be directed by signals, which had been invented for
the purpose by Peter, and had been translated into the different
languages.   He himself brought Gordon a copy for translation
into English, for the use of the English Captains.   The wind
was for a long time unfavourable, and, even after getting to the
mouths of the Dvína, the seafaring company could do nothing
but divert itself by mutual feasts on the various islands.   Peter,
however, who must always have something on hand, discussed

a project for great military manœuvres in the autumn on his return to Moscow, and, under the direction of General Gordon,
made plans of bastions and redoubts, and composed lists of all
the necessary tools and equipments. Finally the fleet set out
on August 21, and with various fortune—General Gordon
nearly going to pieces on a small island to which his pilot had
taken him, thinking the crosses in the cemetery on the shore to
be the masts and yards of the other vessels. With some difficulty he got safely off, and on the 27th the whole fleet reached
Sviatói Nos, the most extreme point which separated the White
Sea from the Northern Ocean. It had been Peter's intention to
venture upon the open sea, but a violent wind rendered it not
only difficult but dangerous. The signal was therefore given,
and, taking leave of the merchant vessels, the three ships of
Peter's navy returned to Archangel, arriving there on the 31st.
Three days longer were all that Peter could stay. On the
evening of September 2, Gordon says, ' We were all at feast
with the Governor, and were jovial.' The next morning they
set out for Moscow.

Immediately after the arrival of the party at Moscow, arrangements were made for the great manœuvres which Peter
had planned. Two armies were formed. In one were included six Streltsi regiments and two companies of cavalry, in
all 7,500 men, under Buturlín, who took the title of King
of Poland, probably on account of the increasing difficulties
with that country. The other, the Russian force, was under
the command of Prince Ramodanófsky, and included the Preobrazhénsky and the Seménofsky regiments, the two select regiments, and a collection of the men fit for military service sent by
the nobility of twenty towns in the neighbourhood of Moscow,
some of the orders being despatched as far as Uglitch, Súzdal,
and Vladímir. The strength of this army is not stated, but it
was probably not inferior to the other, and it required two hundred and sixty wagons for the transport of its ammunition and
equipments. The place chosen for the manœuvres was a wide
valley on the right bank of the river Moskvá, back of the village
of Kozhúkhovo, a little more than a mile from the Símonof
monastery, so celebrated now for its lovely view of Moscow.
Here, in the angle formed by a bend of the river, a small fort

had been begun, even before the departure of Peter for Archangel. These manœuvres, though common enough nowadays
in all military countries, must have been a great surprise to the
inhabitants of Moscow, accustomed to their quiet and almost
pastoral streets. In order to take their positions, both armies,
in full parade, passed through Moscow by different routes. In
the Russian army appeared what was also a new thing to the
Muscovites—the Tsar as Peter Alexéief marching with two of
his comrades as bombardiers, in front of the Preobrazhénsky regiment. What would now seem droll is that both armies had—
what does not now enter into military staff—companies of scribes
and singers, and, in one, twenty-five dwarfs, of course unarmed.

It is useless to recapitulate the story of the manœuvres,
which lasted for fully three weeks, and which are described
with great humour by General Gordon in his diary, and by
Zheliabúzhky in his memoirs. Sufficient to say that there was
fighting which sometimes was only too real, for the bombs,
though without powder, did hurt, and fire-pots burst and burned
faces and maimed limbs. A bridge had to be thrown across
the river Moskvá, and the fort was to be mined and counter-
mined, according to the proper rules of war. Unfortunately
banquets and suppers had too great a predominance in this campaign, and after a very good dinner given by General Lefort on
his name's day, it was decided to storm the enemy's fort.
Flushed with wine as they were, the conquest was easy. Everyone was satisfied except Peter, who was not content with this
summary proceeding. He therefore gave up all the prisoners,
ordered the Polish King again to occupy his fort, and insisted
that mines should be made until the walls should be blown up,
and the conquering army properly walk in. This was done,
and the place was finally taken in the most approved way on
October 27. One incident of the campaign seems to have been
a fight of the singers, headed by Turgénief, the court fool,
against the scribes of the Polish camp.

This was the last time that Peter played at war. Fate ruled
that thenceforth real battles were to take the place of mimic ones.[1]

---

[1] Ustriálof, II. vi. vii. ; Soloviéf, xiv. ; Gordon's *Diary ;* Zheliabúzhky,
memoirs, Posselt, *Lefort ;* Brückner, *Culturhistorische Studien.*

XXV.

Peter had derived so˙ much satisfaction from his visits to Archangel that he thought favourably of various projects of travelling throughout his country, and of beginning new enterprises. Even while at Archangel Lefort wrote to his family at Geneva that there was talk of ' a journey, in about two years' time, to Kazán and Astrakhán. Still, this idea may pass away before two years are over. However, I shall be ready to obey all orders. There is also an idea of constructing some galliots and going to the Baltic Sea.' Later, on September 23, Lefort wrote : 'Next summer we are going to construct five large ships and two galleys, which, God willing, will go two years hence to Astrakhán, for the conclusion of important treaties with Persia.' The ideas of Witsen about the Persian and Asiatic trade, and the many conversations on that subject in the German suburb about the advantages connected with this traffic, which French, Dutch, and English all desired to get into their hands, had evidently stimulated Peter's mind.

Suddenly, however, and apparently to the surprise of everybody, it was resolved to enter upon an active campaign against the Tartars, in the spring of 1695—nominally for the purpose of reducing the Crimea ; actually, the plan of the campaign included opening the Dniéper and the Don, two Russian rivers which were useless for trade so long as their mouths were in possession of the Mussulmans. The only mention that is made of this plan before it was formally announced, is a passage in a letter of General Gordon to his friend Kurz, in Vienna, dated the end of December, 1694, in which he says: 'I believe and hope that this coming summer we shall undertake something for the advantage of Christianity and our allies.' It is difficult

TARTAR CAVALRY ATTACKING A RUSSIAN COMMISSARIAT TRAIN.

to tell what were the real reasons for this campaign. Apparently it was not, as has generally been thought, on the initiative
of Peter himself, for as yet he had not meddled in the concerns
of the Government. The statements that the expedition against
Azof was planned for the purpose of getting a harbour in the
Black Sea, in which to create a navy, or because the success of
the manœuvres near Moscow made Peter desirous of real war,
or because he had already the intention of going to Europe, and
wished to signalise himself by great exploits before he appeared
in the West, rest merely on surmise. The campaign was an
incident in the war against the Tartars, which had been begun
by Sophia, in consequence of her treaty with Poland, and which
had never come formally to a conclusion. No peace had ever
been made. Although, after the unsuccessful close of Golítsyn's
second expedition, in 1689, there had been a practical armistice,
yet this armistice had never been ratified by any convention,
and was frequently broken by the Tartars. The border provinces were constantly exposed to their predatory incursions, and
in 1692 twelve thousand Tartars appeared before the Russian
town of Nemírof, burnt the suburbs, carried away many prisoners, and made booty of a very large number of horses. The
Russians, with the few troops of Cossacks and the local levies
that remained on the border, had confined themselves strictly
to the defensive.

Meanwhile, there had been a growing dissatisfaction in
Moscow with the conduct of Poland. The Russian Resident at
Warsaw constantly wrote that no dependence whatever could
be placed on the King of Poland or on the Emperor. He reported them as desirous of making a separate peace with
Turkey, without the slightest regard for the interest of Russia.
When application was made to Vienna, the Emperor replied
that he was not in league with Moscow, but that, without
doubt, the Polish King kept the Tsars informed of everything
that passed. King Jan Sobieski professed the utmost friendship for the Tsars, but made complaints that they did not assist
him in his operations against the Mussulmans ; that, under the
treaty, they had no right to confine themselves to defensive
warfare alone ; and that, unless they sent either an ambassador
to Vienna with full powers, or sent one to go with his envoy to

the Crimean Khan, it would be impossible for him to satisfy
the Muscovite demands, as he did not know sufficiently what
the demands of Muscovy were. Intrigues had been going on
between Mazeppa, the Hetman of Little Russia, and various
Polish magnates, and it was believed in Moscow that these
were with the knowledge and contrivance of the King. Russia
had finally become so bitter on this point that Sobieski hastened to declare that all the letters intercepted were forgeries,
and a monk, on whose person, it is said, had been found forged

letters and forged seals of
Mazeppa, was surrendered to
the Russians. The explanation was accepted, and the
monk was executed by Ma-
zeppa's orders.

Fearing to be left en-
tirely alone—for it had been
ascertained, by means of
Adam Stille, an official translator at the foreign office in
Vienna, who had been bought
up by the Russian envoy,
and who furnished the Government at Moscow with reports of the negotiations
going on at Vienna, and
sometimes with copies of papers, that no mention, of any
kind whatever, of the in-

Mazeppa.

terest of Russia had been made in the whole of the negotiations at Vienna between Poland, Austria, and Turkey—and
fearing lest a separate peace might be made without them,
which would enable the Sultan to turn all his forces against
them, the Russians resolved to see what they could effect themselves. For this purpose, agents had been sent to the Crimea
to ascertain upon what basis the Khan would make a permanent peace. The Russians were unwilling to agree to the
same state of things that had existed before the campaigns of
Golítsyn. They insisted that the prisoners on both sides should

be delivered up without a ransom, and upon the suppression of the money tribute which had previously been annually sent to the Crimea. On the suggestion of Dositheus, the Patriarch of Constantinople, who had written several letters to the Tsars urging the renewal of hostilities, they made also a request that the Holy Places in Jerusalem should be taken away from the Franks and restored to the Greek clergy.' As to the Holy Places, the Khan replied that the solution of that question depended on the Sultan alone; but, for the other matters, he declined to accept anything but a renewal of the old treaty of Baktchiserai, insisted on the tribute due to him, and refused to give up the captives without a ransom. Not only were these overtures ineffectual, but alarm was caused by the appearance of the Polish magnate, Rzewuski, at the court of the Khan, with propositions from the King. Rzewuski went subsequently to Adrianople, in the hope of making peace with the Sultan on conditions favourable to Poland. This plan fell through ; but the Turks finally consented to open negotiations for a general peace. Information about this reached Moscow in a letter from King Jan Sobieski, in the latter part of July, 1694, and the Tsars were requested to send a proper and fit man to meet the Turkish and Tartar plenipotentiaries. It was, in all probability, the despair of obtaining any favourable conditions for Russia, and the fear that their plenipotentiaries would not be admitted to the congress, that induced the Government at Moscow to resolve on active operations.

The campaign once resolved upon, Peter threw himself into it with all his heart and soul. He looked personally after the artillery, as he had the intention of accompanying one of the armies, in the capacity of bombardier. He even went to Pereyaslávl, to look over the artillery stores which he had left there, in order to see what would be available for the purposes of the expedition. Full of ardour at the thought of active war, he wrote to Apráxin : ' Although for five weeks last autumn we practised in the game of Mars at Kozhúkhovo, with no idea except that of amusement, yet this amusement of ours has be-

---

¹ It is interesting to see how early the question of the Holy Places became a subject of dispute between Russia and Turkey.

come a forerunner of the present war.' And again he wrote:
'At Kozhúkhovo we jested. We are now going to play the
real game before Azof.'

The plan of operations was that the boyár Boris Sheremétief, with 120,000 men, assisted by the Cossacks of the Ukraine
under Mazeppa, should go down the Dniéper and attempt to
take possession of the fortresses of Otchakóf and Kazikermán,
which, with three similar forts, guarded the mouth of that
river. The army of Sheremétief was composed entirely of
troops drilled in the old Russian style. The two regiments
made up of the play-troops of Peter, together with the regiments of soldiers drilled according to foreign tactics and the
best of the Streltsi regiments, were to compose an army
of about 31,000 men, the aim of which was the capture of
Azof.

This fortress town, situated on one of the arms of the Don,
about ten miles from the Sea of Azof, was the chief hinderance
to the Russian access to the Black Sea. In the early times, as
the half-Greek city of Tanais, and in the Middle Ages, as the
Genoese colony of Tana, it had been a great commercial emporium for the Asiatic trade. Destroyed by Tamerlane, and
afterward fortified by the Turks, it had been captured by the
Don Cossacks in 1637, and held by them for six years against
tremendous odds, until they were ordered to abandon it by
the Tsar Michael, Russia being unwilling to engage in a war
with Turkey for its retention. It was then rebuilt by the
Turks, who kept 26,000 men at work for several years in
strengthening its fortifications. What is particularly to be
noticed is that, in sending an expedition to Azof, the Russians
were attacking the Turks, and not the Tartars.

The plan of this campaign was decided upon about the
middle of February, in a council of war held at the artillery
head-quarters. The army was to be divided into three corps,
respectively under the command of Avtémon Golovín, Lefort,
and Gordon; but, strangely enough, there was to be no supreme commander. The command of the army was to be
entrusted to a council composed of these three generals, and
none of their decisions could be carried into effect without the
approbation of the bombardier sergeant of the Preobrazhénsky

regiment, Peter Alexéief, as the Tsar chose to be styled. This arrangement, as might easily have been foreseen, proved productive of great calamities.

The division of General Gordon marched the whole distance, and starting from Moscow in March, arrived at the rendezvous before Azof in the middle of June. The 'great caravan,' as it was called, consisting of the other troops, left Moscow in May, by water, but owing to the constant bad weather (there was snow in Moscow even on June 7), the careless way in which the barges were constructed, and the stupidity and inexperience of the boatmen, had great difficulty in reaching Nízhni-Nóvgorod, on the Volga, where it was found necessary to transship all the troops, equipments, and artillery. As Peter wrote to Vinius, from Nízhni-Nóvgorod:

'Strong winds kept us back for two days at Dedínovo, and three days at Múrom, and most of all the delay was caused by stupid pilots and workmen, who call themselves masters, but in reality, are as far from being so, as the earth is from heaven.'

Fortunately, the barges from Vorónezh were in waiting at Panshín, on the Don, to reach which a short land march was made, and the caravan reached the rendezvous without much trouble on the festival of St. Peter and St. Paul, the name's-day of the Tsar ($\frac{\text{June } 29}{\text{July } 9}$). Gordon at once sent to the Tsar to congratulate him, and asked him to dinner. But Peter busied himself the whole day with disembarking his troops, and came only to supper. Gordon had taken up a position on some low hills within sight of Azof, and had entrenched himself. The other troops did the same, and at the council of war it was resolved to begin siege works at once.

This siege continued for fourteen weeks, with varying success. There was a want of discipline among the Streltsi, there was a want of harmony in the councils of the generals, there was a want of knowledge and experience in the engineers; and, more than that, there was a breakdown of the commissariat. For a long time, the troops were entirely without salt. Everything went on slowly, and it sometimes seemed, as Gordon said, ' that we acted as if we were not in earnest.'

One advantage obtained by the Don Cossacks cheered up the army. They succeeded in storming one of the two small

forts called Kalantchí, which guarded the junction of the Ka-
lantchá—one of the larger arms of the Don, which branches off
above Azof—and which prevented the passage of the Russian
barges with provisions for the army, and compelled everything
to be taken some distance around, exposed to the attack of the
Tartar cavalry. After one fort had been taken by assault, such
a fire was kept up against the other that the Turkish troops
abandoned it in the night. It was, therefore, possible for the
Russians to construct a floating bridge over the Don, and
greatly to facilitate their communications and all their operations. As a set-off to this success, that very afternoon a man
named Jacob Janson went over to the enemy. He was originally a Dutch sailor, who had entered the Russian service at
Archangel, and had adopted the Russian religion; he had been
lately serving as a bombardier, and from some fancy Peter had
become extremely intimate with him and had communicated to
him all his plans and ideas with regard to the siege. This rene-
gade and deserter exposed to the Turkish Pasha all the Russian
plans, and especially the disposition of the troops. One of the
many Russian dissenters who had found a refuge at Azof from
the persecution of the Church and Government was immediately sent by the Pasha to verify this, and, by calling himself
a Cossack, easily succeeded in passing the Russian sentinels and
penetrating into their camp. The Russians, even in the field,
had kept up their old habit of taking a long nap immediately
after their midday meal. Informed of this practice, the Pasha
made a sortie, surprised the Russians in their trenches, and was
only beaten back after a three hours' fight, in which the Russians experienced very severe losses, and General Gordon, who
did his best to rally the troops, came very near being taken prisoner. After this, frequent sorties and attacks greatly annoyed
the Russians and hindered the siege works. General Gordon,
who was really the only officer of great experience, wished to
complete the trenches on the left side as far as the river, for
there was still a vacant space along the river through which the
Tartar cavalry kept up communications with the town. He also
wished to continue the trenches until they were close to the
walls. All his suggestions, however, were overruled by the impulsiveness of Peter and the inexperience of Lefort and Golo-

vín, who voted to please the Tsar. There was great desire for an immediate assault, which was opposed by Gordon, who represented how dangerous it would be to carry the town by storm when there were no trenches close to the fortifications in which the troops could take refuge in case of repulse. His remonstrances were of no avail, and an assault was finally attempted on August 15. It failed completely. The Russians were driven back with a loss of 1,500 men—a very heavy one, considering their numbers. Later on, in spite of the protests of Gordon, two mines were exploded long before they had reached the part of the walls intended to be blown up. No damage was done to the town, but the explosion threw the *débris* back into the Russian trenches with considerable loss of life. The troops began to despair, but Peter resolved to attempt one more assault before giving up the siege, for the weather was now so cold that it was difficult for the men to remain in the trenches. This assault was no more successful than the first, although some of the Cossacks penetrated into the town on the river side. Finally it was determined to raise the siege, and on October 12 the Russians began to withdraw, hotly pursued by the enemy, who made constant attacks on the rear-guard. The severe weather and high water prevented the Russians from crossing the river to the safer side, and many were the privations and great was the distress endured on the homeward march.

The Tartars attacked the rear-guard, and on one occasion, after killing about thirty men in the regiment of Colonel Swart, took prisoner the colonel and the greater part of the regiment, with several standards. This caused great panic at the time, and produced an impression at home which lasted for many years, as is evident from the way in which Pososhkóf brings it forward as an instance of the bad discipline of the army. The troops suffered much from the rains and floods, and afterward from the extreme cold. The steppe, which Gordon, in the spring, had found 'full of manifold flowers and herbs, asparagus, wild thyme, marjoram, tulips, pinks, melilot and maiden gilly flowers,' was now bare and naked. All the vegetation had been burnt off, and frequently the soldiers could not even find a piece of dry wood with which to kindle a fire. The Austrian agent, Pleyer, who had been with the army through the siege,

but who was obliged by a fever to remain a month at Tcherkásk, wrote in his report to the Emperor Leopold :

'I saw great quantities of the best provisions, which could
have kept a large army for a year, either ruined by the bad
weather, or lost by the barges going to the bottom.   What was
left was divided among the Cossacks.   On the way I then saw
what great loss the army suffered in the march, although no
enemy pursued it, for it was impossible not to see without tears
how through the whole steppe for eight hundred versts men
and horses lay half eaten by the wolves, and many villages were
full of sick, half of whom died, as well as many others infected
by them, all of which was very painful to see and to hear.'

The only success of the campaign was the capture of the two
forts, in which a garrison of 3,000 men was left, so as to be
ready for subsequent operations the next spring.   Lefort, in a
letter to his brother, says that had they had 10,000 more troops,
the town would certainly have been taken.   This additional
number would have enabled the trenches to have been drawn
entirely around the town, and its communications would have
been entirely cut off.   But the failure is ra'her to be ascribed
to the want of knowledge and experience on the part of the
officers, and to the impulsiveness of the Tsar, than to the smallness of the army.

Peter himself was indefatigable.   As a bombardier, he filled
bombs and grenades with his own hands, and worked at the
mortars like any common soldier.   With all this, he took part
in the councils of war, supervised all the plans of action, and,
in addition, kept up a constant correspondence with friends.
These letters are all brief.   Some of them refer simply to matters of business, such as the forwarding of material and provisions.   In them he endeavoured to keep up his own spirits as
well as those of his friends, still maintaining the jesting tone
which he had long ago adopted, always addressing them by
their nicknames, and carrying out the fiction of making regular
reports to Ramodanófsky as the generalissimo of the army, and
signing himself, with expressions of great respect, the ' Bombardier Peter.'   There is much talk about ' plowing the field of
Mars,' and there are other classical allusions.   But twice he
shows real feeling—with reference to the death of his friend

Prince Theodore Troekúrof, who was killed on September 17, and to the deaths of his comrades and orderlies Yekím Vorónin and Gregory Lúkin—who had been two of the most intelligent men in his guard, and had been also of great assistance to him in his boat-building at Pereyaslávl—killed at the final assault. He writes to Ramodanófsky on separate scraps of paper, enclosed with the formal letters to him as generalissimo :

' For God's sake, do not trouble yourself because the posts are late. It is certainly from the bad weather, and not, God forbid! because of any accident. Thou canst judge thyself that, if anything had happened, how would it be possible to keep it quiet? Think over this, and tell those that need it. Prince Theodore Ivánovitch, my friend, is no more. For God's sake, do not abandon his father. Yekím Vorónin and Gregory Lúkin by God's will have died. Please don't forget Gregory's father.'

The Tsar accompanied the troops until they had reached Valúiek, the first Russian town. He then went on in advance, but stopped for several days near Túla, at the ironworks built by the Dane Marselis, which were now owned by his uncle, Leo Narýshkin. Here he amused himself by hammering three large iron sheets with his own hands.

The army reached Moscow on December 2, and, in spite of the failure of the campaign, Peter made a triumphal entry into the city, with a captive Turk led before him. The only excuse for this was the partial success of Sheremétief and Mazeppa, who had taken by storm two of the Turkish forts at the mouth of the Dniéper—Kazikermán and Tagán—and had forced the abandonment of two others.[1]

---

[1] Soloviéf, xiv.; Ustriálof, II., viii., ix.; Gordon's *Diary;* Posselt, *Lefort.*

XXVI.

THE CAPTURE OF AZOF.—1696.

PETER undoubtedly felt disappointed, humiliated, and angry at the result of the campaign. Despite the dangers and difficulties which beset his childhood, he had nearly always succeeded in having his own way. He was Tsar, he was self-willed, and he was obstinate. He had undertaken the siege with such confidence of success that he had caused Lefort to write letters to be communicated to the different courts of Europe, informing the world of his designs, and he had returned almost empty-handed.

The difficulties of the homeward march must only have served to increase his obstinate adherence to his purpose, and every hammer-blow which he gave to those iron plates in the forge at Túla drove away a regret and fixed a resolution. He no sooner returned to Moscow than every preparation was made for another campaign. Indeed, he had formed some plans even before this, for, on the march, just after he had escaped from the burning steppe, he wrote to the Emperor, to the King of Poland, and to the Elector of Brandenburg, informing them of the efforts which he had made against the Turks, and of his failure, owing partly to the lack of cannon and ammunition, but especially to the want of skilful engineers and miners, and, in the name of friendship and for the success of their common cause against the Turk, he begged that skilful men be sent to him.

This time, the number of troops designed for the expedition was much greater, amounting in all, with the help of the Cossacks and the regiments from Little Russia, to 75,000 men. Having seen that the failure of the last campaign was owing, in great part, to the divisions in command, Peter appointed a single commander-in-chief for the whole of the forces before Azof, with the title of generalissimo. He at first chose Prince Michael Tcherkásky, a grandee, who was much respected for his character and his great services, but who was then very old; and when Tcherkásky refused this appointment on account of his extreme age and infirmity, his choice fell upon the boyár Alexis Shéïn, more noted for distinguished family—he was the great-grandson of the celebrated defender of Smolénsk in the Troublous Times—than for actual service and experience, but, at the same time, in the opinion of his contemporaries, a man of ability and sound judgment. The appointment of a native Russian to such high rank was doubtless intended to silence the complaints of the ultra-national party, who had again talked of this last defeat being owing to the employment of so many foreigners. The boyár Borís Sheremétief and the hetman Mazeppa were ordered to remain on the defensive and protect the frontier from Tartar incursions.

Alexis Shéïn.

In his first campaign, Peter had seen the absolute necessity of a flotilla in order to prevent the Turks from communicating with Azof, and to keep the command of the river. It is needless to say that his love for the sea strengthened his opinion. He therefore resolved to build a fleet of transport barges, and, at the same time, galleys and galliots that could be armed and used for the defensive if not for the offensive. For the construction of this fleet he chose the town of Vorónezh, on the river Vorónezh, about three hundred miles south of Moscow. All this region had once been covered with a thick virgin forest, and here, from the early years of the reign of Alexis, numerous barges had been constructed every winter for the transport of the grain and wine sent as salary to the Cossacks of the Don. These barges were like those now built on the rivers in the

north of Russia for the transport of timber, hides, and grain—
rude vessels made entirely of wood, without the use of even an
iron nail.   They were good simply for the voyage down the
river, and never returned.   On their arrival they were broken
up, and used either as timber or as fire-wood.   They were usually about a hundred feet long and twenty feet wide, and held
about two hundred quarters of grain.   To such an extent had
barges been built in this locality—at the rate of five hundred
to a thousand a year—that in many places the forests were entirely cut down.   Vorónezh is now a thriving town, the capital
of a province or *gubérnia*, with a population of 45,000, and a considerable trade.   Its greatest reminiscences are those connected
with Peter, and the construction of this flotilla—some of the
boat-houses being still standing; but it also prides itself on the
peasant-poet Nikítin, and possesses an agreeable and cultivated
society.   Here Peter ordered the construction of a wharf on
the low left bank, the side of the river opposite to the town,
for it is a peculiarity of most Russian rivers that the right bank
is high, of bluffs or low hills, and the left flat.   During the
winter of 1696, upwards of 30,000 men, under the command of
officials sent from Moscow, laboured at the construction of more
than thirteen hundred barges for conveying troops, ammunition,
and provisions to the mouths of the Don.   In addition to this,
Peter sent to Archangel for all the ship-carpenters who were
wintering there, promising that they should return for the opening of navigation.   It was his intention to build thirty galleys of
various sizes, some of two and some of three masts, although
they would depend chiefly on oars for their swiftness.   A model
galley, constructed in Holland, which had arrived at Archangel,
was brought by the Dvína to Vológda, and then overland to
Moscow.   Several of those which Peter had himself built at
Pereyaslávl were, according to Lefort, transported on sledges over
the easy snow roads to Vorónezh.   Four thousand men, selected
from various regiments, were told off into a naval battalion or
marine regiment, for service both by sea and land.   Lefort was
made admiral, Colonel Lima, a Venetian who had been for
eight years in the Russian service, vice-admiral, and a Frenchman, Colonel Balthazar de Losier, rear-admiral.   Peter himself
took the rank of captain, and commanded the van-guard.

It is from Peter's return from his first campaign against
Azof that the real beginning of his reign should be dated.   It
was then, for the first time, that he took an active concern and
participation in all affairs of government.   By a singular coin-
cidence, it was about this time also that he became the sole
ruler of the Russian state; for, on February 8, 1696, his brother
Iván, who had greatly improved in health since his marriage,
suddenly died.   Peter had been much attached to Iván, and
the care which he afterwards manifested for his wife and
family[1] showed that he kept the tenderest recollections of him.
He had, however, now but little time to grieve, for the preparations for the campaign entirely absorbed him, though a
bodily ailment rendered him for the moment powerless.   An
injury to his foot had produced a malady which kept him long
in bed, and which, for a time, excited the fears of his family
and his friends.   As soon as he got better, he started southward with a small suite, and, contrary to habit, took a week
for the journey to Vorónezh.   His illness and the bad state of
the roads were sufficient reasons for this.   Once there, he forgot his troubles and immediately set to work, and five days
later, in writing to the boyár Stréshnef to send immediately
some ash timber from the woods of Túla for oars, as such could
not be found near Vorónezh, adds: 'According to the divine
decree to our grandfather Adam, we are eating our bread in
the sweat of our face.'   The ship-carpenters were slow in arriving, and many of the workmen deserted, the weather was most
unfavourable, for the thaw was succeeded by so violent a cold
that the river froze again, and storms of hail and sleet were so
severe that on two occasions the men were prevented from working for three or four days.   Peter was obliged not only to set an
example, but to act at once as overseer and master-shipwright.

All this time Lefort was ill in Moscow with an abscess in
his side, occasioned by a fall from his horse on the march from
Azof.   He did what he could, and at all events cheered the
Tsar somewhat with his constant friendly letters.

---

[1] Three of the five daughters of the Tsar Iván survived their father—
Catherine, Anna, and Prascovia.   Anna became Empress of Russia, Catherine
married the Duke of Mecklenburg, and her infant grandson occupied the
Russian throne for a short time as Iván VI.

Finally, on April 12, three galleys, the 'Principium,' chiefly
the work of Peter himself, the 'St. Mark,' and the 'St. Matthew,' were launched with due ceremony, and two others followed shortly after. Almost the same day, the troops collected at Vorónezh began to load the barges, and on May 1 the
generalissimo Shéïn raised on his galley the great flag bearing
the arms of the Tsar—a representation of the sea with ships,
and St. Peter and St. Paul in the corners—which had been embroidered at a convent in Moscow, and brought to Vorónezh by

Peter in the Dress he wore at Azof.

Franz Timmermann. This
flag is still preserved at Moscow. Two days later, the first
division of the great caravan
of galleys and barges set out.
The voyage down the rivers
Vorónezh and Don took three
weeks, but Peter, with his
lighter and swifter galleys,
overtook the advance, and,
on May 26, reached the town
of Tcherkásk, the capital of
the Don Cossacks, where he
came up with the division of
General Gordon, which had
preceded him by ten days,
and that under General Rige-
man, which had marched
from Tambóf. While wait-
ing for his main forces, he
busied himself with drawing up regulations for the new fleet
while in action, and with loading on barges the artillery and
stores which had been brought from the camp to Tcherkásk the
previous autumn.

On the night of May 28, a messenger arrived from Flor
Mináef, the Ataman of the Don Cossacks—who, with two hundred and fifty men, had been sent to make a reconnoissance at
the mouth of the river—that he had seen two Turkish ships and
had vainly attacked them. Peter immediately communicated
this fact to Gordon and hastened off down the river, followed by

Gordon and his troops.   He stopped at the forts of Kalantchí, where the arrival of the army was hailed with joy.   At a council of war, it was resolved that the Tsar, with his nine galleys, on which he embarked one of Gordon's regiments, and Flor Mináef, with forty Cossack boats holding twenty men each, should steal down the river and attack the Turkish ships, while General Gordon made a military diversion in front of Azof. Unfortunately, a strong north wind blew, which rendered the shallow channel still more shallow.   The galleys got aground, and were at last obliged to return to Kalantchí, or, as it was then called, Nóvo-Sérghiefsk, in commemoration of St. Sergius, the protector of the country of the Don.   Peter had himself embarked on a Cossack boat and gone to the mouth of the river, where he found not two but thirty large Turkish ships, with a considerable number of galleys, barges, and lighters.   It seemed to the Tsar too great a risk to attack these large ships with the light Cossack boats, and he therefore returned to the fort, where he arrived about midnight.   The next morning, at ten o'clock, he visited Gordon and told him the story, ' looking very melancholy and grieved,' but at three o'clock he came back with other news.   What he had not been willing to order, the river pirates of the Don had done of their own accord.   By his directions, the Cossacks had waited at the mouth of the river for observation.   During the day, either not noticing the Cossacks, or disregarding them, the Turks had transshipped to the lighters a quantity of stores and ammunition, and sent them under a convoy of Janissaries up the river to Azof.   A force of about five hundred Janissaries was landed at a mouth of the river, and succeeded in getting to the town with a considerable number of arms.   When night came on, the Cossacks, who were on the watch, attacked the lighters, and succeeded in capturing ten of them with all their contents, while the Turkish soldiers, thoroughly frightened, after almost no resistance, went back to their ships.   The news of this attack wrought such consternation that the whole of the Turkish fleet weighed anchor and sailed off, with the exception of two vessels, which could not be got ready soon enough.   One of these the Turks themselves sank, and the other was burnt by the Cossacks.   In this way, a large quantity of stores and ammunition was obtained, and thirty men were taken prisoners. Two hours later, Peter was again on his way to the mouth of the river, and was speedily followed by Gordon with a detachment of troops.

In the course of a few days, the remainder of the army and of the fleet arrived at Nóvo-Sérghiefsk, and Peter stationed himself, with his whole flotilla of twenty-nine galleys, at the mouth of the river, and completely cut off the Turkish communications with Azof. By his directions, General Gordon began to erect two small forts, which were completed under his personal supervision, and when they were thoroughly armed and garrisoned, he wrote to Ramodanófsky : 'We are now entirely out of danger of the Turkish fleet.'

The garrison of Azof had apparently not expected the return of the Russians, and had taken no precautions to fill up the trenches dug in the previous year. The besieging troops had, therefore, little more to do than to take their old places ; and owing to their increased numbers, they were able fully to occupy the necessary positions, and especially to guard the approaches along the river-bank. At first there was little opposition on the part of the garrison. One small sortie was made, which was speedily repulsed. On June 20, the Tartars from the steppe crept up to the camp, and attacked it in force, but the noble cavaliers from Moscow repulsed them for several miles. Nuradín Sultan himself went off with an arrow in his shoulder, shot by a Kalmuk. Ayúka-Khan had promised to send all his Kalmuks to the Russian assistance, but only a small body came in time ; the main body arrived a few days after Azof was taken.

A large Turkish fleet which came up to the mouths of the Don was for two weeks inactive, and finally, when about to land some troops to relieve the siege, the Pasha was so frightened at the appearance of the Russian flotilla, that the fleet immediately set sail, and went out to sea.

Peter lived chiefly on his galley 'Principium,' looking after the Turkish fleet, coming from time to time to the camp before Azof to see how operations were progressing, and personally opening the cannonade on the evening of June 26th. The Tartars in the steppe made several other attacks, which were repulsed, and on the name's-day of the Tsar, the Russians, believing that the beseiged were in sore straits, shot an arrow into

THE MESSAGE TO AZOF ON THE NAMES-DAY OF THE TSAR.

the town with a letter offering the garrison honourable terms, and promising to permit them to leave the city with all their arms and baggage. The answer was a cannonade.

Meanwhile, the soldiery were discontented even at this short siege, and the general opinion was that the work should be prosecuted in the old fashion, by means of piling up an enormous mound of earth, which could be gradually pushed forward so as to fill up the ditch and topple over upon the wall. General Gordon resolved to comply with this feeling, and no less than 15,000 men worked daily on the construction of this enormous mound. On July 21, when the mound had already become so high and so great that the streets of the town could be seen, and the Russian and Turkish soldiers came even to hand-to-hand conflicts, the engineers arrived who had been sent by the Emperor Leopold in compliance with the Tsar's request. They had not hastened on their way, for they had been fully three months in going from Vienna to Smolénsk, two weeks more from Smolénsk to Moscow, and about a month from Moscow to Azof. They excused the slowness of their journey by the fact that at Vienna they did not expect such an early start, and could learn nothing from the Russian envoy Nephimónof, who professed to have no knowledge of the military operations. Their words were confirmed by Ukráintsef, the official in charge of the foreign office, who naïvely reported that he had sent no information about the army to Vienna, lest Nephimónof should publish it. Peter was irritated by what seemed to him stupidity, and with his own hand wrote to Vinius the following amusing letter:

'Thy brother-in-law has mightily angered me that he keeps Kosmá (Nephimónof) without any news of our war. Is he not ashamed? Whatever they ask about he knows nothing, and yet he was sent for such a great matter. In his despatches to Nikíta Moiséievitch (Zótof) he writes about Polish matters when there was no need at all, but he has forgotten the side of the Emperor, where was all our hope of alliance. Has he any healthy good sense? Entrusted with state matters, yet he conceals what everybody knows. Just tell him that what he does not write on paper I shall write on his back.'

The imperial engineers were surprised at the magnitude of the mound, but, nevertheless, expected little profit from it. They advised mines and trenches in the ordinary way, and immediately gave instructions about the placing of batteries, by which an impression was soon made on one of the bastions. Hitherto no injury had been done, except to the houses in the town, which had all been ruined.

The Zaporovian Cossacks had become disgusted with the slowness of the siege and with the heavy work on the mound, and were, besides that, experiencing a shortness of commons. They therefore made a private arrangement with the Cossacks of the Don, and, on July 27th, without orders, two thousand of them, headed by Lizogúb, their chief, and Flor Mináef, the Ataman of the Don, stormed the fortification from the mound, and made an entry into the town. Had they been properly supported by the soldiery and Streltsi—who remained inactive in their camp—they would have taken it. As it was, they were beaten back, and obliged to take refuge in the corner bastion, which they held. Here they were at last reinforced by the troops of General Golovín, and succeeded in taking another bastion. The next day, the commander-in-chief resolved on a general assault, but meanwhile the Turks decided to surrender on condition that, with their wives and children, they should be allowed to leave the place with all the honours of war. This was granted. The Pasha surrendered all the Russian prisoners without question, and gave up those Dissenters who had taken refuge in Azof, and who had not already become Mussulmans. The only dispute was about the deserter and traitor Janson, who had become a Mussulman. The Russians insisted on his surrender, and the Pasha finally yielded. Janson was brought into the Russian camp, tied hand and foot, screaming to his guards:

'Cut off my head, but don't give me up to Moscow!'

The next morning, the garrison, fully armed, with all their banners, marched through the Russian lines, some to the Turkish fleet, and others on their way to the steppe. Crowded together and without order, they presented a sorry spectacle, and only the Pasha kept up his dignity. On reaching the place of embarkation, where the generalissimo Shéïn was on his horse awaiting him, the Pasha thanked him for the manner in which he had kept his word, lowered his standards to him as a token of respect, and bade him good-by.

After the departure of the Turks, ten Russian regiments marched into the utterly ruined town, where not one house was uninjured. The Zaporovian Cossacks could not be restrained, and went everywhere in search of plunder. Nothing of any importance was found, although cellars and secret recesses were dug up in all directions. There came, however, to the Government a considerable booty in the shape of cannon and powder, but there were almost no small arms, and bullets were entirely wanting. Indeed, during the last resistance offered to the Cossacks in the final assault, it was necessary to cut gold ducats into small pieces to furnish ammunition. The little fort of Lútik, situated at the mouth of the Dead Donetz, was not included in the capitulation, but speedily surrendered, and the Russians were left in full possession of the mouths of the Don.

One of the first tasks which Peter set himself was to find a suitable harbour for his flotilla, and for that purpose he explored the coast on each side. The mouths of the Don, which were shallow or deep according to the wind, afforded no secure refuge, and it was necessary to find a place which might be turned into a safe port. After a week spent in surveying, when he slept on the bench of a galley, almost fasting, Peter decided on an anchorage under a cape long known to the Cossacks as Tagan-róg, or the Tagan Horn. Here he ordered the construction of a fortress, as well as of another a little beyond, at Otchakóf-róg, and then entrusted the imperial engineer Laval with the task of properly fortifying the town of Azof, so that it should be impregnable to assaults by the Turks. The town was cleared as speedily as possible of its ruins, Turkish mosques were quickly transformed into Christian churches, and there Peter heard divine service before starting on his homeward march.

The fall of Azof produced great consternation at Constantinople. The Bey of Konieh and two other officials were executed, all the Janissaries who could be found were arrested and their goods sequestered, while the poor commandant who had surrendered the town, Kalaïlikóz Ahmed Pasha, was obliged to fly to save his life, and lost the whole of his property, which was confiscated to the Treasury.[1]

---

[1] Soloviéf, xiv.; Ustriálof, II., x., xi.; Gordon's *Diary;* Posselt, *Lefort;* Zheliabúzhky, *Memoirs* (Russian); Yelághin, *History of the Russian Fleet* (Russian), St. Petersburg, 1864; Veselago, *Sketch of Russian Naval History* (Russian), St. Petersburg, 1875; A. Gordon, *History of Peter the Great,* Aberdeen, 1755.

XXVII.

THE EFFECT OF THE VICTORY.—BUILDING A FLEET IN EARNEST.—1696-7.

It can be imagined with what delight the news of the sur-render was received at Moscow. 'When your letter came,' wrote Vinius to the Tsar, 'there were many guests at the house of Leo Kirílovitch (Narýshkin). He immediately sent me with it to the Patriarch. His Holiness, on reading it, burst into tears, ordered the great bell to be rung, and, in the presence of the Tsaritsa and of the Tsarévitch, gave thanks to the Almighty. All talked with astonishment of the humility of their lord, who, after such a great victory, has not lifted up his own heart, but has ascribed all to the Creator of heaven, and has praised only his assistants, although every one knows that it was by your plan alone, and by the aid you got from the sea, that such a noted town has bowed down to your feet.'

All Peter's friends burst into a chorus of praise for his bravery, his genius, his humility, likening him to St. Peter, to Samson, and to David. In reply to the congratulations of Vinius, Peter quoted the verse 'the labourer is worthy of his hire,' and suggested that it would be a meet and proper thing to honour him and the generalissimo with a triumphal arch, which might be placed near one of the bridges over the Moskvá. While the arch was being built and the preparations made for the solemn entry of the troops, Peter busied himself for several weeks in visiting the ironworks in the neighbour-hood of Túla. Here he undoubtedly met the celebrated black-smith Nikíta Demidof, who subsequently received those grants of mining land in the Urál which have led to the immense fortune of the present Demídof family. Nikíta Demídof was already known to Peter, at least by reputation, as the cleverest smith and iron-forger in all this region. Mazeppa met the Tsar on the road from Vorónezh to Túla, presented him with a magnificent sabre, the hilt and scabbard of which were studded with precious stones, and informed him of the brave deeds done by the Zaporovian Cossacks during the summer. It seemed that about fifteen hundred of these braves sailed down the Dniéper past the fortifications of Otchakóf, and hovered along the Crimean coast until they met three merchant vessels sailing under the Turkish flag to Caffa. Two of these they captured and burned, after they had transferred the cargoes, the guns, and forty prisoners to their boats. Coasting still further along, they met three more ships coming out from the Azof Sea, and had already captured one of them, when three Turkish galleys came up. In the fight, the Cossack commander was killed, and some confusion ensued, in consequence of which they turned tail, vigorously pursued by the enemy. Unfortunately for them, the Turkish commander at Otchakóf was on the look-out, and they were obliged to take refuge on a desert island, where they concealed their booty. Crossing to the mainland, they then burnt their boats, and marched home with their prisoners. The small detachment left to guard the booty was betrayed by a Turk, and was captured after a long struggle.

After the Tsar had finished his inspection of the ironworks, he met his troops at Kolómenskoe, and made his triumphal entry into Moscow on October 10. It had been very long since the Russians had had a real victory to celebrate, not, indeed, since the early days of the Tsar Alexis, and, in any case, a sight like the present was new to Moscow. The gilded carriages of the generalissimo and the admiral, the gorgeous trappings and rich costumes of the boyárs, the retainers in armour and coats of mail, the Streltsi in new uniforms, the triumphal arch with its pictures and inscriptions, presented a brilliant spectacle ; but it was with great surprise, and not without displeasure, that the people of Moscow saw their Tsar in German dress and hat—the uniform of a ship-captain—walking in the suite of Admiral Lefort.

The success of the Russian arms created a deep impression everywhere in Europe, sometimes of astonishment, sometimes of admiration. In Warsaw, it was not hailed with great enthusiasm by the governing classes.   King Jan Sobieski had died during the summer, and the diet had as yet been unable to elect a successor.   The French were intriguing for the election of the Prince de Conti, a nephew of the great Condé, and had succeeded in getting the election transferred to a general assembly of the Polish nobility.   Another party was supporting the claims of Augustus the Strong, Elector of Saxony, and it was believed in Moscow that the Pope had recommended the choice of the exiled James II. of England.   Even before the surrender of Azof, a Frenchman, Fourni, who was returning through Warsaw after having conducted some foreign officers to Russia, spoke to some of the nobles with praise of the Russian deeds in front of Azof, and especially of the acts of the young Tsar. The senators listened, shook their heads and said : ' What a careless and reckless young man !   What can be expected of him now ? '   The voievode Mazincki remarked : ' The Moskals ought to remember what they owe to the late King Jan, how he raised them up and made them a mighty people, for if he had not concluded an alliance with them, they would have paid tribute to the Crimea until now, and would have set quietly at home, while now they are getting polished.'   To this the voievode of Plock remarked : ' It would have been better if they still sat at home.   It would be no hurt to us.   After they have got polished, and have smelt blood, you will see what will come of it ; though may the Lord God never let it come to this ! '

Nikítin, the Russian Resident at Warsaw, received the news of the capture of Azof on September 8, during divine service, and immediately ordered a Te Deum, and fired a salute, amid the hurrahs of the worshippers.   Four days later, Nikítin, in a solemn session of the Senate, gave to the Primate the Tsar's formal letter announcing the event, and made a speech in which, with all the flowery language of the time, he spoke of the triumph over the heathen, urged the Poles to advance towards Constantinople, and assured them that perhaps Arabia itself would be open to the free Polish eagle ; that now was the time for a crusade against the infidel ; that now was the time to conquer countries and gain new and *lawful* titles for the Polish crown, instead of using titles forbidden by treaties.   In reply to the threat in the concluding words, Nikítin was shortly afterwards informed by the imperial ambassadors that the senators had been frightened, and had resolved that in future the King should not use the title of Grand Duke of Kíef and Smolénsk, but added that the nobility were not very glad of the capture of Azof, although the common people were delighted. A few days later, formal congratulations were sent to the Resident, Te Deums were chanted in all the churches, and a salute fired ; but, at the same time, negotiations were begun with the Tartars and with Mazeppa. Sapieha, the hetman of Lithuania, even tried to diminish the success of the Russian arms by saying to Nikitin that Azof had not been captured by arms, but had surrendered.

If there were any at Moscow—either magnates or peasants —who, in the general joy, thought that with the capture of Azof the day of sacrifices was past, they were grievously disappointed. They little knew what ideas were already fermenting in Peter's mind. While in front of Azof, and even before its capture, Peter had written to the Venetian Senate, begging them, for the profit of all Christians, to send to Moscow thirteen good shipwrights who could construct all sorts of vessels of war. He had already the design of establishing a large fleet on the Black Sea. No sooner had the festivities in Moscow ended than, at a general council of the boyárs, it was decided to send 3,000 families of peasants and 3,000 Streltsi and soldiers to populate the empty town of Azof, and firmly to establish the Russian power at the mouth of the Don. At a second council, Peter stated the absolute necessity for a large fleet, and apparently with such convincing arguments, that the assembly decided that one should be built. Both civilians and clergy were called upon for sacrifices. Every landed proprietor possessing 10,000 peasant houses, every monastery possessing 8,000, was obliged to construct a ship fully equipped and armed, which should be entirely completed not later than the month of April, 1698. The merchants were called upon to contribute twelve mortar-boats, all other landed proprietors who possessed not less than 100 peasant houses were ordered to Moscow to enrol themselves into companies for the construction of ships. Details are known about sixty-one of these companies, of which nineteen were composed of the clergy. The

PETER BUILDS HIS FIRST FLEET.

ships and galleys were to be built at Vorónezh. The Government found the timber, but the companies were to provide the metal-work, the cordage, and all the other equipments, as well as the armament. Some of these companies found that so much time was lost in getting the material together that there was danger of their not fulfilling the precise orders of the Tsar, and of being exposed to heavy penalties. For that reason, nearly all the vessels were built by contractors, who were chiefly foreigners from the German suburb. Among those we notice particularly Franz Timmermann, who was also a Government contractor, the Danish Resident, Butenant von Rosenbusch, and Ysbrandt Ides, who had recently returned from his mission to China. This arrangement was approved by the Tsar, and most of the ships were ready at the appointed time. Ten large vessels were also built by the state.

The Venetian Senate, in reply to the request of the Tsar, sent a number of shipwrights under the command of Captain Giacomo Moro, who arrived in January, 1697, and who showed such great skill in the construction of galleys that the Tsar, on sending them home at the completion of their work, expressed to the Venetian authorities his liveliest gratitude. There were, besides, many shipwrights from Denmark, Sweden, and Holland, obtained through the intervention of Franz Timmermann and of the Danish Resident. Let us quote again from the preface of the Maritime Regulations, where Peter says:

' On this account he turned his whole mind to the construction of a fleet, and when, on account of the Tartar insults, the siege of Azof was begun, and afterwards that town was fortunately taken, then, according to his unchangeable will, he did not endure thinking long about it. He quickly set about the work. A suitable place for ship-building was found on the river Vorónezh, close to the town of that name, skilful shipwrights were called from England and Holland, and in 1696 there began a new work in Russia—the construction of great war-ships, galleys, and other vessels; and so that this might be for ever secured in Russia, and that he might introduce among his people the art of this business, he sent many people of noble families to Holland and other states to learn the building and management of ships; and that the monarch might not be

shamefully behind his subjects in that trade, he himself undertook a journey to Holland; and in Amsterdam, at the East
India wharf, giving himself up, with other volunteers, to the
learning of naval architecture, he got what was necessary for a
good carpenter to know, and, by his own work and skill, constructed and launched a new ship.'

For the purpose mentioned in the preceding extract, Peter
sent abroad fifty nobles, representatives of the highest and most
distinguished families in the empire. Twenty-eight were ordered to Italy, especially to Venice, where they might learn the
art of building galleys, the remainder to Holland and England.
Each was accompanied by a soldier. According to their instructions, they were to make themselves familiar with the use
of charts, compasses, and navigation; they were to learn thoroughly the art of ship-building, and were to become practised
in the duties of common sailors. No one was to return without permission, and without a certificate attesting his profi-
ciency, on penalty of the confiscation of all his property. They
were obliged to pay their own expenses. Most of them were
married and had children, and we can imagine their feelings,
and those of their families, on being thus summarily sent to
unknown and heretical lands to become common sailors. In
point of fact, several of them turned their stay abroad to profit,
and like Kurákin, Dolgorúky, Tolstói, and Hilkóf, became skilful diplomatists, able administrators and useful servants of
Peter and his successors; but not one distinguished himself in
naval matters.[1]

[1] Soloviéf, xiv.; Ustriálof, II., xii.; Yelághin; Veselágo; Posselt, *Lefort.*

XXVIII.

DURING the reign of Iván the Terrible and his son Theodore, young Russian theological students were sometimes sent to Constantinople to learn Greek, and Boris Godunóf, as has been already said, sent a number of youths of good family to Lübeck, France, and England, for the completion of their education. These last found foreign life so attractive that only two of them returned. Under the Tsar Alexis, the children of foreigners living in Moscow were sometimes sent abroad at the expense of the Government to study medicine, and even a Russian, Peter Postnikóf, the son of a high official in the Foreign Office, was sent, in 1692, to Italy for the same purpose. He passed a distinguished examination at Padua in 1696, and received the degree of Doctor of Medicine, as well as that of Doctor of Philosophy. He did not, however, long pursue the practice of the healing art, for on account of his knowledge of Latin, French, and Italian, the Government employed him in diplomatic affairs.

With these exceptions, most of the Russians who had travelled abroad up to this time, had been either pilgrims or diplomatists.[1] To some of these pilgrims we owe highly interesting accounts of Constantinople and the Holy Land, both before and after the occupation of the Imperial city by the Turks. The Abbot Daniel describes his meeting with Baldwin, King of Jerusalem, in 1115. The Deacon Ignatius was present at the coronation of the Emperor Manuel in 1391, and Simeón of

---

[1] Occasionally, but rarely, a Russian merchant ventured abroad. We know of the mishaps of Laptéf (see p. 230), and we should not forget the brave merchant of Tver, Athanasius Nikítin, who has left us an entertaining story of his journey through India in 1468.

Suzdal accompanied the Metropolitan Isidore to the council of Florence in 1439.

The pilgrims were occupied chiefly with relics and with religious ceremonies. The diplomatists, although, like all good Christians, they did not neglect these, were more busied with court ceremonies and with formal official relations. Not understanding the language of the countries to which they were sent, their reports are very dry and meagre, and taken up almost exclusively with exact accounts of the interviews they had with the ministers of foreign affairs, of their audiences with the sovereigns, and of their disputes on points of etiquette. They say almost nothing about the political state of the countries in which they travelled. Indeed, they were not in a condition to obtain information on these subjects. They had not sufficient experience of political life, much less of a political life differing from that of Russia, to know to what points to direct their attention, or how to make inquiries through an interpreter. It is difficult to see what impression even was made on them by foreign countries, or whether they were pleased by a life so different from that at home. Incidentally, we know that their stay abroad must have been agreeable to them, for frequently some members of their suite ran away in order not to return to Russia. We can see, too, that they were greatly interested in the canals and quays at Amsterdam, Bologna, and Verona. They were much pleased with the magnificent gardens of Holland and Italy, to which those made for the Tsar Alexis were so far inferior, and in these their admiration was especially excited by the fish-ponds and fountains. Works of art they were too uncultivated and unrefined to enjoy. The theatre pleased them more, but here they were chiefly struck by the costumes and the scenery. Ignorance of the language prevented them from appreciating the play or the acting, and the greatest opera-singers were to them so many 'wenches.' Zoological gardens and the collections of curiosities, which at that time contained a mixture of the scientific, the rare, the monstrous, and the odd, interested them greatly. Their deepest impressions were, perhaps, those of the comfort, as well as of the luxury, of Western life. The comfort, probably, they appreciated the more. For the introduction of luxury, little more than a command of money was

required; for the appropriation of comfort, there were necessary an organisation of social life and a careful management
which it took many long years to naturalise in Russia. Some
of the more observing diplomatists did indeed learn something
of public life, and gained ideas which were useful to them at
home. The financial and economical reforms of Alexis Kurbátof were the immediate fruits of what he had learned when
accompanying the boyár Sheremétief. Ukráintsef would never
have been the skilful diplomatist he was, had it not been for his
experience in several embassies, and Zheliabúzhky owed much to
his stay in London, and his journey to Italy. In nearly all cases,
even though on their return the travellers sank back into Russian life and Russian ways, their experience in the West must
have given them a certain enlargement of mind, and a certain
readiness to receive new ideas must have sensibly weakened
their prejudices against what was foreign, and have powerfully
aided in the Europeanization of Russia.

The most illustrious traveller of that day was the boyár
Boris Sheremétief. He had gone to Lemberg in 1686, to receive the ratification of the Russian-Polish treaty by King Jan
Sobieski, and had afterwards announced it at Vienna; but, in
1697, after the fatigue of his campaigns against the Turks and
Tartars, he asked permission to go abroad as a simple traveller
for the purpose of fulfilling a vow which he had made when in
danger, to pray at the tombs of the Holy Apostles Peter and
Paul at Rome. This request, which fell in so well with the
views of Peter at that time, was readily granted, and Sheremétief was given letters by the Tsar to the King of Poland, the
Emperor Leopold, the Doge of Venice, Pope Innocent XII.,
and the Grand Master of Malta. Although he travelled simply
as a tourist, he apparently had instructions to inquire into the
relations of Venice, and especially of Malta, with the Orient,
and to see what dependence could be placed on them, or what
aid be expected from them, in case of the continuation of the
war with Turkey. Sheremétief left Moscow in July, 1697, and
did not return until the end of February, 1699. He took with
him a numerous suite—among them as his secretary and treas-
urer, Alexis Kurbátof, who afterwards became distinguished as
a financial reformer. Sheremétief travelled with great state,

and his whole journey cost him the sum of 20,550 rubles, equivalent then to about $42,500, fully ten or twelve times the salary usually received by the ambassadors. He was received with great ceremony and honour by the rulers of the countries he visited, was feasted and entertained by the nobles of Venice, Rome, and Naples, all of which cities were then in the height of their social splendour; was courted by the Jesuits, who hoped to convert him, and through him to unite the Russian with the Catholic Church; he was made a Knight of Malta, and was the first Russian who ever received a foreign decoration.

In general, the diplomatists were very badly paid. They were usually given twice the salary which they received from their official positions at home, in addition to presents of furs and provisions, and on their return usually further presents of furs. Only a small portion of their salary was paid in advance, and that chiefly in furs, which they had to sell at their post of duty in order to raise money. It was difficult for them to draw either on the Government or on their private property, as the commercial relations of Russia with foreign countries were at that time such that bills of exchange on Amsterdam were the only means of sending money abroad. They were therefore obliged to travel chiefly at their own expense, and frequently had great difficulty in getting paid when they came home. General Gordon was obliged to wait years for the payment of his expenses when on a special mission to England. The burden thus laid on diplomatists was not inconsiderable. Their suites were great. Likhatchéf, for example, had twenty-eight persons with him; and the attendants of Tchemodánof were so numerous that he was obliged to charter two vessels from Archangel, as they could not all be accommodated on one. They were enjoined also to give proper presents in the proper places, and always strictly to pay their debts, that dishonour might not accrue to the Government. The manner of payment by furs and other articles of commerce, which they were obliged to sell in order to raise money, gave them sometimes more the air of commercial travellers and merchants than of ambassadors, and as they were naturally desirous of getting these wares—which were money to them—through the custom-houses free of duty, disputes with foreign Governments, as we have seen,[1] were not unfrequently brought about. Besides this, too, they were sometimes commissioned to make sales of articles abroad for the benefit of the Government. Thus Tchemodánof took to Italy, on behalf of the Government, 3,600 pounds of rhubarb, worth, according to Russian calculations, 5,000 rubles, and sables to the amount of 1,000 rubles. The speculation was unsuccessful. No purchasers could be found for the rhubarb, because it had been injured at sea, and on account of the difficulty of its transport over the Apennines, Tchemodánof was obliged to leave Leghorn. But few of the sables were sold, and these at very low prices.

In some cases the Government assisted its envoys by lending them embroidered robes of state, jewels, plate, and horse-trappings, which had to be exactly accounted for, and given back to the Treasury on their return.

Not the least interesting information contained in the reports of the Russian diplomatists is that concerning the difficulties of travel in those days. Journeys by water were always easier and cheaper than those by land, and the embassies sent to England, Holland, France, or Italy usually went by sea from Archangel, although in so doing they were obliged to spend much time, and in the Mediterranean to expose themselves to imminent danger of capture by Turkish and Barbary pirates. The voyages of Likatchéf and Tchemodánof from Archangel to Leghorn occupied between four and five months, and besides the pirates, they encountered icebergs and severe tempests. As to land travel, the journey through Turkey was too dangerous and difficult to be for a moment considered. In Poland, the hostile attitude of the magnates was such, especially during the constant intestine difficulties, that it was generally desirable to avoid that country, and there were often reasons for not passing through the territory of Riga. In travelling by land, too, there were frequent delays arising from difficulties of obtaining horses, and the bad manner in which Russian carriages were constructed. Sheremétief, who took five months and a half for his journey from Moscow to Cracow, travelled, as long as he was on Russian soil, with his own horses. After crossing

---

[1] See page 146.

the frontier, he hired them. He frequently made only five or six miles a day. Even outside of Russia, a journey by land was necessarily slow. Sheremétief took a whole month to go from Vienna to Venice, and sixteen days for his return. Tchemodánof was eight weeks in going from Venice to Amsterdam, and Likatchéf five and a half weeks from Florence to Amsterdam.

Even in England, the roads were so bad that in 1703 the Spanish Pretender Charles III. (VI.) was fourteen hours in driving from London to Windsor, although he stopped only when the carriage was overturned or stuck in the mud. There were great difficulties in crossing the mountains, whether in Switzerland or between Vienna and Venice. Sheremétief was put to much trouble and expense by the snow near Pontebba, on the road from Tarvis, and was obliged to go for some distance on foot. Likatchéf was detained three days by a snowstorm on the St. Gothard. Stage-coaches were introduced into some parts of Europe, especially into Brandenburg, where in 1676 a Frenchman going to Berlin expressed his astonishment that one could travel in a coach by night. A pamphlet which appeared in England in 1673 tried to prove that stage-coaches were injuring trade in England, that fewer saddles, boots, spurs, and pistols were bought than formerly, and that clothes were not worn out so fast since men could keep dry by sitting in the coaches, by which the use of manufactured articles was limited. It was alleged that travelling by stage-coach produced effeminacy, because people were not exposed to the weather, and that travelling by night was very unhealthful.

The expenses of travelling were sometimes very great, even for a small party. Likatchéf paid for four carriages, a baggage-wagon and four riding-horses, to go from Bologna to Modena, a distance of about twenty-four miles, the sum of 154 thalers, a great amount in those days.

In the larger towns, there were sometimes good inns. Sheremétief put up at the 'Golden Bull' at Vienna, and at an inn in Naples. Montaigne, we all remember, when in Rome lodged at the Albergo dell' Orso, which he found too expensive for him. The account given by the President des Brosses, in 1739, of the inns in the Italian towns, especially in Rome, shows that they were not particularly comfortable. In the smaller towns and villages, the inns scarcely provided more than shelter for the horses, and travellers were obliged to take lodgings in some private house. The Russian diplomatists usually had recourse first to the merchants at Archangel, and then to the Dutch merchants in Amsterdam who had relations with Russia, and from them received information as to their road—for they knew almost nothing of geography—and letters to correspondents in different towns who obtained for them accommodation. On reaching their destination, they usually had accommodation provided for them by the Government to which they were accredited. This sometimes happened in other places. Zheliabúzhky was lodged in Massa at the Ducal castle, and in Trent Tchemodánof was entertained by the archbishop. Both at Rome and at Vienna, Sheremétief was able to hire large furnished apartments in palaces.[1]

---

[1] Brückner, *Culturhistorische Studien;* Kotóshikhin, *Russia in the Reign of Alexis* (Russian), St. Petersburg, 1856 ; *Diplomatic Monuments* (Russian), vol. x., St. Petersburg, 1831 ; *Documents Relating to Russia from the Florentine Archives* (Russian and Italian), Moscow, 1871 ; *Old Russian Travellers* in Sákharof's *Account of the Russian People* (Russian), St. Petersburg, 1841 ; Sheremétief, *Journal du Voyage,* Paris, 1858.

XXIX

THE JOURNEY OF PETER TO WESTERN EUROPE.

THE Tsar's feeling was so strong with regard to what might be learnt about ship-building in foreign countries that, after he

had sent off many of his subjects to study the trade, he resolved to go himself. Without ascribing to this journey all the importance which Macaulay gave to it when he said, 'His journey is an epoch in the history, not only of his own country, but of ours, and of the world,' we must admit that it was a remarkable event, and one fraught with much consequence. Since the exiled Izyasláv visited the court of the Emperor Henry IV., at Mainz, in 1075, no Russian ruler had ever been out of his dominions. Peter's journey marks the division between the old Russia, an exclusive, little known country, and the new Russia, an important factor in European politics. It was also one of the turning points in the development of his character, and was the continuation of the education begun in the German suburb. In one way, it may be said that Peter's appearance in the German suburb was really more startling, and of more importance, than

Peter In the Dress of Western Europe.

his journey westward, for that journey was the natural consequence and culmination of his intercourse with foreigners at
Moscow.

This sudden and mysterious journey of the Tsar abroad exercised the minds of Peter's contemporaries no less than it has
those of moderns.   Many were the reasons which were ascribed
then, and have been given since, for this step.   There was
even a dispute among the students of the University of Thorn
as to the motives which had induced the Tsar to travel.   Pleyer,
the secret Austrian agent, wrote to the Emperor Leopold that
the whole embassy was 'merely a cloak for the freedom sought
by the Tsar, to get out of his own country and divert himself
a little.'   Another document in the archives at Vienna finds
the cause of the journey in a vow made by Peter, when in danger on the White Sea, to make a pilgrimage to the tombs of
the Apostles St. Peter and St. Paul, at Rome.   According to
Voltaire, 'He resolved to absent himself for some years from
his dominions, in order to learn how better to govern them.'
Napoleon said: 'He left his country to deliver himself for a
while from the crown, so as to learn ordinary life, and to re-
mount by degrees to greatness.'   But every authentic source
gives us but one reason, and the same.   Peter went abroad,
not to fulfil a vow, not to amuse himself, not to become more
civilised, not to learn the art of government, but simply to become a good shipwright.   His mind was filled with the idea
of creating a navy on the Black Sea for use against the Turks,
and his tastes were still, as they had always been, purely mechanical.   For this purpose, as he himself says, and as his prolonged residence in Holland shows, he desired to have an opportunity of studying the art of ship-building in those places
where it was carried to the highest perfection, that is, in Holland, England, and Venice.

In order to give the Tsar greater freedom of action, and to
save him from too much formality and ceremony, which he
exceedingly disliked, an attempt was made to conceal the purpose of his journey by means of a great embassy, which should
visit the chief countries of Western Europe, to explain the
policy of Russia toward Turkey, and to make whatever treaties
it was found possible, either for commercial purposes or for the

war against the Turks. The embassy consisted of three extraordinary ambassadors, at the head of whom was General Lefort. Besides the other rewards he had received for the campaigns against Azof, he had been given the honorary title of Governor-General of Nóvgorod. The other ambassadors were the Governor-General of Siberia, Theodore Golovín, who had already distinguished himself by the treaty of Nertchínsk with the Chinese; and the Governor of Bólkhof, Prokóp Voznítsyn, a skilful and experienced diplomatist. In the suite of the ambassadors were twenty nobles and thirty-five others, called volunteers, who, like those previously sent, were going abroad for the study of ship-building. Among these was the Tsar himself. These volunteers were chiefly young men who had been comrades of Peter in his play regiments, in his boat-building, and in his campaigns against Azof. Among them may be particularly remarked Alexander Menshikóf and Alexis Golítsyn, two Golovíns, Simeon Narýshkin, and the Prince Alexander Bagrátion of Imeritia. Including priests, interpreters, pages, singers, and servants of various kinds, the suite of the embassy numbered as many as two hundred and fifty persons. The Tsar himself travelled under the strictest incognito. It was forbidden to give him the title of Majesty—he was always to be addressed simply as *Min Her* Peter Mikháilof—and it was forbidden, under pain of death, to mention his presence with the embassy.

During the absence of the Tsar, the government was entrusted to a regency of three persons—Leo Narýshkin, Prince Boris Golítsyn, and Prince Peter ProzoRófsky, who were given supreme power. Prince Ramodanófsky was charged with maintaining order in Moscow, and he had verbal instructions to follow up, in the severest way, the slightest movement of discontent or rebellion. The boyár Shéïn, assisted by General Gordon, had charge of the defence of the southern frontier on the side of Azof, while Prince Jacob Dolgorúky succeeded the boyár Sheremétief in charge of the defences against the Tartars on the frontier of Little Russia, and was ordered to get galleys ready for the siege of Otchakóf in the spring of 1698. Sheremétief, who had already served two years in that country, obtained leave of absence and permission to travel abroad.

Preparations were nearly finished for the departure of the embassy, when an unexpected delay occurred. Gordon expressed it thus in his diary: ' A merry night has been spoiled by an accident of discovering treason against his Majesty.' The Colonel of the Streltsi, Iván Zickler, of foreign birth or extraction, and two Russian nobles of high rank, Alexis Sokóvnin and Theodore Púshkin, were accused of plotting against the life of the Tsar. They were accused on the testimony of Lárion Yelisárof, who was one of the denunciators of the alleged plot against Peter's life in 1689, when he took refuge at Tróïtsa. In all probability there was no plot whatever, but simply loose and unguarded talk between discontented men. Zickler had always been well treated by the Princess Sophia and Shaklovíty, but when he saw the preponderance on the side of Peter he went to Tróïtsa and made denunciations. He did not, however, receive the reward and favour which he expected, but, on the contrary, was looked upon askance, and had recently been sent to Azof. He was naturally irritated against the Tsar, and in unguarded moments probably expressed his feelings too strongly. Sokóvnin was a virulent dissenter, and the brother of two ladies well known for their opposition to the Patriarch Níkon, and their encouragement of dissent in the reign of Alexis—Theodora Morózof and the Princess Avdótia Urúsof. He was therefore opposed to many of Peter's innovations ; and his father-in-law, Matthew Púshkin, who had been appointed Governor of Azof, had excited the anger of the Tsar because he had refused to send his children abroad. Theodore Púshkin was one of the sons, and had uttered vague threats of revenge in case the Tsar should have his father whipped to death for his refusal, for rumours to that effect were being industriously circulated. Torture produced confessions of various kinds, and among them repetitions by Zickler of the old accusations against the Princess Sophia. The prisoners were speedily condemned, and were beheaded on the Red Place, after having their arms and legs chopped off. Their heads were exposed on stakes. The confessions of Zickler, and the renewed accusations against his sister Sophia, excited Peter's mind against the whole of the Miloslávsky family, and in his rage he even went to the length of taking up the body of Iván Miloslávsky—who had been dead fourteen years—of dragging the coffin by swine to the place of execution, and of placing it in such a position that the blood of the criminals spurted into the face of the corpse.

Even at this time there was much popular discontent and hostile criticism of Peter. Not all of those who saw that re-forms were absolutely necessary approved his measures and his conduct. A rumour was spread that the Tsar Iván had publicly proclaimed to all the people: ' My brother does not live accord-ing to the Church. He goes to the German suburb, and is acquainted with Germans.' There was talk, too, of the way in which Peter had abandoned his wife and family, and family affairs probably caused the quarrel between Leo Narýshkin and the Lopúkhins, the relatives of Peter's wife. What exactly happened is not known, but Peter Lopúkhin, the uncle of the Tsaritsa and the Minister of the Palace, was accused of bri-bery and extortion, and for this, or some other cause, was ex-iled, together with his brothers, one of them the father of the Tsaritsa. A report was circulated among the common peo-ple, and was widely believed, that Peter had assisted with his own hands in applying the torture to his wife's uncle. One man, the monk Abraham, dared to make himself the exponent of the popular feeling, and presented to Peter a petition in which he made mention of the abandonment of his wife, of the relations which he had formed in the German suburb, and of the bad feeling which had been excited by the Tsar lower-ing himself to work at boats, and to appear on foot in the tri-umphal procession, instead of taking his proper place. As was natural, the petition gave rise to a trial; Abraham was sent to a distant monastery, and three other men who were impli-cated were punished with the knout, and sent to Azof.

When these trials were completed, the embassy set out, on March 20, 1697. It was intended to go first to Vienna, then to Venice and Rome, then to Holland and England, and to return by the way of Königsberg. The trouble in Poland, con-sequent on the interregnum, made travelling through that country dangerous, and the only way in which Vienna could be reached was by a roundabout journey through Riga, Königs-berg, and Dresden. The plan was therefore changed.

The first experience of the Tsar in a foreign country was an unfortunate one. The Governor of Pskov, who had been ordered to make the arrangements for Peter's journey through Livonia, had neglected to say in his letter to Eric Dahlberg, the Governor of Riga, how many persons accompanied the embassy. Dahlberg replied, asking the number of people he should expect, and saying that, while he would do his best, he hoped they would overlook some inconveniences, as a great famine was unfortunately reigning in the country. Major Glazenap was sent to the frontier to escort the embassy, but Peter was so impatient, and travelled so fast, that they arrived at the frontier before the proper arrangements had been made to receive them. They therefore found no conveyances, and were obliged to go on to Riga in the carriages brought from Pskov, and trust to their own provisions. A short distance from Riga, light carriages and an escort were waiting for them, and they were ceremoniously received in the town with a military parade, while a guard of fifty men was placed near their lodgings. The next day the ambassadors sent two of their nobles to thank the governor for his kindness, and a return visit was paid by one of his adjutants. Immediately afterward, Peter wrote to Vinius that they 'were received with great honour, and with a salute of twenty-four guns, when they entered and left the fortress.' Unfortunately, the embassy was detained at Riga for a whole week by the breaking up of the ice on the Düna, which made crossing impossible. Peter preserved his incognito, and went out to see the town. His military curiosity naturally led him to inspect the fortifications and measure the width and depth of the ditches, when he was somewhat rudely ordered away by the sentinel. Discontented at this, a complaint was made, and the governor apologised, assuring Lefort that no discourtesy was intended. Lefort was satisfied, and said that the sentinel had merely done his duty. It must be remembered that Riga was a frontier town, that Livonia was an outlying province of Sweden, and that the embassy was not accredited to the Swedish court. Dahlberg was coldly, formally polite; he did all that propriety demanded, but nothing more. He knew perfectly well that the Tsar was with the embassy, but he respected his incognito. As the ambassadors did not pay him a visit in person, he did not pay a personal visit to the ambassadors. Nothing was done in the way of amusement or diversion for the Tsar, besides the first reception. The ambassadors were left to pay for their lodgings and their provisions, and to get on as best they might. They paid high prices for everything, but times were hard, and the people naturally tried to make the most they could out of the distinguished strangers. As there was nothing to be seen, either in a military or naval way, as there were no feasts or amusements of any kind prepared for him, Peter became bored, especially as he was anxious to continue his journey. He left the rest, ventured across the river in a small boat, and remained waiting two days on the other side. In a letter to Vinius, of April 18, he says: 'Here we lived in a slavish way, and were tired with the mere sight of things.' Nevertheless, the embassy took its leave with all form and ceremony, and crossed the river on a vessel carrying the royal flag of Sweden, and with a salute. When it was necessary to find a pretext for a war with Sweden, the reception at Riga was made one of the reasons, and even in 1709, when the siege of Riga was undertaken, Peter, after throwing the first three bomb-shells into the town, wrote to Menshikóf: 'Thus the Lord God has enabled us to see the beginning of our revenge on this accursed place.' We should add here that Peter's feelings about his reception at Riga probably increased with time. In other countries where he went, there was a sovereign with a court, and although, in a certain way, the Tsar was incognito, yet he was privately and familiarly received and entertained. It was unfortunate for him that his first venture was in an outlying province, the tenure of which was not too secure, and in a commercial rather than in an aristocratic city.

Mitau is now a dull provincial town, and the Hebrew signs on the street corners show the great Jewish population. Its greatest object of interest to travellers is the old Ducal Castle, almost entirely rebuilt in the last century, with its reminiscences of the residence and sudden departure of the exiled Louis XVIII., and with the mummified body of the Duke John Ernest Biren (the lover of the Empress Anne, and the ancestor of the Sagan family), which lies in its coffin attired in velvet and ruffles, but by some malice lacking the tip of the nose. In 1697 Mitau was the capital of the little Duchy of Curland, which maintained a semi-independence by becoming a fief of the Polish crown. The reigning Duke, Frederic Casimir, was an old friend of Lefort. It was with him that Lefort had served in Holland. Although he was poor, he did everything that he could to make the time pass pleasantly for Peter and for the embassy. Here the Tsar consented to give up in part his incognito, made visits to the Duke, and received them in return. A week was quickly passed in amusement and pleasure, but even with this Peter found time to exercise himself in a carpenter's shop.

From Mitau Peter proceeded to Libau, where he was detained by bad weather for a week, until he finally took passage on a small ship going to Pillau, the port of Königsberg. During his stay at Libau, he passed for the skipper of a Russian privateer, though he was able to give no satisfactory explanation to an acquaintance, who frequently met and drank with him in a small beer-shop, as to why it was a privateer, and not a merchant vessel that he commanded. Besides the beer-house, Peter often visited an apothecary's shop, and wrote to Vinius that he had seen there 'a wonder which was ordinarily considered untrue, a real salamander preserved in spirits in a bottle,' which he had taken out and held in his hand. The embassy proceeded by land. The Tsar went by sea, to avoid passing through Polish territory.

Blomberg, whom we have already cited about the election of Patriarch, met the embassy in Curland, and says of their entertainment: 'Open tables were kept everywhere, with trumpets and music, attended with feasting and excessive drinking all along, as if his Tsarish Majesty had been another Bacchus. I have not seen such hard drinkers; it is not possible to express it, and they boast of it as a mighty qualification.' Of Lefort's drinking he remarks: 'It never overcomes him, but he always continues master of his reason.' Leibnitz, writing from private information received from Königsberg, says much the same thing: 'Lefort drinks like a hero; no one can rival him. It is feared that he will be the death of some of the Elector's courtiers. Beginning in the evening, he does not leave his pipe and glass till three hours after sunrise, and yet he is a man of great parts.'

Frederick III., Elector of Brandenburg, then on the eve of

transforming himself into the first King of Prussia, was greatly
interested to know whether the Tsar was really with the embassy, and beside sending a secret agent into Curland to find
out, he gave directions about the treatment of the embassy, in
case it were simply intending to pass through his dominions,
or in case it were directed also to him. Peter was therefore
met at Pillau by an officer who proffered the hospitality of the
Elector, but an answer was returned that there was no person
of distinction on board, except the Prince of Imeritia, and that
no visits could be received. A similar occurrence took place at
the mouth of the Pregel, and it was not until Peter arrived at
Königsberg itself that he was willing to allow himself to be
known to the Elector. After taking small lodgings in a street
on the Kneiphof, he went out in a close carriage, late at night,
and paid a visit to the Elector, entering the palace by a private
staircase. The interview lasted for an hour and a half, and the
sovereigns were mutually pleased. Although, in order to keep
his incognito, Peter refused to receive a return visit, yet he saw
the Elector several times again, and was entertained by him at his
country house, witnessed a bear-fight, and appeared at a hunting
party. His curiosity and vivacity, his readiness to be pleased, and
his appreciation of the manners and habits of the country, made
a favourable impression. He astonished by his natural capacity
and his dexterity, even in playing the trumpet and the drum.

The embassy arrived eleven days after Peter, and was splendidly received. Great advantages were expected to Brandenburg from an intimacy with Russia, and the Elector, therefore,
spared no money. Peter's visit is said to have cost him 150,000
thalers. Under the skilful guidance of Lefort and Von Besser,
all ceremonial observances were strictly complied with, and, for
the first time in the history of Russian missions abroad, there
was no unseemly wrangling over points of precedence and etiquette. The members of the embassy appeared officially in
Russian costume, although they wore foreign dress in private.
The Elector told the Tsar afterwards that he had hard work to
keep from laughing, when, according to custom, he had to ask
the ambassadors how the Tsar was, and whether they had left
him in good health. Peter had just before been standing at
the window to see the entry of the embassy, and was well

satisfied. At a supper given in honour of the ambassadors, great pleasure was caused by the fireworks, one piece representing the Russian arms, and another the victory at Azof.

The two rulers were so well disposed towards each other, that a treaty of friendship was speedily concluded. The Elector was greatly desirous that there should be inserted an article of alliance for mutual defence and protection; but the Russians were too cautious for this, and although the treaty contained clauses giving additional privileges to merchants, especially as regarded the Persian trade, and for the surrender of criminals and deserters, yet the Elector had to be satisfied with a verbal agreement and oath 'not to let a favourable occasion escape of being useful to each other by giving each other their mutual help, as far as possible, against all their enemies, but particularly against the Swedes.'

On June 20, after nearly a month's stay, Peter went to Pillau, with the intention of taking ship directly to Holland, for he found it more convenient to defer his visit to Vienna till his return. Before leaving, he sent a ruby of large size as a present to his host. At Pillau he was detained three weeks longer, by the necessity of watching affairs in Poland, where the interregnum consequent on the death of Sobieski had produced more than the usual trouble. The threatened intervention by the French, to support the Prince de Conti on the Polish throne, would have been greatly against the interest of Russia. The Tsar occupied his leisure with active and thorough studies in artillery, under the guidance of the chief engineer of the Prussian fortresses, Colonel Steitner von Sternfeld, who gave him a certificate of remarkable progress and knowledge.

An unfortunate incident, arising from Peter's hasty temper, marked the conclusion of his stay. He had remained a day longer to celebrate his name's-day, and had expected the Elector to visit him. He had even made some fireworks for the occasion. Frederick had been obliged to go to Memel, to meet the Duke of Curland, and therefore sent Count von Kreyzen and the Landvogt von Schacken to present his compliments and his regrets. Peter was childishly vexed, and in his disappointment at not being able to show his fireworks, vented his rage on the envoys. He took it amiss that they had left the room after dinner to 'refresh themselves' after their journey, and had them brought back. Looking 'sourly' at Count von Kreyzen, he remarked in Dutch to Lefort, that 'The Elector was very good, but his counsellors were the devil.' Then, thinking he saw a smile steal over the face of Kreyzen, who was about to retire, he rushed at him, cried, 'Go! go!' and twice pushed him backwards. His anger did not cool until he had written to his 'dearest friend,' the Elector, a letter half of complaint and half of apology.

Instead of going by sea from Pillau to Holland, Peter went no farther than Colberg, as he was fearful of falling in with the French squadron, which was said to be escorting the Prince de Conti to Poland. From that place he travelled by land as speedily as possible, stopping only to look at the famous ironworks near Ilsenburg, and to ascend the Brocken for the view.

The journey of the Tsar produced as much commotion and excitement in the minds of curious people of that time as did those of the Sultan and Shah in our own day. Among those most anxious to form a personal acquaintance with the Tsar were the philosopher Leibnitz, who had long been interested in Russia, chiefly for philological reasons, and his friends, Sophia, the widowed Electress of Hanover, granddaughter of James I. of England, and her daughter Sophia Charlotte, wife of the Elector of Brandenburg. Sophia Charlotte was on a visit to her mother, and had therefore missed the visit of Peter to Königsberg, though she had had full accounts of it from a constant correspondent. Leibnitz was unable at this time to see the Tsar, but the two Electresses, attended by several young princes and members of their court, made a hasty journey from Hanover to Koppenbrügge, through which they found Peter was to pass. They invited him to sup with them, but it took a discussion of an hour to persuade him to accept, and he did so only on the assurance that he would be received in the simplest way. He finally succeeded in avoiding the curious eyes of the attendants, and in getting into the supper-room by the back staircase. After supper there was a dance, and the party did not separate until four in the morning. Perhaps the princesses can tell their own story best. Sophia Charlotte says in a letter:

'My mother and I began to pay him our compliments, but he made Mr. Lefort reply for him, for he seemed shy, hid his face in his hands, and said: "*Ich kann nicht sprechen.*" But we tamed him a little, and then he sat down at the table between my mother and myself, and each of us talked to him in turn, and it was a strife who should have it. Sometimes he replied with the same promptitude, at others he made two interpreters talk, and assuredly he said nothing that was not to the point on all subjects that were suggested, for the vivacity of my mother put to him many questions, to which he replied with the same readiness, and I was astonished that he was not tired with the conversation, for I have been told that it is not much the habit in his country. As to his grimaces, I imagined them worse than I found them, and some are not in his power to correct. One can see also that he has had no one to teach him how to eat properly, but he has a natural, unconstrained air which pleases me.'

Her mother wrote, a few days afterwards:

'The Tsar is very tall, his features are fine, and his figure very noble. He has great vivacity of mind, and a ready and just repartee. But, with all the advantages with which nature has endowed him, it could be wished that his manners were a little less rustic. We immediately sat down to table. Herr Koppenstein, who did the duty of marshal, presented the napkin to his Majesty, who was greatly embarrassed, for at Brandenburg, instead of a table-napkin, they had given him an ewer and basin after the meal. He was very gay, very talkative, and we established a great friendship for each other, and he exchanged snuff-boxes with my daughter. We stayed, in truth, a very long time at table, but we would gladly have remained there longer still without feeling a moment of *ennui*, for the Tsar was in very good humour, and never ceased talking to us. My daughter had her Italians sing. Their song pleased him, though he confessed to us that he did not care much for music.

'I asked him if he liked hunting. He replied that his father had been very fond of it, but that he himself, from his earliest youth, had had a real passion for navigation and for fireworks. He told us that he worked himself in building ships, showed us his hands, and made us touch the callous places that had been caused by work. He brought his musicians, and they played Russian dances, which we liked better than Polish ones.

'Lefort and his nephew dressed in French style, and had much wit. We did not speak to the other ambassadors. We regretted that we could not stay longer, so that we could see him again, for his society gave us much pleasure. He is a very extraordinary man. It is impossible to describe him, or even to give an idea of him, unless you have seen him. He has a very good heart, and remarkably noble sentiments. I must tell you, also, that he did not get drunk in our presence, but we had hardly left when the people of his suite made ample amends.'

In another letter she says:—

'I could embellish the tale of the journey of the illustrious Tsar, if I should tell you that he is sensible to the charms of beauty, but, to come to the bare fact, I found in him no disposition to gallantry. If we had not taken so many steps to see him, I believe that he would never have thought of us. In his country it is the custom for all women to paint, and rouge forms an essential part of their marriage presents. That is why the Countess Platen singularly pleased the Muscovites; but in dancing, they took the whalebones of our corsets for our bones, and the Tsar showed his astonishment by saying that the German ladies had devilish hard bones.

'They have four dwarfs. Two of them are very well-proportioned, and perfectly well-bred; sometimes he kissed, and sometimes he pinched the ear of his favorite dwarf. He took the head of our little Princess (Sophia Dorothea, ten years old), and kissed her twice. The ribbons of her hair suffered in consequence. He also kissed her brother (afterwards George II. of England, then sixteen years old). He is a prince at once very good and very *méchant*. He has quite the manners of his country. If he had received a better education, he would be an accomplished man, for he has many good qualities, and an infinite amount of natural wit.'[1]

---

[1] Ustriálof, III., i. ii. and appendix; Soloviéf, xiv. ; Posselt, *Lefort ;* Brückner, *Die Reise Peters des Grossen in Ausland,* in the *Russische Revue* for 1879; Lamberty, *Mémoires pour servir à l'histoire du XVIII. siècle,* i., La Haye, 1724 ; Blomberg, *Account of Livonia ;* Erman, *Mémoires pour servir à l'histoire de Sophie Charlotte,* Berlin, 1801 ; Theiner, *Monuments historiques ;* V. Guerrier, *Leibnitz and Peter the Great* (Russian), St. Petersburg, 1871-73; F. Martens, *Recueil des Traités et Conventions de Russie,* V., *Traités avec l'Allemagne,* St. Petersburg, 1880.

XXX.

A short sail from Amsterdam, up the gulf of the Y, brings the traveller to the picturesque little town of Zaandam, extending along the banks of the river Zaan. From the windows of the coffee-house, built on the dam or dyke which connects the two parts of the town, one can see on one side the placid pool of the Binnenzaan, with gardens sloping to the shore, and cottages painted blue, green, and pink, half concealed in the verdure, and on the other the port with its wharves and ship-yards, the many sails on the Y, and the multitudinous windmills, which surround the town like guardian towers. At the end of the seventeenth century, Zaandam, with the neighbouring villages, was the centre of a great ship-building business. There were not less than fifty private wharves in Zaandam, at which merchant vessels were constructed, and so great was the crowd of workmen, and so rapid the execution, that a vessel was often ready to go to sea in five weeks from the time the keel was laid. The windmills then, as now, supplied the motive power for sawing the necessary timber. At Vorónezh, at Archangel, and elsewhere, Peter had met shipwrights from Zaandam, who had praised so much their native town, that he was convinced that only there could he learn the art of ship-building in its perfection. His journey from Koppenbrügge and down the Rhine had been rapid, and passing through Amsterdam without halting, the Tsar reached Zaandam early on the morning of August 18, having with him only six volunteers, including the Prince of Imeritia and the two brothers Menshikóf. On the way he saw an old Moscow acquaintance, the smith Gerrit Kist, fishing in the river. He hailed him, and told him for what purpose he had come to Zaandam. Binding him

to absolute secresy, the Tsar insisted on taking up his quarters
in his house; but it was necessary first to persuade the woman
who already lodged in this small wooden hut to vacate it, and
then to prepare it a little for the illustrious guest. Peter therefore took refuge in the ' Otter' Inn, for it was Sunday, and the
streets were thronged with people, and although he was in a
workman's dress, with a tarpaulin hat, yet the Russian dress of
his comrades excited the curiosity of the crowd. The next day,

Peter at Work at Zaandam.

he entered himself as a ship-carpenter at the wharf of Lynst
Rogge, on the Buitenzaan.

Peter's stay in Zaandam lasted a week only, and as, during
this time, he visited nearly all the mills and factories in the
neighbourhood, at one of which he made a sheet of paper
with his own hands, and as the next day after his arrival he
bought a row-boat, and passed much of his time on the water,
supped, dined, and talked familiarly with the families and relations of men whom he had known in Russia, he could not
have done much work. The popular curiosity proved too an-
noying for him. There were rumours that the Tsar was in the
town. These rumours brought large and inquisitive crowds from
Amsterdam. Finally, one day when Peter had bought a hatful

PETER THE GREAT AT ZAANDAM.

of plums, and was eating them as he walked along the street, he met a crowd of boys, with some of whom he shared his fruit. Those to whom he had refused to give began to follow him, and, when he laughed at them, to throw mud and stones. Peter was obliged to take refuge in the 'Three Swans' Inn, and send for the Burgomaster. He had to make some sort of explanation to the Burgomaster, and an edict was immediately issued, forbidding insults to ' distinguished personages who wished to remain unknown.' One man, too, had received a letter from his son in Moscow, speaking of the great embassy, and saying that the Tsar was with it, and would in all probability visit Zaandam. The Tsar, it was said, could easily be recognized by his great height—nearly seven feet—by the twitching of his face, by his gesturing with his right hand, and by a small mole on the right cheek. This letter was seen by the barber Pomp. When, soon after, the Muscovites came into his shop, he immediately recognised Peter as answering to this description, and at once circulated the news. When Peter sailed on the Zaan in the new yacht which he had bought, and to which he had himself fitted a bowsprit, he was followed by crowds of curious people. This put him out of patience, and leaping ashore, he gave one of them a cuff on the cheek, to the delight of all the spectators, who called out: ' Bravo ! Marsje, you are made a knight.' The angry Tsar shut himself up in an inn, and could only return late at night. The next day, Saturday, had been appointed for drawing a large ship built by Cornelius Calf across the dyke, from the Binnenzaan to the Vorzaan, by means of rollers and capstans, a difficult and even critical operation. Peter, who was greatly interested, had promised to come, and a place had been set apart for him. The news of his expected presence having spread, the crowd was so enormous that the guards were driven back, the palisade broken down, and the reserved space encroached upon. Seeing the crowd, Peter refused to leave his house, and although the Schout, the Burgomasters, and the other authorities came in person to him, they got nothing more than ' Straks, straks' (immediately), and finally, when he had stuck his head out of the door and seen the crowd, a blunt refusal : ' Te veel volks, te veel volks' (too many people). Sunday, it seemed as if all Amsterdam had come for a sight of him, and

Peter, as a last resource, managed to get to his yacht, and although a severe storm was blowing, and every one advised him not to risk it, he sailed off, and three hours later arrived at Amsterdam, where his ambassadors were to have a formal reception the next day. With some difficulty he made his way to the *Oude zijds Heeren logement*, where they were living.

After the ambassadors had been received, Peter, in com-

Sham-Fight on the Y.

pany with them, visited the town hall (now the Royal Palace), considered by all good burghers of Amsterdam as a *chef-d'œuvre* of architecture, inspected the docks and the admiralty, went to a special representation of a comedy and ballet, took part in a great dinner, saw a splendid display of fireworks on the Amstel, and, what interested him most of all, witnessed a grand naval sham-fight on the Y, which lasted for a whole day, under the direction of the Vice-Admiral Giles Scheij.

PETER'S HOME AT ZAANDAM.

The house in which Peter lived at Zaandam has been a place of pilgrimage for a century, beginning with a royal party, which included the Emperor Joseph II., Gustavus III., King of Sweden, and the Grand Duke of Russia (afterward the Emperor Paul), then travelling as the Comte du Nord. Even Napoleon visited it. Bought in 1818 by a Russian princess, at that time Queen of Holland, it is now preserved with great care inside a new building. In itself it is no more worth visiting than any other house where Peter may have been forced to spend a week. It is only of interest as being the spot where the ruler of a great country sought to gain knowledge of an art which amused him, and which he thought would be beneficial to his people. His real life as a workman was all in Amsterdam.

During the festivities Peter asked the Burgomaster Witsen, whose personal acquaintance he had at last made, whether it would not be possible for him to work at the docks of the East India Company, where he could be free from the public curiosity which so troubled him at Zaandam. The next day, at a meeting of the directors of the East India Company, it was resolved to allow 'a high personage, present here incognito,' to work at the wharf, to assign him a house in which he could live undisturbed within the precincts, and that, as a mark of their respect, they would proceed to the construction of a frigate, in order that he might see the building of a ship from the beginning. This frigate was to be one hundred or one hundred and thirty feet long, according to the wish of the Tsar, though the Company preferred the length of one hundred feet. The Tsar was at the dinner of state given to the embassy by the city of Amsterdam, when he received a copy of this resolution. He wished to set to work immediately, and was with difficulty persuaded to wait for the fireworks and the triumphal arch prepared in his honour; but as soon as the last fires had burnt out, in spite of all entreaties, he set out for Zaandam on his yacht in order to fetch his tools. He returned early the next morning, August 30, and went straight to the wharf of the East India Company, at Oostenburg.

For more than four months, with occasional absences, he worked here at ship-building, under the direction of the Baas

Gerrit Claes Pool. Ten of the Russian 'volunteers' set to work at the wharf with him. The rest were sent to other establishments to learn the construction of masts, boats, sails, and blocks, while Prince Alexander of Imeritia went to the Hague to study artillery, and a certain number of others were entered as sailors before the mast. The first three weeks were taken up with the preparations of materials. On September 19, Peter laid the keel of the new frigate, one hundred feet in length, to be called 'the Apostles Peter and Paul,' and on the next day wrote to the Patriarch at Moscow as follows:

'We are in the Netherlands, in the town of Amsterdam, and by the mercy of God, and by your prayers, are alive and in good health, and, following the divine command given to our forefather Adam, we are hard at work. What we do is not from any need, but for the sake of learning navigation, so that, having mastered it thoroughly, we can, when we return, be victors over the enemies of Jesus Christ, and liberators of the Christians who live under them, which I shall not cease to wish for until my latest breath.'

Peter allowed no difference to be made between himself and the other workmen, and it is said that, when the Earl of Portland and another nobleman came from the king's château at Loo to have a sight of him, the overseer, in order to point him out, said: 'Carpenter Peter of Zaandam, why don't you help your comrades?' and Peter, without a word, placed his shoulder under the timber which several men were carrying, and helped to raise it to its place. In the moments of rest, the Tsar, sitting down on a log, with his hatchet between his knees, was willing to talk to anyone who addressed him simply as Carpenter Peter, or Baas Peter, but turned away and did not answer those who called him Sire or Your Majesty. He never liked long conversations.

When Peter came home from the wharf, he devoted much of his time to learning the theory of ship-building, for which he had to make additional studies in geometry. His note-books, which have been carefully preserved, show the thoroughness with which he worked. But, besides that, he had many letters to answer, and now that he was away from home he took more interest in at least the foreign policy of his Gov-

ernment. Every post from Moscow brought him a package of
letters, some asking questions and favours—for, in spite of the
Supreme Regency, many matters were still referred to him—
some giving him news, and others containing nothing but good
wishes or friendly talk about social matters. To all these
Peter endeavored to reply by each Friday's post, but, as he
wrote once to Vinius, 'sometimes from weariness, sometimes
from absence, and sometimes from *Khmelnítzky*,' one cannot
accomplish it.' He was the first to communicate to Moscow
news and congratulations on the battle of the Zenta, where.
Prince Eugene of Savoy defeated the Turks commanded by
the Grand Vizier, for which he ordered *Te Deums* and festivities at home, and had a banquet given by his embassy in Holland. The defeat of the Tartars near Azof, and the splendid
defence of Taván against the Turks, made an occasion for another feast. Until the Prince de Conti ignominiously returned
by post from Danzig, after he had gone there with a French
squadron, the Tsar was much troubled with Polish affairs. He
had also to thank Charles XII. of Sweden for his timely gift
of three hundred cannon to arm his infant fleet, while, at the
same time, Lefort was asking the Chancellor Oxenstjerna for
explanations about the attitude of Sweden in regard to Poland.
He was in constant communication with the great embassy, and
used his best efforts to persuade William III. to join in the
league against the Turks. Partly for this purpose he went to
Utrecht together with Lefort and Witsen, where he had an
interview with the King in the Toelast Hotel. Although the
details of this interview have never been known, it was thought
worthy of a commemorative medal. The Government of the
Netherlands, fearing for its Smyrna and Eastern trade, was
unwilling to enter into any such alliance, and made no offer of
money nor of a loan, which, indeed, the Russians had not
asked, and it was with some difficulty even that men could be
found to enter the Russian service as officials, engineers, or
craftsmen. Those who went, did so without the recommendation of the Government, and on their own responsibility.

---

[1] *Iváshka Khmelnítzky*, from *Khmel*, hops, is the Russian substitute for
Bacchus.

The Tsar was also greatly interested in the conferences at Ryswyk, which at last resulted in a treaty. He understood well that if the Emperor were freed from the war in the West, he could so much the more readily devote himself to operations against the Turks. Nevertheless, he had little confidence in the duration of the treaty, even before it was signed. Not understanding how necessary it was for England and the Netherlands, he believed it to be simply a manœuvre on the part of France for gaining time, and expected a new war soon. We know the history of the negotiations at Ryswyk, the struggles for precedence, and the interminable disputes on etiquette. Now that Russia had made up her mind to enter upon regular diplomatic intercourse with other nations, it was important that she should make her *début* properly. No better stage could be found than the Hague, where the most skilled diplomatists of all European countries were then assembled. On the whole, Russia did well. The embassy was splendidly received at the Hague, and lodged in the Oude Doelen Hotel, as the palace of Prince Maurice, the usual ambassadorial lodging, was already full. The ambassadors were men of good presence, Lefort had wit and good breeding, the liveries were new and gorgeous, the entertainments were sumptuous, the presence of the Tsar (for he had gone on to the Hague for a few days, to witness the ceremonies) gave additional effect. Visits were made to all the foreign ambassadors except to the French. The feeling created by Prince Dolgorúky's report of his mission, in 1687, was still so strong, added to the irritation of Peter against the French intrigues in Poland and at Constantinople, that he would not permit his ambassadors to call on the French. In this he was unwise, for it was in consequence of this that certain persons continually tried to cause difficulties in his negotiations, and that untrue and malicious reports with regard to the embassy, and to the Tsar in particular, had circulation then, and have since found credence.

In his hours of recreation, Peter's curiosity was insatiable. He visited factories, workshops, anatomical museums, cabinets of coins, botanical gardens, theatres and hospitals, inquired about everything he saw, and was soon recognised by his oft-repeated phrases: 'What is that for? How does that work?

That will I see.' He journeyed to Texel, and went again to Zaandam to see the Greenland whaling fleet. In Leyden he made the acquaintance of the great Boerhave, and visited the celebrated botanical garden under his guidance, and in Delft he studied the microscope under the naturalist Leeuwenhoek.

1. Peter in the Museum of Jacob de Wilde.　　2. Peter's Lodging at Leyden.

He made the intimate acquaintance of the Dutch military engineer Baron Van Coehorn, and of Admiral Van Scheij. He talked of architecture with Simon Schynvoet, visited the museum of Jacob de Wilde, and learned to etch under the direc-

tion of Schonebeck. An impression of a plate he engraved—
for he had some knowledge of drawing—of Christianity victorious over Islam, is still extant. He often visited the dissecting
and lecture room of Professor Ruysch, entered into correspondence with him, and finally bought his cabinet of anatomical preparations.[1] He made himself acquainted with Dutch
home and family
life, and frequented
the society of the
merchants engaged
in the Russian
trade. He became
especially intimate
with the Thessing
family, and grant-
ed to one of the
brothers the right
to print Russian
books at Amster-
dam, and to intro-
duce them into Rus-
sia. Every market
day he went to the
Botermarkt, min-
gled with the peo-
ple, studied their
trades, and followed
their life. He took
lessons from a trav-
elling dentist, and
experimented on his
servants and suite;
he mended his own

Copy of Etching by Peter.

clothes, and learned cobbling enough to make himself a pair
of slippers. He visited the Protestant churches, and of an
evening he did not forget the beer-houses, which we know

[1] It now forms part of the Museum of the Academy of Sciences at St.
Petersburg.

so well through the pencils of Teniers, Brouwer, and Van Ostade.

The frigate on which Peter worked so long was at last launched, and proved a good and useful ship for many years, in the East India Company's service. But Peter, in spite of the knowledge he had acquired, as is shown by the certificate of his master, Baas Pool, was not satisfied with the empirical manner in which the Dutch built ships. He had laboured in vain to acquire a theory in ship-building which, with a given length, or the length and the width, would show him the necessary best proportions. For this he had written to Witsen, from Arch-

angel, 1694, and had then been told that every ship-builder made the proportions according to his experience and discretion. Peter's dissatisfaction was evident in two ways—by his sending an order to Vorónezh, that all the Dutch ship-carpenters there should no longer be allowed to build as they pleased, but be put under the supervision of Danes or Englishmen, and by resolving to go to England for several months, to see what he could learn in English ship-yards. He had, indeed,

Peter's Evening Pipe.

been recently delighted by receiving a truly royal present from King William. This was the King's best yacht, the 'Transport Royal,' which had just been constructed on a new plan, was light, of beautiful proportions, and armed with twenty brass cannon. In answer to the letter of Lord Caermarthen, which spoke of it as the best and quickest vessel in England, Peter sent to London Major Adam Weyde, who had just come back from a special mission to Vienna, and from taking part in the battle of the Zenta. Weyde was also instructed to obtain the King's consent to the visit of the Tsar, with a request that his incognito should be as far as possible preserved. Together with a favourable answer, came English vessels for himself and the great embassy, and on January 17, 1698, Peter, leaving his embassy in Holland, set out for England.[1]

---

[1] Ustriálof, III., iii. ; Brückner, *Reise, etc. ;* id. *Peter der Grosse ;* J. Scheltema, *Peter de Groote in Holland,* Amsterdam, 1813 ; id. *Rusland en de Nederlanden,* Amsterdam, 1817 ; G. Verenet, *Pierre le Grand en Hollande,* Utrecht, 1863 ; Posselt, *Lefort ;* Pekársky, *Science and Literature under Peter the Great* (Russian), St. Petersburg, 1862.

MEETING OF PETER THE GREAT AND WILLIAM III. OF ENGLAND.

XXXI.

VISIT OF THE TSAR TO ENGLAND.

The weather was stormy, and the ships of Admiral Mitchell could carry but half their canvas, but the wind was in the right direction, and early in the morning of January 30 they were coasting along Suffolk, and the Tsar was saluted by the guns of the fort at Orford. Leaving its convoy at the mouth of the Thames, the yacht anchored at St. Katherine's, and Peter was rowed in a barge past the Tower and London Bridge, and landed at a house in Norfolk Street, Strand, which had a few years before been the refuge of William Penn, when under accusation of treason and conspiracy.[1] The Tsar was immediately waited upon by a chamberlain, with the congratulations of the King, who, at his request, appointed Admiral Mitchell to be in constant attendance upon him. Three days later, the King came in person to see him. Peter was without his coat, but made no ceremony, and received him in his shirt sleeves. He slept in one small room, together with the Prince of Imeritia and three or four others. When the King entered, the air was so bad that, notwithstanding the very cold weather, it was necessary to open a window. This visit the Tsar returned a few days afterwards, when he made the acquaintance of the Princess Anne, the heiress to the throne, and her husband, Prince George of Denmark. The Princess Anne apparently made a deep impression, for four years after, when she

[1] Tradition says that at this time the door was never opened without the servant first reconnoitring through a loop-hole to see whether the visitor looked like a constable or a dun. The house is now No. 21 Norfolk Street, and is converted into a lodging-house and private hotel. Authorities differ somewhat as to the house Peter occupied. One account gives a house in the Adelphi; an official tablet has been placed on the front of No. 15 Buckingham Street, Strand. Luttrell's *Relation* confirms the statement in the text.

had come to the throne, Peter remarked, in a letter to Apráxin, that she was 'a veritable daughter of our church.'

The first days of Peter's stay were occupied in seeing the sights of London, and making acquaintances. He visited the Royal Society, the Tower, the Mint, the Observatory, was much in the society of the eccentric Lord Caermarthen, with whom he used to sup at a tavern near the Tower, now the 'Czar of Muscovy,' visited Caermarthen's father, the Duke of Leeds, and frequently went to the theatre. One of the favourite actresses of the day, Miss Cross, pleased him so much, that his relations with her became very intimate, and continued so during his

Sayes Court.

stay in England. More than all he was attracted by the docks and the naval establishments, although 'the exceeding sharp and cold season,' which the Londoners jestingly said the Russians had brought with them, and the ice in the Thames, at first impeded his movements. For greater convenience, and to get rid of the crowds who watched for his appearance, he removed to Deptford, where he occupied Sayes Court, the house of John Evelyn. For forty-five years the accomplished author of 'Sylva' had been making the plantations and laying out the gardens, and it grieved him to the heart to have such bad tenants as the Muscovites evidently were. While the Tsar was still there,

Evelyn's servant wrote to him : ' There is a house full of people, and right nasty. The Tsar lies next your library, and dines in the parlour next your study. He dines at ten o'clock and six at night, is very seldom at home a whole day, very often in the King's Yard, or by water, dressed in several dresses. The King is expected there this day; the best parlour is pretty clean for him to be entertained in. The King pays for all he has.' The great holly hedge, the pride of the neighbourhood, was ruined, as is said, by the Tsar driving a wheelbarrow through it. The King had already remarked, after receiving Peter's first visit, that he was indifferent to fine buildings and beautiful gardens, and cared only for ships. After Peter had gone, Evelyn writes in his diary : ' I went to Deptford to see how miserably the Tsar had left my house after three months making it his court. I got Sir Christopher Wren, the King's surveyor, and Mr. London, his gardener, to go and estimate the repairs, for which they allowed 350*l.* in their report to the Lords of the Treasury.'[1]

With the exception of a week spent in going to Portsmouth, where he was gratified by a review of the English fleet off Spithead, and in visiting Windsor and Hampton Court, and a couple of days at Oxford, where he received the degree of Doctor of Laws, Peter remained very steadily at work at Deptford until the beginning of May. He had come to England expecting to stay but a short time, but he found so much to interest and attract him, both at the ship-building establishments at Deptford and at the Royal Arsenal at Woolwich, which he frequently visited, that, in spite of the rumours which reached him of troubles at Moscow, he constantly put off his departure, and went only when he had satisfied himself that he had acquired all the special knowledge which he could obtain in England. He evidently formed a high opinion of English shipbuilders, for he subsequently said to Perry that had it not been

---

[1] Sayes Court had been let by Evelyn in 1696 to Captain, afterwards Admiral, Benbow, who underlet it with the furniture to the Tsar. It is not therefore quite certain which tenant caused all the damage. The petition and the report of Wren are printed in *Notes and Queries*, 2nd S., No. 19, May 10, 1856, pp. 365–7. In 1701, Sayes Court was let to Peter's friend, Lord Caermarthen, who had a similar taste for things maritime.

for his journey to England, he would always have remained a bungler. One thing, however, he could not learn there, and that was the construction of galleys and galliots, such as were used in the Mediterranean, and would be serviceable in the Bosphorus, and on the coast of the Crimea. For this he desired to go to Venice.

Peter, who prided himself on being a good judge of men, spent much of his time in England in looking for suitable persons to employ in Russia, and in examining their qualifications. The night after his return from Portsmouth, together with Golovín, who had come over from Holland for the purpose, he signed contracts with about sixty men, many of whom had been recommended by Lord Caermarthen. The chief of these were Major Leonard van der Stamm, a specialist in ship-designing, Captain John Perry, an hydraulic engineer, whom he appointed to construct a canal between the Volga and the Don (for Colonel Breckell, a German engineer who had already begun this work, had run away), and Professor Andrew Fergharson, from the University of Aberdeen, who was engaged to found a school of navigation at Moscow. For officers in the fleet, he seems to have preferred Dutchmen to Englishmen, and succeeded in persuading Captain Cornelius Cruys, a distinguished Dutch officer, a Norwegian by birth, to enter his service. Cruys brought with him three other captains, and officers, surgeons, and sailors to the number of five hundred and seventy. The officers were chiefly Dutchmen, the sailors Swedes and Danes. Among the surgeons, who had been recommended by the anatomist Ruysch, were several Frenchmen. More than a hundred other officers, including Greeks, Venetians and Italians, who promised to find sailors acquainted with the navigation of the Black Sea, were also taken into the Russian service at this time. With mining engineers, however, Peter found it difficult to enter into any arrangements, as they demanded what he considered exorbitant salaries. He had at first endeavoured to find such men through Witsen, but Witsen had always deferred giving advice from day to day, and nothing was done. Finally, the Tsar decided to find some, if possible, in Saxony. He was the more anxious for this, as during his absence Vinius had written to him that magnetic iron ore

of the very best quality had been discovered in the Ural Mountains, and was begging in every letter that mining engineers be
sent as soon as possible.

The mere hand-money which had to be paid to the foreigners entering the Russian service was a great expense, and the
treasury of the embassy became so reduced that it was necessary to draw on Moscow for very large sums. One method
was found by Peter for obtaining a supply of ready money,
and that was by a privilege which he gave to Lord Caermarthen
for the monopoly of the tobacco trade in Russia. Smoking
tobacco or using it in any form had been forbidden by the
Tsar Michael in 1634, under pain of death, and religious and
old-fashioned Russians had the greatest prejudices against this
narcotic herb. Nevertheless, the use of tobacco spread so fast
in spite of pains and penalties, that before his departure for
abroad, Peter made a decree authorising its use, and even then
entered into temporary arrangements for its sale, as he expected
by the duties to realise a large sum for the treasury. A Russian merchant, Orlenka, had offered 15,000 rubles for the monopoly, and even General Gordon had offered 3,000 rubles in
1695, but the Marquis of Caermarthen was willing to give
more than three times as much as Orlenka, viz., 20,000*l.*, or
48,000 rubles, and to pay the whole in advance. For this, he
was to be allowed to import into Russia a million and a half
pounds of tobacco every year, and Peter agreed to permit the
free use of tobacco to all his subjects, notwithstanding all previous laws and regulations. Lord Caermarthen acted here as the
representative of a group of capitalists. The monopoly had
previously been offered by the Tsar to the Russia Company,
and had been declined.

The personal relations of the Tsar and King William had
become very cordial. Peter had always admired William, and
a close personal intercourse caused the King to speak in much
higher terms of Peter towards the end of his visit than he
had used at first. As a souvenir of the visit of the Tsar, the
King persuaded him to have his portrait painted, and the remarkable likeness of him by Sir Godfrey Kneller, then in the
height of his celebrity, still hangs in the Palace of Hampton
Court.

The Imperial ambassador, Count Auersperg, in a letter to the Emperor Leopold, says:

'As concerns the person of the Tsar, the Court here is well contented with him, for he now is not so afraid of people as he was at first. They accuse him of a certain stinginess only, for he has been in no way lavish. All the time here he went about in sailor's clothing. We shall see in what dress he presents himself to Your Imperial Majesty. He saw the King very rarely, as he did not wish to change his manner of life, dining at eleven o'clock in the morning, supping at seven in the evening, going to bed early, and getting up at four o'clock, which very much astonished those Englishmen who kept company with him.'

Peter and Golovín took their leave of the King at Kensington Palace, on April 28. We are told that, as a slight token of his friendship and his gratitude, not only for the kind reception he had had, but for the splendid yacht which had been presented to him, Peter took out of his pocket a small twisted bit of brown paper and handed it to the King, who opened it with some curiosity, and found a magnificent uncut diamond of large size. This may not be true, but it is thoroughly characteristic. The last days of Peter's stay he had again consecrated to sight-seeing. He was present at a meeting of Parliament, when the King gave his assent to a bill for raising money by a land tax, but he was so unwilling to have his presence known that he looked at the House through a hole in the ceiling. This gave rise to a *bon mot* which circulated in London society. Some one remarked that he had 'seen the rarest thing in the world, a king on the throne, and an emperor on the roof.' Hoffmann wrote to the Austrian Court that Peter expressed himself unfavourably to the limitation of royal power by a parliament; but according to a Russian account he said: 'It is pleasant to hear how the sons of the fatherland tell the truth plainly to the King; we must learn that from the English.'

A spirit of proselytism, a desire to propagate one's own religious, social, and political views, is implanted in the Anglo-Saxon breast at least, if indeed it be not common to the human race. A young monarch who was liberal or curious enough to visit Quaker meetings [1] and Protestant cathedrals became the natural prey of philanthropists and reformers, who saw a way opened by Providence for the introduction of their peculiar notions into remote Muscovy. Such an enthusiast was 'the pious and learned Francis Lee, M.D.,' who gave 'proposals to Peter the Great, etc., at his own request, for the right framing of his Government.' [2]

That Peter should visit the churches of different denominations in Holland, made many simple-minded or fanatical Dutch

---

[1] Two Quakers, Thomas Story and Gilbert Mollyson, succeeded in getting an interview with the Tsar and presented him with Latin translations of *Barclay's Apology* and other books. They had a long conversation with him, and even preached him a sermon. Peter, who seemed interested in what they said, on taking the books asked: 'Were not these books writ by a Jesuit? It is said there are Jesuits among you.' This was a plain allusion to the reports then prevalent of the Quakers, and especially William Penn, being the intermediaries between the Jesuits and Jacobites abroad and their friends in England. William Penn, on hearing of this interview, went himself to Deptford privately and had a long talk with the Tsar in Dutch, which he spoke fluently, presenting him at the same time with some Dutch translations of Quaker books. 'The Tsar appeared to be much interested, so that the visit was satisfactory to both parties. Indeed, he was so much impressed by it, that afterwards, while he was at Deptford, he occasionally attended the meeting of the Quakers there, where he conducted himself with great decorum and condescension, changing seats, and sitting down, and standing up, as he could best accommodate others. Nor was this impression of short duration, for in the year 1712—that is sixteen years afterwards, when he was at Frederickstadt, in Holstein, with five thousand men, to assist the Danes against the Swedes, one of his first inquiries was, whether there were any Quakers in the place; and being told there were, he signified his intention of attending one of their meetings. A meeting was accordingly appointed, to which he went, accompanied by Prince Menshikóf, General Dolgorúky, and several dukes and great men. Soon after they were seated the worship began ; Philip Defair, a Quaker, rose up and preached. The Muscovite lords showed their respect by their silence, but they understood nothing of what was said. The Tsar himself occasionally interpreted as the words were spoken, and when the discourse was over, he commended it by saying that whoever could live according to such doctrines would be happy.'—Clarkson's *Life of William Penn*, pp. 253, 254.

[2] These proposals related to the institution of seven committees or colleges :—1. For the advancement of learning. 2. For the improvement of nature. 3. For the encouragement of arts. 4. For the increase of merchandise. 5. For reformation of manners. 6. For compilation of laws. 7. For the propagation of the Christian religion. They were printed in 1752 in a rare book entitled, 'Ἀπολειπόμενα, *or dissertations, etc., on the Book of Genesis.* It is hardly possible to take Lee's phrase, 'at his own request,' in its most literal interpretation.

believe that he was inclined to Protestantism, and that the object of his journey was to unite the Russian and Protestant churches. It was reported that he had already taken the communion with the Elector of Brandenburg, and that he was inviting doctors of all sciences to establish colleges and academies in his dominions. In like way, in Vienna, it was widely believed that Sheremétief had already become a Catholic, and that the Tsar was inclined to become one. When Peter was in Vienna, the nuncio reported to Rome that the Tsar had shown a special respect for the Emperor Leopold, as the head of Christianity, that he had dined with the Jesuits, and wished to be taken into the bosom of the true church. From Poland the Jesuit Vota wrote to Cardinal Spada, with great satisfaction, of the reverential demeanour of Peter during the Catholic service, and of the humility with which he had accepted his blessing.

Churchmen in England were led into similar beliefs, and entertained hopes of a similar union of the two churches. It was probably not simple politeness that led the Archbishop of Canterbury and other English prelates to visit Peter. Among them was Gilbert Burnet, Bishop of Salisbury, who, in his 'History of his Own Time,' gives the following opinion of the Tsar:

'I waited often on him, and was ordered, both by the King and the archbishop and bishops, to attend upon him, and to offer him such information of our religion and constitution as he was willing to receive ; I had good interpreters, so I had much free discourse with him ; he is a man of a very hot temper, soon inflamed, and very brutal in his passion ; he raises his natural heat by drinking much brandy, which he rectifies himself with great application ; he is subject to convulsive motions all over his body, and his head seems to be affected with these ; he wants not capacity, and has a larger measure of knowledge than might be expected from his education, which was very indifferent ; a want of judgment, with an instability of temper, appear in him too often and too evidently. He is mechanically turned, and seems designed by nature rather to be a ship-carpenter than a great prince. This was his chief study and exercise while he stayed here ; he wrought much with his own hands, and made all about him work at the models of ships ; he told me he designed a great fleet at Azuph, and with it to attack the Turkish empire ; but he did not seem capable of conducting so great a design, though his conduct in his wars since this, has discovered a greater genius in him than appeared at that time. He was desirous to understand our doctrine, but he did not seem disposed to mend matters in Muscovy ; he was, indeed, resolved to encourage learning, and to polish his people by sending some of them to travel in other countries, and to draw strangers to come and live among them. He seemed apprehensive still of his sister's intrigues. There is a mixture both of passion and severity in his temper. He is resolute, but understands little of war, and seems not at all inquisitive that way. After I had seen him often, and had conversed much with him, I could not but adore the depth of the providence of God, that had raised up such a furious man to so absolute an authority over so great a part of the world.'

The phrase 'he did not seem disposed to mend matters in Muscovy,' evidently referred to the religious question, and Burnet, as well as others, was much surprised that this apparent free-thinker and liberal should hold so firmly to the orthodox faith. It had been the fashion, either from too little knowledge or from too great patriotism, sharply to criticise Burnet's opinion of Peter's character; but considering what Burnet knew of Peter, and even what we know of Peter, is it, after all, so far out of the way? Peter's tastes led him to navigation and to ship-building, and he sincerely believed that it was through having a fleet on the Black Sea that he would be able to conquer Turkey—the idea at that time uppermost in his mind. But he did not show the same disposition to master the art of war as he did that of navigation. Many a wide-awake boy of fifteen will nowadays equal and surpass Peter in special accomplishments and general knowledge. Many a young man, with a far better education than Peter, has the same mechanical and scientific turn, carried even further. At this time only one idea possessed Peter's mind—navigation. His own studies, the fact that men of the best Russian families were sent abroad to become common sailors, and nothing else, are proof enough. Hoffmann writes to Vienna:

'They say that he intends to civilise his subjects in the manner of other nations. But from his acts here, one cannot find any other intention than to make them sailors; he has had intercourse almost exclusively with sailors, and has gone away as shy as he came.'

During his journey abroad he saw something of the effects of a greater civilisation; he saw comforts and conveniences which he thought it would be well to introduce among his people, but he paid little or no attention to anything concerning the art of government, or to real civil and administrative reform.

The stay of Peter in Holland and in England gave rise to numberless anecdotes. The stories of Dutch carpenters who had assisted him in Russia, the tales told by the English captains of his familiarity at Archangel, of his bathing with them in public, and of his drinking bouts and familiar conversation, had, in a measure, prepared the public mind, and the spectacle of the ruler of a great country who went about in sailor's clothing, and devoted himself to learning ship-building, rendered it possible and easy to invent. Many of these anecdotes are, in all probability, untrue. They are of the same class of stories as are told now of any remarkable individual—the Shah, the Sultan, the Khedive—on his travels. Sometimes there may be a basis of truth, but it has been distorted in the telling.

After the interview with King William, Peter delayed still three days, which were chiefly taken up with visiting the Mint, for he had been struck with the excellence of the English coinage, and had already ideas of recoining the Russian money. On May 2, he left Deptford in the yacht, the 'Transport Royal,' given to him by King William, but even then could not resist running up to Chatham to see the docks there, and arrived at Amsterdam on the 19th.[1]

Twice the embassy at Amsterdam had been in great dis-

---

[1] The 'Transport Royal' was sent to Archangel under the command of Captain Ripley, and took a part of the collections of curiosities and military stores which Peter had collected in Holland. By the Tsar's order, Franz Timmermann met it there, to take it to Vológda, and thence partly overland to Yarosláv. It was intended afterward to convey it to the Sea of Azof, as soon as the canal between the Volga and the Don should be finished, but as the yacht drew nearly eight feet of water, Timmermann could not get it farther than Holmogóry, and it went back to Archangel, where it remained ever after.

NICHOLAS WITSEN, BURGOMASTER OF AMSTERDAM.

tress about Peter, for after his departure for London the storms
were so great and the colds so intense, that it was three weeks
before any news was received from him.   Again, from February 18 to March 21, no letters arrived in Amsterdam.   People
in Moscow were still more troubled, and Vinius showed his
consternation by writing to Lefort, instead of to Peter, to ask
what the matter was.   Peter replied on May 23, blaming his
friend very severely for being so troubled by a miscarriage of
the post, and adding fuel to the flame at Moscow when he
ought to have been more courageous and not to have doubted.
Lefort had written from Holland several letters by every post,
taken up with longing for his return, with inquiries about his
health, with talk of the necessity of going to Vienna, and of
his personal desire to visit Geneva, and begging him to send
something fit to drink.

On arriving at Amsterdam, Peter found several relatives of
Lefort who had come from Geneva for the purpose of seeing
him.   They had already been sumptuously entertained by the
embassy, and now had the pleasure of being presented to the
Tsar, and being amicably received by him.   The accounts
which they give in their letters home of the position of their
uncle, and the ceremony which everywhere attended him, show
the rank which he held above the other ambassadors, as being
the friend and favourite of Peter.   With regard to the Tsar
himself, Jacob Lefort writes:

'You know that he is a prince of very great stature, but
there is one circumstance which is unpleasant—he has convul-
sions, sometimes in his eyes, sometimes in his arms, and sometimes in his whole body.   He at times turns his eyes so that
one can see nothing but the whites.   I do not know whence it
arises, but we must believe that it is a lack of good breeding.
Then he has also movements in the legs, so that he can scarcely
keep in one place.   He is very well made, and goes about
dressed as a sailor, in the highest degree simple, and wishing
nothing else than to be on the water.'

There was every reason now to hasten Peter's departure.
Troubles at Moscow with some Streltsi who had run away from
the army, troubles in Poland, where the Polish magnates were
not as well disposed toward Russia as was the King himself,

troubles at Vienna—for it was reported to him that the Austrians were intending to make a peace with the Turks, without the slightest regard for the interests of either Poland or Russia —all rendered him uneasy. In addition to this, he was both surprised and astonished to learn that King William had accepted a proposition made to him to act as mediator between Austria and Turkey, and that the States-General of Holland were to take part with him. The troubles at Moscow he believed to be over; at all events, they seemed no more serious than the troubles which arose in Moscow on the eve of his departure, but he felt it necessary to get soon to Vienna, in order that he might have a personal interview with the Emperor Leopold, and ascertain the views of the Austrian court, and, if possible, make them fall in with his own. Beside that, he wished to go on to Venice, to complete his studies in naval architecture.[1]

---

[1] Ustriálof, III., iv. ; Posselt, *Lefort ;* Perry, *State of Russia*, London, 1716; Brückner, *Reise Peters des Grossen;* the Austrian despatches in Sadler, *Peter der Grosse als Mensch und Regent*, St. Petersburg, 1872, p. 239 ; Narcissus Luttrell, *Brief Historical Relation of State Affairs*, Oxford, 1857; Phillimore, *Sir Christopher Wren*, London, 1881. See also the description of the Tsar's visit in Macaulay's *History of England*, and the London newspapers and other authorities then referred to.

XXXII.

In spite of his haste, it took Peter a month to reach Vienna, where he arrived on June 26, and yet he travelled every day, with the exception of one day at Leipzig and two at Dresden. He also visited the linen factories at Bielefeld, surveyed the fortifications of Königstein, and walked through the beautiful park at Cleves, where he carved his name on a birch-tree. In Dresden he was delighted with the curiosities of the Green Vaults, where he went immediately after his arrival, and stayed all night. He also carefully examined the arsenal, and astonished his entertainers by displaying the knowledge he had acquired at Königsberg and Woolwich, and by pointing out and explaining the defects in the artillery. He paid a visit to the mother of the Elector, for Augustus himself was then in Poland, and twice supped with Prince von Fürstenburg. At the Tsar's special request, ladies were invited, and among others the famous Countess Aurora von Königsmark, the mother of Maurice de Saxe, then a child in arms. Peter had met her accidentally on his way to the arsenal, and had doubtless been informed of her intimacy with Augustus. At these suppers, he was ' in such good humour that in the presence of the ladies he took up a drum, and played with a perfection that far surpassed the drummers.' Peter had a strange shyness, which seemed to grow upon him. He hated to be stared at as a curiosity, and the more he met people of refinement, versed in social arts, the more he felt his own deficiencies. Nothing but the excitement of a supper seemed to render general society possible to him. His visits of ceremony were brief and formal. It was very hard at Dresden to keep people out of his way, and allow him to go about unobserved. After the Tsar had gone,

Fürstenburg wrote to the King: 'I thank God that all has
gone off so well, for I feared that I could not fully please this
fastidious gentleman.' And General
Jordan reported that the Tsar was
well content with his visit, but that
he himself was 'glad to be rid of
such a costly guest.'

Strangely enough, in spite of Peter's
desire to find mining engineers, he did
not stop at Freiberg, where quarters
had been got ready for him.

In Vienna, all the difficulties of
ceremonial and etiquette were renewed. The Holy Roman Empire, as
the only empire in the world, and as
the lineal descendant of the old empire of Rome, claimed for its sovereign
a superior rank to other monarchs,
and insisted greatly on punctilio. The
authorities at Vienna were unwilling
to grant to the Russian embassy the
same honours which had been given
to it in other countries, or to do anything which might seem to place the
Tsar on the same level with the Emperor. For that reason, it took four
days before the details of the entry
into Vienna could be arranged, and
even then, through a general coming
from exercise on the Prater insisting
on marching all his troops across the
route selected, it was night before
the ambassadors could take up their
lodging in the villa of Count Königsacker, on the bank of the river
Vienna at Gumpendorf—for Peter
had particularly requested that his

Spire of St. Stephen's Cathedral, Vienna.

quarters should be in the suburbs, and
not in the middle of the town. The Russians were little

pleased at the manner of their reception, and even the Papal Nuncio spoke of the slight pomp displayed. After this, more than a month elapsed before the ambassadors had their solemn reception by the Emperor, and it was only then, on account of Peter's great desire to take Lefort and Golovín with him to Venice, that he waived certain points of ceremonial which had up to that time been insisted upon. If the Congress of Vienna in 1815 did no other good, it at least accomplished much in putting all States on the same rank, abolishing national precedence, and simplifying court ceremonial as respects ambassadors and ministers.

In the meantime, however, Peter had been privately received by the Emperor, the Empress, and their eldest son, Joseph, the King of the Romans, in the imperial villa of Favoriten, where, with truly Austrian ideas of maintaining his incognito, he was not allowed to go in at the principal entrance, but was taken through a small door in the garden, and was led up a small spiral staircase into the audience-hall. Leopold also paid a personal visit to Peter, and toward the end of his stay, entertained him at a great masquerade, called a *Wirthschaft*, in which all the society of Vienna, and many foreign princes sojourning there took part, dressed in the costumes of different countries. Peter appeared as a Frisian peasant, and his partner, who was assigned to him by lot, and was dressed in the same costume, was the Fräulein Johanna von Thurn, of the family now called Thurn und Taxis. The festivities were kept up until morning, and the Tsar was most merry, and danced '*senza fine e misura.*' At the supper-table, where there was no precedence, the Emperor and Empress sitting at the foot of the table, Leopold arose, and, filling his glass, drank to Peter's health. This was immediately responded to, and the same ceremony was performed with the King of the Romans. The cup used for this purpose—which was of rock-crystal, the work of di Rocca, and valued at 2,000 florins—was sent the next day to the Tsar, as a souvenir. This was the first great festivity given at court since the beginning of the war with Turkey. Economy had been the order of the day. Peter Lefort wrote to Geneva:

'I must admit that I was greatly disappointed on my arrival here, for I had expected to see a brilliant court; it is quite the contrary. There are neither the splendid equipages nor the fine liveries we saw at the court of Brandenburg. There are many great lords here, but they are all very modest in their dress.'

On St. Peter's Day the embassy gave a great ball, with music and fireworks, which lasted all night, and at which a thousand guests were present.[1] It is worth notice that, at the state dinner which followed, the solemn audience of the

West Front of St. Stephen's Cathedral, Vienna.

ambassadors, the healths of the Empress and the Tsaritsa were omitted, although it had been agreed beforehand to drink them. There were reasons for thinking it might be disagreeable to the Tsar. During the dinner, there being much talk about Hungarian wine, Baron Königsacker sent Lefort a salver, with six kinds as specimens. After tasting them, Lefort begged permission to pass them to his friend, who stood behind his chair. This was the Tsar himself, who had come in this way to witness the feast.

It has been already said that the Papal court was greatly excited at the possibility of converting Russia to Catholicism, and the despatches of the nuncio and of the Spanish ambassador show with what care every movement of the Tsar was watched. The deductions of these prelates seem to us now to

---

[1] Notwithstanding the statements in the despatches of the nuncio as to the small amount of money given by the Imperial Government for the support of the embassy, we know, from Russian official documents, that the whole expense of the feast was paid by the Emperor's treasury.

be based on very narrow premises. They evidently believed what they wished to believe, and reported what they knew would please. The Cardinal Kollonitz, Primate of Hungary, gives, among other things, an account of the person and character of Peter :

'The Tsar is a youth of from twenty-eight to thirty years of age, is tall, of an olive complexion, rather stout than thin, in aspect between proud and grave, and with a lively countenance. His left eye, as well as his left arm and leg, was injured by the poison given him during the life of his brother; but there remain now only a fixed and fascinated look in his eye and a constant movement of his arm and leg, to hide which he accompanies this forced motion with continual movements of his entire body, which, by many people, in the countries which he has visited, has been attributed to natural causes, but really it is artificial. His wit is lively and ready; his manners rather civil than barbarous, the journey he has made having improved him, and the difference from the beginning of his travels and the present time being visible, although his native roughness may still be seen in him; but it is chiefly noticeable in his followers, whom he holds in check with great severity. He has a knowledge of geography and history, and—what is most to be noticed—he desires to know these subjects better; but his strongest inclination is for maritime affairs, at which he himself works mechanically, as he did in Holland; and this work, according to many people who have to do with him, is indispensable to divert the effects of the poison, which still very much troubles him. In person and in aspect, as well as in his manners, there is nothing which would distinguish him or declare him to be a prince.'

Inquiries were made by the Tsar as to the intentions of the Emperor to conclude a peace with Turkey, to which the Emperor frankly replied that the Sultan had himself proposed a peace through the intervention of Paget, the English ambassador at Constantinople, and had requested that the King of England should be a mediator, to which he had assented. At the same time, he showed the Tsar the original letters. Peter then had an interview with Count Kinsky, in which he tried to convince him that it would be better for the Austrians to continue the war, that it was scarcely fair to the allies to make peace without consulting their interests, and that if peace were made, a war would be begun with France about the Spanish succession, and the Turks would take

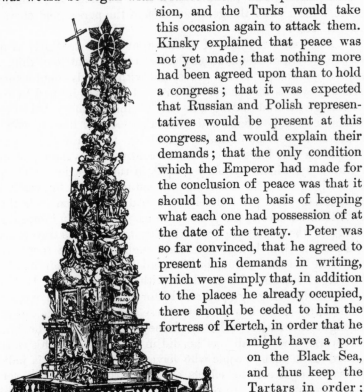

Trinity Column, Vienna.

this occasion again to attack them. Kinsky explained that peace was not yet made; that nothing more had been agreed upon than to hold a congress; that it was expected that Russian and Polish representatives would be present at this congress, and would explain their demands; that the only condition which the Emperor had made for the conclusion of peace was that it should be on the basis of keeping what each one had possession of at the date of the treaty. Peter was so far convinced, that he agreed to present his demands in writing, which were simply that, in addition to the places he already occupied, there should be ceded to him the fortress of Kertch, in order that he might have a port on the Black Sea, and thus keep the Tartars in order; that if this condition were not agreed to, the Emperor should not make peace, but continue the war until a more advantageous treaty, or until 1701, by which time he hoped to have gained great advantages over the Turks. The reply which Leopold sent to Peter was that, while he found the demand for the cession of Kertch to be a just one, he saw a great difficulty in the way, 'for the Turks are not accustomed to give up their fortresses without a fight, and even what has been extorted from them by arms, they try in every way to get back.' He therefore urged Peter to use his efforts to get possession of Kertch before the treaty should be made, and to send a representative to the congress, and promised again that he would sign no peace without his consent. Peter was so satisfied with this that he was on the point of starting for Venice, and even had ideas of continuing his journey into Italy, and perhaps visiting France before his return.

Passports were obtained, and part of his small suite had already started for Venice, where great preparations were made for his reception, when suddenly a letter was received from Ramodanófsky, announcing that the Streltsi regiments on the frontier had revolted and had marched on Moscow, but that Shéïn and Gordon had been sent to put them down. Nothing was said of the cause of the revolt, or of the intentions of the Streltsi. The letter had been on its way for a whole month, and the Tsar was still in ignorance as to whether the revolt had been put down, or whether the rioters were in possession of Moscow, and his sister Sophia ruling in his place. Nevertheless, he decided to start at once, and, to the astonishment of the Austrians, who knew nothing of this news, his post-horses took the road for Moscow, and not for Venice. Before he went, he wrote to Ramodanófsky:

'I have received your letter of June 27, in which your grace writes that the seed of Iván Mikhaílovitch (Miloslávsky) is sprouting. I beg you to be severe; in no other way is it possible to put out this flame. Although we are very sorry to give up our present profitable business, yet, for the sake of this, we shall be with you sooner than you think.'

Peter travelled day and night, and refused even to stop in Cracow, where a banquet had been prepared for him. Immediately afterward, he received quieting intelligence that the insurrection had been put down, and the ringleaders punished. He was therefore able to travel more leisurely, looked carefully at the great salt mines of Wieliczka, and at Bochnia inspected the Polish army, which was encamped there. At Rawa, a small village of Galicia, he met King Augustus on August 9, and was his guest for four days.

Peter had expected to pass by the way of Warsaw, and it was with great surprise that the King received a courier announcing the Tsar's visit for the same day. Arrangements were at once made, and 'the King waited in vain for him all night, for he did not arrive until the next morning at dinner-time. As he desired, he was conducted to his lodging without formality or ceremony, and shortly after was visited by the King. The tenderness and mutual embraces, the kisses, and the expressions of love and esteem which they gave each other, are scarcely credible. The Tsar, knowing well the esteem of

the King, was carried away by sympathy, and immediately struck up with him a more than fraternal friendship, never ceasing to embrace and kiss him, and telling him that he had come almost alone, with very few followers, to put himself into his hands, and confide his life to him, being ready, however, to serve him in need with a hundred

Column of the Virgin, Vienna.

thousand men or more.' Augustus and Peter dined and supped together, and the two following days were taken up with amusements, with reviews of troops, and sham fights, which greatly pleased the Tsar, and with political talk. The Jesuit Vota, who was introduced to the Tsar by the King himself, argued in favour of maintaining the Polish alliance, and continuing the war against Turkey. Peter, after saying that he thought the Russians, Poles, and Saxons were sufficient, and that once Otchakóf were taken, Constantinople would be in the death-struggle, applied the old fable that it was useless to divide the skin before the bear was killed. The impression produced on

Peter by Augustus was strong and lasting: Peter had supported the candidacy of Augustus, and had sent an army to the
frontier on political grounds, but the sympathy produced by
personal contact had an important influence. It was greatly
owing to this that Peter two years later was induced to enter
the Northern League, and to declare war against Sweden. The
day after the Tsar's arrival at Moscow, in speaking of the foreign sovereigns he had visited, he made honourable mention of
the King of Poland. 'I prize him more than the whole of you
together,' he said, addressing his boyárs and magnates that
were present, 'and that not because of his royal pre-eminence
over you, but merely because I like him.' He still proudly
wore the King's arms, which he had exchanged with that monarch for his own, in order to proclaim that their bond of
friendship was more solid than the Gordian knot, and never to
be severed with the sword.

After leaving the King, Peter went on to Moscow through
Zamosc, where he was entertained by the widow of the castel-
lan. He met there the Papal Nuncio, who begged permission
for missionaries to pass through Russia on their way to China,
and was much struck with the amiability of the Tsar, especially
as Lefort had put him off with polite excuses. In thanking
the Tsar for his promise, he asked him to give him a written
document. Peter, replying that when he arrived at Moscow
he would immediately send him a diploma, said : 'My word
is better than ten thousand writings.' At Brzesc-Litewski
there was an unfortunate adventure with the Metropolitan
of the Uniates, who, in talking to the Tsar, had the bad
taste, to say the least, to use the word schismatic, in regard
to the members of the Russian Church. The Tsar replied
that he could not stand such impertinences of language, and
people as indiscreet as he in Moscow would have been whipped
or hanged. Not content with this, Peter asked the Governor to send away the Metropolitan, saying that he was not
sure that he would be master of his own hands if he met him
again.

Notwithstanding these delays, Peter arrived at Moscow
much sooner than he was expected—on September 4, at six
o'clock in the evening. He did not stop at the Krémlin, nor

see his wife, but accompanied Lefort and Golovín to their houses, then called to inquire for General Gordon, who was away on his estate, and went that night to Preobrazhénsky.[1]

[1] Ustriálof, III., v. ; Theiner, *Monuments Historiques ; Fontes rerum Austriacarum*, Abth. II., vol. 27, Vienna, 1867, p. 429, ff. ; *Archiv. für sächsische Geschichte* (1873) XI., p. 127, ff.; Posselt, *Lefort ;* Bruckner, *Reise Peters des Grossen ;* id. *Peter der Grosse.*

XXXIII.

THE REVOLT AND THE PUNISHMENT OF THE STRELTSI.

As soon as he arrived in Moscow, Peter threw himself with feverish haste into the investigation of what had been the cause of his sudden return—the revolt of the Streltsi regiments.

Ever since the downfall of Sophia, the Streltsi had had abundant reasons for complaint. They had passed long terms of service on the southern frontier, taking them away from their wives and families, and from their business affairs, for we must not forget that the Streltsi were more in the nature of a national guard or militia than of a regular army, living at home, and in ordinary times carrying on occupations of peace. They had been treated with distrust, and even with something like contempt by Peter; in his sham-fights the Streltsi had always formed the enemy's troops, and had always been defeated, and were thus placed in opposition to the regular soldiery, and to the play-troops of Peter. At the two sieges of Azof they had suffered much; they had lost many men in the assaults; they had endured many privations on the march; and they had been severely punished for want of discipline. All of this they ascribed to the influence of the foreigners. Seeing how the Tsar protected and encouraged foreigners, how he enjoyed their society, and how he had almost transferred his capital to the German suburb, their hatred was very natural. After the siege of Azof, four regiments were left there for the protection of the colony. When Peter was in Brandenburg, and received news of the double election to the Polish throne, and of the possibility that the Prince de Conti might make an attempt to employ force, he, in order to be ready to assist King Augustus, ordered to the Polish frontier an army composed partly of Streltsi and partly of levies in the old Russian style—that is, retainers of the great noblemen. For this purpose, instead of sending to the frontier of the Streltsi then in Moscow, six regiments were sent from that place to Azof, and the four regiments already at Azof were ordered to the frontier. These men had been a long time at Azof engaged in severe labour—building fortifications—they had made a long march, and they were not even allowed to pass through Moscow, much less to halt there for a short time to see their wives and families. Some of them resolved to return to Moscow at any cost. There were gradual desertions from the army, and in the latter part of March one hundred and fifty-five runaways appeared in Moscow, with petitions that they should all be allowed to return, as they were suffering from want of provisions and want of pay. This sudden arrival threw the boyárs into consternation, and the deserters were ordered to leave Moscow by April 18, and rejoin their regiments. At the conclusion of their respite, the Streltsi, instead of going away, came in a noisy crowd to their department and demanded to be allowed to present their case. Prince Troekúrof agreed to receive four deputies, but no sooner had they begun to speak than, with the political unwisdom so characteristic of the hasty-tempered boyárs of that time, he commenced abusing and scolding them, and had them arrested. On their way to prison they were rescued by their comrades, and it became necessary to expel them from the town. In the conflict one man was killed, and another was arrested and sent to Siberia.

The Streltsi returned to Toropétz, where the army was then encamped, bringing not only their complaints, but strange reports of what they had heard and seen at Moscow. They had found what all Russians had so long hated—a Government of boyárs, accompanied with extortion, bribery, injustice, and misrule.[1] The Tsar was away, and it was said that he had become entirely German, that he had abandoned the orthodox faith, that the country was to be given up to the foreigners, and that for true Russians there was no hope. For weeks nothing had been heard from the Tsar, and the alarm which was evident among the rulers and among Peter's friends, as shown by the

---

[1] According to Guarient, the Austrian ambassador, this charge was only too true.

letters of Vinius and Ramodanófsky, easily spread, with exaggerations, to the common people. It was reported that the Tsar was dead, that the life of the Tsarévitch was in danger, that the ears of the Tsaritsa had been boxed by the boyárs, that the princesses were almost starved and had to ask aid of their friends, and that the boyár Tíkhon Stréshnef desired to make himself Tsar. The reports of these deserters had sufficiently excited the minds of their comrades, when a decree arrived dispersing the army, but ordering the Streltsi, instead of returning to Moscow, to take up their quarters in the towns of Viázma, Biélaya, Rzhef, Volodomírovo, and Dorogobúzh, while the deserters were to be sent into exile, with their wives and children, on the frontier of Little Russia. Neither Prince Michael Ramodanófsky, the general-in-chief, nor their colonels, could restrain the riotous disposition of the Streltsi. Those who had been already arrested were released by their comrades, and the deserters easily succeeded in concealing themselves among the different regiments, sure of protection. Their surrender was refused, and finally, after some halts and hesitations, the Streltsi began to march toward Moscow. The news of their approach excited a general panic, well-to-do people began to leave the capital, and the Government was at its wits' end. Fears were entertained of an insurrection of the serfs and common people, and there were disputes among the boyárs as to the proper measures to be taken. At last it was decided to send against them the boyár Shéïn, General Gordon, and Prince Koltsóf-Massálsky, with four thousand regular soldiers and twenty-five cannon. The troops came up with the rioters at the village of Vozkresénsky, about thirty miles north-west of Moscow; where the Patriarch Níkon had established his still celebrated monastery of the New Jerusalem, and while Shéïn was engaged in negotiations and in receiving the complaints of the rioters, Gordon, after taking up a commanding position, gradually surrounded the camp of the Streltsi with his troops. General Gordon was himself sent to the camp of the Streltsi, and, as he says, 'used all the rhetoric I was master of, but all in vain.' The foreigner having failed, a Russian, Prince Koltsóf-Massálsky, then undertook to persuade the rioters to submit. He had no better success, but, as a final epitome of their complaints and griefs, the sergeant Zorin gave him a draft of an unfinished petition, which recited 'the faithful services of themselves, their fathers, and their ancestors to the Tsars according to the common Christian faith; that they had always intended to keep to orthodoxy, as prescribed by the holy Apostolic Church, ... that they had been ordered to serve in different towns for a year at a time, and that, when they were in front of Azof, by the device of a heretic and foreigner, Fransko Lefort, in order to cause great harm to orthodoxy, he, Fransko, had led the Moscow Streltsi under the wall at a wrong time, and, by putting them in the most dangerous and bloody places, many of them had been killed; that by his device a mine had been made under the trenches, and that by this mine he had also killed three hundred men and more.' With much other complaining about the losses they had met with at Azof, the hard service which they had endured ever since, and the bad treatment they had to suffer from their generals, the petition concluded by saying that 'they had heard that in Moscow there is great terror, and for that reason the town is shut up early, and only opened at the second or third hour of the following day, that the whole people are suffering great insolence, and that they had heard that Germans are coming to Moscow who have their beards shaved, and publicly smoke tobacco, to the discredit of orthodoxy.' It was, of course, impossible for Shéïn to comply with Zorin's request that a paper which, in disguise of a petition, was an attack on the favourite of the Tsar, on the Tsar himself, and on all his ideas, should be read publicly before the army. The Streltsi showing no signs of giving in, twenty-five cannon were fired over their heads. Encouraged, rather than discouraged, by this, the Streltsi beat their drums and waved their banners, the priests chanted prayers, and they advanced to attack the troops. A few more rounds were fired, and the Streltsi dispersed in all directions and sought refuge in the houses and barns of the village, after losing fifteen killed and thirty-seven wounded. The whole affair occupied about an hour. Those who ran away were caught. An investigation was immediately made by Shéïn, accompanied by torture and torment, 130 men were executed, and 1,860 imprisoned in various monasteries and strongholds.

On the way home from Vienna, Peter had received letters from Gordon and others, telling him of Shéïn's victory, and of the punishment meted out to the rebellious. Vinius wrote :
'Not one got away ; the worst of them were sent on the road to the dark life with news of their brethren to those already there, who, I think, are imprisoned in a special place ; for Satan, I imagine, fears lest they may get up a rebellion in hell, and drive him out of his realms.'

When Peter came to learn the details of the revolt, and the proceedings of the trial of the ringleaders, he was dissatisfied. Two questions disturbed his mind, and on neither of them was there thrown any light—How far was Sophia implicated in this disturbance ? and had there been any plot against his life on the part of the dissatisfied members of the nobility ? To sat- isfy himself on these points, he had all those Streltsi who were kept under guard in the prisons and monasteries brought in batches to Preobrazhénsky, where he instituted a criminal in- vestigation on a tremendous scale.   A criminal investigation at that time meant the application of torture to obtain confessions, and he established fourteen torture chambers, which were pre- sided over by the Russians he had most confidence in for that sort of work.[1]   In these chambers about twenty men were ex- amined daily, except Sunday. The Tsar was himself present at the torture, and personally questioned those who seemed most criminal.   Torture at that time in Russia was, as it had long been, of three kinds—the *batógs*, the knout, and fire. In administration of the *batógs*, a man was held down by two per- sons, one at his head and the other at his feet, who struck at his bare back in turn with *batógs*—little rods of the thickness of the finger—'keeping time as smiths do at an anvil until their rods are broken in pieces, and then they take fresh ones until they are ordered to stop.' 'The knout is a thick, hard thong of leather, of about three feet and a half long, with a ring or kind of swivel like a flail at the end of it, to which the

---

[1] These were Prince Peter Prozorófsky, Prince Michael Tcherkásky, Prince Vladímir Dolgorúky, Prince Iván Troekúrof, Prince Boris Golítsyn, Shéïn, Prince Michael Ramodanófsky, Stréshnef, Prince Theodore Stcherbá- tof, Prince Peter Lvof, Iván Golovín, Simeon Yazýkof, Prince Theodore Ramodanófsky, and Zótof.

thong is fastened.' The executioner strikes the criminal 'so many strokes on the bare back as are appointed by the judge, first making a step back and giving a spring forward at every stroke, which is laid on with such force that the blood flies at every stroke, and leaves a wheal behind as thick as a man's finger ; and these *masters*, as the Russians call them, are so exact at their own work that they very rarely strike two strokes in the same place, but lay them on the whole length and breadth of a man's back, by the side of each other, with great dexterity, from the top of the man's shoulders down to the waistband of his breeches.' The criminal was usually hoisted upon the back of another man, but sometimes his hands were tied behind him, and he was then drawn up by a rope, while a heavy weight was affixed to his feet, so that he hung there with his shoulders out of joint. In torturing a man by fire, ' his hands and feet are tied, and he is then fixed on a long pole, as upon a spit, which being held at each end by two men, he has his raw back roasted over the fire, and is then examined and called upon by a writer to confess.' In this way 1,714 men were examined, and Guarient and Korb write that thirty fires were daily burning at Preobrazhénsky for this purpose.

In spite of all these horrors, Peter ascertained almost nothing. No boyár or person of distinction was found to have taken part in any plot, or to have instigated the riot. Nothing more could be brought out than the discontent of the Streltsi, their hatred to foreigners, and their subsequent rebellion. With regard to Sophia, it was a long time before any revelations were made at all, and finally all that was alleged, under the severest torture, was that two letters purporting to be from Sophia had been read in the Streltsi camp. These letters urged the Streltsi to come to Moscow, to attack the town, and to call Sophia to the throne. The wives of the Streltsi, all the bed-chamber women and attendants of the princesses, even poor beggars who had received their charity, were examined and tortured ; the princesses themselves were personally examined by Peter without torture, and yet nothing could be found which in any way traced these letters to Sophia. The most that was discovered was that her sisters sometimes sent Sophia notes hidden in linen and clothing, and that they had informed her that

THE PRINCESS SOPHIA AS THE NUN SUSANNA IN THE
NOVODEVITCHY MONASTERY.

the Streltsi were all coming to Moscow, and would probably be punished; to which she was reported to have replied that ' she was very sorry for them.' No great evidence of guilt this! Sophia herself said to her brother that she had never sent any letter to the Streltsi, and that as to calling her to the throne, it needed no letter from her, as they must well remember that up to 1689 she had ruled the state. Many Streltsi declared, under torture, that they believed the Tsar to have died abroad; that they therefore intended to revenge themselves on the foreigners and destroy the German suburb, to kill the boyárs who had oppressed them, and then to ask Sophia to rule them; and that had she refused, they would have asked the Tsarévitch, or the other princesses, and as a last resort, ' Prince Basil Golítsyn if he were still alive, for he had always been merciful to them.'

The written depositions of all the persons examined in this investigation are still in existence in the Russian archives, and on a careful analysis they seem to prove very little. Peter, how-ever, chose to be satisfied of the complicity of his sister, and, as the only method of preventing her from again engaging in in-trigue, he forced her to take religious vows. Under the name of the nun Susanna she was confined under the strictest surveil-lance, guarded by a hundred soldiers, in the Novodevítchy con-vent, where she had already lived for nine years. In close con-finement, not allowed to see even the members of her family, except under the greatest precautions, she lived on until 1704. Her sister Martha was also made a nun in a convent at Alexán-drofsky, under the name of Margaret, and died there in 1707. The Princess Catherine, who was strongly suspected, on account of certain relations which she had had with a deacon, succeeded in escaping. She was proved to be guilty of nothing more than dallying with sorcery and witchcraft, heinous as that offence was.

The execution of the first batch of Streltsi examined (341 men) took place on October 10. Only 201 were actually put to death—five were beheaded at Preobrazhénsky, 196 were hanged along the walls of Moscow and at the gates—a hundred who were under twenty years of age were branded in the right cheek and sent into exile, and the remaining forty were detained for further examination. These executions took place, at least in part, in the presence of the Tsar himself and of most of the

foreign ministers and ambassadors, who were specially invited to
be present. Of the second batch, 770 men were executed—some
hanged, some beheaded, and others broken on the wheel. Of
this number, 195 were hanged on a large square gallows in front
of the cell of Sophia at the Novodevítchy convent, and three remained hanging all the winter under her very window, one of
them holding in his hand a folded paper to represent a petition.
Long files of carts carried the Streltsi to the place of execution.
Each cart contained two men seated back to back, with lighted
candles in their hands. Their wives and children ran weeping
and shrieking alongside ; the populace stood silent, cursing the
Tsar under their breath ; except the nobles and the foreigners, everyone sympathised with the criminals. In general the
Streltsi met their death with great stolidity 'there was a kind
of order among the unfortunate wretches ; they all followed one
another in turn, without any sadness on their features, or any
horror of their imminent death.' 'When the execution was over,
it pleased the Tsar's majesty to sup at General Gordon's ; but he
showed no sign of cheerfulness, insisting to several upon the
obstinacy and stubbornness of the criminals. He detailed with
indignant words to General Gordon and the Muscovite magnates
present that one of the condemned was so insolent that he dared,
just as he was about lying down upon the beam, to address the
Tsar with these words : "Make way, my Lord—it is for me to
lie here." '

Further executions took place during the winter, and some
of the trials were actually prolonged for several years without great result. One execution was delayed until 1707. The
heads of many were placed on spikes and their bodies remained
heaped up at the place of execution, while others stayed nearly
the whole winter hanging to the gallows and to beams put
through the battlements of the walls. About the middle of
March, 1,068 bodies were taken down and heaped up outside the
town along the roads. Here they remained two weeks more
before they were buried, and commemorative pillars with heads
spiked on top were erected on the spot. It is necessary to add
that this proceeding was only possible in such a large town because the weather in Moscow in winter is always below freezing
point.

The times were cruel, and people in Russia were accustomed to scenes of blood,[1] yet such general horror was felt at these tortures and executions that the Patriarch felt it his duty to take a picture of the Virgin and exhort the Tsar to mercy. But Peter, resenting the intervention, inveighed against the Patriarch: 'What wilt thou with thy image, or what business is it of thine to come here? Hence forthwith, and put that image in the place where it may be venerated. Know that I reverence God and His most holy Mother more earnestly, perhaps, than thou dost. It is the duty of my sovereign office, and a duty that I owe to God, to save my people from harm, and to prosecute, with public vengeance, crimes that tend to the common ruin.'

Disagreeable as it is to believe, the evidence of several personal observers is that Peter compelled many of his courtiers and nobles to act as executioners, and on one day, in the presence of the Tsar, 109 persons were beheaded at Preobrazhénsky by the nobles of his court. It is said that Menshikóf especially distinguished himself by his cruelty. Whether Peter was himself guilty of immersing his own hands in his subjects' blood remains a question. It is positively asserted both by Guarient, the Austrian ambassador, in his official reports, and by his secretary Korb, in his diary,[2] but both admit that they were not present, and had it from hearsay, while Gordon and Zheliabúzhky, who were certainly better informed, make no mention of this, though they speak of the executions by the nobles. At all events, these horrible occurrences inspired the common people with a belief in the cruelty and blood-thirstiness of Peter. It was said that neither he nor Ramodanófsky could sleep until they had tasted blood. Prince Ramodanófsky

---

[1] Kotóshikhin, writing in the time of the Tsar Alexis, said that there were fifty executioners in Moscow, and that none of them was ever idle.

[2] The diary of Korb is excellent authority for the details of the tortures and executions. It is to be corrected in some respects by the official reports. But it cannot be read without horror. It was published in 1700 at Vienna, with the imperial privilege for copyright. The book was offensive to Peter, and the privilege was wrongly interpreted. On the request of the Tsar many copies were destroyed, and scarcely a dozen are now known to exist. It is accessible in an English translation by Count MacDonnell (Diary of an Austrian Secretary of Legation), which I have quoted after verifying it with a copy of the original in the library at Frascati, founded by the Cardinal Duke of York.

seems to have excelled everyone in Russia as a criminal judge.
He could even rival Jeffreys. Once the anger of Peter, then
in Holland, was aroused by Jacob Bruce coming to him with
scars which he ascribed to the fire-torture of Ramodanófsky.
Peter put an angry postscript to a letter he wrote : 'Beast!
How long are you going to burn people ? Even here people
have come wounded by you. Cease your acquaintance with
Iváshka, or it will be taken out of your wretched skin.' Ramodanófsky, in justifying his treatment of Bruce, defends himself
from the charge of drunkenness, for which he says he has no
time, and leaves that to Peter :

'I have no time to keep acquaintance with Iváshka. *I am
always washing myself in blood.* It is your affair in your leisure to keep up acquaintance with Iváshka, but we have no
leisure.'

It is hard to conceive how a man of the natural good
humour and good disposition of Peter, especially impulsive as
he was, could lend himself to such excesses. It shows what
remarkable obstinacy and strong will he had when following a
fixed idea. At the same time, it leads us to reflect with what
responsibility a man is weighted who uses an authority over
millions in this way to carry out ideas in which few besides
himself believe.

While the examinations were going on at Moscow, the six
regiments of Streltsi at Azof had become excited over the news
of the rebellion of their comrades, and showed signs of acting
in a like manner. They were insubordinate; they complained
bitterly of being kept so long away from home, of the hard
work they did on the fortifications, and especially of the bad
treatment they met with from the foreign officers. Among
them were men who had taken part in the rebellion of Sténka
Rázin, and many wished those times to return. They threatened, with the help of the Don Cossacks, to march back to
Moscow, kill the boyárs and foreigners, and assert their own
will. One of them pithily summed up their complaint by saying : 'There are boyárs in Moscow, Germans in Azof, demons
in the water, and worms in the earth.' The reports which subsequently reached them of the punishments of their comrades
at Moscow, after Peter's return, proved to them that it was

THE STRELTSI GOING TO EXECUTION.

better to keep quiet. Nevertheless, investigations had already begun, and they came in for their share of the punishment.

When the trials were all over, a decree was issued abolishing the Streltsi. Their houses and lands in Moscow were taken from them, and they were all sent into exile in the country, and became simple villagers. It was strictly forbidden to receive them into the military service as soldiers, and it was forbidden to protect or to give assistance to the widows or children of those who had been executed. It was only afterward, in 1702 and 1704, when there was every need of troops against the Swedes, that some regiments of soldiers were formed out of the former Streltsi.

The Streltsi of other towns, who had taken no part in the revolt of their comrades in Moscow, were continued in existence, and subsequently did good service in the Swedish war. After the revolt of Astrakhán they were also abolished.[1]

---

[1] Ustriálof, III., vi. vii. viii. ; Soloviéf, XIV, ; Posselt, *Lefort;* Gordon's *Diary ;* Zheliabúzhky, *Memoirs ;* Korb, *Diarium Itineris,* Engl. Transl. of Count MacDonnell; Perry, *State of Russia ;* Sadler, *Peter der Grosse.*

XXXIV.

THE TSARITSA IS SENT TO A CLOISTER.

WE have already said that Peter did not visit his wife on his arrival at Moscow. He at once took steps to have her removed to a convent, and made inquiries as to why his previous orders on the subject had not been obeyed. Monks and nuns were dead to the world, and to force a wife to take the veil in a convent was, in those days, the customary method of divorcing her. Peter had long wished for a separation, and had resolved on this plan. Hints of it had got out, and his intentions were gossiped about in letters to Leibnitz and others. The Tsar had written from London to Stréshnef, to Leo Naryshkin, and to her confessor, to persuade the Tsaritsa voluntarily to take religious vows. She obstinately refused to comply. On returning to Amsterdam, Peter renewed his request, and this time pressed Ramodanófsky to use his influence. The Patriarch excused himself to the Tsar for having accomplished nothing, and laid the blame on several priests and boyárs who had hindered it. Peter at last had a personal interview with his wife in the house of Vinius, and argued with her for four hours. Three weeks afterward, the Tsarévitch Alexis, now nearly nine years old, was taken from his mother and confided to the care of Natalia at Preobrazhénsky. The Tsaritsa Eudoxia, willingly or unwillingly, was put into a common post-cart, and taken without suite or attendants to the Pokrófsky convent, at Suzdal, where ten months afterward, by a decree of the Tsar, she was forced to take the veil under the name of the nun Helen.

Once there, Peter seemed to forget all about her. Sophia and Martha still received the same income as the other princesses, and were allowed to have personal attendants, while

no money was sent to Eudoxia, all her servants were taken
from her, and she was reduced to the condition of a simple
nun.   At times she was really in want, and had recourse to
her brother Abraham Lopúkhin and his wife.   In one of her
secret letters, she asks them to send her some wine and fish.
'Although I do not drink myself,' she wrote, 'yet I must have
something to offer to people.   Here there is nothing at all;
everything is bad.   Although I am very troublesome to you,
yet what am I to do?   While I am alive kindly give me drink
and food, and clothe me.'   Her family was generous to her,
and the Tsaritsa did not long keep the veil or the attire of a
nun, and in throwing them off she also threw off the special
virtues of the cloister.   She lived in a cell arranged in worldly
style, wearing the attire and the diadem of a Russian princess,
enjoying the friendship and intimacy of some of the people of
the vicinity as well as of a major on recruiting service there,
visiting the neighboring convents, and exchanging secret correspondence with her family and others.   Strangely enough, so
little thought was taken of her by Peter, that all this remained
unknown to him, or at least unnoticed by him, for nearly
twenty years.   She never lost the hope of being recalled to
Moscow.   In 1703, she wrote to Streshnef: 'Have mercy on
me, a poor woman; beg our Lord for grace.   How long must I
live thus without seeing him or my son, or hearing from him?
This is now my fifth year of misery, and my Lord shows no
mercy.   Petition my Lord to let me hear of his health, and to
see my relations.'   After twenty years we shall meet with her
again.

The exact cause of the separation of Peter from his wife is
unknown.   There apparently was no one charge imputed to
her, although Peter long afterward speaks of her as having
been made a nun on account of her 'opposition and suspicions.'
What is perfectly well known is that the marriage had not
been one of love on Peter's part, that Eudoxia was without
education, and adhered to the old-fashioned ways in which she
had been brought up, and that she hated foreigners, especially
Lefort, and those whom Peter liked the most.   It is always
dangerous to the peace of the family when a wife endeavors to
alienate her husband from his friends.   To this, Eudoxia added

jealousy, and Peter knew that he was not blameless. Her attempted interference with his friendships and amusements made him angry ; her jealousy and suspicions of his relations in the German suburb annoyed him ; her marks of affection, her letters, and her attempts to keep or regain his love wearied him.

With the German goldsmith's daughter, Anna Mons, who was the cause of Eudoxia's jealousy, Peter's relations became daily more open and public. Together with the Tsar, she stood as sponsor at the christening of a son of the Danish Envoy, and on her birthday the Tsar dined at her mother's house. She was very pretty, fairly well educated, bright and quick in conversation, and there is every reason to believe that she might have succeeded in supplanting the Tsaritsa on the throne as well as in the Tsar's affections, had it not been that she sometimes exercised her power too plainly, that she was grasping, ever eager for money and presents, and used her favour to push forward her own relations and friends. A handsome house, almost a palace, was built for her, and a fine and productive estate given to her. Her relations with Peter continued uninterruptedly until the end of 1703, when Peter for the first time met the Esthonian girl, Catherine, who subsequently became Empress. Thinking, perhaps, that she would attach the Tsar more firmly to herself by making him jealous, Miss Mons began to coquet with the Prussian Minister Kayserling, who fell deeply in love with her, and, proud to be a rival of the Tsar, offered to marry her. Seeing that she was losing the Tsar's affections, and wishing to establish herself, she was ready to accept this proposal, and asked the Tsar's consent, not in person, but through Menshikóf, who disliked her, and was putting Catherine forward with ends of his own in view. Peter was indignant, revoked the grant of her estate, and took away his portrait set in diamonds, saying that she could have no further use for it, as she had preferred a wretched slave to the original. Together with her mother and her sister, she was placed under arrest in her own house. Two years later, when Peter's anger had somewhat cooled down, the members of the Mons family, although still nominally under arrest, were allowed to visit the Lutheran church, and were shortly afterward given full liberty. In 1707, at Lublin, at a banquet given by Prince Menshikóf on Peter's name's day, Kayserling, whose love was still ardent, and who was still desirous of the marriage, tried to persuade the Tsar to take her brother, Wilhelm Mons, into the military service.[1] Peter had been in very good humour, but no sooner was the name of Mons mentioned than he flew into a passion, and said : 'I educated the girl Mons for myself, with the sincere intention of marrying her, but since she was enticed and inveigled away by you, I do not want to hear or know about her or any of her relations.' Kayserling undertook to defend her, when Menshikóf, taking the side of the Tsar, expressed strong opinions about her. Both got angry, Menshikóf gave Kayserling a blow on the breast, and Kayserling slapped Menshikóf's face, while vile epithets were used on both sides. Kayserling, finding his sword gone, tried to retreat, but, as usual at feasts of this kind, the doors were locked. The Tsar, who after trying to reconcile them had left the room, came back and asked Kayserling what he was plotting, and whether he were not trying to fight. 'I myself am plotting nothing,' Kayserling answered, 'and cannot fight because they have taken away my sword; but if I do not receive the satisfaction I desire from your Majesty, I am ready in any other place to fight with Prince Menshikóf.' Peter then exclaimed that he would fight Kayserling himself, and drew his sword, as did also Menshikóf. Shafirof threw himself in front of them, and begged them not to touch the Minister. The bystanders, to protect Kayserling, pushed him out of the room, but the soldiers who guarded the door, out of excess of zeal, gave him a good drubbing. The Minister, in spite of messages from Peter and Menshikóf, reported this accident to his sovereign and demanded ample satisfaction ; but it did not suit the King of Prussia to quarrel, and the matter was arranged. Kayserling wrote most humble letters of apology to the Tsar

---

[1] Wilhelm Mons subsequently entered the Russian service and became Court Chamberlain. He embittered the last days of the Tsar by an intrigue with the Empress Catherine, for which he was executed in 1724. This was not the last time the Mons family caused trouble to the Tsars. A niece of Anna and Wilhelm married a cousin of the Tsaritsa Eudoxia ; both were accused of plotting against the Empress Elisabeth (the daughter of Peter and Catherine), and both were sent into exile in Siberia in 1743.

and to Menshikóf, in which he ascribed the whole affair to a drunken misunderstanding. A few days later he had a public reconciliation with Menshikóf. Peter, taking Kayserling aside, said to him: 'As God knows my soul, I am right sorry for what has happened, but we were all "full," and now, thank God! all is over and settled.' Two of the guards who had struck Kayserling were condemned to death after Kayserling had agreed to pardon them. Kayserling reported that he had received the 'most complete satisfaction,' and in 1711 married Miss Mons, and died on his wedding journey to Prussia. With the exception of the incident just recounted, Anna Mons disappears from Peter's life after 1704, and while preparing for a second marriage—this time with a Swedish captain, a prisoner of war—she died in the foreign suburb of Moscow in 1714.[1]

[1] Ustriálof, III., vii.; Esipof, *Life of Prince Menshikóf*, in *Russian Archives* for 1875; Semefsky, *The Mons Family*, Moscow, 1862; id. *Avdotia Lopúkhin* in *Russian Messenger* for 1859; Alex. Gordon, *History of Peter the Great*, Aberdeen, 1755.

XXXV.

FOREIGN FASHIONS AND FIRST REFORMS.

THE report of the Tsar's arrival spread quickly through Moscow, and all the boyárs and chief Muscovites hastened to Preobrazhénsky early the next morning to pay their court. Korb says:

' The Tsar received all that came with an alacrity that. showed as if he wished to be beforehand with his subjects in eagerness. Those who, according to the fashion of that country, would cast themselves upon the ground to worship Majesty, he lifted up graciously from their grovelling posture and embraced with a kiss, such as is only due among private friends. If the razor, that plied promiscuously among the beards of those present, can be forgiven the injury it did, the Muscovites may truly reckon that day among the happiest of their lives. Shéïn, general-in-chief of the Tsar's troops, was the first who submitted the encumbrance of his long beard to the razor. Nor can they consider it any disgrace, as their sovereign is the first to show the example. Nor was there anybody left to laugh at the rest. They were all born to the same fate. Nothing but superstitious awe for his office exempted the Patriarch. Prince Michael Tcherkásky was let off out of reverence for his advanced years, and Tíkhon Stréshnef out of the honor due to one who had been guardian to the Tsaritsa. All the rest had to conform to the guise of foreign nations, and the razor eliminated the ancient fashion.'

Five days afterward, on the Russian first of September, there was a feast at Shéïn's.

' A crowd of boyárs, scribes, and military officers almost incredible was assembled there, and among them were several common sailors, with whom the Tsar repeatedly mixed, divided apples, and even honoured one of them by calling him his

brother.   A salvo of twenty-five guns marked each toast.   Nor
could the irksome offices of the barber check the festivities of
the day, though it was well known he was enacting the part of
jester by appointment at the Tsar's court.   It was of evil omen
to make show of reluctance as the razor approached the chin,
and was to be forthwith punished with a box on the ears.   In
this way, between mirth and the wine-cup, many were admon-
ished by this insane
ridicule to abandon
the olden guise.'

A Contemporary Caricature.

To the orthodox,
old-fashioned Rus-
sian, the beard was
then as sacred as it
is now to a Turk,
or as the queue
is to a Chinaman.
The Patriarch
Adrian, shortly
after his accession,
had promulga-
ted a fulminating
edict against all
who were so irre-
ligious, unholy, and
heretical as to
shave or cut their
beards, an orna-
ment given by
God, and which
had been worn by
all the holy prophets and apostles, and by the Saviour himself.
Only such men as Julian the Apostate, Heraclius the Heretic,
Constantine the Iconoclast, Olgerd the Idol-worshipper, and
Amurath the Mussulman, had forced their subjects to shave,
while Constantine the Great, Theodosius the Great, and Vladímir
the Great had all worn beards.[1]   Peter, in his eagerness to adopt

---

[1] See also page 205.

the usages of Western Europe, chose to consider the beard as the symbol of what was uncivilised and barbarous. He was not content with repealing the decree of Alexis, and saying that his subjects might shave, but he said that they *must* shave. For Peter himself it was easy; he had little beard, and even his moustache, which he allowed to grow, was always very thin. What had begun in jest was soon done in earnest. Decrees were issued that all Russians, the clergy excepted, should shave, but those who preferred to keep their beards were allowed to do so on condition of paying a yearly tax, fixed at a kopék (two cents) for the peasantry, and varying from thirty to a hundred rubles (from $60 to $200, a ruble being worth at that time about $2) for the other classes, the merchants, as being the richest and most conservative, paying the highest sum.

On the payment of this duty they received a bronze token, which they were obliged always to wear about their necks, and to renew yearly.[1] Many were willing to pay this very high tax in order to keep their beards, but

Token for Beard Duty.

most conformed to the Tsar's wishes, some through policy, some through ' terror of having their beards (in a merry humour) pulled out by the roots, or taken so rough off, that some of the skin went with them.' The Tsar would allow no one to be near him who did not shave. Perry writes:

' About this time the Tsar came down to Vorónezh, where I was then on service, and a great many of my men who had worn their beards all their lives were now obliged to part with them, amongst whom one of the first that I met with, just coming from the hands of the barber, was an old Russ carpenter

---

[1] Although the restrictions on the wearing of beards by the peasantry and the middle classes soon disappeared, yet, until the accession of Alexander II., all public officials were obliged to be shaved. This gradually became relaxed in practice, but it was only in the year 1875 that a decree was issued permitting the officers and soldiers of the army, except the Imperial Guard, to wear their beards when in service.

that had been with me at Camisbinka, who was a very good
workman with his hatchet, and whom I always had a friendship for.   I jested a little with him on this occasion, telling
him that he was become a young man, and asked him what he
had done with his beard.   Upon which he put his hand in his
bosom and pulled it out and showed it to me; further telling
me that when he came home, he would lay it up to have it put
in his coffin and buried along with him, that he might be able
to give an account of it to St. Nicholas, when he came to the
other world, and that all his brothers (meaning his fellow-workmen who had been shaved that day) had taken the same care.'

Soon after compelling his courtiers to shave their beards,
Peter began a crusade against the old Russian dress.   On
October 9, Lefort and Golovín, the only two members of the
Great Embassy then in Moscow, entered the town in solemn
state.

'No one was allowed to appear except in German dress,
which was especially meant to irritate Prince Ramodanófsky
with the sight of what he liked not, for when it was told to
him that the ambassador Golovín had put on the German dress
at Vienna, he answered: "I do not believe Golovín to be such
a brainless ass as to despise the garb of his fatherland."'

A few months afterward, Peter himself gave a carnival
entertainment, at which the boyár Sheremétief, who had just
returned from his visit to Italy, appeared in full foreign dress,
wearing the cross of Malta, which many envied him.   The
Tsar cut off, with his own hands, the sleeves of some of his
officers which seemed to him to be too long.   He said: 'See,
these things are in your way.   You are safe nowhere with
them.   At one moment you upset a glass, then you forgetfully
dip them in the sauce.   Get gaiters made of them.'   On January 14, 1700, appeared a decree commanding all the courtiers
and the officials, as well in the capital as in the provinces, to
wear nothing but foreign clothing, and to provide themselves
with such suits before the end of the carnival.   This decree
had to be repeated frequently throughout the year, and models
of the clothing were publicly exposed.   According to Perry,
these patterns and copies of the decree were hung up at all the
gates of the towns, and all who disobeyed these orders were

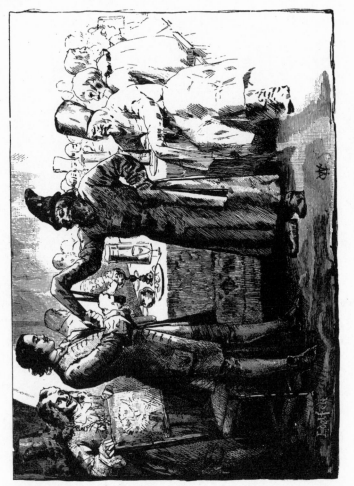

THE TSAR CUTTING THE LONG SLEEVES OF THE BOYARS.

obliged either to pay a fine, or ' to kneel down at the gates of
the city, and have their coats cut off just even with the ground,
so much as it was longer than to touch the ground when they
kneeled down, of which there were many hundreds of coats
that were cut accordingly ; and being done with a good humour,
it occasioned mirth among the people and soon broke the custom of their wearing long coats, especially in places near Moscow and those towns wherever the Tsar came.'   As this decree
did not affect the peasantry, it was less difficult to put it into
execution.   Even the women were compelled to adopt foreign
fashions, and to give up the old Russian costumes.   Peter's sisters set the example.   Here the women, as might perhaps be expected, were less conservative than the men.   They saw, in the
adoption of foreign fashions of dress, a great opening to variety
of costume.   Decrees were even issued against high Russian
boots, against the use of Russian saddles, and even of long Russian knives.

There is no absolute and real connection between costume
and civilisation.   Shaved faces and short garments made the
Russians no more civilised and no more European than they
were before, although they made them conform in one respect
to the usages of civilised people.   It is the natural spirit of imitation, the desire not to be different from the rest of the civilised world, that induces peoples rising in the scale of civilisation
to adopt the fashion of the garments of more highly cultured
nations, even though the new costume may be both unbecom-
ing and inconvenient.   This we have seen in our own day
among the Japanese.   We see it also in the way peasant costumes constantly disappear, and even the neat white cap gives
place to a tawdry imitation of a lady's bonnet, and the comfortable and convenient knee-breeches and long stockings to the
awkward trousers.   At the same time, there is often a tendency
to see in European dress something necessary to modern and
Western life ; there is a tendency to the false reasoning that a
man becomes civilised because he wears European garments.
This tendency is sometimes seen in missionaries, who immediately put what they call Christian clothing on their new con-
verts, to the great inconvenience of the latter ; and this feeling
seems to have had some influence on Peter when he changed

the costume of Russia by an edict. Only in one way can such an arbitrary and forced change be defended—that it might, perhaps, render the people more ready to accept Western ideas. If they had violently broken with the traditions of their fathers in point of costume, they might be more easily led to break with them in other respects. Still, even without decrees of this kind, had people been left free to dress as they liked, as European notions and European habits crept into Russia, the change of dress would naturally follow. It had been begun before, and even a forced change of costume was no new idea. Yury Krýzhanitch, the learned Serbian Panslavist, to whom we have referred several times before, in his book on Russia, which he wrote in his exile at Tobolsk from 1660 to 1676, set out a project for reforming Russian costume of very much the same sort as that adopted by Peter. He was in favour of the same violent measures, and had the same abhorrence to the clothing of every description worn by the Russians and other Slavs. He accused it of being effeminate uncomfortable, a hinderance to work and action, and a cause of great and unwarrantable expense. It is true that the Russians who appeared abroad in Russian clothing were laughed at in the streets, but so nowadays is anyone stared at and pointed at in London or New York who appears in a costume different from that ordinarily worn. It is only in the East that all costumes pass without remark. The fashion of dress is one of the weak points of the highly cultured nations, and one on which they are most intolerant. It was natural that Peter, while imbibing foreign ideas, should in a way, too, imbibe foreign prejudices. Hence he preferred a short coat to a gown, a shaven chin to a beard, and a peruke to natural hair. Even with us it does not require such a very long memory to recall the time when English and Americans were as fanatical on some points as were the orthodox Russians of Peter's day. A full beard was looked upon almost as a mark of a revolutionist or a freethinker, and a moustache showed a tendency for adopting foolish foreign notions of all kinds. That prejudice, fortunately, has passed away, and people nowadays have even come to see that a great-coat down to the heels, of almost the same fashion as those which Peter had cut off at the gates, is more comfortable in a cold climate than

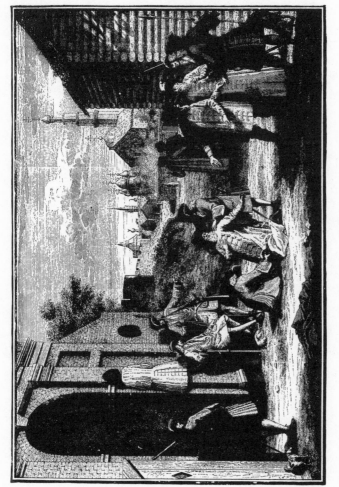

CUTTING OFF THE LONG ROBES OF THE BOYARS.

a short jacket. The red shirt, the loose trousers tucked into
the high boots, and the sleeveless caftan of the peasant, are
worn now as a student fashion in Russia to show Slavophile
feelings, and since the time of Catherine II., the fixed court
dress for Russian ladies is the old costume, which may be seen
at the Winter Palace on any state occasion.

There were some importations from abroad which promised
more advantage to
the State than did
the foreign gar-
ments and the
shaved faces. Such
was the introduc-
tion of stamped
paper. This was
recommended by
Alexis Kurbátof,
who had travelled
abroad with Boris
Sheremétief as his
steward and treas-
urer. As Kurbátof
was of low birth
and yet was not a
ship-carpenter, the
only way in which
he could make the
recommendation to
the Tsar was to en-
close his project in
a letter, directed to

Catherine II. in National Costume.

be delivered into the hands of the Tsar without being unsealed,
and drop it on the floor of one of the public offices. This was
the manner in which all denunciatory letters were delivered,
and it may be imagined that it was a pleasure to Peter to find,
not an accusation of crime, but a project for increasing the
revenues of the State. Kurbátof was given the rank of secretary, and was appointed chief of the new municipal department.

Peter had been struck in Holland by the wealth, the comfort, and the independence of the middle classes; by the fact that it was from them that the Government received the greater part of its revenues, and that on them depended the welfare of the State. At this time in Russia, the middle and the commercial classes, who were small in number and inhabited only the towns, were entirely in the hands of the Voievodes, or governors, who (as was even officially stated in the decree promulgating the reform we shall speak of) exhausted the patience and the pockets of the towns-people by exactions of every kind—by taking percentages on their bargains, by levying contributions in money and in kind, and by extorting bribes to do justice or to prevent injustice. Peter had seen that in other countries the towns-people governed themselves by elected burgomasters and councillors. But even in Little Russia, such elective institutions already existed, under the name of the 'Magdeburg Right.' This it was resolved to apply to the whole of Russia, and in Moscow, as well as in the other towns, the merchants were permitted to choose good and honest men, one from every guild or ward, who should form a council having charge of the collection of taxes, of the disputes between the citizens, and, in general, of municipal affairs. Each of these councillors was to act in turn as president for the space of a month. All of these new municipal bodies were placed under the charge of a new department, which had no connection with the existing Ministries, but could report directly to the Tsar. This foreign institution was called by a foreign name, one of the first importations of German terms, the *Búrmistr* (burgomaster) Department, or *Rátusha* (*rath-haus*). As a compensation for being freed from the exactions of the Voievodes, and for the introduction of municipal government, the merchants were obliged for the future to pay double taxes. It always takes time to become accustomed to independence which has not been given gradually, but has been thrust on a nation, and one of the first results of the municipal institutions was that the merchants elected rulers out of their own body who were as bad as those they supplanted. Corruption and bribery speedily found their way here. The first case brought before the notice of the Tsar —that of the town of Venev—was severely punished; both bribers and bribe-takers were beaten with the knout, and sent, with their wives and children, to hard labour at Azof. It was decreed that such offences should in future be punished with death; but even that did not avail.

Shortly after the introduction of stamped paper and of municipal councils, came another decree, which also had reference to the increase of general prosperity and of the State revenues. That was the re-organisation of the monetary system. The only coins at that time circulating in Russia were small, oval bits of silver called kopéks (two cents), very badly stamped with St. George on one side and the title of the Tsar on the other. The quality of the silver and the size of the coin had varied at different periods. In the time of the Tsar Alexis, an attempt was made to reform the currency with advantage to the State, by diminishing the size of the kopék, and at the same time stamping copper coins of the same size and weight, and of the same nominal value. The natural result of this was that the silver all left circulation ; and, as the real value of the copper was so far below its nominal value, the price of articles increased in the ratio of one to fifteen. The dearness of provisions caused a riot, which was only quelled with difficulty and with great effusion of blood. It was found necessary to return to the old system. Although the kopék was the only coin, yet accounts were kept in *rubles, altýns*, and *déngas;* a *dénga* being the half of a *kopék*, an *altýn* being three *kopéks*, and a *ruble* one hundred *kopéks*. It was necessary, therefore, for the purposes of small change, to use bits of stamped leather, or to cut the kopéks into halves and quarters. Undeterred by the failure of his father, Peter resolved on a rational reform, and began by coining copper for the purposes of small change, of the same—or nearly the same—real value as the silver ; it was necessary, therefore, to make a copper kopék forty-five times as heavy as a silver one. Consequently, the copper pieces, being not tokens but actual coins, were of very large size, which, though inconvenient, gave satisfaction to a primitive people. After the copper came a gold coinage of single and double ducats, with the portrait of the Tsar on one side and the arms of Russia on the other ; then a silver coinage of *grivenniks* (ten kopéks), quarter and half rubles, and finally rubles. In this way, the new coinage was introduced without

difficulty, and the old withdrawn from circulation.   In the first
three years there were coined in this way over nine millions of
rubles ($18,000,000).

Another measure removed a barrier, though but a slight
one, between Russia and the rest of the world.   The Russians
had been in the habit of beginning the new year on September
1 (it being believed that the world was created in the autumn,
when all the fruits of the earth were in perfection), and of
dating their years from the beginning of the world.   On
December 20 (O.S.), 1699, appeared a decree ordering the year
to begin on January 1, and the date to be that from the birth
of Christ, and not from the creation of the world—*i.e.*, the year
was to be 1700, and not 7208.   It was stated in the decree that
this change was made in order to conform to the custom of
other countries, and Peter defended the change to those who
exclaimed that the world could not have been created in the
depth of winter, by desiring them 'to view the map of the
globe, and, in a pleasant temper, gave them to understand that
Russia was not all the world, and that what was winter with
them was, at the same time, always summer in those places
beyond the equator.'   In order to impress this event on the
people, special New Year services were held in all the churches,
the inhabitants of Moscow were ordered to congratulate each
other on the New Year, evergreens were placed on the door-
posts of the houses and in the corners of the rooms, fire-works
and bonfires were lighted on the Red Place and in the streets,
and there was to be a general illumination of private houses for
seven days.   Feasting went on until Epiphany, when there
took place the semi-annual blessing of the river Moskvá.
Contrary to previous custom, the Tsar did not seat himself
with the Patriarch on his throne, but appeared in uniform at
the head of his regiment, drawn up together with other troops,
amounting to twelve thousand men, on the thick ice of the river.
The new arms and the brilliant uniforms made an excellent impression.

It is unfortunate that, when this change was made, the Gregorian calendar was not adopted.   But at that time Protestants,
as well as Orthodox, had a suspicion of the Gregorian calendar as being something peculiarly Romish and Papistical.   It

was not finally adopted in England until the year 1752. For various reasons, it has never been found convenient to adopt the new style in countries where the Orthodox Church prevails. The chief objection is that in this church there are many saints' days, and it is feared that there would be disturbances among the ignorant peasants and common people if in one year they should be suddenly deprived of twelve days, for at no period of the year could these be taken together without including some great holidays. Still, with Peter's fearlessness and firmness, the change would probably have been made at that time if the new style had been in use in England.[1]

---

[1] Korb, *Diary ;* Perry, *State of Russia ;* Gordon's *Diary ;* Posselt, *Lefort ;* Ustriálof, III., vii. ; Soloviéf, xiv. ; Russian Laws, ii., iii. ; Brückner, *Ein Kleiderreformprojekt vor Peter dem Grossen* in *Russiche Revue ;* Kryzhanitch, *Works*, i.

XXXVI.

PETER'S DEJECTION, ANGER, AND GRIEF.

No matter how pleasant the journey abroad had been, Peter was glad to be again in the society of his friends. It was partly that, and partly, perhaps, the desire to counteract the effect of the trials and executions, that banquets, festivities, and masquerades were given almost nightly. Dinners with his friends, christenings and weddings in the German suburb, the receptions of foreign ambassadors, carols at Christmas time, daily feasts at the new club-house, called Lefort's Palace, absorbed all his leisure time. According to Korb—

'A sham Patriarch and a complete set of scenic clergy dedicated to Bacchus, with solemn festivities, the palace which was built at the Tsar's expense, and which it has pleased him now to have called Lefort's. A procession thither set out from Colonel Lima's house. He that bore the assumed honours of the Patriarch was conspicuous in the vestments proper to a bishop. Bacchus was decked with a mitre and went stark naked, to betoken lasciviousness to the lookers-on. Cupid and Venus were the insignia on his crozier, lest there should be any mistake about what flock he was pastor of. The remaining route of Bacchanalians came after him, some carrying great bowls full of wine, others mead, others, again, beer and brandy, that last joy of heated Bacchus. And, as the wintry cold hindered their binding their brows with laurel, they carried great dishes of dried tobacco-leaves, with which, when ignited, they went to the remotest corners of the palace, exhaling those most delectable odours and most pleasant incense to Bacchus from their smutty jaws. Two of those pipes through which some people are pleased to puff smoke—a most empty fancy—being set crosswise, served the scenic bishop to confirm the rites of consecration.'

During the carnival, on the very day when a hundred and eighty-six Streltsi were executed, there was a feast at Lefort's house, with a grand display of fire-works, which was witnessed by the Tsarévitch and by the Tsar's sister Natalia from another apartment. The next day, the envoy of Brandenburg had a solemn leave-taking, and Mr. de Zadora-Kesielsky was accepted as Resident in his stead.

'The Tsar commanded him to stay for dinner, which was splendid, and at which the envoys of foreign princes and the principal boyárs were also present. After dinner was over, the Councillor Zótof, who was mimic Patriarch when the Tsar wished, began giving toasts. He that drank had on bended knee for mockery to revere the sham ecclesiastical dignitary, and beg the favour of his benediction, which he gave with two tobacco-pipes, set in the shape of a cross. He alone, of all the envoys, withdrew furtively, for he held the sacred sign of our Christian faith too holy to approve of such jests. The same prelate added to the decency of the dancing by opening it with pontificals and crozier. The inner apartment, next the room in which the festivities were going on, was again occupied by the Tsarévitch and the Tsar's sister Natalia; thence they saw the dancing and all the gay tumult, the curtains with which the place was most handsomely decorated being drawn a little; and they were only seen through a lattice by the guests. The natural beauty of the Tsarévitch was wonderfully shown off by his civilised German dress and powdered wig. Natalia was escorted by the most distinguished of the married ladies. This day, too, beheld a great departure from Russian manners, which up to this forbade the female sex from appearing at public assemblies of men, and at festive gaieties, for some were not only allowed to be at dinner, but also at the dancing afterward. The Tsar had arranged to go off to Vorónezh that night, for which reason, as Carlowitz was about to return to his sovereign in Poland, after a deal of flattering and envied compliments, he gave him a kiss, telling him to bear it to the King as a manifest token of his everlasting affection. He also gave Carlowitz his picture, exceedingly rich set with a profusion of diamonds, a fruit of that royal goodwill which Carlowitz had managed to win.'

With the trouble in his own family, with the suspicions that his step-sister had been plotting against his life, with the numerous executions, Peter's mind was in such a state that he could not always be quieted by dissipation. At some of these festivities he was morose, and melancholy, and dejected; at others, the slightest cause roused him to anger. A few days after his arrival, at a grand dinner given by Lefort, the Tsar left the room in a rage with his generalissimo Shéïn, with whom he had been warmly disputing, and nobody knew what he was going to do. Korb relates:

'It was known later that he had gone to question the soldiers, to learn from them how many colonels and other regimental officers that general-in-chief had made without reference to merit, merely for money. In a short time when he came back, his wrath had grown to such a pitch that he drew his sword, and facing the general-in-chief, horrified the guests with this threat: 'By striking thus, I will mar thy mal-government.' Boiling over with well-grounded anger, he appealed to Prince Ramodanófsky, and to Zótof; but finding them excuse the general-in-chief, he grew so hot that he startled all the guests by striking right and left, he knew not where, with his drawn sword. Prince Ramodanófsky had to complain of a cut finger, and another of a slight wound on the head. Zótof was hurt in the hand as the sword was returning from a stroke. A blow far more deadly was aiming at the general-in-chief, who beyond a doubt would have been stretched in his gore by the Tsar's right hand, had not General Lefort (who was almost the only one that might have ventured it), catching the Tsar in his arms, drawn back his hand from the stroke. But the Tsar, taking it ill that any person should dare to hinder him from sating his most just wrath, wheeled round upon the spot, and struck his unwelcome impeder a hard blow on the back. He is the only one that knew what remedy to apply; none of the Muscovites is more beloved by the Tsar than he. This man so mitigated his ire that, threatening only, he abstained from murder. Merriment followed this dire tempest: the Tsar, with a face full of smiles, was present at the dancing, and, to show his mirth, commanded the musicians to play the tunes to which (so he said) he had danced at his most beloved lord and brother's, when that most august host was entertaining exalted

PROCESSION IN HONOR OF BACCHUS.

guests. Two young ladies departing by stealth were, at an
order from the Tsar, brought back by soldiers.'

In the case of Shéïn, there was probably just cause for the
Tsar's anger. We learn that when it was known that the Tsar
was coming back so quickly, the astonished boyárs held councils
twice a day, and, under threat of the whip, forced the merchants' clerks to make out their accounts for them. The pro-
motions of officers made by Shéïn in the Tsar's absence were
all cancelled.

On another occasion, finding Menshikóf dancing with his
sword on, he taught him to lay it aside by cuffing him with
such force that the blood spouted from his nose. At a dinner
at Colonel Chambers', Korb says:

' An inexplicable whirlwind troubled the gaieties. Seizing
upon General Lefort and flinging him on the floor, the Tsarish
Majesty kicked him. He that is next to the fire is nearest to
burning.' On another occasion, in a dispute between Leo
Narýshkin and Prince Boris Golítsyn, the Tsar 'loudly threatened that he would cut short the dispute with the head of one
or the other, whichever should be found ·most in fault. He
commissioned Ramodanófsky to examine into the affair, and
with a violent blow of his clenched hand thrust back General
Lefort, who was coming up to mitigate his fury.'

We involuntarily ask ourselves the question why Peter,
whose presence was so awe-inspiring, was so frequently obliged,
then and afterward, to use the stick, and to resort to the personal chastisement of his ministers and friends. Much is to be
explained by the character of the times. The nation was un-
developed and unripe. No strong power nor strong will was
restrained by self-respect or by public opinion. Besides this,
Peter had lowered himself in his dealings and intercourse with
his subjects. He had not only thrown off the dignity and safe-
guards which formerly surrounded the Tsar, but he had conde-
scended to be the equal, if not the inferior, of his subjects, by
his manual occupations and his love of practical joking. It
was natural, therefore, that even in serious things his subjects
sometimes forgot themselves, and looked upon him as their
equal. There are princes nowadays who have been accused of
lowering their royal dignity by being too careless of the com-

pany with which they associated, but who yet carry themselves in such a way that no man has ever dared to take a liberty with them. This is the effect, partly of personal character, and partly of modern society and well-disciplined and well-organised public opinion. In Peter's time this last was lacking.

It was at Vorónezh, where Peter went three times in the first winter after his return, where he was away from the society of Lefort and his friends, looking after his ships, that he most gave way to melancholy and despondency. The forced labour in the ship-yards was very hard for the poor peasants, who had to bring their own hatchets, and sometimes their horses, to cut and float timber, and to work at the ships under pain of death. The mortality was so great, owing to bad sanitary conditions, that the wharves had to be fenced in and guarded to prevent desertion. Runaways, when found, were well beaten, and their wives and children were cast into prison. There was bribery and peculation among the officials, and the country as far as Moscow suffered from the disorder to work and the bad administration. Firm as was Peter's will, and strong as was his belief in himself, he even began to doubt whether, after all, he was on the right road. He wrote to Vinius on November 2, 1698, from Vorónezh: 'Thank God! we have found our fleet in an excellent condition, and have approved the magazine. But still a cloud of doubt covers my mind whether we shall ever taste of this fruit, like dates, which those who plant never gather. However, we hope in God and in St. Paul. "The husbandman that laboureth must be the first partaker of the fruit."' In another letter he writes: 'Here, by God's help, is great preparation; but we only wait for that blessed day when the cloud of doubt over us shall be driven away. We have begun a ship here which will carry sixty guns.' His doubts and his hesitations were being rapidly driven away by hard work, when he received from Moscow the melancholy news of the sudden death of General Lefort. Lefort had entertained the envoys from Denmark and Brandenburg, on the eve of their departure for Vorónezh, where they were going by permission of the Tsar, to see his new fleet. The banquet had lasted so long that they had finished it by drinking in the open air, in the cold of February. The next

day, Lefort was taken alarmingly ill with a burning fever, and
died a week after in delirium.   The Tsar immediately returned
from Vorónezh to be present at the funeral.   At the news of
the death, he burst into thick sobs, and, with a flood of tears,
broke out in these words : ' Now I am left without one trusty
man.   He alone was faithful to me; in whom can I confide
henceforward?'   He frequently spoke of his loss, and years
after, when Menshikóf gave an entertainment which was to his
taste, said : ' This is the first time that I have really enjoyed
myself since Lefort's death.'   It is to be mentioned to Lefort's
honour that, with all the opportunities he had for making himself rich, he died almost penniless.   The Tsar maintained in his
service Peter Lefort, the nephew and steward of the general,
and sent to Geneva for Henry Lefort, the only son of the de-
ceased, saying that he always wished to have one of the name
near his person.

A few months later, on November 29, 1699, the Tsar lost
another and an older friend, with whom we have had much to
do—General Gordon.   Peter visited him five times during his
short illness, was with him twice on the last night, and closed
his dying eyes with his own hand.   The last entry in Gordon's
diary is on the last day of December, 1698, when, as if antici-
pating his death, he wrote : ' In this year I have felt a sensible
failing of my health and strength—but Thy will be done, O
my gracious God ! ' [1]

---

[1] Korb, *Diary;* Posselt, *Lefort;* Gordon, *Diary;* Veselago, *Sketch of
Russian Naval History.*

XXXVII.

ONE of the Great Embassy, Prokóp Voznítsyn, had been left in Vienna, and was made delegate to the Congress that was to settle the terms of peace with the Turks, and which met shortly afterwards at Carlowitz, near Peterwardein, on the Danube. It was, as we remember, greatly against Peter's will that he consented to take any part in the negotiations. He was dissatisfied that peace should be made by Austria, for he knew that Russia alone was unable to cope with the Turkish Empire, which, in spite of its recent defeats, was still strong. All his efforts at ship-building, so far as they had any national importance, were in order to create a fleet which could fight the Turks on their own waters, the Black Sea. He objected also to the principle on which the peace was to be made, that of the *uti possidetis*. Voznítsyn, therefore, had instructions to insist not only on keeping all that Russia had acquired by force of arms—that is, Azof and the forts on the Lower Dniéper—but also on the cession of Kertch. Subsequently, when the Tsar found that Austria would, in any event, make peace, he instructed his envoy, in case the Turks were obstinate, not to insist too strongly on Kertch, provided Azof and the forts on the Dniéper could be retained. He soon saw that the negotiations at Carlowitz proceeded too quickly for him to make any effort at new conquests before the conclusion of a treaty. Austria and Turkey were both sincerely desirous of peace—Austria because she did not wish to risk the conquests she had gained, and wanted to have her hands free, Turkey because the Sultan and his Vizier feared still further defeats. England and the Netherlands desired peace because they foresaw the war of the Spanish succession, and wished to use the whole force of Aus-

tria to counterbalance that of France. The Austrian and Turkish commissioners, assisted by the mediators, Lord Paget and
Colyer, in a few secret cessions, quickly established the terms
of peace, in spite of all the intrigues of Voznítsyn. The Russian envoy had at first applied to the Austrian ministry, and
then to the Emperor himself, asking that, on the basis of the
treaty of 1697, by which each party bound itself not to make
a separate peace, the overtures of the Turks should be rejected,
unless the Russian demands were satisfied. Finding this of no
avail, he endeavoured to work on the Turks through his old
acquaintance Alexander Mavrocordato, a Greek by birth, the
dragoman of the Porte and one of the Turkish commissioners.
He insisted to the Turks that this was no time for them to
make peace, as Austria would soon be at war with France, and
they would have the chance, not only of reconquering all they
had lost, but, perhaps, of gaining additional advantages. These
negotiations were carried on through the chaplain of Mavrocordato and Doctor Postnikóf, who had returned with his doctor's
diploma from Padua. In order to escape observation, they
took long circuits through the plains surrounding Carlowitz,
and met at distant points. Mavrocordato sent flattering messages, and willingly accepted presents and bribes. When he
hinted that it was cold, Voznítsyn sent him his own embroidered caftan lined with blue-fox fur. In return for the caviare,
smoked fish, and salted sturgeon, Mavrocordato gave tobacco,
coffee, pipes, and writing-paper. The ruse was too transparent;
all were astonished that the Russian envoy should take the side
of the Turks, and his plans came to naught. The Turks, sure
of the peace with Austria, refused to make concessions, either
to the Poles or the Venetians, and demanded from the Russians
the evacuation of the Lower Dniéper. They would hear nothing of the cession of Kertch, were with difficulty prevailed upon
to allow Azof still to remain in the Russian possession, and
absolutely refused to give up the Dniéper. They wished, by
all means, to keep to themselves the Black Sea. Voznítsyn
then brought forward the proposition which he had held in
reserve, that a two years' truce should be made, which Peter
thought would allow him sufficient time to have his fleet in
readiness for active offensive operations. This the Turks re-

fused, said they had come to terms with the other powers, and that they were able to fight and conquer Russia. At this Voznítsyn took a firmer and more threatening attitude, and replied that if they wished war they could have it. This had an effect, and before the arrival of a new proposition from Peter that the forts on the Dniéper should be rased to the ground and not be rebuilt by either side, Voznítsyn had concluded a truce for two years. In defending himself for this, he said that the Congress was over, the treaty signed,[1] and the Turkish commissioners could not be found this side of Constantinople; that the Turks were little disposed to cede anything except what was too far off for them to defend and maintain, as they wished to use all their strength in reconquering the Morea. He therefore advised Peter, instead of running the chances of war, to send a special embassy to Constantinople, headed by some man of quickness and capacity, to see on what terms the Turks were willing to make peace, but not to ask for a peace, and to refuse all terms inconsistent with the dignity and power of Russia.

This advice Peter took, and appointed as his ambassador Emelian Ukráintsef, who had long been in the Russian Foreign Office, and had been entrusted with several delicate and important negotiations. In order to give dignity to the mission, and at the same time to impress the Turks with the new naval power of Russia, he resolved that Ukráintsef, instead of prosecuting his journey by land, should sail from Azof on a frigate, while he, with all the other ships disposable, would accompany him as far as Kertch. Golovín was made general-admiral of the fleet, and invested with the insignia of the new order of St. Andrew. This order Peter created after the model of those decorations he had seen in other countries. He had found out how convenient and cheap a way this was of rewarding services to the state.

---

[1] By the Treaty of Carlowitz, which, after discussions lasting seventy-two days, was signed on January 26, 1699, Austria regained Transylvania, the Banate, and all of Hungary northwest of the Theiss; Venice kept Dalmatia and the Morea; and Poland received Kamenetz and Podolia, while all tributes to the Porte from these three powers, whether paid as such or as honorary presents, were done away with. It was the beginning of the decadence of Turkey. From that time, Europe felt no fear of the Turkish arms.

On his visit to Vorónezh, in the autumn of 1698, Peter found his infant fleet in a far greater state of forwardness than he had expected. Many ships were already built and armed, and ready for a cruise. The magazines were full of material. In this, and in subsequent visits, he laboured to make good all the deficiencies, and Cruys, who had arrived from Holland, inspected all the vessels, and recommended that many of them be strengthened, and in part rebuilt. Peter was glad to find that many of his fellow-workmen at Amsterdam and Deptford had already arrived, and he himself set heartily to work, and laid the keel of a new frigate, one hundred and thirty feet long, to be called the 'Predestination.' By the
spring of 1699, there
were ready eighty-six
ships and boats of all
kinds, including
eighteen which car-
ried from thirty-six
to forty-six guns, be-
sides five hundred
barges for transport-
ing provisions and
munitions. The fleet,
under the command
of Admiral Golovín,
left Vorónezh on May
7, and reached Azof

The Apostle Peter.

on June 3. Peter went as commander of the forty-four-gun ship the 'Apostle Peter.' Cruys, in his journal, gives a full account of the voyage, and after describing the lovely country through which they passed, tells, among other things, how at Pánshin, where they arrived just in time to prevent the assem-bled Cossacks and Kalmuks from coming to blows over cattle-lifting and pasturage, Peter came to see him, and found his men engaged in cleaning some tortoises which they had caught on the banks of the Don. The Tsar asked what they were for, and being told ' to make a fricassee for dinner,' immediately ordered a similar dish to be prepared for his own table. Tortoises were

considered unclean animals. The Russian nobles who dined
with him, not knowing of what the dish was composed, but
thinking, from its taste, that it was made of young chickens,
ate it with satisfaction. When the dish was empty, Peter
ordered a servant to bring in the feathers of these excellent
chickens, which, to the general astonishment and consternation,
turned out to be tortoise-shells. Most of them laughed at the
joke, except Shéïn and Sóltykof, who became sick at having
eaten food so repugnant to all their ideas. Peter was fond of
practical jokes of this kind, and at a supper at Moscow, not long
before, had seized Golovín, who hated oil, and stuffed salad
down his throat till the blood ran from his nose.

After inspecting the fortifications at Azof and Taganróg,
drawing up and correcting maritime regulations, and trying the
qualities of the vessels in manœuvres and a sham fight, Peter
started for Kertch with all his fleet. The forty-six-gun ship
'Fortress,' under the command of Captain van Pamburg, who
had been engaged in Holland, was selected to take Ukráintsef
to Constantinople.

Negotiations with the Pasha of Kertch lasted ten days.
First an absolute refusal was given to the passage of the ship
without orders from Constantinople ; then a journey by land
was recommended. When Peter threatened to force the passage with his whole fleet in case of an absolute refusal, the
Pasha consented, as there were only four Turkish ships in the
harbour, but still excuses were made on account of the bad
weather. When it seemed that everything had been arranged,
Peter returned with his squadron to Taganróg, and in a few
days to Vorónezh. His departure seemed to give the Turks
hope that they might create new delays. Finally, Ukráintsef
was forced to give the order for the immediate departure of his
vessel, in spite of all the dangers that were set before him by
the Turks, who said : ' You do not know our sea. Not without
reason is it called Black. In time of danger, men's hearts grow
black on it.' Refusing the request of the Turkish vessels that
convoyed him, to stop at Balakláva, Ukráintsef directed his
course straight to Constantinople, and after sighting land at
Heracléa, speedily came into the Bosphorus, and anchored at
sundown, on September 13, opposite the Greek village of Yení-

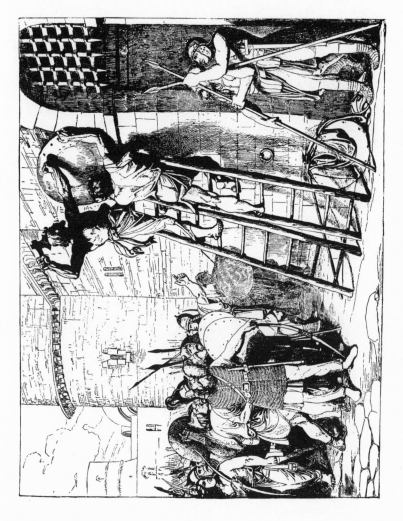

OLEG NAILING HIS SHIELD TO THE GATE OF CONSTANTINOPLE.

keui. A message of congratulation came from the Sultan, and boats and caïques were sent to take the embassy to Stambúl. Ukráintsef, wishing to keep within the spirit of his orders, refused to go in the Sultan's caïques unless the frigate preceded him. He was received at the landing-place by high officials sent to meet him, mounted a splendidly caparisoned horse, and, accompanied by an immense crowd, went to the house prepared for him near the church of the Virgin of Hope, at the Sand Gate, on the shore of the Sea of Mármora. Owing to the fall of the wind, the frigate had been obliged to anchor opposite the Jewish village of Kusgundjík, near Scútari, but on the next day it took an excellent position directly in front of the palace on the Seraglio Point, to the astonishment of the Sultan, the ministers, and all the people. The Turks could not understand how such a large vessel could get out of the shallow mouths of the Don, and were only quieted by the belief that it was flat-bottomed and unfit for bad weather. They expressed their annoyance at the fact that so many Dutch and Englishmen were in the Russian service, for they had hitherto considered those nations to be particularly friendly to the Porte.

The boats of a few Cossack pirates had advanced as far as the mouth of the Bosphorus ; but no Russian vessel had been seen at Constantinople since the times of the old Greek Empire. In the tenth century, the early Russian princes had kept Constantinople in terror by their incursions, which had been greatly magnified by patriotic tradition. It is said that Oleg fitted wheels to his ships, and drew them over the peninsula to the Sea of Mármora, and hung his shield as a defiance on the Golden Gate. His son, Igór, was less successful, and his fleet was destroyed by Greek fire, with terrible loss. But those days were long past, and the exploits of Oleg and Igór were unknown to the Turks. To the Russians they were kept alive by popular songs and the chronicle of Nestor.

The Russian frigate was visited by all classes of the motley population of Constantinople, and even by the Sultan himself, who was greatly interested and carefully inspected the vessel in detail. Rumours magnified the prowess and intentions of the Russians, and it was said that ten vessels had entered the Black Sea and were cruising off Trebizond and Sinope. A thoughtless act of Captain Pamburg added to the general excitement. He had invited to dinner a number of his French and Dutch acquaintances. After entertaining them till midnight, he fired a salute of all his guns, to the consternation of the Sultan, his wives, and the whole city, who believed that this was a signal given to the fleet of the Tsar to approach Constantinople. Early the next morning, the Grand Vizier sent Mavrocordato to Ukráintsef to express his displeasure, and to request the punishment of the captain. If this were refused, the Sultan ordered the captain to be arrested by Turkish troops and imprisoned, and his ship to be seized and towed up to the Admiralty. Ukráintsef replied that if the salute had been displeasing to the Sultan, it would not be repeated; but that he had no power over the commander of the vessel. Matvéief, who was then at the Hague, reported that news had come there from the Dutch agent at Smyrna, that the Sultan in his anger sent three hundred men to Captain van Pamburg, to forbid his firing again. Pamburg declared to them that they had better not attempt to board him, for he would blow up the ship the moment they had all reached the deck.

The conferences at Constantinople, twenty-three in all, between Ukráintsef and the secretary Tcheredéief, on the one side, and the Reis-Effendi Mehmed Rami and Mavrocordato, the dragoman of the Porte, on the other, lasted from the middle of November, 1699, to the end of June, 1700. The conditions of the Russians—which at the request of the Grand Vizier were given in writing, in Latin and Russian—were composed of sixteen articles, the chief of which were that the towns and lands conquered by Russia were to be ceded to Russia, according to the principle of *uti possidetis* accepted at the treaty of Carlowitz; that neither the Khan of the Crimea, nor the Tartars under his control, nor the Turks, should vex Russia with incursions, nor should, under any pretext, ask the Russian Government for a tribute of money or for presents; that Russian commercial vessels should have the right of sailing on the Black Sea; that the prisoners should be mutually exchanged; and that the Holy Sepulchre at Jerusalem should be taken away from the Catholics and given back to the Greeks. The disputes, the delays, the quibblings were endless, and at one time the ne-

gotiations were almost entirely broken off, and could not be renewed until Zhérlof arrived from the Tsar, bringing as a final
concession the alternative proposition that the towns on the
Lower Dniéper should remain in the possession of Russia six
or seven years, and then be rased, or that they should be entirely destroyed and occupied by neither power. The Turks
claimed that the *uti possidetis* basis was impossible, and had
actually been given up in the treaty of Carlowitz, as the Austrians, for the purpose of simplifying the frontier, had restored
some small districts to Turkey. They insisted on the surrender of the Lower Dniéper, and refused to mention in the
treaty the maritime towns and villages on the Sea of Azof.
They even refused to cede more than the distance of a cannon-
shot from the walls of Azof, although finally they granted surrounding territory to the distance of ten days' journey. Even
after the plenipotentiaries had agreed upon the terms of the
treaty, the Sultan for a time refused to sign it, unless the Russians consented to destroy all the new forts which had been
constructed, such as Taganróg, Pávlofsky, and Miúsky, and the
new fortifications of Azof. With regard to the Holy Sepulchre, the Sultan claimed that this was a question entirely within
his jurisdiction, which he could not mention in the treaty, but
that if after the treaty the Tsar chose to make representations,
he would doubtless be willing to oblige him in some respects.
Mavrocordato, who, after the treaty of Carlowitz, had been
made a Count of the Holy Roman Empire, and was long the
guiding spirit of Turkish diplomacy, promised on his faith as
an orthodox Christian to assist in this pious purpose. It was
found impossible to get any concession from the Porte with
regard to the Black Sea. The Turks said: 'The Black Sea
and all its coasts are ruled by the Sultan alone. They have
never been in the possession of any other power, and since the
Turks have gained sovereignty over this sea, from time im-
memorial no foreign ship has ever sailed its waters, nor ever
will sail them. More than once, and even now, have the
French, Dutch, English, and Venetians begged the Porte to
allow their trading ships on the Black Sea, but the Porte always
has refused them and always will refuse them, because the sovereignty of this sea belongs to no one else than the Sultan. The

Ottoman Porte guards the Black Sea like a pure and undefiled virgin, which no one dares to touch, and the Sultan will sooner permit outsiders to enter his harem than consent to the sailing of foreign vessels on the Black Sea. This can only be done when the Turkish Empire shall have been turned upside down.' All that could be obtained on this point was that, after the conclusion of peace, the plenipotentiary who should come to Constantinople for its ratification should be empowered to engage in negotiations for advantageous and mutual commerce. Ukráintsef reported that on this point the Turks were rendered still more obstinate by the advice of the foreign ministers, especially the English and French, who had great commercial interests in the East, and wished to reserve all the trade for themselves. They therefore saw with jealousy and displeasure the possibility that the Russians might have a commercial fleet either on the Black Sea or at Archangel. Ukráintsef believed that the foreign representatives did all they could to hinder the success of his mission, even in other respects, as they did not desire that Russia should get on too friendly and intimate terms with Turkey. With the representatives of other powers the Russian envoy had no intercourse, except as mutual messages of congratulation and compliment were sent. The Porte kept him under surveillance, and refused to allow him to visit the foreign legations, who lived at Gálata in free intercourse with all the world, and they, in their turn, replied to his pressing request for aid in this matter, that they were sure of being refused by the Porte, and they did not wish to expose themselves to the affront.

At last it was possible to sign a thirty years' truce—for the Sultan refused to sign a permanent peace on the ground that sufficient concessions had not been made to him. The Turks of that time always preferred a truce to a peace. By a truce nothing was settled, except for the moment. The signers abandoned no claims, and were bound to nothing. When the truce expired, all questions were again open, as if war had never ceased. The chief articles of this truce were that the towns on the Dniéper were to be destroyed within thirty days, and the land on which they stood returned to Turkey; that Azof and all its towns both new and old, were to remain in the possession of Russia; that a belt of waste and uninhabited country should separate the whole Crimea from the Russian dominions; that the tribute and presents heretofore paid to the Tartar Khan were given up; that prisoners should be exchanged or ransomed on honourable terms; that Russian pilgrims should be allowed to go to Jerusalem without being taxed, and Russian ecclesiastics living in Turkish dominions protected from oppression and insult; and that the Resident of the Tsar in Constantinople should have the same rights and privileges as those enjoyed by the representatives of other Christian powers.[1]

---

[1] Ustriálof, III., ix. x. ; Soloviéf, xiv.; Posselt, *Lefort ;* Brückner, *Peter der Grosse ;* Yelágin, *History of the Russian Fleet ;* Veselago, *Russian Naval History ;* Hammer, *Histoire de l'Empire Ottoman,* XII.

XXXVIII.

DURING the spring of 1700, the Tsar was very uneasy at receiving no favourable news from Constantinople, for he had
made engagements to declare war upon Sweden, and he saw the
favourable time passing by without being able to take advantage
of it. He could not yet tell whether he might not be obliged to
use all his forces in the South, and, at any rate, he did not wish
to have two wars on his hands at the same time.

The idea of recovering for Russia the border provinces which
had been seized by Sweden during the Troublous Times, and
ever since retained, appears to have come into Peter's mind
after his visit to Vienna, when he found that the Emperor was
determined on making peace with the Turks. He saw that it
would be difficult for him to make war alone against the still
formidable Ottoman Empire, and now that he had used so
many exertions for the purpose of creating a fleet, it was necessary for him to find a sea for it to sail upon. Although he may
have felt a passing anger at his reception at Riga, it was so
completely effaced by what was done for him at Königsberg
that he did not openly complain of it. His secret agreement
with the Elector of Brandenburg had, it is true, been aimed
against Sweden, but it had been devised by the Elector for his
own advantage, and had with difficulty been accepted by Peter.
The Tsar's mind was then so occupied with Turkey and with
the idea of getting a harbour on the Black Sea, that he never
seemed to think of moving in the North. In Holland the Great
Embassy had been on the best footing with Baron Lilienroth,
the Swedish ambassador at the Ryswyk Congress. The Tsar
had been grateful for the three hundred cannon sent by the
Swedish King, and Lefort had shown, in his correspondence

with the Chancellor Oxenstjerna, the desire of his master to be
on the most friendly terms with Sweden. It was not until
after Peter had left Vienna, and had become intimate with the
King of Poland, that he suggested his adventure at Riga as a
possible cause of war. Peter was young, and felt the charm of
the finished man of the world. In an outburst of enthusiasm,
at a supper with Count Flemming, Peter had promised Augustus to aid him against his Polish subjects if they rebelled, and
in return asked his assistance to avenge himself on Sweden. It
was a light and trifling talk over the wine, about which neither
party thought much at the time, nor, indeed, for months. For
a long time after Peter's return to Russia he apparently had
not the remotest idea of anything hostile to Sweden. After
the lapse of nearly a quarter of a century, Peter told of this
conversation in his autograph corrections of the 'Journal' of
the Swedish War.

In October, 1698, there appeared at Warsaw a gentleman
from Livonia, Johann Reinhold Patkul, with a plan for uniting
the neighboring states in a war against Sweden. All had suffered loss to the profit of that country. Livonia, as well as
Esthonia and Curland, had up to the middle of the sixteenth
century belonged to the Order of the Teutonic Knights. After
the severe defeats inflicted on the Order by Iván the Terrible,
Esthonia placed herself under the protection of Sweden, Curland became a separate duchy, the vassal of Poland, the islands
of Oesel and Dagö were taken by the Danes, and Livonia was
united to the Grand Duchy of Lithuania, and in that way
formed a component part of the Kingdom of Poland. By a
royal privilege of November, 1561, Sigismund II. (Augustus)
granted to Livonia religious freedom and self-government, and
guaranteed the nobility in the possession of all their estates.
The attempts of the subsequent Polish kings to introduce the
Polish language and laws and the Catholic religion, caused great
dissatisfaction in that province, which revolted and called in the
Swedes. After a long and bloody war, the victories of Gustavus Adolphus confirmed the Swedish supremacy, and by the
Treaty of Oliva, Livonia, as well as the islands of Oesel and
Dagö, became part of Sweden, on the same conditions on which
they had been annexed to Poland.

The aristocracy in Sweden, which had rapidly increased in power since the death of Gustavus Adolphus, had succeeded in making itself so hated by all the other classes of the population that the Diet restored to King Charles XI. all the preceding royal, despotic, and absolute power. One of the measures taken against the nobility was the so-called 'reduction,' which restored to the royal domain all the crown lands which had been at different times granted to the nobles on varying tenures, and had been wrongfully treated by them as hereditary estates, sold and alienated. The measure was legally defensible, but it caused great distress, and many innocent and honest purchasers were reduced to beggary. Although in 1678 Charles XI. had granted a charter to the Livonian nobility confirming all their rights to their estates, and expressly promising that they should not be subjected to any 'reduction,' yet in 1680 the 'reduction' was applied in Livonia, and even to lands which had never been in the possession of the Swedish crown, but which had once belonged to the Order of the Teutonic Knights, its grand-masters, or its chapters, or to the bishops and archbishops. More than five-sixths of the lands of the Livonian nobles were thus confiscated, and out of 6,236 separate estates only 1,021 were left in their possession, and even for those they were required to produce documentary titles dating back to 1561. Protests were made, but were disregarded by the King, who said that the 'reduction' had been resolved upon as a measure necessary for the common weal, and that no exception could be made in favor of Livonia. The measure was unjust, and—if written charters and royal signatures mean anything—illegal; a brutal and irritated governor-general carried it out with unnecessary harshness. The Landrath Budberg and Captain Patkul were sent to Stockholm to explain and defend the privileges of the Livonian nobility, and did it with such eloquence that the King was moved, touched Patkul on the shoulder, and said: 'You have spoken like an honest man for your fatherland. I thank you.' But evil counsellors prevailed, several high nobles were arrested, and Patkul was condemned to death on a charge of high treason. He succeeded in escaping from Stockholm, and passed several years in wandering over Europe, devoting himself to study, and, among other things, translating into French the book of Puffendorf on the duties of a man and a citizen. But he was watching for an opportunity to revenge himself, and do what he could for his native country. This opportunity he thought had come on the death of King Charles XI., when Sweden was left to the rule of a boy. Patkul was a singularly able and brilliant man, but we cannot at once admit that he was truly patriotic. He defended only the rights of his class, which included his own. That there existed in Livonia any other class besides the nobility whose rights were worth respecting, seems not to have entered his mind any more than the mind of many nobles nowadays in the Baltic provinces, who claim that an exclusive regard to their rights and privileges should have precedence over the general welfare of the community. In the protest to the Swedish Government, there was no discussion of the point whether the 're-duction' was or was not better for the mass of the population. All that was claimed was that it infringed on the rights of the no-

Patkul.

bility. Patkul knew that it would be impossible for the small province of Livonia to become an independent State, and if it threw off the Swedish yoke it must immediately take upon itself that of some other power. Poland was a republic of nobles, and under such rule the nobility could be sure of keeping their rights. The King, too, was a German prince who could sympathise with Germans.

It seemed to him that the misery and distress inflicted upon the population by a war were of far less moment than that the nobility should be reduced from wealth to comparative pov-

erty. Indeed the address of the Diet at Wenden, which was
drawn up by Patkul, had said this very thing, 'that Livonia
was reduced by the "reduction" to such despair, that if it
pleased God to give them the choice of a devastating invasion
of an enemy or the unendurable persecution which they were
now undergoing, they would unquestionably choose the former
rather than the latter misfortune.' Apart from the natural
feelings which make a military nobility stand up for its rights
and property, there might also have been the calculation that
they would suffer on the whole less by losing their revenues for
a few years, even if the houses of the peasantry were destroyed
and the common people reduced to beggary, than they would
if their property was entirely taken away from them, and the
peasantry remained untouched.

Patkul therefore proposed to King Augustus a coalition
against Sweden of Poland, Denmark, Brandenburg, and Russia, and, as an incentive to action, recalled to him that Livonia
had previously belonged to the Polish crown. In his memo-
rials given to the King, especially that of April, 1699, he explained the chances of the coalition, and the difficulties it might
meet with from other powers. Denmark, he thought, would
be the easiest of all to persuade, on account of the known hostility of the Danes to the Swedes, and especially of the dispute
between the Danish King and the Duke of Holstein-Gottorp,
who had married the sister of the Swedish King, Charles XII.,
and was bound to him by ties of personal friendship. If the
Elector of Brandenburg could not be persuaded to join the union,
his neutrality at least could be assured by promising to aid
him in his efforts to secure for himself the title of King. The
Duke of Lüneberg was in the same way to be persuaded to assist
them, by promising to make him Elector. The assistance of Russia was in every way necessary to the success of the plan, and
it was thought the Tsar might get the aid of Austria in his negotiations with the Porte, if he should promise the Catholic missionaries permission to travel freely through his dominions to
China, and that in this way he would also get the goodwill of
Venice and the Pope, and especially of the influential College
of the Propaganda at Rome. In making an arrangement with
Russia, it was desirable that an agreement should be made for

the Tsar to assist the King both with money and with troops, especially infantry, 'who would be most serviceable for working in the trenches, and for receiving the enemy's shots; while the troops of the King could be preserved and used for covering the approaches.' It would also be absolutely necessary 'to bind the hands of the Tsar in such a way that he should not eat before our eyes the piece roasted for us, that is, should not get hold of Livonia, and should restrict himself to Ingermanland and Karelia. He should not even be allowed to attack Narva, for in that case he could threaten the centre of Livonia, and take Dorpat, Reval, and the whole of Esthonia almost before it could be known at Warsaw.' As to other countries, Austria had too much to avenge for what she suffered during the Thirty Years' War, and at the Peace of Westphalia, to do anything to the advantage of Sweden. France would have enough on her hands, in view of the approach of a war for the Spanish succession. Although England and Holland would 'doubtless make loud cries about the harm done to their trade,' they would probably do nothing. In any case, it would be best to assure them that all the hindrances to commerce which had existed in Livonia under the Swedish rule would be done away with. As further inducements, Patkul assured the King of the easy conquest of Livonia, gave him exact accounts of the fortifications of Riga, and showed him from letters, that he had already formed a conspiracy in Riga itself, and was only waiting for the proper moment to act.

The King entered into Patkul's views, and agreed to the coalition and to the war. In order to cover up the secret negotiations with Denmark, he sent the Senator Galecki as ambassador to Charles XII. The greatest difficulty in the way of Augustus was how to induce the Polish Diet to agree to the war. If the matter were discussed before the Diet, there would be great delay, and Sweden would take the alarm, and there might even be opposition and a refusal to engage in the war. If the matter were not presented to the Diet, there might be jealousy on the part of the Polish nobles, who would suspect the King of designs for aggrandising his own family, and of taking possession of Livonia—an old Polish province—for the benefit of Saxony. Besides, there was the difficulty of getting permission for the Saxon troops to remain on Polish territory. The matter was placed before the meeting of the privy council, under the presidency of the King's friend and favourite, Flemming, and it was decided to work upon Cardinal Radziejowski, the Primate of Poland. The Cardinal hesitated, but Flemming and Patkul knew well how to overcome his scruples. After they had promised him the sum of 100,000 thalers, and given him notes for that amount, he agreed to induce the Diet, which was constantly demanding the withdrawal of the Saxon troops from Poland, to consent to 7,000 men being left in Curland, under the pretext of fortifying the port at Polangen, but in reality for attacking Riga. As an additional argument for him, he was shown a convention between the King and Patkul, as the representative of the Diet of Livonia, by which Livonia recognised the supremacy of Augustus, and united itself for ever to the Republic of Poland, preserving its internal administration, laws, and institutions. In a secret article, which was not shown to the Cardinal, the Livonian nobility agreed to recognise the sovereignty of Augustus and his successors, and to send the taxes directly to them, even in case they were no longer kings of Poland.

To secure the entrance of Russia into the alliance, General Carlowitz, who had previously accompanied Peter from Poland on his journey home, and was much liked by him, was sent as special envoy to make a secret treaty. He was accompanied by Patkul, disguised under the name of Kindler. To prevent any rumours or suspicions, Carlowitz took with him twelve Saxon mining engineers who had been engaged for the Russian service.[1]

[1] Ustriálof, III., xi. xii. xiii.; Soloviéf, xiv.; O. A. Wernich, *Johann Reinhold v. Patkul und seine Zeitgenossen*, Berlin, 1849; O. Sjögren, *J. R. Patkul* in *Historisk Bibliotek*, Stockholm, 1880; E. Herrmann, *Geschichte des Russischen Staates*, vol. iv., Hamburg, 1849.

XXXIX.

AFTER King Charles XII. had been declared of age, and the government of Sweden had been handed over to him by his grandmother, Hedwiga Eleanora, he sent word to Moscow that he would speedily send an embassy to confirm the treaty of Cardis, as was customary on the accession of a new ruler. Knipercrona, the Swedish Resident at Moscow, was informed that the embassy would be received with pleasure if it should arrive before the end of the Carnival, because after that the Tsar was going to the south of Russia for a prolonged absence. Nothing, however, was heard of it during the winter, and it was only in the middle of June, 1699, when the Tsar was with his fleet at Azof, that the Swedish ambassadors appeared on the frontier. Although Apráxin, the Voievode of Nóvgorod, gave them all facilities, they were still two months on their way to Moscow. Leo Naryshkin received them politely, but expressed his inability to understand why they should have chosen that time to come, when they must have known that the Tsar was absent, if his message had been properly delivered by the Swedish Resident. He added that the Tsar was so far off that it was impossible for them to go to him, and that they had better deliver their letters of credence to the ministry, as other envoys had done. As they were not envoys, but ambassadors come to ratify the treaty of Cardis, and could deliver their letters to no one except His Majesty, there was nothing for them to do but to wait, and Peter did not arrive at Moscow until the 7th of October. He found there two embassies waiting for him—that of the Swedes to confirm the treaty of peace, and that of King Augustus, asking him to make war on Sweden. The Tsar was glad of the proposition of Augustus, and was perfectly ready to join in the alliance of Poland and Denmark, but on condition that he should have no open rupture with Sweden before the conclusion of peace with the Turks. He had already made a treaty of alliance and mutual aid with Denmark, but it was general in its terms and not particularly directed against Sweden. The negotiations with the Swedes went on openly at the Foreign Office; that with the Poles was carried on secretly at Preobrazhénsky, and besides Peter and Carlowitz, none except Golovín, the Danish minister Heins, and Shafírof, who acted as interpreter, were admitted to the secret. It was known that negotiations of some sort were going on with Carlowitz, but it was thought that they were for the purpose of concluding a treaty between the King and the Tsar, in consequence of the rumoured intentions of Augustus to overthrow the republic and establish an absolute monarchy in Poland. Some strength was perhaps given to this belief by the oft-repeated expression of Peter, that he loved the King of Poland as a brother, but that the Poles were good for nothing, even to the devil. The Swedes themselves apparently suspected nothing. They were received with great honour at the palace, where they gave the presents they had brought, including among others a full-length portrait of King Charles XII.[1] In the absence of news from Turkey, it was necessary to go through the form of confirming the previous treaties with Sweden, but it was a little salve to the conscience of the Tsar that he could avoid taking an oath on the Gospels to keep them. This oath was insisted upon by the ambassadors, but was refused by the Tsar on the ground that he had already taken it when he first came to the throne, and that it was neither necessary nor customary to repeat it. In proof of this, the Russians adduced the journal of the proceedings on the occasion of the accession of Queen Christina, when the Tsar Michael did not repeat the oath which he had sworn once before. At the same time, complaints were made by the Russians of the treatment which the Grand Embassy and the Tsar himself had undergone at the hands of the Governor of Riga, and a demand was made

---

[1] This portrait was burnt, in 1706, by a fire that destroyed the house of Prince Menshikóf.

for satisfaction. The ambassadors were unable to explain the affair at Riga, of which they said they had never heard, and promised to report it to the King. After many conferences, they finally agreed to accept the precedent of Queen Christina, on the faith of the Russian documents, as the Swedish ones had been consumed in a fire, and at their farewell audience received, instead of the Tsar's oath on the Gospels, a formal letter from him to the King, confirming all the previous treaties of peace exactly the same as if he had sworn to them anew.

Nine days before this, Peter had signed a treaty with Carlowitz agreeing to make war upon Sweden. This duplicity may have been necessary, and may have formed a part of the received diplomacy of those times, but luckily in the present day sovereigns are shielded from personal moral responsibility, because they do not themselves appear in the negotiations, which are carried on by ministers, more or less constitutional. At that time Peter acted as his own prime minister, and took personal part in the negotiations.[1]

After the treaty was signed, Patkul, who had up to this time remained in the back-ground, was presented to the Tsar, and explained his plan for the conquest of Livonia, and for the concerted action of the allies. Two weeks later, Carlowitz took his departure for the Saxon army in Curland, intending to stop on the way at Riga and inspect the fortifications and defences of the town, in order to discover their weakest places, for it had been arranged that the war was to begin on the part of the Poles on Christmas-day, by a sudden attack upon Riga, without any preliminary declaration of war. Carlowitz was to return to Russia after Riga was taken, and it was then Peter's intention to send with him his son Alexis for education in Germany. King Augustus had promised to take charge of him, and treat him as his own child. Lefort's son Henry was to join him in Dresden, and be brought up with him. The

---

[1] Ustriálof, who may be considered almost as the official historian of Peter, says : ' Peter was not afraid either of the taunts of his contemporaries or of the judgment of posterity. Advantages gained to his country were for him higher than all other considerations, and he regarded nothing in a matter which tended to increase the greatness of his beloved Russia.' Vol. III., ch. xiii.

speedy death of Carlowitz and the war put an end to these projects.

Peter now began to make serious preparations for war, and the greatest of them all was the formation of a regular army after the model of the four regiments that already existed—the Preobrazhénsky, Seménofsky, Lefort, and Butýrsky. For this purpose he ordered the prelates and monasteries to send one man for every twenty-five peasant houses, and the nobles one for every thirty to fifty, according to their means, choosing especially those useless men who were not actually at work, but were hanging about the kitchens of the monasteries and the stables of the great lords. These were to be sent to Preobrazhénsky in December, 1699, and January, 1700, and, in addition to this, a call was made for volunteers from Moscow, who were promised good pay. The recruits thus collected were instructed at Preobrazhénsky under the personal supervision of the Tsar himself, assisted by General Avtémon Golovín, the commander of the guard, the brigadier Adam Weyde, and the lieutenant-colonel of the Preobrazhénsky regiment, Prince Nikíta Répnin, each of whom was ordered to form a division of nine regiments. General Gordon was already dead. The work of instruction went on very fast. The greatest difficulty was found with the officers, many of whom were drunken worthless fellows, who could not even learn the use of the musket. To supply the place of those who were cashiered, many courtiers, after a little preliminary training, were enrolled as officers, and they advanced so quickly that the Tsar was delighted, and exclaimed: ' Why should I spend money on foreigners when my own subjects can do as well as they ? ' Subsequently, nearly all the chamberlains and palace officials entered the service. The soldiers were uniformed after the pattern of the German infantry, in dark-green cloth coats, and low cocked hats, and armed with muskets and bayonets. They were taught to stand firmly side by side, to march evenly, to fire by platoons, to charge with the bayonet, to give absolute attention to the word of command, and for the least infraction of discipline were severely punished. A special commissariat was created, with Simeon Yazýkof as commissary-general, while Prince Jacob Dolgorúky was intrusted with the direction of military justice. The artillery, which was numerous and well arranged, was put under the command of Prince Alexander of Imeritia, who had studied artillery at the Hague. The articles of war were drawn up by Adam Weyde, who had thoroughly studied the organisation of the Austrian army under the command of Prince Eugene of Savoy, and had taken part in the battle of the Zenta. In this way, in the course of three months, an army of 32,000 men was formed, consisting of twenty-nine regiments of infantry, two regiments of dragoons, and a special detachment at Nóvgorod. The drill and general conduct won high praise from the Saxon general, Baron Langen, in a report to King Augustus.

Toward the end of February, 1700, Peter went to Vorónezh, and busied himself about getting ready more ships for the Sea of Azof. Early in May he was able to launch his new frigate, the 'Predestination,' in the presence of his son, his sister, and many boyárs, who, by command of the Tsar, were obliged to bring with them their wives. Many ladies of the German suburb were also present. While at Vorónezh, he received the news that Augustus had begun the war against Sweden. It had been arranged, as we have said, that the attack upon Riga should be made on Christmas Day. The plot in Riga was ripe, the Saxon troops had been collected in Curland, close to the Livonian frontier, and yet the Swedes, and even Dahlberg, who had been so suspicious at the time of Peter's visit, apparently mistrusted nothing. But this very time had been chosen by Flemming to leave his army and to go to Saxony, to marry a lady of the famous house of Sapieha. General Paykull, a Livonian by birth, who commanded the Saxon troops in his absence, knew nothing of the plot in Riga, and, however much Carlowitz tried to persuade him, refused to advance. The secret got out, and Dahlberg took such measures that any sudden attack was impossible. When Flemming returned, in February, he wrote to the King that he would immediately attack Riga, and began to move his troops on the very day on which Peter left Moscow for Vorónezh. But it was too late. All his efforts were vain, and Carlowitz was killed in an attack on Dünamünde. Flemming then went back to Warsaw, and Paykull, in spite of his proclamations, was, by the vigor of the Swedish generals, forced to retreat into Curland.

'By dissipation and inexcusable thoughtlessness, much precious time has been lost,' Golovín reported to Peter.

'It is a pity,' Peter replied; 'but there is nothing to be done. I have not heard from Constantinople.'

He, however ordered Golovín to send a young engineer, Kortchmín, to Narva to buy some cannon—six, nine, and twelve pounders—that he heard were for sale, and, at the same time, to pay particular attention to the defences and fortifications of the town, and, if possible, penetrate as far as Oréshek, 'and if that be impossible, at least alongside of it. That position there is very necessary. It is the outlet from Lake Ládoga to the sea— look on the map—and very necessary to keep back the reinforcements. The boy, I think, is not stupid, and can keep a secret. It is very necessary that Kniper (Knipercrona), who knows that he has been well taught, should not find out about it.'

Soon after, the news came to Moscow that the King of Denmark had begun war by invading Holstein-Gottorp with 16,000 men, and laying siege to Tönning. The time was propitious for action on Peter's part, but as yet there was nothing decisive from Constantinople. He had had no direct reports for some time from Ukráintsef, but rumours came from all directions that the Turks were making preparations for war. These rumours disturbed Peter so much that he considered it necessary to reassure the King of Sweden as to his peaceful intentions by sending an embassy. At the end of April he therefore appointed Prince Jacob Dolgorúky, Prince Thedore Shakhofskóy, and the scribe Domnín as ambassadors, and sent in advance Prince Andrew Hílkof to announce their arrival, and to obtain information as to the actual policy of Sweden. He was instructed to make formal inquiries against whom the King of France had concluded an alliance with Sweden, why a war had broken out between King Charles and King Augustus, why Saxon troops had attacked Riga, whether there were any Polish troops with them, and whether Sweden was at war or peace with Denmark and Brandenburg. Knipercrona, the Swedish Resident at Moscow, spoke in high terms of the members of the embassy, especially of Prince Dolgorúky, and, as an evidence of the peaceful intentions of the Tsar, reported to King Charles, on May 26, as follows:

'His Tsarish Majesty, on the next day after his return from Vorónezh, visited my house, and jestingly blamed my wife for having written to her daughter at Vorónezh that Russian troops were preparing to march into Livonia, which had made a great panic among all the Swedes at Moscow, "Your daughter," said the Tsar, "cried so much that I could hardly appease her. 'You foolish creature,' I said to her, 'do you really think that I would consent to begin an unjust war, and to break an eternal peace that I have just confirmed?'" We were all so much moved by his words that we could not refrain from tears; and when I asked him to excuse my wife, he embraced me, adding, "Even if the King of Poland should take Riga, it would not remain in his possession. I would tear it out of his hands."'

Prince Dolgorúky was told not to hasten, but Prince Hílkof set out for Stockholm at the end of June. He passed through Narva, inspected its fortifications, and made a report on them to the Tsar, but arrived in Sweden too late to find the King, who had already departed for the Danish war; and he was finally presented to Charles XII. in the camp before Copenhagen, at the end of August, after the conclusion of the peace. Following Hílkof, Prince Yúry Trubetzkóy was sent on a secret mission to Berlin to state to the Elector Frederick the intention of the Tsar to make war on Sweden as soon as he had arranged affairs with Turkey, and begging him to take part in the league on the basis of the mutual engagement by which the Tsar and the Elector had bound themselves to assist each other. This invitation was not accepted. In July, King Augustus went in person to his army before Riga, and sent Baron Langen to Moscow to persuade the Tsar immediately to send auxiliary troops and to attack Ingria, in order to draw off the Swedes from Riga. In his letter he said: 'Dear brother, I beg you to spare the bearer of this from strong drinks, because they do mortal harm to his life.' Peter replied that he had no intention of injuring Langen, but that drink was evidently no novelty to him, as his gout showed. Langen was very well received, and, at his request, entirely without ceremony.

'The Tsar sent his ministers out of the room, and, with tears in his eyes, said to me in broken Dutch how grieved he was at the delay in concluding peace with Turkey, through the intrigues of the opposite party, notwithstanding that he had ordered his ambassador at Constantinople to conclude a peace or a truce in the quickest possible time, even to his own loss, so as to have his hands free to aid the allies with all his forces.'

To Langen's earnest entreaties, Peter finally consented to give two-thirds of the cannon then in Smolénsk, and to send a few regiments of Little Russian Cossacks, but refused to come to an open rupture, because, although he was now sure of peace, 'it was not yet signed, and the Porte had been informed by the Polish Minister of the secret league, and had begun to be obstinate again as soon as it had heard of the war in the North.' He said, however, that he ' was waiting for a courier from hour to hour, and if he received news of peace to-day, he would move his troops against the Swedes to-morrow.' Peter kept his word. On August 18, the despatch of Ukráintsef, announcing the signature of the treaty, arrived. That evening, the peace with Turkey was celebrated with ' extraordinary fireworks,' and on the very next day war was declared in the usual form by proclamation from the Bed-Chamber Porch, ' for the many wrongful acts of the Swedish King, and especially because during the journey of his Majesty through Riga, much opposition and unpleasantness was caused to him by the inhabitants of Riga.' The troops were ordered to march at once, and were put under the command of Golovín, who was created field-marshal. The same day, Peter despatched an autograph letter to Augustus, informing him of the fact—'and we hope, by the help of God, that your Majesty will not see other than profit.' [1]

---

[1] Ustriálof, III., xii. xiii. ; Soloviéf, xiv.; A. Fryxell, *Lebensgeschichte Karl's des Zwölften*, Ger. Transl of Jenssen-Tusch, vol. i. Braunschweig, 1861. O. Sjögren, *Otto Arnold Paykull*, in *Historisk Tidskrift*, Stockholm, 1881.

XL.

CHARLES THE TWELFTH.

No more unpropitious time for declaring war could have been chosen. The attempt of King Augustus and his Saxon troops on Riga had failed, and the King of Denmark had been awed into submission by the Swedish forces, and, on the very day that the news of the treaty with the Turks arrived at Moscow, had concluded with Charles XII. the peace of Travendal. A new and unexpected element had spoiled all the calculations of the allies. They had counted upon the youth and carelessness of the Swedish King. They were grievously disappointed. Charles XII. of

Queen Ulrica Eleanora.

Sweden, the son of Charles XI., was born in 1682, and was therefore just ten years younger than Peter. His early years were tenderly cared for by his mother, Ulrica Eleanora, a Danish princess, whose many virtues made her beloved by all save her husband. Without being precocious, the mind of

Charles was bright and active, and it was rapidly developed under the guidance of his tutor Norcopensis. His native language he neither wrote nor spoke well; German, which was then the court language of the North, he learned to speak as his mother tongue; Latin he spoke better than either, but he was only induced to learn it when told that the King of Denmark and the King of Poland habitually used it. To the study of French he always showed a repugnance, and could rarely be induced to speak it; but he understood it, read it, and enjoyed the French theatre. History he studied eagerly, whether it treated of the deeds of Cæsar and Alexander, or of the Reformation and of his great predecessor, Gustavus Adolphus. He was well drilled in the principles of religion and morals, and showed a quick intelligence and much power of application, though, at the same time, great self-will and determination. His education was well begun, but the death of his mother, and then of his tutor, when he was not twelve years old, brought changes and interruptions, and it was not so carefully continued.

In his early years his health was delicate, and grief for his mother threw him into a long fever, which terminated in an attack of small-pox; but his constitution was strong, his passion for physical sports gave him health and strength, and at the age of fourteen he was tall, slim, and wiry, and seemed almost like a grown man. He had been put on the back of a pony at the age of four, and had even ridden at reviews of the troops. He speedily became a perfect horseman. His love of hunting developed with equal rapidity. When seven years old he had shot a fox, and before he was twelve had killed a bear. His taste for military exercises and the art of war now took a more decided turn, and his military education was confided to General Stuart. His father delighted in the promise of the lad, and loved to take him on his hunting-parties and military inspections. In this way much time was lost from study.

In April, 1697, Charles XI. died. By his will, he appointed a regency, under the presidency of his mother, the Queen Hedwiga Eleanora, but fixed no time at which his son should be declared of age. By custom, the majority of Swedish princes had been fixed at the age of eighteen, but in the present case there had been such disputes between the regents themselves, and among the nobles—who were divided into Danish and French factions—such jealousy of the nobility on the part of the other estates, such dislike to the influence of the Queen-mother, such a general appreciation of the abilities and good qualities of the young prince, and such a desire to gain his favour by being the first to please him, that little opposition was manifested to the project of declaring him of age in November of the same year, when he was just fifteen years old. The plan was matured and executed within ten hours.

King Charles XII.

Charles had given every reason for confidence. Though still a minor, he had been admitted to the meetings of the council, and had impressed every one not only by his good sense and quick decision, but by his power of silence. He had at times a gravity and determination which were far beyond his years. During the conflagration of the royal palace, shortly after his father's death, he had shown a calmness and self-restraint which were in striking contrast to the excitement and nervousness of the Queen-mother and which produced a favourable impression on everyone. No sooner was he declared of age, and the sole and absolute ruler of the country, than he seemed to change. The nobles who had counted on a mitigation of the 'Reduction' edicts of Charles XI., were disappointed. The young King upheld and defended all the acts of his father. He manifested an excessive amount of self-will and obstinacy, and made it a point of honour never to draw back from a resolution

which he had once made. He at the same time showed a cold-
ness and haughtiness in his demeanour in public which had not
before been noticed. At the meetings of the council he would
calmly listen for a while to the arguments and statements, and
then interrupt by saying that his mind had long been made up.
Once having said this he would hear no more, for his will was
supreme. Some of the courtiers took advantage of this side of
his character to flatter him, hoping thus to advance themselves.
It was owing to this that he refused to be crowned in the ordinary way, claiming that while it was proper for elected kings
to be solemnly crowned, he, as being born to the throne, had
no need of it. In spite of the representations of the more conservative and moderate statesmen, in spite of the entreaties of
his grandmother, the utmost that he would yield was to allow
himself to be consecrated by the archbishop, in order that he
might carry out the biblical injunction and be the anointed of
the Lord. But the ceremony was called not the coronation but
the consecration, and Charles rode to the church with his
crown on his head, and refused to take the oath to govern well
and justly, which, on the part of the ruler, corresponds to the
oath of allegiance on the part of the subject. The superstitious
found many omens for the future of the King and country;
there was a violent snow-storm during the ceremony; the procession looked dismal in the black dress required by the court
mourning; the King amused himself during the sermon with
picking the black specks out of his robe; and, worst of all, the
archbishop dropped the anointing horn, and the crown fell from
the King's head and rolled upon the ground. Wise and prudent men saw more serious signs of trouble and danger in the
conduct of Charles toward the Diet, in his views with regard
to the coronation oath, and in the systematic way in which he
tried to lower the importance of the members of the council.
Too late they repented of having put themselves at the mercy
of a wayward and wilful youth, jealous of his own power and
careless of the rights of others. Determined to show himself
the supreme master, Charles constantly humiliated the old
councillors and ministers by keeping them waiting for hours in
the ante-rooms while he discussed affairs with his favourites,
Piper and Wallenstedt. He transacted the weightiest affairs of

CHARLES XII. BEAR HUNTING.

State without their knowledge or advice, convoked the Council only at rare intervals in three years, to decide questions of law, or to go through the form of signing his decisions, and even went so far as to appoint a generalissimo, to send troops out of the country, and almost to declare war, before the Council was informed or consulted.

The education of Charles was naturally at an end. What time he could spare from his duties as a ruler was devoted to military exercises and to field sports. The more dangerous the amusement, the greater attractions it had for him. He took up the idea that it was cowardly to attack beasts with fire-arms, and went bear-hunting armed with nothing but a pike or a cutlass. Soon the victory seemed to him too easily gained even in this way, and he forbade the use of cold steel as well as of fire-arms, and all were armed with strong wooden forks. The sport was to wait until the bear rose on his hind legs, catch him in the neck with the fork and throw him over backward, when the huntsmen sprang out and wound a net around his hind legs. Charles rode fast and furiously, up and down hill, through forest and stream. Frequently his horse fell with him, and he returned black and blue. Once, the snow was so deep that his horse fell upon him : he could not move, and as he had far outstripped his companions, he was nearly frozen when rescued. At another time, he rode up the side of a cliff so steep that both horse and rider fell backward, and it was considered a miracle that his life was saved. On another occasion, starting out from the palace at four o'clock in the morning, attended only by a page and a captain of his guards, he came to one of the gulfs near Stockholm, which was covered with a sheet of ice so thin from the spring rains that even foot passengers scarcely dared to trust themselves upon it. In spite of the remonstrances of his attendants, he ventured upon it, and found at the other side a clear space of water fifteen feet wide. He could not go back, plunged in, and luckily reached the shore. Finally, the old equerry, Hord, summoned up courage to remonstrate with him, and told him that God had saved his life twice in such dangers, and would be excused if, the third time, He did not interpose. 'God has created beasts for the service of men, but not to help them break their own necks.' In winter

Charles amused himself with sledging parties of the most dangerous character. Sometimes the sledges were fastened together in a long file, and the horses were then whipped to the top of their speed down the steep hills. Once he found a peasant's sledge laden with wood, and with two or three companions mounted it, and set off down a steep which had been made like glass with several coats of ice. It was impossible to steer the sledge, and they came up against a heavy stake at the bottom. His companions were severely injured; he remained unhurt.

The military sports were, if possible, still more dangerous. As under Peter's direction in Russia, the sham fights in Sweden were carried on with pasteboard hand-grenades, and frequently cost many lives. In taking a snow intrenchment, the King had his clothes nearly torn off him, and many others were seriously injured. Sometimes there were sea-fights of a peculiar character. The boats were armed with fire-engines, and the crews with large squirts, with which they fought. On one occasion, Arfvid Horn, one of Charles's great friends, stripped himself to his shirt, rowed away from his yacht in a small boat, and attacked the King and his suite. He was repelled with such vigour that his boat soon filled with water, and began to sink. Jumping out, Horn swam once around the yacht. Charles at last asked him if swimming were difficult. 'No,' said Horn, 'if one is not afraid,' at which the King immediately jumped into the water, but found that courage did not make up for want of skill, and would have drowned had not Horn caught him by the clothes and brought him a long distance to land. Another day the guards were divided into two parties, led by Charles and Horn. The horses were not allowed to be saddled, and the men were armed with nothing but stout hazel sticks. No one was spared. The blows given by Horn were so vigorous, that Charles, in a moment of excitement, aimed a blow at his face, and hit a boil on his cheek. Horn fell fainting to the ground, and the pain and the heat combined threw him into a violent fever, which nearly cost him his life. Charles repented, frequently visited him, and gave him 2,000 thalers for his cure, promising to repeat the prescription as often as he was again wounded. All this Charles did, not for amusement alone, but in order to harden and inure himself to the fatigues of real war. He would frequently rise from bed, and sleep the rest of the night half-naked on the bare floor. One December, he slept three consecutive nights without undressing on the hay in the stables. Nothing annoyed him so much as his delicate skin and fair complexion. He used every means to get sunburned, so as to appear manly, and took a childish pride in some pock-marks on his face. He dressed simply; he wore a wig until his first campaign in Denmark, when he threw it aside for ever. He ate but little, and always plain and coarse dishes. Wine he gave up after finding its effects too strong for his self-control.

Cold of temperament, of love Charles knew nothing, and cared little for the society of ladies. Six princesses sought his hand in vain, and the very mention of marriage distressed him.

The freaks of Charles, even when not dangerous, were disagreeable to those about him. Their worst point was reached during the visit of his cousin Frederick III., Duke of Holstein-Gottorp, who came to Stockholm in 1698 to marry the Princess Hedwiga Sophia. The Duke was as foolhardy as his brother-in-law, and soon acquired great influence over him. Then began what was called the 'Gottorp Fury.' The royal cousins rode races till they had broken down several horses; they coursed a hare in the parliament-house; for days they practised on beheading sheep, in order to see which had the greater force of hand, and the greater knack with the sword—all this, too, in the private apartments of the palace, till the floors and staircases were running with blood. This was to the great astonishment of the passers-by, for the bleeding heads were thrown out of the windows.[1] They sallied into the streets at night, and broke the windows of the peaceful citizens. In broad daylight they made cavalcades from the palace with no costume save their shirts, and with drawn sabres in their hands. They jerked off the hats and wigs of all who came near them. At dinner, when they had tired of snapping cherry-stones into the

---

[1] It is impossible to avoid comparing the occupations and amusements of the three strong men of that time: Charles riding horses to death and beheading sheep and bullocks; Augustus the Strong, with his 260 illegitimate children, straightening horseshoes and rolling up silver plates with one hand; Peter hammering out iron bars, filling fireworks, and building ships.

faces of the privy-councillors, they would knock the dishes out
of the servants' hands, and then break all the furniture, and
throw the fragments through the closed windows, shivering
both glass and frame. They broke all the benches in the
palace chapel, so that the congregation had to hear service
standing. Fortunately the Duke was unable to lead Charles
to acts of immorality. The people began to murmur. They
accused the Duke of wishing to bring the King to his death,
in order that, as the next heir, he might inherit the crown.
Things got to such a pass that, on one Sunday morning, three
clergymen preached on the same text: 'Woe to thee, O land,
when thy king is a child.' This remonstrance seemed to affect
Charles, who was sincerely pious. When the Duke went away
he entirely changed his manner of life, became quiet and reflec-
tive, and devoted himself with renewed ardour to his duties as
a ruler.

A year later, in consequence of his war with Denmark, the
Duke came again to Stockholm. The follies of the preceding
year were not repeated, but in their turn were masquerades,
balls, and festivities of all sorts. The court of Stockholm, renew-
ing the traditions of the reign of Christina, became suddenly
the most brilliant in Europe, except that of Louis XIV., and,
of course, at enormous expense. There were balls which cost
40,000 thalers each, given with so much elegance that foreigners declared they were unsurpassed in Paris. A French company played the works of Molière, Corneille, and Racine during
the whole winter, and the King was nearly always a spectator.
There were processions of masks through the streets, which
were laid with blue cloth. All the lords and gentlemen followed
the example of the court, not even excepting the clergy. The
pastor of the great city church, Iser, gave such a sumptuous
dinner that everyone went home with the headache. The King
took no part in the drunken bouts, but danced sometimes until
nine or ten o'clock in the morning, which necessitated several
changes of clothing. Tessin, who arranged the court festivities
with such taste, was rewarded with a title of nobility, and frequently went home with his pockets stuffed with gold by an
unseen hand. Again this manner of life was broken by a sermon. When the court clergy did not dare to speak, Svedberg

MAD FROLIC OF CHARLES XII.

persuaded the palace chaplain to let him occupy his pulpit, and delivered a thundering sermon against the project of having a masked ball on a Sunday evening. The ball was given up. Just then came the news of the invasion of Livonia by Augustus, and the festivities were for ever at an end.

This intelligence arrived when Charles was hunting bears at his favourite country seat of Kungsör. It seemed to make little impression on him at the time, for he turned to the French ambassador, and smilingly said : ' We will make King Augustus go back by the way he came,' and the sport continued. When it was over, Charles returned to Stockholm, looking firm and severe. He said to the assembled Council: ' I have resolved never to begin an unjust war, but also n^ver to end a just one without overcoming my enemy;' and on another occasion : ' It is curious that both my cousins' (for Augustus, as well as King Frederick IV. of Denmark, was cousin to Charles) ' wish to make war on me. So be it ! But King Augustus has broken his word. Our cause is then just, and God will help us. I intend first to finish with one, and then I will talk with the other.'

Military preparations were pushed on with great vigour both by land and sea. The clergy and the civil officials were each ordered to furnish a regiment of dragoons, the burghers of Stockholm a regiment of infantry. A few of the higher nobility followed the old custom of arming single companies. The fleet in Karlskrona was fitted for sea, and all the vessels in Stockholm were seized on behalf of the Government for transport service. The financial difficulty was the greatest. There was no money. Charles XI. had collected a large treasure for military purposes, and had left more than four and a half million of thalers. All this Charles XII. had spent in two years by the extravagance of his court, and by his lavish generosity to the Duke of Holstein-Gottorp, to his friends and favourites, and even to families of the nobility who had been impoverished by the ' Reduction.' Even all the plate in the ' Elephant Vault ' had been melted down. During the ' Gottorp Fury,' Charles had spent twenty thousand thalers of pocket-money in four days, and no one knew what had become of it. Besides large sums which he gave openly as presents, he had a habit, in order to escape thanks, of secretly filling with money the pockets of his favourites. A chest of jewels, which had stood for years in the ' Elephant Vault,' was brought to Charles's bed-chamber and was speedily emptied. There had been left in the military chests of the fortresses and regiments, by the economy of Charles XI., savings to the amount of six hundred and seventy thousand thalers. Great sums had been taken even from this. Not enough remained in the treasury of the state to pay all the expenses of his sister's marriage, and Charles wished to raise a loan by pledging Pomerania or Bremen. Now that money was still more necessary for war, it became imperative to re-impose the war tax, which had been abolished by Charles XI. This brought in a million thalers, but as it was insufficient, the King called for voluntary contributions. Piper, Wrede, and Stenbock gave among them twenty thousand thalers, though this example found few followers. The citizens of Stockholm contributed thirty thousand thalers. In order to excite enthusiasm among the nobility, Charles finally decided to cancel any further proceedings under the ' Reduction ' laws of his father. This important edict was signed on April 23, 1700, and on the same evening the King took leave of his grandmother and his sisters, in order, as he said, to go for some time to Kungsör. In the night he quietly left the palace, and turned southward. He never again saw Stockholm, his grandmother, or his elder sister.

There would have been no need of a war with Denmark had it not been that Charles had promised the Duke of Holstein-Gottorp, when he came to him for protection in 1699, that he would right him, even though it cost him his crown. This agreement was greatly blamed by all the King's counsellors, but too late—the King's word had been given. Everyone disliked the Holstein-Gottorp family, and all feared the cost of a war. What the disputes were between Denmark and Holstein-Gottorp it is difficult and unnecessary to explain. The King of Denmark knew that the forts in Slesvig were occupied by Swedish garrisons, and he knew, too, the Swedish threats of interference in case he attacked the Duke. Nevertheless, in conjunction with Poland and Russia, he had resolved to run the risk.

Now that war was come, in consequence of Charles's rash promise, it was certainly wiser to finish with Denmark, the nearer and more dangerous foe, before attacking King Augustus. After leaving Stockholm, Charles made a hasty journey through the southern provinces, to assure himself of the military preparations. The fleet immediately set sail and occupied the Sound in connection with the fleets of England and Holland, who also guaranteed the peace between Denmark and Holstein. Charles resolved now to cross over to Zealand, and make an attack on Copenhagen while the Danish King was occupied with the siege of Tönning. This plan was successful. With six thousand men, which were all the troops at that time collected at Malmö, Charles crossed the straits on August 3, 1700, waded ashore at the head of his men, under the enemy's fire, and secured a firm position between Copenhagen and Helsingör. The next day was stormy, and had the troops and militia of Copenhagen attacked the Swedes, they might have given them a severe check. But the time passed, and, on the next day, which was clear, seven to eight thousand more men crossed, and made the force of Charles too large for the little Danish army to resist. The assault on Tönning by the Danish troops was unsuccessful, and the King hastened back to protect his capital. He saw himself powerless, and signed a peace at Travendal on August 18, in which he agreed to recognise the sovereignty of the Duke of Holstein-Gottorp, and to pay him a war indemnity of two hundred and sixty thousand thalers. In two weeks from the crossing of the straits, this almost bloodless war was over. Charles for a moment thought of carrying on an independent war on his own account against the Danes; but for once—the last if not the first time of his life—he listened to good counsel and desisted. He won more fame by this than he would have done by taking Copenhagen. By the manner in which he had treated them he had already secured the respect and esteem of the population of Zealand, who still remembered his mother with affection. He recrossed the Sound to Sweden on September 2.[1]

---

[1] Fryxell, vol. i. ; Voltaire, *Charles XII.* ; F. F. Carlson, *Carl. XII.'s första regeringsär*, in *Historisk Tidskrift*, Stockholm, 1881.

XLI.

THE BATTLE OF NARVA.—1700.

THE great object of Peter in making war upon Sweden was to obtain possession of the provinces of Ingria and Karelia on the Finnish gulf, which had once belonged to Russia, but had been seized by Sweden during the Troublous Times. Ingria, or, as the Swedes called it, Ingermanland, known in the old Russian chronicles as the land of Izhóra, was a comparatively narrow strip of country extending along the southern coast of the gulf from the Neva to the Naróva. Karelia included the country between the gulf and Lake Ládoga, as far as Kexholm and Viborg. The possession of this region would give to Russia the river Neva, and, besides the possibility of having a seaport, would furnish Nóvgorod with free access to the Baltic by the way of the river Vólkhof, Lake Ládoga, and the Neva, and would also enable an easy communication, for the most part by water, to be made between the Gulf of Finland and Archangel. The annexation of Narva, the frontier fortress of Esthonia, was not included in Peter's plans, but he believed, especially at the time when war was declared, that the surest way for him to secure the coveted territory was to attack and capture Narva, by which means the communications of Livonia and Esthonia with the Neva would be entirely cut off. Near Narva the Russian boundary was only about twenty miles from the sea.

The orders to march on Narva were much to the distaste of Patkul, and of Baron Langen, the envoy of King Augustus. Langen wished these provinces to come to his master ; Patkul, as a Livonian, did not wish his country to be conquered by anyone, especially by the Russians, and hoped that, as the result of the war, it would gain a position of semi-independence.

The command-in-chief of the troops was given to Theodore

Golovín, admiral and ambassador, now created field-marshal, and who was actually Minister of Foreign Affairs. There were three divisions, respectively under Avtémon Golovín, Adam Weyde, and Nikíta Répnin. Altogether, including a force of Cossacks, 63,520 men were assigned to this expedition. The Tsar himself, as an officer of the Preobrazhénsky regiment, accompanied the advance. At Tver, he received a message from Augustus, that King Charles with 18,000 men would soon land at Pernau, from which he would be within striking distance both of Narva and Riga. The news was premature, but it caused Peter great perplexity, because, if true, it meant that the Danes had been beaten, and that the Swedes had finished with one ally and were free to deal with the others. Orders were given to stop the advance, but as Peter became convinced, by the examination of prisoners, that the garrison of Narva was small, and that no troops had yet arrived from Sweden, he resolved to prosecute the war, and arrived at Narva on October 4. With the assistance of General Hallart, who had been sent by King Augustus, he immediately began to get ready for a siege. Peter now found that, even although he had begun the war late, he had not made sufficient preparations for it. The roads were in a fearful state, and everyone who knows what a Russian road is now, can imagine what they were in a rainy autumn, when *chaussées* were unknown. The means of transport were utterly insufficient. No provision had been made for it, except to seize the horses and carts in the towns and villages through which the troops passed. There was no artillery harness, the carts were all weak, and the horses broke down with the bad roads and the heavy service. Peter kept sending urgent summonses from his camp before Narva, and Golovín did his utmost to hurry them on, but it was not until October 29 that the troops from Moscow and Nóvgorod arrived, suffering from cold, hunger, and exposure. The division of Répnin, which had come from the Volga country, was far behind, and the Cossacks did not make their appearance. In all, there were rather less than forty thousand men.

Narva (called also in old Russian chronicles Rugodív), which was built by the Danes in the thirteenth century, on the right bank of the river Naróva, eight miles from its mouth, was then a seaport of considerable importance for the trade coming from Nóvgorod and Pskof. In the flourishing times of the Hanseatic League it was not unknown, but it suffered so terribly from the frequent border wars that its trade at that time received no great development. The city was surrounded by a stout wall, consisting, on the land side, of six bastions, built of earth and partly faced with stone, and of a wall and three bastions of stone on the river side. At the southern end, on a half-detached hill, was the citadel, with its old tower, still known as *Der lange Hermann*. Connected by a good stone bridge was the old and still picturesque castle of Ivángorod, built by the Russians in 1492 to overawe Narva, but at this time forming part of the defences of the town. The fortress was well armed, but the garrison, under the command of Rudolph Horn, was small, consisting of thirteen hundred infantry, two hundred cavalry, and about four hundred armed citizens. In appearance, Narva was like many an old German town, and even now, from the public garden, the old brick gables rising above the trees and walls have a picturesque and thoroughly un-Russian air. The political and social importance of Narva has now diminished, but the foreign trade is still not inconsiderable, and the rapids of the Naróva, just above the town, furnish water-power for large cloth and linen factories.

The Russian line of circumvallation, which was entirely on the left or western side of the river, extended from near the rapids above the town—about where the factories are now situated—to the village of Vepsa-kylä, two miles below the city walls. In all it was about seven miles in length. Earthworks were also thrown up opposite to the castle of Ivángorod. The lines were laid out under the personal supervision of the Tsar, who took up his quarters near Vepsa-kylä, on the little grassy island of Kamperholm, which, from changes in the river's current, has long since disappeared. At Kamperholm the river was crossed by a bridge; here was the nucleus of the Russian camp, and here the stores and ammunition were concentrated. The artillery at last arrived, and was put into position, and on October 31 the bombardment began from eight batteries on the Narva side, and also from the trenches in front of Ivángorod. The artillery fire continued day and night for two weeks without success. The constant sorties of the Swedes troubled the Russians, and the gun-carriages were so badly made, or so injured by transportation, that they usually fell to pieces after three or four discharges. The powder also was bad. On November 17, it was found that there was not sufficient ammunition to carry on the bombardment from the new breach batteries for even twenty-four hours. It was necessary, therefore, to stand still until new supplies arrived. At the same time, information was received that King Augustus had retired from before Riga, and had shut himself up in Kokenhusen, and that Charles XII. had landed at Pernau with an army magnified by rumour to thirty-two thousand men. Sheremétief had been sent to Wesenberg, eighty miles west of Narva on the road to Reval, with a force of five thousand irregular cavalry, to observe the Swedish movements. At Purtis he had a meeting with the enemy, and got a slight advantage, taking a few prisoners. After ravaging and burning the country, he wisely retreated to Pyhäjöggi, a strong pass, capable of easy defence, and blocking the only road to Narva. This pass Sheremétief desired to fortify, but the Tsar, who did not fully appreciate the situation, rejected the advice, blamed the retreat as well as the devastation of the country, and sent Sheremétief back toward Wesenberg. Instead of occupying Pyhäjöggi in force, it was decided to fortify the Russian camp on the land side against an attack by the Swedes, and meanwhile vigorously prosecute the siege. Two assaults were attempted on Ivángorod, but as no breaches had been made in the wall, they were easily repulsed.

As the first siege of Azof was marked by an act of treachery, so, now, Hummert, an Esthonian by birth, an officer who had been much favoured and liked by Peter, and who had recently been promoted to be major of the Preobrazhénsky regiment, went over to the enemy. He had left his wife and children in Moscow, and it was for a time thought that he had been killed or taken prisoner, and message was sent to the town to treat him well, under threat of reprisals. Soon it was found out that he had deserted. Subsequently, Hummert, pretending that he had gone to Narva as a spy, with the design of aiding the Russians, wrote to the Tsar several letters, asking for money, and giving counsels about carrying on the war, and criticisms on the siege. He ascribed the failure to the want of discipline, to the unwillingness of the Russian officers to work and to obey orders, and to bad generalship. Hummert's letters were unanswered, and the only revenge of Peter was to hang him in effigy before the house he had given him in Moscow, of which his wife remained in undisturbed possession. The suspicious Swedes hanged him in reality. The desertion of Hummert caused a general panic. The troops in the trenches were strengthened against a sortie, and the Tsar was begged to take safer quarters.

On the 28th of November, Peter left the army and went to Nóvgorod; partly in order to hurry up the ammunition and reinforcements—for everything moved faster when he put his hand to the wheel—and partly to have an interview with King Augustus, and decide on the future conduct of the war. He showed, at other times, proofs enough of his personal bravery to refute the charge of cowardice brought against him by his enemies, even though we remember his ignominious flight to Tróïtsa in 1689. The conduct of Augustus in withdrawing from Riga seemed suspicious to him, and he had already sent Prince Gregory Dolgorúky to the Saxon camp to find out what was really going on, and whether there was any talk of overtures of peace, and to arrange an interview for him with the King. Baron Langen, in writing to the King on the very day of the Tsar's departure, presses him to appoint a place for an interview, as he could easily go from Warsaw to the Düna in four days. The Tsar would start as soon as the courier returned. He, Langen, would go to Mitau during the Tsar's absence. All this seemed to show, not fear, but over-confidence. With the slowness of the Russian operations, neither Peter nor those about him appreciated the rapidity of the Swedish movements under Charles, nor really understood the danger. It was expected that the siege would be still going on when Peter should return.

The Tsar took with him the field-marshal Golovín, who, as Minister of Foreign Affairs, was necessary to conduct the negotiations with Augustus, and especially with Poland. Peter still had hopes of drawing the Republic into the war; the treaty had been made with Augustus as Elector of Saxony, and the Republic was as yet not engaged. The command of the army was intrusted to the Duke de Croy. Charles Eugene, Duke de Croy, Prince of the Holy Roman Empire, Margrave, Baron, and Lord of many lands, had served with distinction for fifteen years in the Austrian wars against the Turks, and had risen to be field-marshal and commander-in-chief. Having been for some reason relieved of his command, and crying out against Austrian ingratitude, he presented himself to the Tsar in Amsterdam in 1698. No arrangement was made with him at the time, and the Duke entered the service of King Augustus, and was sent by him to the Tsar just before the siege of Narva. Peter was pleased with him, took him to Narva, and had the intention of appointing him commander-in-chief, but the execution of the project was delayed. He was only forty-nine years old, and certainly had greater military knowledge and experience than any officer of the Russian army. Had he been appointed sooner, he might have served the Tsar in good stead, but it was now too late.[1] The Duke himself saw this, and pleaded his ignorance of the language and his want of acquaintance with the officers as reasons for refusing. He at last consented, and Peter gave him written instructions with absolute power over the whole army. In these instructions he was ordered to wait for the arrival of the ammunition before beginning the attack, and meanwhile to keep a sharp look-out for the approach of the Swedes, and prevent them from relieving the town. Langen, in writing to the King, said : ' I hope when the Duke de Croy shall have the absolute command that our affairs will take quite another turn, for he has no more wine or brandy ; and being therefore deprived of his element, he will doubtless double his assaults to get nearer to the cellar of the commandant.' Evidently, no one in the least expected what a surprise was in store for them all in only a few hours' time.

Charles, after his return from Denmark, was in the south of Sweden, pressing the preparations for the expedition to Livonia, when he received the news of the appearance of the Rus-

---

[1] On hearing of the death of the Duke in 1702, Peter said : ' If I had given him the command of my camp fourteen days sooner, I should not have suffered the defeat of Narva.'

sian troops before Narva. This made him still more anxious
to start, and he was so busy that he would not even see the
court, which was in the neighbouring town of Christianstad,
saying that he had no time to receive ladies. A private letter
from Karlshamn, written about this time, gives us a notion of
the feelings of the King.

'We had the hope that His Majesty would return to Stockholm, but he is resolved to go to Livonia, cost what it may.
That the King has acted as though he would return to Stockholm has been in order to deceive, and especially to keep the
French and Brandenburg ambassadors from coming here. For
he tries to avoid meeting these gentlemen, in order not to be
obliged to listen to proposals of peace, which, it is said, they
are commissioned to place before him. He wishes, at any
price, to fight with King Augustus, and is annoyed at anything
which seems likely to hinder his doing this. One evening, as
he was just about getting into bed, Count Polus came and said
that important intelligence had arrived, which needed to be
immediately communicated to him. The King turned hastily
toward-Polus, and made him one bow after another until, in
this way, he had complimented him out of the door. He was
afraid that Polus and Åkerhjelm, in their reports, might let
fall some words about peace and arrangement, and carried this
so far that those gentlemen could never get his signature to the
papers they had to send, unless when Piper came to their aid.'

The whole preparations for the new war lasted less than six
weeks, and, leaving Karlskrona on the 11th of October, after
spurning all appeals for delay on account of the stormy season,
Charles arrived at Pernau, on the Gulf of Riga, on the 16th,
having suffered severely from sea-sickness on the journey.
Some of the troops landed at Pernau, and others were driven
by stress of weather to Reval—about 8,000 in all. The fleet
returned to Sweden for 4,000 more men and the rest of the
artillery. The first intention of Charles was to attack Augustus, but he soon received the news that the Saxons had given
up the siege of Riga, and had retired into winter quarters at
Kokenhusen. Time was necessary for the arrival of all the
troops, and for obtaining accurate information of the position
and movements of the enemy; but on the 15th of November

Charles was able to set out from Reval, and on the 23d began the march from Wesenberg. The troops were allowed to take no baggage except their knapsacks, and in spite of the cold, the swamps, the bad food, and the difficulties of the march, reached Pyhäjöggi in four days. The pass was not fortified, and the troops of Sheremétief were quickly driven back toward Narva. The strong pass of Silämäggi was also left without defence, and on the morning after Peter's departure, Sheremétief came into camp saying that the Swedes were closely following him. A council of war was at once held in the Russian camp, additional rounds of ammunition were served out, and the vigilance redoubled. But that day and night passed quietly. The next morning, November 30, at about eleven o'clock, the Swedish forces appeared in battle-array from behind the woods on the top of the Hermannsberg. There were only 20,000 Russians fit for service, and these were extended along a line of seven miles. Although the Swedes did not number 9,000 men, it was comparatively easy for them in their sudden onset, under cover of a cannonade, to pierce the thin Russian lines. They were assisted in this by a sudden snow-storm, which blew in the face of the Russians, and prevented their seeing more than twenty feet from them. The Russians were panic-stricken, and, with the want of confidence which they had in their new general, cried out 'The Germans have betrayed us,' and fled in confusion. Sheremétief was one of the first to run. With his cavalry, he headed immediately for the river Naróva, near the cataracts, and succeeded in getting across, although very many men were lost in the rapids. The majority went the other way to the Kamperholm bridge. The bridge broke down, and many men were lost. Two regiments, the Preobrazhénsky and the Seménofsky, which were protecting the artillery park, and had surrounded themselves with a little fortification, held their ground. With them were the Duke de Croy, General Hallart, and Baron Langen. Although the Russians stood firm against the enemy, yet they were in great confusion. They cried out against the foreign officers, and killed several of them. Seeing this, and fearing for his life, the Duke de Croy said to those near him, 'The devil could not fight with such soldiers,' and made his

way through the swamps toward the Swedish lines, followed by
Hallart, Langen, and Blumberg, the commander of the Preobrazhénsky regiment. Stenbock, who for a long time could
not be found in the darkness, received them politely and took
them to the King. The Russian generals, Prince Dolgorúky,
Prince Alexander of Imeritia, Avtémon Golovín, and Buturlín, after holding a council in a bomb-proof, decided to surrender. They wished to keep their artillery, but the King was
inexorable, and finally it was agreed that on the next day they
should retreat with their banners and arms, but with only six
guns. General Weyde, who was on the extreme right flank,
and was wounded, knew nothing of the defeat till Buturlín sent
him word of the capitulation. He then followed the example.
Count Wrede wrote to his father a few days afterward :
    ' Yet if he had had the courage to attack us, he would have
infallibly beaten us, for we were extremely tired, having scarcely
eaten or slept for several days, and besides this, all our men were
drunk with the brandy that they had found in the Muscovite
tents, so that it was impossible for the few officers that remained
to keep them in order.'
    The confusion and panic of the Russians were very great.
Hallart says :
    ' They ran about like a herd of cattle, one regiment mixed
up with the other, so that hardly twenty men could be got into
line.'
    The next day the bridge to Kamperholm was repaired, and
the Russians were allowed to retreat, but the generals were all
declared prisoners of war, on the ground that the troops had carried away with them the army chest, containing 300,000 rubles,
in contravention of the capitulation. Nothing, however, had been
said in the agreement on this point. The Russian loss was about
5,700 men. Seventy-nine officers, including nine generals, were
taken prisoners. The Swedes captured, in addition, 149 cannon
and 32 mortars, including many of the guns which Charles
himself had given to Peter before the war, and 146 banners.
The Swedish loss in killed and wounded was less than 2,000.
    Charles had constantly exposed himself to great personal
danger. He was always in the thick of the fight, and in order
to get around a mound of corpses fell into a morass, from which

THE BATTLE OF NARVA.

he was extricated with difficulty, and where he was obliged to leave his horse, his weapons, and one of his boots. He immediately mounted another horse, which was soon killed under him, while he himself was hit by a spent ball, which was deadened by his necktie, and was afterward found in his clothes. An officer immediately sprang from his saddle and offered him his horse. The King in mounting said laughingly: ' I see that the enemy want me to practise riding.' [1]

[1] Soloviéf, xiv. ; Ustriálof, IV. i. ii. ; Fryxell, I. ; K. Lundblad, *Geschichte Karl des Zwölften* (German Transl. of G. V. v. Jensen), Hamburg, 1835 ; C. v. Sarauw, *Die Feldzüge Karl's XII.*, Leipzig, 1881 ; Gólikof, *Actions of Peter the Great* (Russian), Moscow, 1837 ; *Journal of the Swedish War* (Russian), St. Petersburg, 1770.

XLII.

THE fate of prisoners of war in those days was not enviable. General Hallart was obliged to give up all his private papers and the memoranda he had made of the siege, and, more than that, experienced the personal anger of King Charles because the answers to his questions with regard to the number of troops were not to his liking. Charles insisted that the Russians had at least 80,000 men, whereas Hallart could not make out more than 30,000, including the disabled. All the prisoners were sent under strict guard to Reval, and the next spring to Sweden, except the Duke de Croy, who was allowed to remain at Reval with Dr. Carbonari, the body physician of the Tsar. The King respected the high personal and military rank of the Duke, and immediately after the battle sent him 1,500 Swedish ducats and food and wine from his own table, when the other prisoners were almost starving. While at Reval, De Croy wrote to Peter, Menshikóf, and Golovín, asking for money, and explaining how he had paid out of his own pocket the expenses of the foreign officers who had accompanied him to Russia, and what great expense he was put to at Reval. In reply to his first letter Peter sent him 6,000 rubles, but he was so lavish that this amount did not go far, and by no means sufficed for his needs. At his death, in the spring of 1702, his debts were so great that his creditors put into force an old law refusing burial to insolvent debtors. His body was kept in the cellar of the church of St. Nicholas, the antiseptic properties of which prevented it from decaying, and up to a few years ago—when by an order of the Russian Government it was finally interred—it was still shown to travellers as a curiosity. Baron Langen and General Hallart were exchanged in 1705, but the other prisoners remained in Sweden for many years, as did Prince Hílkof, who had been arrested by royal order as soon as it had become known that the Russians had declared war. Hílkof, who had sincerely believed in the Tsar's peaceful designs, and, it is said, complained bitterly of those who had persuaded him to accept the mission to Sweden, had to pay in person for the double-dealing of his master. He was treated with great severity; all writing materials were taken from him, and at first a guard of soldiers was stationed even in his bedroom. Later the authorities contented themselves with placing a guard outside his house. He never again saw his country, but died in Vesterås in 1715. Prince Alexander of Imeritia was held by the Swedes at a high price. At one time they demanded ten kegs of gold; at another they agreed to exchange him for twenty captains, twenty lieutenants, and twenty ensigns. His father begged the Tsar to do this, but the Prince himself, who was heavily in debt, suffering from cold, and without enough to eat, wrote from Stockholm in 1710:

'It has never come to my tongue nor even into my mind to ask for anything to the detriment of the Empire in order to free me, or even those a thousand times better than me. For that are we called—to suffer and to die in the interest of our Lord and of the Empire.'

The Prince was finally exchanged in 1711, together with Prince Trubetskóy, for Count Piper, but died in Finland on his homeward way. Few of these Russian prisoners returned home until after the battle of Poltáva, in 1709, which produced sufficient effect upon the Swédes for them to desire an exchange of prisoners.

The treatment of Hílkof influenced that of Knipercrona, the Swedish Resident at Moscow. When war was declared, a guard of twenty-four soldiers was placed at his door, but he was given permission to return to Sweden either by way of Smolénsk or Archangel. The Smolénsk route was dangerous on account of the Polish war, and that to Archangel tedious from the autumn rains. He therefore preferred to remain in Moscow. When the news came of the bad treatment of Hílkof, Knipercrona was not allowed to leave his house, and was separated from his wife and four children. This lasted till August, 1701, when his family was restored to him. He was afterward sent to Stockholm, where he was living in freedom in 1709, while Hilkof was still confined in the castle.

In the early part of the war the Russians took few prisoners. The garrisons of the fortresses they captured were generally allowed to march off under the terms of the capitulations. A time came, however, when large bodies of men surrendered, and in the autumn of 1709, after the battle of Poltáva, there were in Russia about twenty thousand Swedes, prisoners of war, including nearly two thousand officers, besides a great number of chaplains and civil officers. There were then so few Russians in Sweden that the exchange of prisoners made scarcely a sensible difference in the numbers. The Swedish officers received money for their support from their own Government, and many of them obtained. besides, civil employment in Russia, and sometimes assistance from kind-hearted Russian governors. The soldiery were employed on the estates of the nobility, in the mines in the Ural, in the most distant provinces of Siberia, and even in the building of St. Petersburg. After the peace of Nystad, in 1721, all were allowed to go home, but some did not get away until 1724, and even later. As far as can be ascertained, only about five thousand soldiers returned to Sweden. Some of them had not seen their native land for twenty years.

The battle of Narva created a great impression throughout Europe. Glowing accounts of the victory were published in many languages, and the praise of the youthful monarch was the theme for orations and poems, while satire and raillery found subjects in the ' flight ' of Peter and the conduct of the Russian troops. Swedish diplomatists published a refutation of the reasons and additional explanations offered by Patkul in justification of the Russian declaration of war, and even Leibnitz, who had shown so much interest in Russia and the Russians, expressed his sympathy with the Swedes in no measured terms, and his wish that he could see their ' young King reign in Moscow and as far as the river Amur.' Medals were struck in honour of Charles with the inscriptions, ' *Superant superata fidem*,' and ' At last the right prevails.' There was another commemorative medal of a different kind : on one side the Tsar was represented warming himself over the fires of his mortars

which were bombarding Narva, with the inscription, 'And
Peter warmed himself at the fire'; and on the other, the Russians were shown running away from Narva, with Peter at their
head; his hat had fallen off, his sword had been thrown away,
and he was wiping away his tears with his handkerchief, and
the inscription read: 'He went out and wept bitterly.'

The victory at Narva was, however, in the end more disas-
trous to the Swedes than to the Russians. From this time on,
Charles made war the great object of his life. He became persuaded that he was invincible. Certain traits of his character,
especially his cold-bloodedness, his indifference to the loss of
life, and even to the suffering of his soldiers, became accentuated.
He even seemed to take delight in carnage. This is very plain
from letters descriptive of the fight at Narva, written by Swedish officers to their friends at home. Axel Sparre rode over
the field of battle afterward with the King, who pointed out to
him all the places of interest, and said:

'But there is no pleasure in fighting with the Russians, for
they will not stand like other men, but run away at once. If
the Naróva had been frozen, we should hardly have killed one
of them. The best joke was when the Russians got upon the
bridge and it broke down under them. It was just like Pharaoh in the Red Sea. Everywhere you could see men's and
horses' heads and legs sticking up out of the water, and our
soldiers shot at them like wild ducks.'

Carl Cronstedt, afterward the celebrated Field-marshal, General Stenbock, and Carl Magnus Posse, all express themselves
in nearly the same terms about the King's obstinacy, his belief
in his mission, and his refusal to listen to advice. Stenbock
wrote a few weeks after the battle of Narva:

'The King thinks now about nothing except war. He no
longer troubles himself about the advice of other people, and he
seems to believe that God communicates directly to him what
he ought to do. Piper is much troubled about it, because the
weightiest affairs are resolved upon without any preparation, and
in general things go on in a way that I do not dare commit to
paper.'

Posse, writing in December of the same year, says:
'In spite of the cold and scarcity, and although the water is

standing in the huts, the King will not yet let us go into winter quarters. I believe that if he had only 800 men left he would invade Russia with them, without taking the slightest thought as to what they would live on ; and if one of our men is shot, he cares no more about it than he would for a louse, and never troubles himself about such a loss.'

The counsellors of Charles were of opinion that he should immediately accept the propositions of peace offered by King Augustus, invade Russia, take up winter quarters in the enemy's country, and use all means to foment the discontent existing there, even to proclaiming Sophia. After such a defeat, the Russians were unprepared to resist, and it would be possible to advance even to Moscow. In any case, the Swedes could get advantages of much the same sort as they had had in the Troublous Times, and could for ever secure their rule in the provinces already possessed by them. Charles was at first inclined to this opinion, and forbade his troopers foraging over the frontier, lest the country should become barren, and nothing be left for the invading army. But he speedily changed his mind. His contempt for the Russians rapidly grew, and he despised them as a people not worth fighting against. He had a personal feeling of hostility toward his cousin 'Augustus for his treachery, and feared, or pretended to fear, that if peace were made with him, he would break it the moment the Swedes had entered Russia. More than all, he desired to put down the third enemy by force of arms.

No doubt many of those who surrounded him secretly worked on his feelings of ambition, in order that these plans might be carried out, for they feared the march through the deserted and cold districts of Northern Russia, where, with the King's temperament, they would be obliged to suffer many privations. Sending, therefore, a small force to the region of Lake Ládoga and the Neva, Charles took up his winter quarters in the castle of Lais, a few miles from Dorpat. The troops were quartered in the villages and in the open country round about. Although he might have taken up pleasanter winter quarters in Narva, Riga or Pernau, he did not visit these towns once during the course of the winter, and it was not until the beginning of June that he even went to the neighbouring university town of Dorpat.

The time passed merrily enough in the castle, where General Magnus Stenbock invented all sorts of amusements—suppers, masquerades, spectacles, and even a great sham fight, with snow castles and snowballs. Charles paid little attention to governmental affairs, and busied himself solely with plans of war. He frequently visited the detachments of troops, but simply in order to see them drilled and go through their exercises, and not for the purpose of inquiring into their condition. Meanwhile, owing to the cold and privations, fever was making tremendous ravage in the army ; 270 of the Dalecarlian regiment died, and 400 in that of Vestmanland, so that on the return of spring less than half the troops were fit for action. The King's cousin, the Count Palatine Adolph Johann, died from fever, as well as many of the royal servants. The lack of provisions, and even of clothing, caused the soldiers, in spite of the severe orders, to pillage and plunder the villages and houses of the inhabitants. The people wondered that the King should thus harass his own subjects, when he could have lived on the enemy in the neighbouring Russian province of Pskof, and the discontent which was caused among the nobility of Livonia and Esthonia by the ' Reduction' now extended to all classes of the population.

Peter had not got far from Narva when he received the news of the defeat. It surprised him, and almost stunned him by its unexpectedness and its magnitude, but it did not dispirit him. On the contrary, it roused him to new effort. He had the heroic qualities of perseverance and determination, difficulty but spurred him on, and, Antæus-like, he rose after each fall, with new energy and new courage. At a later time, after the battle of Poltáva, he was able to judge the matter calmly, and said:

'Our army was vanquished by the Swedes—that is incontestable ; but one should remember what sort of an army it was. The Lefort regiment was the only old one. The two regiments of guards had been present at the two assaults of Azof, but they never had seen any field-fighting, especially with regular troops. The other regiments consisted—even to some of the colonels— of raw recruits, both officers and soldiers. Besides that, there was the great famine, because, on account of the late season of the year, the roads were so muddy that the transport of provisions had to be stopped. In one word, it was like child's play. One cannot, then, be surprised that, against such an old, disciplined, and experienced army, these untried pupils got the worst of it. This victory was then, indeed, a sad and severe blow to us. It seemed to rob us of all hope for the future, and to come from the wrath of God. But now, when we think of it rightly, we ascribe it rather to the goodness of God than to his anger ; for if we had conquered then, when we knew as little of war as of government, this piece of luck might have had unfortunate consequences. . . . That we lived through this disaster, or rather this good fortune, forced us to be industrious, laborious, and experienced.'

But there was no time then for calm consideration of the causes and consequences of the Russian defeat. Every moment was necessary for action. The Swedes might at any time invade the country. Peter met, near Lake Sámra, Prince Nikíta Répnin, who had collected his division in the Volga country, and was marching toward Narva. He was at once turned back to Nóvgorod, and instructed to bring into order the regiments which had left Narva ' in confusion.' Work was immediately begun on the fortifications of Nóvgorod, Pskof, and the Petchérsky monastery near Pskof. Men, women, and children were all put to the work, and the services in the churches were given up in order that the priests and monks could help. Houses were pulled down and churches were destroyed where they stood in the way of the new fortifications. Peter set the example by labouring with his own hands at the first intrenchment at Nóvgorod, and then entrusted it to Lieutenant-Colonel Shénshin. On coming back afterward and not finding Shénshin there, he had him mercilessly whipped at the very intrenchment, and then sent him to Smolénsk as a common soldier. At Moscow, Leontius Kókoshkin was hanged because he had taken a bribe of five rubles when engaged in receiving carts at Tver, and another official, Poskótchin, was hanged at Nóvgorod for a similar offence.

Three weeks after the battle, when the stragglers had all come in, it was found that, out of the three divisions of Golovín, Weyde, and Trubetskóy, there remained 23,000 men. Adding

to these the division of Répnin, Peter still had an army of
33,000 men. The irregular cavalry and the local levies had
practically disappeared, and were unserviceable. Orders were
at once given to Prince Boris Golítsyn to make new levies, and
especially to raise nine regiments of dragoons of 1,000 men
each. Volunteers were also again asked for from Moscow, but
the prohibition against enlisting the old Streltsi was still kept in
force. In a few months, the army was much larger than before,
and, according to the testimony of foreigners, was in excellent
condition.

Peter stayed two weeks in Nóvgorod, to do what was most
indispensable for the protection of the frontier. He then went
to Moscow, and his activity was visible everywhere.

It was necessary to make new artillery, for nearly all had
been captured by the Swedes. Vinius was charged with this
task, and, in default of other metal, was ordered to melt down
the bells of the churches and monasteries. The old man set to
work with all his energy, and, in spite of the difficulty in finding
workmen, in spite of the delays of the burgomasters in sending
on metal, he was able, by the end of 1701, to furnish 300 cannon, and prided himself on having done this so well, for not
only were the pieces faultless, but they had been made at a sav-
ing of 10,000 rubles over previous cost. Besides this, he had
founded a school, where 250 boys were learning to become artil-
lerymen and skilled workmen. Old as he was, in 1702 he even
undertook a journey to Siberia to investigate the copper found
there. Vinius perhaps exaggerated the difficulties under which
he laboured, but what he complained of most was that, in being appointed inspector of the artillery, he had been deprived of
the charge of the post-office, and inquired whether it was on account of any anger toward him. Peter replied :

'I have received your letter, in which you write about the
readiness of the artillery, and how you are working at it. The
business is very good and necessary, for time is like death. You
ask me if the post was not taken away from you so unexpectedly from some anger of mine. But does not your conscience
at all accuse you ? For I long ago talked to you about it, and
you are quite aware that many people talked about it, and even
gave something. The post was taken from you for no other

reason than that, while you had it, it was not a profit to the State, but only to you; for, often as I have talked to you about correspondence with other places, my words were vain. For that reason it has been given to another, from whom, also, if such rumours be truly spread, it will be taken away again.'

For a long time Vinius did wonders, but finally his energy began to flag, and he too openly filled his pockets at the expense of the State. In 1703, Peter came to Schlüsselburg, and was very indignant to find that there had been great delay in forwarding the artillery and the medical stores. Vinius was at the same time Director of the Medical Department, the Artillery Department, and the Siberian Department. Peter immediately wrote to Prince Ramodanófsky:

'There is great delay to our work here. It is impossible even to begin. I myself have often spoken to Vinius, but he answered me with the Muscovite "immediately" (*seitchas*). Be good enough to inquire of him why he manages so carelessly such an important matter, which is a thousand times dearer than his head. Not an ounce of medicine has been sent from the medical stores. We shall be forced to cure those who take so little care.'

Vinius, who tried to excuse himself, and threw the blame on others, was subsequently accused by Menshikóf, who was charged with another investigation, of giving him large bribes to let the matter drop. The wrath of Peter could not be appeased. Vinius lost his friendship for ever, was deprived of the direction of the Siberian and Artillery departments, and was fined 13,000 rubles.[1]

---

[1] Soloviéf, xiv. ; Ustriálof, IV. iii. ; Fryxell, I. ; Lundblad, I. ; Sarauw; Gólikof ; *Journal of the Swedish War ;* Guerrier, *Leibnitz.*

XLIII.

EVEN before the battle of Narva, Prince Gregory Dolgorúky had been sent on a mission to King Augustus. Subsequently Captain Theodore Sóltykof was sent on a similar errand, and instructions were given to both to inform the King of the Russian defeat, to arrange for an interview, and to state, although in cautious terms, the firm resolution of the Tsar to maintain the alliance. Dolgorúky found the King at Warsaw, and received from him every assurance that he would allow no change of fortune to alter his plans. At the same time, on December 30, Augustus wrote to the Tsar saying that about March 1 he would be at Dünaburg, where he would be most glad to see him. Peter, who was in Moscow when he received the King's letter, set out in the middle of February ; but when he arrived at Dünaburg, after a journey of two weeks, he found that the King was eighty miles farther at Birze, an old fortified castle which had formerly belonged to the Radziwill family, and was then the property of the young Princess of Neuburg. Augustus was just starting for Dünaburg, and his sledge was standing ready at the door when Peter arrived, so unexpectedly that he could scarcely meet him on the threshold. In the ten days which Peter spent here, the chief business was negotiations and political discussion, but the King and the Tsar made also an excursion to Dünamünde, the fortress below Riga, at the mouth of the river, which had been renamed Augustusburg, in honour of the King, and Peter went also to Bausk and Mitau. Time enough was left for feasting and amusement. One day the Tsar and the King fired at a mark, from cannon mounted on different bastions. The King hit the mark twice, but the Tsar, although an experienced artillerist, never hit it at all. The

next day there was a great dinner, which lasted so late that the
King overslept himself the following morning, and the Tsar
only went to mass. He attentively followed the service, and
was curious about all the ceremonies. This led one of the Polish senators to say to him that it was in his power to unite the
Greek and Roman Churches. Peter replied : ' Sovereigns have
rights only over the bodies of their people—Christ is the sovereign of their souls. For such a thing a general consent is necessary, and that is in the power of God alone.' It was not the
union of the Churches, but the alliance of the Republic of Poland, as well as of the King, that Peter had come to Birze to
secure. On this subject he had a conversation with Sczuka, the
Vice-chancellor of Lithuania. Peter suggested that now was the
very best time for the Poles to join the Russians and Saxons,
and tear away Livonia from the Swedes. Sczuka replied that
Poland was exhausted by her preceding wars, and needed rest
and repose. Besides that, Livonia was not enough. Poland
needed some more solid advantages. ' What are they ? ' asked
the Tsar. ' The whole matter is in your Majesty's hands,' said
the Chancellor, and finally explained that Poland could only be
induced to fight by the return of some of its frontier provinces
occupied by Russia—as, for instance, Kíef and the neighbouring districts. The Tsar replied that this was impossible, and
left the room. The negotiations were continued by Golovín,
but with no better result. He said the cession of Kíef would
cause disturbances at Moscow. ' If this is hard for Moscow,'
said Sczuka, ' war is still harder for the Republic.' The negotiations with Poland ended here, but a new treaty was concluded
with Augustus, by which the allies bound themselves to continue
the war with all their forces, and not to end it without mutual
consent. The Tsar promised to aid the King with from 15,000
to 20,000 well-armed infantry, to send to Vitebsk 100,000
pounds of powder, and, besides paying certain expenses, to give
him within three years the sum of 100,000 rubles. The King
was to attack the Swedes in Livonia and Esthonia, so as to allow
the Tsar a clear field for operations in Ingria and Karelia. Livonia and Esthonia were, when conquered, to belong to the
King and to Poland without any claim on the part of Russia.
But as the issue of the war was uncertain, and as the War of the

Spanish Succession might endanger the German possessions of the King, it was agreed to listen to any offers of mediation made by, Austria, France, England, Prussia, or Holland; and in a secret article Peter promised 20,000 rubles to buy up Polish senators.

Peter was followed to Moscow by an aide-de-camp of the King for the money. This was hard to raise. All was collected that could be found in the different ministries and departments—even the foreign money left over from the journey of the Tsar, and some Chinese gold which had been sent from Siberia. Finally, 1,000 gold pieces were obtained from the Tróïtsa monastery, 420 were given by Menshikóf, and 10,000 rubles by the rich Moscow merchant Filátief, and the sum of 150,000 rubles was made up. The auxiliary force of 20,000 men was placed under the command of Prince Répnin, and started out for Pskof about the end of April to join the King at Dünaburg. New orders were given by the King, and Répnin was obliged to go on to Kokenhusen, where he arrived at the end of June. The Russian troops were much praised by Fieldmarshal Steinau: ' They are all good men—except perhaps about fifty who need drilling—armed with Dutch muskets, and some regiments have swords instead of bayonets. The soldiers march evenly, work zealously and quickly, and do all that the field-marshal orders them. Especial praise must be given them that they have not among them any women nor any dogs, and the Muscovite general in the council of war requested that the wives of the Saxon musketeers be forbidden to come into the Russian camp morning and evening to sell wine, because the Muscovites are greatly given to drinking and debauchery. General Répnin is forty years old (in reality he was only thirty-three), knows little of military affairs, but nevertheless is of an inquiring mind and very respectful. The colonels are all Germans, old and incompetent men, and the officers are without experience.'

After sending off his money and his men, Peter passed a few days at Preobrazhénsky, and then went to Vorónezh, to build new ships and prepare and inspect that fleet which could be of no possible service unless there might be war with Turkey, and a port could be gained on the Black Sea. He was accompanied by most of the court, and by many ladies of the German suburb.

In spite of the dangers which threatened his empire, Peter
remained at Vorónezh at his favourite occupation for three
months, paying a visit on the way back to Moscow to the Iván
Lake, where he proposed to dig a canal between the Oká and
the Don. Three days after his return to Moscow there was a
frightful conflagration in the Krémlin. On the afternoon of
June 29, a fire started in the hostelry of the Saviour, rapidly
spread across the river, and burned nearly all the buildings in
the Krémlin—the ministries, departments, and other public
offices, with all their documents, the monasteries, the houses,
the great stores of provisions and ammunition. The palace was
entirely destroyed; the princesses living in it escaped with great
difficulty ; the bells of the cathedrals fell down, and the largest
bell of the Iván tower, weighing 288,000 pounds, was broken to
pieces. In one church all the sacred pictures, ornamented with
pearls and precious stones to the value of a million and a half
of rubles, were a prey to the flames. Two thousand houses were
burned, and it was only owing to the great personal exertions of
the Tsar that the stone bridge was saved.

During all this time the Tsar was engaged in negotiations of
two kinds—to find alliances which would aid him in carrying on
the war, and to find mediators who could persuade the King of
Sweden to make a peace advantageous to Russia. In January,
1701, a secret treaty was concluded with the King of Denmark,
by which he was to send to Windau at the opening of navigation three regiments of infantry and three of cavalry, in all
4,500 men, to be paid by the Russian Government. This treaty
was never carried out, for the victories of Charles XII. had
made his name so formidable that the King of Denmark did
not dare move a finger.

Matvéief, who had been sent on a mission to Holland, endeavoured to persuade the Netherlands to mediate between Sweden and Russia, and he was ordered to give the following account of the battle of Narva : ' The Swedes burst into the in-
trenchments, and found themselves between the division of
Weyde and the regiments of the guards. Seeing that the
Swedes were surrounded, the Russians three times sent a trum-
peter with a proposal of a truce. The armistice was concluded,
but on the next day, when the Russians began to cross the Na-

róva, the Swedes attacked them in spite of the royal promise, robbed them of everything, and seized the artillery and ammunition.' Matvéief asked the States-General not to allow the Swedes to hire troops or buy military stores in Holland before the mediation was decided. The truth was too well known in Holland for much attention to be given to the requests of the Russian minister, and the libels and pasquinades against Peter and his people were in lively circulation at The Hague. The Dutch were in a difficult position. They tried to prevent the war, which was injurious to their commercial interests in the Baltic. They were bound by a treaty with Sweden to furnish that country with money and aid; but they did not wish to break with Russia and lose their Archangel trade, and they feared the growing intimacy between Sweden and France. They would not openly help the Russians, and they tried to avoid assisting the Swedes. They explained that the money which the States-General and England had sent to King Charles was not intended to aid him in carrying on the war. At the same time, Witsen managed it so that muskets were bought in Amsterdam for the Russians. The Dutch were desirous of peace, but while William III. made vague promises of mediation in connection with the King of Prussia, the States-General did not like to offend Charles XII., who, in order to avoid discussion, had sent their minister away from Livonia, and told him to go to Stockholm to confer with the Council of State, which, as everyone knew, had no power.

Prince Peter Golítsyn, the brother of Boris, who had already been in Italy for the purpose of studying naval affairs, was sent to Vienna to ask the mediation of the German Emperor. He was ordered to go incognito and as speedily as possible. Yet he took three months for the journey, ' suffering,' as he wrote, ' all sorts of discomforts and privations.' His negotiations were carried on through the Jesuit Father Wolf, the confessor of the Emperor, by means of an interpreter, Linksweiler or Rothwell, who had already served the boyár Boris Sheremétief on his journey from Vienna to Malta. The interpreter was much to the taste of Golítsyn, and not at all to that of Wolf, who accused him of letting out what had been said. Golítsyn was received by the Emperor in private audience, but was able to effect nothing. After the battle of Narva, Peter had sunk very low in German opinion, and all sorts of rumours were current of new Russian defeats. Golítsyn wrote that Count Kaunitz laughed at him, and that the French and Swedish ministers made him the subject of jests. ' People here are well known to you,' he wrote to Golovín ; ' not only the men, but even the wives of the ministers, take money shamelessly. Everybody here gives them valuable presents, while I can only give them flattering words. It is necessary to try in every way possible to get a victory over the enemy. God forbid that the present summer should pass away with nothing ! Even though we conclude an eternal peace, yet how shall we wipe out an eternal shame ? It is absolutely necessary for our sovereign to get even a very small victory, by which his name may become famous in Europe as it was before. Then we can conclude a peace ; while now people only laugh at our troops and at our conduct of the war.' In addition to this, there was the difficulty about the late minister Guarient, who was accused of having written, or at least caused to be published, the journal of Korb, full of details about the punishment of the Streltsi.[1] Golítsyn says that he always spoke disrespectfully of the Russians and called them barbarians, and Guarient found himself obliged, not only to deny having had any part in the book, but to write apologetic letters to Golovín and the Tsar himself. In the way of mediation there was the difficulty that the Russians demanded as a condition of peace that they should be given Ingria and the river Neva, which they had not yet conquered. There was also a further difficulty—that the King of Poland had made a hostile expedition against Riga, without formally declaring war. As Golítsyn writes : ' The Swedish minister spent the morning with the Polish minister, and both talked about curves ; after dinner they discovered that there was a war between their sovereigns.'

In addition to these negotiations, talk of another kind was going on. The Empress, who still retained the favourable impression of Peter that she had received on his visit at Vienna, was anxious to make an alliance between the families, and proposed that her son, the Archduke Charles, who was then six-

---

[1] See note on p. 329.

teen years old, should marry a Russian princess. The only ones who were available—unless we include Peter's sister Natalia, who was then twenty-eight years old—were the three daughters of the Tsar Iván, Catherine, Anne, and Prascovia, of the respective ages of eleven, nine, and seven years. Golítsyn had no instructions on this point, and was obliged to write to Moscow. It was three months before the answer came. The Tsar was pleased at the proposal, and had the Dutch painter, Cornelius Le Bruyn—then on his travels in Russia—paint portraits of the three princesses in German costume, with their hair arranged à l'antique, to be sent to the Empress. Not only was Peter content with the portraits, but the Tsarítsa Prascovia liked them so much that she ordered Le Bruyn to paint duplicates for herself. The most beautiful was Anne, a blonde, who subsequently became Empress of Russia. The other two were brunettes. The negotiations on this point lingered on, to the displeasure of the Russians, and finally came to nothing. To all inquiries on the part of the Russian minister the Austrians said that the first proposal had come from the Russians, and that there were difficulties in the way. The Archduke Charles subsequently, in 1708, married Elizabeth, Princess of Brunswick-Wolfenbüttel, at that time one of the beauties of Europe, and their daughter was the celebrated Empress Maria Theresa. The Empress had also another wish, which was that the Tsarévitch Alexis should be sent to Vienna to receive his education, and both she and the Emperor promised to treat him as one of their own children, and to do everything possible for him. Peter consented to this, but the events of the war interfered with the project, and Alexis first went to Vienna fifteen years later as a fugitive.

Meanwhile the war had been proceeding in a quiet way as regarded Russia, although in a decisive and disagreeable way as regarded King Augustus. Early in the spring of 1701, orders had been given to fortify Archangel, which was at that time the only port of Russia, and when Izmaílof, the Russian minister at Copenhagen, wrote that the Swedes were hiring pilots for Archangel, additional precautions were ordered. Prince Prozorófsky, the governor, had only finished his preparations for defence, when a Swedish squadron of seven vessels, sailing under English and Dutch colours, appeared at the mouth of the Dvina, and anchored off Mudiúg island. The commandant of the island, thinking them trading vessels, sent as usual a detachment of sixteen soldiers, with interpreters and secretary, to inspect them. The men were all taken prisoners. Three of the vessels, guided by a Russian pilot, one of the prisoners, passed up the river, and again a Russian coast-guard was nearly captured, but took the alarm in time, and escaped to land with a loss of five men killed. The vessels went on, but one frigate and a yacht got aground, as the Swedes say, by the treachery, or patriotism, of the pilot. By this time they were known, and they were fired on by the batteries opposite, when their crews immediately abandoned them. The Russian soldiers took possession of them, and turned their cannon against the retiring Swedes. Unfortunately a quantity of powder which was on the deck took fire and blew off the poop of the frigate. After destroying various huts on Mudiúg island and some buildings connected with the salt-works, and committing other ravages along the shore, the Swedish squadron retired.

From Turkey there came good news. All rumours of war were at an end, and the Sultan had confirmed the treaty. But from the banks of the Düna came different intelligence. King Charles, having at last received reinforcements from Sweden, had set out from his winter quarters at Lais, had crossed the Düna in the face of the Saxon troops commanded by Marshal Steinau and Paikull, and had badly beaten them. Without underrating the merits of the Swedish generals and the Swedish troops, the defeat was in some degree due to the fault of Paikull, who, instead of opposing the crossing, allowed a part of the Swedish army to proceed, hoping to beat them afterward and possibly to capture the King. Enough men crossed the river, under the cover of the smoke of damp hay and manure carried in advance, to defeat the Saxons before they had made the necessary dispositions for attacking. Peter learnt of this defeat at Pskof, and was so much troubled that he decided to propose peace to Charles through the intervention of Prussia. But this attempt was as vain as those at The Hague and at Vienna. The Russian troops under Répnin returned to Pskof.

Four regiments, who had been in part of the reserves at the battle, were so frightened that, without waiting for the command, they ran twenty miles to join their comrades at Bórkovitsa.[1]

---

[1] Soloviéf, xiv. ; Gólikof; *Journal of Swedish War ;* Fryxell, I. ; Sjögren, *aykull.*

XLIV.

Two weeks after the battle of Narva, Peter had written to Sheremétief to do something to encourage the soldiers and embarrass the enemy. Accordingly, at the end of December 1700, Sheremétief sent a party against the fortified town of Marienburg, twenty miles from the frontier. The attack was unsuccessful. In revenge for this, Colonel Schlippenbach suddenly invaded the Russian territory, burned many villages, and laid siege to the Petchórsky monastery; but, after an officer had been killed in trying to screw a petard to the gates, he retreated to Livonia. During the winter, other similar forays laid waste the territory on each side of the frontier. After King Charles had marched toward the Düna, in July, 1701, Sheremétief again attacked the detachment of Schlippenbach, who remained in Livonia, at Rauke. He was beaten back, but Schlippenbach sent an urgent message to the King, telling him of his position, and saying that Sheremétief had as many troops as the whole Swedish army. The King replied merely, 'It cannot be,' and ordered 600 men to be sent to the village of Rappin, near the Russian border. This was in spite of the remonstrances of Schlippenbach, who said the force was too small, and proposed a more suitable point of attack. The King could not be moved, and Schlippenbach was obliged to report: 'It happened as I foresaw. Out of the whole detachment only one captain returned; all the rest were killed or taken prisoners by the Russians, together with two cannon.' This was on September 15, 1701, the Russians being commanded by the son of Sheremétief. This skirmish, for it was scarcely more, was the beginning of the Russian successes. In January, 1702, Sheremétief, with 8,000 infantry and dragoons, together with Cossacks, Kalmuks, and Tartars, and fifteen field-pieces, moved against Schlippenbach, who, with 7,000 men, was encamped on the estate of Erestfer, and on January 9, after a battle which lasted four hours, until it became dark, inflicted a severe defeat on the Swedes, who lost, according to their own account, 1,000, and according to the Russian estimate, 3,000 killed and wounded, and 350 prisoners, together with six guns and eight standards. The Russian loss amounted to more than 1,000 men. Sheremétief was glad of his victory, but he was still more pleased that the Swedes did not come out of the forests and attack him when he was in the midst of the deep snows and his men were too worn out to march farther. Peter was delighted, and after receiving Sheremétief's report, exclaimed : 'Thank God! we can at last beat the Swedes.' He immediately appointed Sheremétief field-marshal, and sent by Menshikóf to him the blue ribbon of St. Andrew and his own portrait set in diamonds. All the officers were promoted, and the common soldiers were given a ruble apiece of the newly coined money. At Moscow there was great rejoicing. Te Deums were chanted in the churches, with the ringing of bells and the firing of cannon ; a great banquet was given by the Tsar in a building erected for the purpose on the Red Place—the palace, we remember, had been burned down that winter—and the night closed with fireworks and illuminations. A fortnight later the Tsar made a triumphant entry, having in his train the Swedish prisoners, who were well treated. This was the first of a series of triumphs for small victories, which were indeed ridiculed by the foreign ministers, but which, nevertheless, served to keep up the spirits and arouse the patriotism of the people.

After the victory of Erestfer, Sheremétief made two pressing requests to be allowed to return to Moscow. His wife, he said, was living in the house of a neighbour, and he must find her a place to lay her head. The Tsar at first refused, but finally wrote from Archangel, leaving it to his judgment whether he could be spared from the army, and telling him if he should go, to be back again by Holy Week. On his return, Sheremétief attacked Schlippenbach at Hummelshof on July 29, 1702, and inflicted on him a severe defeat, amounting to a complete rout. The Swedish infantry was almost annihilated, and Schlippenbach with the cavalry retreated to Pernau. The Swedes had only about 5,000 men engaged, and lost at least 2,500 in killed and wounded, besides 300 prisoners, and all their artillery, standards, and drums. The Russian loss was 400 killed, and about the same number wounded.

After the battle of Hummelshof, Livonia remained entirely without defence. In Riga, Pernau, and Dorpat there were comparatively large garrisons, which did not dare leave the fortresses, and in the smaller towns only a few hundred men each. Sheremétief then thoroughly devastated the whole of the country, destroying towns, villages, and farms, taking captive the population, and sending his prisoners to the south of Russia. The Cossacks, Tartars, and Kalmuks in the Russian army had full swing, and Livonia was for a long time unable to recover from the effects of this campaign. Many rich and strong castles built by the Teutonic knights were then destroyed. Sheremétief in his report wrote :

'I send Cossacks and Kalmuks to different estates for the confusion of the enemy. But what am I to do with the people I have captured? The prisons are full of them, besides all those that the officers have. There is danger because these people are so sullen and angry. You know what they have already done, careless of themselves. In order that such plots may not begin again, and that the men may not set fire to the powder in the cellars, or die from their close quarters, much must be done. Considerable money besides is necessary for their support, and one regiment would be too little to conduct them to Moscow. I have selected a hundred families of the best of the natives who are good carpenters, or are skilled in some other branch of industry—about 400 souls in all—to send to Azof.'

That these prisoners included all classes of society may be seen from the fact that Patkul was obliged to petition the Tsar for the release of two daughters of his acquaintance, the Landrath Vietinghof, who had been taken prisoners and formed part of the booty of the Cossacks. So much cattle was taken that it could be bought at nominal prices, and, according to the Austrian Agent Pleyer, a Swedish boy or girl of fifteen years old could be bought at Pskof for two *grivnas*, or twelve groschen. The towns of Menza, Smilten, Ronenburg, and Wolmar were reduced to ruins, as well as Marienburg, which was a strongly fortified place, and offered great resistance. It was to this Sheremétief referred in the above report, for, after the town had been captured, an ensign of artillery, Wulff, continued the defence, and finally set fire to the powder-magazines, and blew himself up. Many Swedes were killed as well as many Russians.

The siege of Marienburg is of interest to us because among the captives was the Provost Gluck, with his family, and in his family was the girl who subsequently became the Empress Catherine I.

In the spring of 1702, Matvéief reported that the Swedes were intending again to attack Archangel. Not satisfied with the measures of protection and defence which had been taken in that region, considering that only 1,900 men were available there for military operations, Peter resolved to go himself to the North, and set out at the end of April, taking with him his son Alexis (then a boy of twelve), a numerous suite and five battalions of the guard, amounting to 4,000 men. He was thirty days on the road from Moscow. In our times of rapid communication it is hard to realise how any regular plan of defence or war could be carried out in a country where such enormous distances were required to be travelled, and where so much time had to be spent on the journey. In a stay of three months, which Peter made at Archangel, there was little which he could do in the way of military preparations. He occupied himself with shipbuilding, and on Trinity Sunday launched two frigates, the 'Holy Spirit' and the 'Courier,' constructed by Eleazar Ysbrandt, and laid the keel of a new twenty-six-gun ship, the 'St. Elijah,' writing at the same time to Apráxin that he could do nothing more, as there was no more ship-timber. In August the early fleet of merchant-ships arrived, much more numerous than usual, for all the trade which had before come through the Swedish ports on the Baltic naturally turned to Archangel. There were thirty-five English and fifty-two Dutch ships, with a convoy of three ships of war. These vessels brought the news that the Swedes had given up any attack on Archangel that summer. Peter therefore felt at liberty to de-

part, and went by sea to Niúktcha, on the Bay of Onéga, stopping by the way for a few days at the Solovétsky monastery.
From Niúktcha to Povienétz, at the northern end of Lake
Onéga, a road eighty miles long had been made through the
swamps and thick forests by the energy and labour of Stche-
pótef, a sergeant of the Preobrazhénsky regiment. Over two
of the rivers it was necessary to build long bridges, strong
enough for the passage of the five battalions of guards which
accompanied the Tsar. From Povienétz Peter sailed through
Lake Onéga and down the river Svir, and finally arrived about
the end of September at the town of Old Ládoga, on the river
Vólkhof near Lake Ládoga. Here he was met by Field-marshal
Sheremétief with his army, who had sailed down the Vólkhof
from Nóvgorod, and also by the artillery which Vinius had collected for him. With a force then of about 12,000 men, Peter
advanced on October 6 to lay siege to the fortress of Noteborg.
Noteborg had been originally built by the people of Nóvgorod
four centuries before, under the name of Orékhovo or Oréshek,
on a small island of the river Neva, just where it leaves Lake
Ladoga. The island was in shape like a hazel-nut, whence both
the Russian and Swedish names. It served for a long time as
a barrier against the incursions of the Swedes and Danes, and
protected the commerce of Nóvgorod as well as of Ládoga. In
1323, peace was concluded there between the Swedes and Russians. In the subsequent wars it was sometimes in the hands
of the Swedes, sometimes in those of the Russians, and finally,
in 1611, was captured again by the Swedes under De la Gardie,
and had since that time belonged to Sweden. Noteborg was
defended by a small garrison of 450 men, with 142 cannon of
small calibre, under the command of the old Colonel Wilhelm
von Schlippenbach, the brother of the Swedish general commanding in Livonia. The Russians took up a position on both
sides of the river, and by a fleet of small boats, which they
brought down from the river Svir through Lake Ládoga, succeeded in completely blockading the fort. On October 11 they
opened fire, and on the 22d, after an unsuccessful storm by the
Russians, in which Prince Michael Golítsyn displayed remarkable bravery and coolness, the commandant capitulated on honourable conditions. His whole garrison, with all their property,

were allowed to depart to the next Swedish fort. On the third day of the cannonade, the wife of the commandant had sent a letter to the Russian field-marshal, in the name of the wives of the officers, asking that they be permitted to depart. Peter, wishing to lose no time, had himself replied to the letter that he could not consent to put Swedish ladies to the discomfort of a separation from their husbands, and if they desired to leave

Bombardment of Noteborg.

the fort, they could do so provided they took their husbands with them.

According to Pleyer, only forty-one Swedes were living to take advantage of the capitulation. The Russians, however, lost more than the whole Swedish garrison, in all 538 men, besides 925 wounded. Peter immediately proceeded to repair the damages done to the fort, renamed it Schlüsselburg, and fastened up in the western bastion the key given him by the commandant, as a symbol that this fort was the key to the whole of the Neva. Ever afterward, when at St. Petersburg, he went to Schlüsselburg on October 22, and feasted the capitulation. Menshikóf, who had shown great military ability, was appointed governor of the newly named fort, and from this time date his intimate friendship with Peter and his prominence in public life.

When the despatch announcing the fall of Noteborg was read to King Charles, who was then in Poland, Piper feared its effect, but the King said with apparent calm : ' Console yourself, dear Piper. The enemy have not been able to drag the place away with them.' But it evidently went to his heart, and on another occasion he said that the Russians should pay dearly for Noteborg.

Peter announced the event to his friends, and in a letter to Vinius said : ' In very truth this nut was very hard ; but, thank God ! it has been happily cracked.' He made another great entry into Moscow, when a laurel wreath was let down upon his head as he passed under the triumphal arch ; but he spent only two months in the capital, and went off to Vorónezh, troubled by reports that there might be difficulties with the Tartars, if not with the Turks. In consequence of these rumours, three regiments of troops were sent from Nóvgorod to Kíef, and battalions of the Preobrazhénsky and Seménofsky marched to Vorónezh. The winter was cold, but there was little snow, and it was therefore possible for Peter to stop at the Iván lake, to inspect the works which had been begun for connecting the Don with the Volga, by means of a canal which would join the Upá, one of the upper branches of the Don, with the Oká. The work had been begun in 1701, and was then being pressed vigorously forward. It was never finished. At Peter's death the work was stopped, and there is now scarcely a trace of it.

On the upper waters of the river Vorónezh, Peter, with all his suite, stopped at a large and handsome country place which he had given to Menshikóf, and in honour of his favourite founded here a city, which he called Oranienburg.[1] He wrote to Menshikóf :

---

[1] Oranienburg, or Ranenburg, as it is now called, is in the province of Riazán, and numbers at the present time about 7,000 inhabitants.

'MEIN HERZ: Here, thank God! we have been very merry, not letting a single place go by. We named the town with the blessing of Kíef, with bulwarks and gates, of which I send a sketch in this letter. At the blessing we drank—at the first bastion, brandy, at the second, sec, at the third, Rhine wine, at the fourth, beer, at the fifth, mead, and at the gates, Rhine wine, about which the bearer of this letter will report to you more at length. All goes on well, only grant, O God! to see you in joy. You know why.'

Although Peter wrote the letter in his own hand, he signed it third as Pitírim Protodiácon, after Yaníki, the Metropolitan of Kíef and Galicia (probably Ivan Mússin-Púshkin), and Gideon, Archdeacon (probably Prince Gregory Ramodanófsky). The letter was signed by twenty others who took part in this mummery.

The sketch sent by Peter represents a nearly regular pentagon, with bastions at the corners named after the five senses respectively—Seeing, Hearing, Smelling, Tasting, and Touching—and gates called Moscow, Vorónezh, and Schlüsselburg. Le Bruyn, the Dutch artist, accompanied the Tsar on this journey. He says:

'One could not enter the house without passing through the gate of the fort, both being surrounded by the same wall of earth, which, however, is not of great extent. There are several fine bastions well garnished with cannon, covered on the one side by a mountain, and on the other by a marsh or kind of lake. When I entered where the Tsar was, he asked me where I had been. I replied: "Where it had pleased Heaven and our drivers, since I neither knew the language nor the road." That made him laugh, and he told it to the Russian lords who accompanied him. He gave me a bumper to punish me, and regaled us in perfection, having a cannon fired at each toast. After the feast he took us upon the ramparts, and made us drink different liquors on each bastion. Finally, he had sledges prepared to cross the frozen marsh and see everything from there. He took me in his own sledge, without forgetting the liquor, which followed, and which we did not spare. We returned to the chateau, where the glasses began again to make the round and to warm us. As the fort had not yet been named, his Majesty gave it the name of Oranienburg.'

After many festivities at Vorónezh, Le Bruyn asked permission of the Tsar to sketch, which he immediately granted, saying : 'We have diverted ourselves well. After that we have reposed a little. Now it is time to work.' In making his sketches, Le Bruyn suffered much from the curiosity of the Russians, who had got up all sorts of stories about him, one being that he was one of the Tsar's servants, executed for some crime by being buried up to his waist at the top of a mountain, with a book in his hand. But when, a few days after, they found that the supposed criminal had changed place, it was necessary to invent another explanation. When he took leave of the Tsar to go back to Moscow, Peter was 'amusing himself, as he frequently did, with an ice-boat. By a sudden change of course his boat was overturned, but he immediately picked himself up. Half an hour afterward he ordered me to follow him alone, and went out in a hired sledge with two horses. One of them fell into a hole, but they soon got it out. He made me sit next to him, saying : " Let us go to the shallop. I want you to see a bomb fired, because you were not here when they were fired before." ' After this had been shown, Le Bruyn was allowed to go. On the road, in the neighbourhood of Vorónezh, he found many post-houses, inhabited by Circassians, which pleased him greatly, as they were very clean, and there were generally some musicians, who played wild airs. He was particularly struck with the half-naked children on the stoves, with the beauty of the women and their costume, and especially with the ruffles around their necks.

Peter stayed at Vorónezh but a month. He was unable to do much on the fleet in the very cold weather, and was troubled, besides, because the stock of iron had given out and an epidemic with great mortality prevailed among the workmen. Good news having come from Constantinople, Peter left Vorónezh and went to Schlüsselburg, scarcely stopping at Moscow. Something there appears to have made him lose his self-control and give way to an outburst of temper, for on reaching Nóvgorod he wrote to Theodore Apráxin : 'How I went away I do not know, except that I was very contented with the gift of Bacchus. For that

reason I ask the pardon of all if I offended anyone, and especially of those who were present to bid me good-bye.'

In pursuance of his plan of gradual conquest, Peter now set
out with an expedition of 20,000 men, and moved down the right
bank of the Neva to the fort of Nyenskanz. This was on the
Neva at the mouth of the little river Okhta, where now is a ship-
ping-wharf, just opposite the Institute of Smólna and the Tau-
rida Palace. The place, though small, was prosperous, deriving
its importance from numerous saw-mills. On three sides of it,

Defeat of the Swedish Flotilla.

at a little distance, were unfinished earth-works, which had been
begun the year before, and which now served excellently the
purposes of the besiegers. Batteries were placed in position, and
the bombardment began on May 11. The next day the very
small garrison capitulated. The fort was renamed Slotburg and
became the nucleus of the future city of St. Petersburg.

That night came news that a Swedish squadron was sailing
up the gulf toward the Neva. It signified its arrival to the fort
by firing two signal-guns, which were immediately answered, in
order to deceive the Swedes and draw them into a snare. A

boat was sent up the river, which was attacked by the Russians, and one sailor was captured. He informed them that the fleet consisted of nine ships, under the command of Vice-Admiral Nummers. Three days after, two Swedish vessels sailed up the river, but came to anchor off the Vasily Island on account of the darkness. The next day, Sheremétief sent Peter and Menshikóf down the river, with two regiments of guards in thirty boats. They concealed themselves behind the islands, and after maturing a plan, attacked the Swedish vessels early on the morning of May 18. After a sharp fight, the ships using their cannon and the Russians replying with hand-grenades and musketry, Peter and his comrades succeeded in boarding and capturing the vessels, and brought them up to Slotburg. Of the seventy-seven men that composed the crews, fifty-eight were killed. The remainder were taken prisoners. For this, the first Russian naval victory, both Peter and Menshikóf were created by Sheremétief cavaliers of the Order of St. Andrew.[1]

While Peter was laying the foundation of his new capital, Sheremétief was sent against the little forts of Kopórié and Yamburg, the latter on the river Lúga, only twelve miles from Narva. Both towns were soon taken.

Peter had now obtained the object for which he had declared war. He occupied the Neva, and could communicate with the sea. He had restored to Russia her ancient province of Ingria, which had so long been in the hands of the Swedes. It is not to be wondered, therefore, that at his triumphal entry into Moscow one of the banners represented the map of Ingria, with the apposite inscription from the Book of Maccabees: ' We have neither taken other men's land nor holden that which appertaineth to others, but the inheritance of our fathers, which our enemies had wrongfully in possession a certain time. Wherefore we, having opportunity, hold the inheritance of our fathers.'

As the capture of Narva at the beginning of the war would have facilitated the conquest of Ingria, so now it was necessary to get possession of this stronghold in order to be certain of re-

---

[1] Peter was the sixth knight of the order which he had founded in 1699 on his return from Europe. The others were Admiral Theodore Golovín, the Cossack Hetman Mazeppa, Sheremétief, the Prussian Envoy Printzen, and the Saxon Chancellor Beichling.

taining the provinces which had already been won. The latter part of the summer of 1703 Sheremétief devoted to a systematic devastation of Esthonia and Livonia as far as Reval and Pernau. The ruin was as great, and the amount of booty and the number of captives even greater, than in his march of the preceding year. In the summer of 1704, after a little wavering as to whether he should not make a diversion into Curland in order to assist King Augustus, Peter decided on attacking both Dorpat and Narva. The Swedish flotilla on Lake Peipus was destroyed or captured, but the siege of Dorpat—a town which had been founded 675 years before by the Russian Grand Duke Yarosláv, under the name of Yúrief—owing to the bad dispositions of Sheremétief, proceeded slowly, and Peter was obliged to go thither in person. He found the troops in good enough condition, but the batteries placed with an utter ignorance of engineering, so that all the ammunition spent was simply wasted. Every man, he says, threw the blame on some one else. He drew up and carried out a new plan of operations, and Dorpat, after a heavy bombardment, was taken by storm on July 24. The siege had lasted five weeks, and 5,000 bombs had been thrown into the town.

Peter Apráxin, the brother of Theodore Apráxin, the Director of the Admiralty, was in the autumn of 1703 given command of Yamburg. The recollections of the great defeat at Narva were still so vivid that both he and his brother were much troubled at this vicinity to the Swedes, and this was increased when he was sent to the mouth of the Naróva, to prevent a Swedish squadron from landing stores and men. Some did manage to slip by him, to the great anger of the Tsar. At the news of the arrival of the Swedish squadron, Peter changed his plan of attacking Kexholm, on Lake Ládoga, and hastened with all his force to Narva, where, about the middle of June, he took up his position in the same entrenchment which he had thrown up four years before. It was a blockade rather than a siege, for the Russian artillery had not yet come up, and Sheremétief and his troops were still detained at Dorpat. When the armies were joined, the Russians had fully 45,000 men and 150 pieces of artillery. The Swedish garrison consisted of 4,500 men, with 432 guns in Narva and 128 in Ivángorod. The

Russians were troubled by the frequent sorties of the garrison, as well as by the constant rumours which reached them that Schlippenbach, with a strong Swedish force, was advancing from Reval. In order to draw the enemy out of the town, on the advice of Menshikóf the Russians resorted to the expedient of dressing up some of their troops in Swedish uniforms, and having a sham fight with them on the road to Wesenberg. The Russians gradually retired as if they had been beaten, and the Swedes came out from the town to attack them in the rear, accompanied even by women and children in the hope of booty. They all fell into the ambush prepared for them: 300 men were killed and forty-six taken prisoners. When Field-marshal Ogilvy, who, through the intervention of Golítsyn and Patkul, had just entered the Russian service for three years, arrived at the camp, he found fault with the siege-works, and said that it would be impossible ever to capture Narva from that side. On his recommendation batteries were placed on the eastern side of the Naróva, and the bombardment began on Sunday, August 10. In the course of ten days over 4,600 bombs were thrown into the town, breaches were made in the bastions, and Horn, the commandant, was urged to surrender, but he repulsed all propositions. On August 20 the Russians carried the place by storm. After they were in full possession, Horn, then too late, tried to capitulate, and himself beat the drum with his fists for a parley, but the Russians refused to listen. The carnage was fearful, and neither women nor children were spared. Out of 4,500 men in the Swedish garrison only 1,800 remained alive. Two hours after the surrender, Peter, Field-marshal Ogilvy, and some others rode about the town, and ordered trumpets to be sounded in all the streets to stop the pillage, and the Tsar himself struck down one soldier who refused to obey his orders. Coming into the town-hall, he threw his sword down on the table before the trembling councillors, and said: 'Do not be afraid. This is not Swedish but Russian blood.' Horn was captured, and after being confined for twelve days in the same prison where the Russian officers had languished, was sent to Russia, where he remained a prisoner for fifteen years. His wife was killed in the assault, and his children—one son and four daughters—were taken charge of by General Chambers and educated at the Tsar's expense. Shortly before the peace of Nystad, Horn, at his own request, was allowed to go to Sweden, on his promise to return in case no one were exchanged for him. He forfeited his word and never came back, and the Swedes even kept the galley on which he went.

The castle of Ivángorod held out for a week longer, but was obliged to surrender when all the provisions had been exhausted. Peter wrote to Ramodanófsky: 'Where we had such grief four years ago we are now joyous victors; for by the scaling-ladder and the sword we have taken this famous fortress in three-quarters of an hour.'

The satisfaction of the Tsar and of the Russian people was great, and the moral effect of the victory was tremendous.[1]

---

[1] Soloviéf, xiv. ; Ustriálof, IV. iv. v. vii. ix. xi. xii. and appendices; *Journal of Swedish War ;* Fryxell, I. ; Lundblad ; Sarauw ; Le Bruyn.

XLV.

MENSHIKÓF AND CATHERINE.

WITH two persons mentioned in the preceding chapter we have now to make a closer acquaintance.

Peter's early intimacy with Menshikóf had produced a

friendship which gradually grew into an affection as the Tsar saw the great qualities and remarkable abilities of his companion develop. It was after the siege of Noteborg that Menshikóf was admitted to the full friendship of his master, became the confidant of his plans and feelings and his trusted adviser, and in every way occupied the place in Peter's friendship which had been vacant since the death of Lefort. For this there were also other reasons of a more private nature.

Menshikóf.

Much obscurity rests upon the parentage of Menshikóf. His father served in the guard, and was buried—together with his wife—at Preobrazhénsky. What his condition in life was we do not know. In the diploma creating Menshikóf a Prince of the Holy Roman Empire, he is stated to be descended from an ancient and noble Lithuanian family. Even at an earlier period than this, some of Menshikóf's enemies admitted his Lithuanian origin, and that many relatives of his were landed proprietors in the neighbourhood of Minsk.

There seems to be no foundation for the story that Menshikóf, in his boyhood, sold pies in the streets of Moscow, whatever he may have done for amusement in the camp at Preobrazhénsky. Born in November, 1673, he was a year and a half younger than Peter, and was, from his earliest boyhood, attached to his service. He was one of the Tsar's play-soldiers, and was among the first enrolled in the Preobrazhénsky regiment. Though he possessed no recognised court rank and bore no official title, he was attached to the personal service of the Tsar as *denstchik*, orderly or adjutant, and in that capacity was with Peter day and night, taking his turn of sleeping in the adjoining room, or on the floor at the foot of his master's bed. A letter from Peter to him in 1700 would seem to show that at that time, at least, he had especial charge of the domestic economy of the palace and of the wardrobe of the Tsar. Handsome, witty, lively, good-humoured, of quick intelligence, and ready at those sports and exercises which Peter preferred, Menshikóf soon became the favourite of the Tsar, and, for a time, popular in Preobrazhénsky, where he was known by the nickname of Alexáshka, or by his patronym Danílovitch. Both he and Gabriel Menshikóf—who was presumably his brother—made their appearance in the 'great company of singers' who sang carols during the Christmas holidays at the house of General Gordon. He took part with Peter in the expeditions against Azof, and accompanied him to Holland as a volunteer, being first in the list of the company of which Peter was the head. He worked by the side of the Tsar at Amsterdam, and was almost his equal in ship-carpentry, being the only one of the volunteers who showed any aptitude for the business. With Peter, he visited England and Vienna, and the passport for the Tsar's proposed journey to Venice was made out in Menshikóf's name. It was after his return, and especially about the time of the executions of the Streltsi, that he came prominently into public notice as one of those who had a certain amount of influence with Peter. After Lefort's death this influence visibly increased, but it was not for several years after that he obtained over Peter the same kind of power as Lefort had, or was as much trusted by him. Up to 1703, Peter always addressed him in his letters as *Mein Herz* and *Mein Herzenchen*. In 1704, it was *Mein Liebste Camerad, Mein Liebste Vrient,* and *Mein Best Vrient,* and after that always *Mein Bruder.* At the end of the letters is the constantly repeated phrase : 'All is well ! Only God grant to see you in joy again ! You yourself know.'

The more opportunity Menshikóf had of exercising his powers, the greater ability he displayed, and his rewards were proportional. After the capture of Noteborg he was made governor of Schlüsselburg, and subsequently of Nyenskanz and St. Petersburg, and not long after governor-general of Ingria, Karelia, and Esthonia. For the capture of the Swedish vessels at the mouth of the Neva, he, together with Peter, was made a cavalier of St. Andrew. In the winter of 1703, Peter, on his journey to Vorónezh, founded near Menshikóf's estate, and in his honour, the town of Oranienburg. In 1703, through the intervention of Golítsyn, the Russian envoy at Vienna, he was made a Count of Hungary, and, in 1705, on his own proposition, the Emperor Joseph created him a Prince of the Holy Roman Empire. This title was confirmed in Russia, and, two years later, when the Tsar had begun to create new titles of nobility, he named Menshikóf Prince of Izhóra, with the title of Highness, and gave over to him the districts of Yamburg and Kopórié. It is interesting to note that, only two weeks afterward, Menshikóf wrote to Korsákof, the Landrichter of Ingria, to ascertain the population, the number of parishes, and estates, and the revenue to be derived from them, and ordered his name to be mentioned with that of the sovereign in the public prayers, both in the Russian and the Lutheran churches.

Unfortunately, Menshikóf misused his powers and position, as well as the confidence which the Tsar so freely gave him. He was ambitious and avaricious. At court he was disliked and feared, and among the people he was hated. In Poland, in Little Russia, in the Baltic provinces—wherever he held command—his greed and his extortions excited the discontent and

the complaints of the inhabitants. The familiar and affection-
ate letters of Peter were interrupted by outbursts of anger and
indignation, when some new misdeed had come to his ears.
Menshikóf wrote abject apologies, and had a powerful protector
in Catherine, and the Tsar always relented. Menshikóf's extraordinary talents, his initiative and his energy rendered him indispensable to Peter in carrying out his ideas and reforms, and his
personal devotion and sympathy made him necessary as a friend.

The immense for-
tune which he had
accumulated was
scarcely affected by
the heavy fines
which the Tsar
from time to time
condemned him to
pay, and after a
short period of dis-
grace he always re-
turned to favour
and power. Affec-
tion made Peter in-
consistent, and pre-
served Menshikóf
from the fate of
Gagárin and Nés-
terof, who expiated
their crimes on the
scaffold. On one
memorable occa-

Guard-Room of the Ancient Terem.

sion, however, the Tsar said to Catherine, after again granting
pardon: 'Menshikóf was conceived in iniquity, born in sin,
and will end his life as a rascal and a cheat, and if he do not
reform he will lose his head.' But his fall, exile, and death were
to come only under Peter's grandson, after he had reached the
zenith of his power, and had been for two years the real ruler
of Russia.

At the old court of the Tsaritsas, in addition to the ladies
of the palace and the dames of the bed-chamber, there were

always a number of young girls of similar age to the Tsaritsa, and to the princesses, who bore the title of Boyár Maidens. Their chief duty consisted in being companions to the princesses, in playing and talking with them, and sharing their amusements. After the death of the Tsaritsa Natalia, the life of all the princesses became freer. The doors of the *Terem*, or women's apartments were more easily accessible to outsiders, and the princesses themselves frequently made excursions into the town and country. Peter's sister Natalia took up her abode with him at Preobrazhénsky, bringing with her a small court. Among other maids of honour were three sisters, Dária, Barbara, and Axínia Arsénief, the daughters of a governor somewhere in Siberia. Menshikóf, as a constant companion of Peter, was admitted to the court of Natalia, and there soon sprang up a strong attachment between him and Dária Arsénief, which on account of his absences brought about a regular correspondence. Presents were also frequently exchanged— sometimes rings and jewels, sometimes shirts, dressing-gowns, bed-linen, and neck-ties—and occasionally a little souvenir was put in for the Tsar. The letters were not long and were often written on scraps of brown paper, yet Menshikóf kept his friends well informed of his movements and his successes, although even then he was frequently upbraided for writing so seldom. The intimacy had begun some time in the year 1700, and when Menshikóf returned to Moscow, in 1703, two of the Arséniefs came to live in the house which his two sisters kept for him. Maria Danílovna Menshikóf in December married Alexis Golovín, the brother of Theodore Golovín, the Director of the Department of Foreign Affairs, after which the family consisted of Anna Menshikóf, Barbara and Dária Arsénief, and their aunt Anísia Tolstói. A few months later a new member was added to the household—Catherine Skavrónsky, better known to us as the Empress Catherine I.

The early history of Catherine is as obscure as that of Menshikóf. She was in all probability the daughter of a Lithuanian peasant named Samuel Skavrónsky, settled in Livonia, and was born in the village of Ringen, not far from Dorpat. At an early age, the little Martha—for so she was then called—was left an orphan and destitute, and was taken into the family of

Pastor Gluck, at Marienburg, where, without being exactly a servant, she looked after the children, took them to church, and made herself useful in the household. A Swedish dragoon fell in love with her. She was betrothed to him, and was to marry him in a week or two, but in the midst of the festivities came an order which sent him to join his company at Riga. He was killed in an engagement in 1705. After the capture of Marienburg in 1702 by Sheremétief, Pastor Gluck and his family were sent to Moscow, but the orphan remained in the service of the field-marshal. She was then seventeen years old and very pretty. Although at this time she could neither read nor write, she had been well taught by Pastor Gluck, possessed quick intelligence and a merry humour. Her hair gradually became dark, and her hands, which were coarse with work, grew whiter and more delicate with time. In the autumn of 1703 we find her in Moscow, bearing the name of Catherine, and an inmate of Menshikóf's house. Menshikóf was in Moscow from August to December 1703, but unfortunately his correspondence with the Arséniefs, from the time he went back to St. Petersburg until the end of July 1704, has not been preserved. Peter did not go to Moscow until the end of October 1703, and remained there until December 5, when he went to Vorónezh. He was again in Moscow from December 28 to March 6, 1704. In one of his visits to the Arsénief ladies, during his stay in the capital, Peter saw and became acquainted with Catherine. He was struck by her appearance, and the readiness of her replies, and formed a 'strong attachment for her. This was just at the time when he broke with Anna Mons, and his relations with Catherine probably began in pique at the infidelity of his old mistress. The acquaintance ripened fast. In August of the same year the family went to visit Peter and Menshikóf at Narva, and remained with them for some months. A child was born during the winter, at least in March 1705 we find Peter writing to the two Arséniefs: 'I am rarely merry here. O mothers! do not abandon my little Petrúshka. Have some clothes made for him soon, and go as you will, but order that he shall have enough to eat and drink, and give my regards, ladies, to Alexander Danílovitch. And you have shown me great unkindness in not being willing to write to me about your health.' Men-

shikóf had just at this time written to them to go to him at
Wilna, and on the back of the letter Peter had added: 'Don't
believe all, but I think it is not far from the truth. If you go
to Alexáshka, remember me to him. Piter.' Owing to the
bad weather the ladies could not get to Menshikóf, who was
then at Vitébsk, until after Easter. Propriety demanded that
the family should keep together. The Arsénief ladies needed
their aunt to matronise them, and Catherine, who was confided
to their charge, could not be left alone in Moscow.

Menshikóf had not long enjoyed the society of the ladies
when he received the disquieting news of the illness of the
Tsar. Peter wrote on May 19: 'I should long ago have been
with you, except that for my sins and my misfortune I have
been kept here in this way. On the very day I was starting
from here, that is, Thursday the 15th, a fever took me and I
was obliged to return. In the morning, after taking some medicine, I felt a little better. The next day I wished to go, but
the fever returned stronger than before. The next day I felt
better, and after that ill again. Thus we know that it is a ter-
tian fever, on account of which I must stay here some time yet,
hoping in the mercy of God Almighty that my illness will not
be prolonged. Hey! how much I suffer from my illness, and
also from grief that time is lost, as well as from my separation
from you! But, for God's sake, do not be sad. I have written
you all the details only that you should not receive them from
others with exaggerations, as usual.'

On the 25th, although Peter was better, he sent for Menshikóf: 'To my illness is added the grief of separation from you.
I have endured it for a long time, but cannot stand it any more.
Be good enough to come as soon as possible, so that I shall be
merrier, as you yourself can judge. Bring with you an English
doctor, and not many followers.' But Menshikóf had already
set out, and reached Moscow on the very day the letter was
written. He immediately informed his friends at Vitébsk that
he had found the Tsar much better, and announced their speedy
arrival. By June 10, Peter was well enough to start, and they
arrived at Vitébsk on the 19th. After a month's longer stay
here, the ladies returned to Moscow, and in October another
son was born and named Paul. The Arséniefs hastened to con-

gratulate Peter, and the mother herself signed the letter ' Catherine with two others.'

What with the visit of the Tsar to Moscow and the sojourn of the ladies in the camp, both Peter and Menshikóf managed to enjoy for a good part of the time the society of their mistresses. Still Peter and Menshikóf were sometimes separated, and the ladies could not be with both at once. Peter had obtained a promise from Menshikóf that he would marry Dária Arsénief, and at times was fearful lest he should not keep his word. He evidently himself wished to marry Catherine, but still had some scruples about it during the lifetime of his wife Eudoxia. In April, 1706, he writes to Menshikóf from St. Petersburg, where the ladies were then staying in Menshikóf's house: 'As you know, we are living here in paradise, but one idea never leaves me, about which you yourself know, but I place my confidence not on human will, but on the divine will and mercy.' But while Peter was in ' paradise,' Menshikóf, in spite of the frequent letters, and the presents of dressing-gowns and shirts, felt lonely, and begged Peter, when he left St. Petersburg, to send the ladies to Smolénsk. Finally, on June 28, Peter and the ladies arrived at Smolénsk from one direction, and Menshikóf from the other. Shortly afterward they all went to Kíef, but Menshikóf had to go off with his dragoons on the campaign, and from the army sent his friend Dária a present of five lemons—all that could be found—and suggested to her to use them some time when the Tsar was present. Peter himself thanked Menshikóf for the lemons, and in a subsequent letter called him to Kíef: ' It is very necessary for you to come by Assumption Day, in order to accomplish what we have already sufficiently talked about before I go.' Menshikóf came to Kíef, and on August 29, 1706, married Dária Arsénief. Two days afterward, Peter, Catherine, and the aunt Anísia Tolstói went off to St. Petersburg. Barbara Arsénief and Anna Menshikóf remained in Kíef. The family was divided, and Catherine now had a matron with whom she could travel.

The day after Peter's arrival in St. Petersburg the Neva overflowed its banks. Boats navigated the streets, and the water was nearly two feet deep in the palace of the Tsar. ' It was very amusing,' wrote Peter to Menshikóf, ' to see how people sat on the roofs and trees, just as in the time of the deluge, and not only men, but old women.' Peter was so merry over this new phase of his beloved town that he sent Menshikóf salutations, not only from Catherine and himself, but also from his favourite dog Lisette.[1]

Menshikóf could scarcely have had a better wife. She, like Catherine, was a true officer's wife, looked after her husband's comforts, and accompanied him in many of his campaigns— sometimes even, it is said, on horseback.

In 1707 Catherine was privately married to Peter at St. Petersburg, but it was not until after the affair on the Pruth, that she was publicly and officially acknowledged as the Tsaritsa.

Long before the formal public nuptials in 1712, Catherine had given up the Catholic religion, in which she had been born, and the Lutheran, in which she had been educated, and had been received into the Russian Church. The Tsarévitch Alexis acted as her godfather, for which reason she added to Catherine the patronym of Alexéievna.

A fatality seemed to attend the many children of this union. The boys all died in childhood or infancy. Two daughters, Anne and Elizabeth, lived, the latter to become Empress.

Even when on the throne Catherine never forgot her origin. The widow of Pastor Gluck was given a pension, his children were well married, or were put in positions at court. She assisted the student Wurm, whom she had known when he lived in Pastor Gluck's house at Marienburg. At her request Peter hunted up her family. Her brother Carl Skavrónsky, a stable-boy at a post-station in Curland, was brought to St. Petersburg and educated, and subsequently created a count. His descendants married into the well-known families of Sapieha, Engelhardt, Bagratión, Vorontsóf, and Korff.

After Peter's death, Catherine's two sisters and their family came to St. Petersburg. Christina, the elder, was married to a

---

[1] This was the dog for which a priest of Kozlóf got into trouble in 1708. On coming back from Moscow he had told his acquaintances: 'I saw the Tsar as he drove out of the court of Prince Menshikóf, and a little dog jumped into his carriage, and the Tsar took up the dog and kissed it on the head.' Some little time afterward the priest was arrested and tried for using improper language about the Tsar.

Lithuanian peasant, Simon Heinrich, who, together with riches and honours, received the name of Héndrikof. Anna, the younger, had married the Polish peasant Michael Yefim, who became the founder of the Yefimófsky family. The Empress Elizabeth gave the title of count to both families.

The opposite of Eudoxia, Catherine was the wife that Peter needed. She rose to his level, and showed a remarkable adaptability in her new position. Her gifts of head and heart were such that she was able not only to share his outward life, his pleasures, and his sorrows, but also to take part in his inner life, enter into his views and plans, and sympathise with his aspirations. Her conversation cheered him, her presence comforted and consoled him, and aided him to bear his sudden attacks of nervous suffering. Their correspondence is simple, unaffected, and familiar, and shows constantly how well suited they were to each other, how warmly they loved each other, and what a human and lovable nature Peter had, in spite of his great faults and imperfections.

Many of the letters are trivial, some are coarse,[1] all are marked by good humour, and are full of personal allusions and little jests. Some of them we shall have occasion to quote in their proper place. The following extracts from others will suffice as examples of their character :

' Moeder,

' Since I went away from thee I have no news of what I want to know, and especially how soon thou wilt be in Wilna. I am bored without thee, and thou, I think, art the same. Here, thank God, all is well. King Augustus has come in and Krassau has gone out ; Leszczynski has let his beard grow because his crown has died out. The Poles are constantly in conference about the affairs of Iváshka Khmelnítsky.[2] . . .

' From Lublin, capital of Iváshka, August 31, 1709.'

' Warsaw, Sept. 24, 1709. . . . Thanks for thy package. I send thee some fresh lemons. Thou dost jest about amuse-

---

[1] The manners of the time permitted a freedom of language that is not tolerated now ; there is, however, nothing in these letters that approaches the tone of much of the correspondence of the Duchess of Orleans.

[2] *I.e.*, are carousing.

ments ; we have none, for we are old and not that kind of people. . . . Give my regards to Aunty. Her bridegroom had an interview day before yesterday with Iváshka, and had a bad fall on the boat and now lies powerless; which break gently to Aunty that she do not go to pieces. . . .'

' Marienwerder, October 16, 1709. . . . Give my regards to Aunty. That she has fallen in love with a monk I have already told her bridegroom, about which he is very sad, and from grief wishes himself to commit some follies.'

Katerinushka, my friend, how art thou !
'We arrived here well, thank God, and to-morrow begin our cure. This place is so merry, you might call it an honourable dungeon for it lies between such high mountains that one scarcely sees the sun. Worst of all there is no good beer. However we hope God will give us good from the waters. I send thee herewith a present, a new-fashioned clock, put under glass on account of the dust, and a seal. . . . I couldn't get more on account of my hurry, for I was only one day in Dresden.— Carlsbad, 14 September, 1711.'

'Carlsbad, Sept. 19, 1711. . . . We, thank God, are well, only our bellies are swelled up with water, because we drink like horses, and we have nothing else to do except. . . . You write that on account of the cure I should not hurry to you. It is quite evident that you have found somebody better than me. Kindly write about it. Is it one of ours or a man of Thorn ? I rather think a man of Thorn, and that you want to be revenged for what I did two years ago. That is the way you daughters of Eve act with us old fellows.'

' Greifswald, August 2, 1712. . . . Thank God, we are well, only 'tis very hard living, for I can't use my left hand, and in my right alone I have to hold both sword and pen. How many helpers I have thou knowest.'

' Greifswald, August 8, 1712. I hear that thou art bored, and I am not without being bored, but thou canst judge that business does not leave me much time for *ennui*. I don't think

I can get away from here to thee quickly, and if the horses have arrived, come on with the three battalions that are ordered to go to Anclam. But, for God's sake, take care not to go a hundred yards from the battalions, for there are many enemy's ships in the Haff, and the men constantly go into the woods in great numbers, and through those woods thou must pass.'

'Berlin, October 2, 1712. I inform you that day before yesterday I arrived here and went to see the King. Yesterday morning he came to me, and last night I went to the Queen. I send you as many oysters as I could find. I couldn't get any more, because they say the pest has broken out in Hamburg, and it is forbidden to bring anything from there.'

'Leipzig, October 6, 1712. I this moment start for Carlsbad and hope to arrive to-morrow. Your clothes and other things were bought, but I couldn't get any oysters. With this I confide you to God's keeping.'

'Carlsbad, October 11, 1712. We began to drink water at this hole yesterday. How it works I shall write, but don't ask for any other news from this wilderness.'

'Lagau, Dec. 2, 1712. . . . Thanks for the clothes, which I put on new on St. Andrew's day. As to what you say about bringing you here, we must put that off for a while, for the time has come for you to pray and for us to work. The Swedes yesterday attacked the Danes to keep them from joining us, and we are starting this moment to help the Danes.'

In 1716, when on his way to the waters, Peter received from Catherine a pair of spectacles. He writes: 'Leaving Altona, May 23, 1716. Katerinushka, my heart's friend, how are you. Thanks for the present. In the same way I send you something from here in return. Really on both sides the presents are suitable. You sent me wherewithal to help my old age, and I send you with which to adorn your youth.'

And again: 'Pyrmont, June 5, 1716. I received your letter with the present, and I think you have a prophetic spirit that you sent only one bottle, for I am not allowed to drink more than one glass a day, so that this store is quite enough for me. You write that you don't admit my being old. In that way you try to cover up your first present so that people should not guess. But it is easy to discover that young people don't look through spectacles. I shall see you soon. The water is acting well, but it has become very tiresome here.'

'Altona, Nov. 23, 1716. . . . Alexander Petrovitch writes that Petrushka has cut his fourth tooth ; God grant he cut all so well, and that we may see him grow up, thus rewarding us for our former grief over his brothers. . . .'

Catherine tells her husband of this boy in a letter written two years later, when the Tsar was cruising in the Baltic: 'July 24, 1718. I and the children, thank God, are in good health. Although on my way to Petersburg Petrushka was a little weak with his last teeth, yet now with God's help he is quite well and has cut three back teeth. I beg you, little father, for protection, for he has no little quarrel with me about you,—namely, because when I tell him that Papa has gone away he does not like it, but he likes it better and becomes glad when one says that Papa is here.' Peter was greatly pleased with this letter, to which he immediately replied in the same vein. In another letter from Reval, dated August 1, 1718, he says : ' Thanks, my friend, for the figs, which came safely. I have had myself shorn here, and send you my shorn locks, though I know they will not be received.'

The next summer Peter again wrote from Reval: 'The new garden is very fine, and the trees on the seaside or the north very well planted, but on the south must be changed. Not one tree has been set out at the espalier, in which Nerónof lied. They are now levelling the court which will be behind the house. All the earthwork is done in the garden. To tell the truth it will be a marvel when finished. I send you some flowers, and some of the mint which you yourself planted. Thank God, all is merry here, except that when one goes out to the villa and you are not there it is very lonesome.'

There still lie between the pages of this letter a little bunch of dried flowers and some mint, as well as a notice cut from a newspaper of a man and woman respectively 126 and 125 years old, who had been married 110 years, arriving at London from Monmouthshire. Catherine, in a long and pleasant letter acknowledging this, says: 'Thanks, my friend, for the present. 'Tis not dear to me because I planted it, but because it comes from thy hands.' Soon after she writes: 'Our only pleasure here is the garden. . . . The Frenchman, who made the new flower-beds, was walking one bad night and met Iváshka Khmelnitsky, and had such a bout with him (*i.e.* got drunk) that he was pushed off the bridge and sent to make flower-beds in the other world.'

Sending Peter some apples and fresh nuts Catherine writes: 'The lion (Leo) sent by Your Grace came to me. Quite wonderful, but he is not a lion, merely a playful cat from the dear Lion. He brought me a letter which pleased me, but kindly send me him whom I call Lion.'

Peter again visits Reval, and writes in July, 1723: 'The garden planted only two years ago has grown beyond belief, for the only big trees which you saw have in some places stretched their branches across the walk, and Aunty's tree, the stem of which was like a middle finger without the nail, has taken splendidly. The chestnuts all have fine crowns. The house is being plastered outside, but is ready within, and in one word we have hardly anywhere such a regular house. I send you some strawberries, which ripened before our arrival, as well as cherries. I am quite astonished that things are so early here, when it is in the same latitude as Petersburg.' [1]

---

[1] Ustriálof, **IV.** v. viii.; Sadler, *Peter der Grosse; Correspondence of the Russian Sovereigns* (Russian), I.; Seméfsky, *The Mons Family;* Soloviéf, **xiv.**; Esipof, *Menshikóf;* Kostomárof, *Russian History,* **vi.**

END OF VOLUME I.

RUSSIA
AT THE TIME OF
PETER THE GREAT.

SCALE OF MILES
0 50 100   200   300

Explanations.

Russia as Peter
Found it.

Peter's
Conquests.